Contents

Figures ix

Tables xiii

Special notices xv

IBM trademarks xvi

Preface xvii
The team that wrote this redbook. xviii
Notice xx
Comments welcome. xx

Chapter 1. Introduction 1
1.1 Introducing the Operational Data Store 2
1.2 Business questions 3
1.3 What is an Operational Data Store (ODS)? 4
    1.3.1 Definition of an ODS 5
    1.3.2 Characteristics of an ODS. 5
    1.3.3 Benefits of an ODS 6
    1.3.4 When to use a separate datastore? 7
    1.3.5 Some differences between an ODS and a DW 8
1.4 How to position the ODS within the BI architecture. 13

Chapter 2. ODS issues 17
2.1 The business requirements. 18
2.2 Mapping the requirements to the ODS issues. 19
2.3 Transferring the data. 22
    2.3.1 Integrating multiple operational sources 23
    2.3.2 ODS data transformations. 24
2.4 Data characteristics. 26
    2.4.1 Near-current data delivery. 26
    2.4.2 Source synchronization. 26
    2.4.3 Current data 26
    2.4.4 Level of detail 27
2.5 The ODS environment. 27
    2.5.1 Mixing updates and queries 27
    2.5.2 Flexible growth path 28
    2.5.3 Uptime. 28

2.6 ODS administration and maintenance. 28
   2.6.1 Administration 29
   2.6.2 Performance tuning and monitoring 30
   2.6.3 Initial loads 31

Chapter 3. ODS architectures. 33
3.1 Business scenarios 34
   3.1.1 Consolidated customer and product information. 34
   3.1.2 Consolidated customer and order information 35
   3.1.3 Detect calling card fraud while the call is in progress 37
3.2 ODS types. 38
   3.2.1 ODS type A: real-time data access/localized update 43
   3.2.2 ODS type B: update transaction trigger 46
   3.2.3 ODS type C: fully integrated 49
   3.2.4 Selecting the right type of ODS. 51
3.3 Data modeling. 52
   3.3.1 ERM modeling. 53
   3.3.2 Dimensional modeling. 54
   3.3.3 Deciding on the modeling technique 55
3.4 ODS layers 57
   3.4.1 Defining the operational data needed 58
   3.4.2 Data acquisition. 61
   3.4.3 ODS workload considerations. 63
   3.4.4 Information catalog 64
   3.4.5 System management requirements 66
   3.4.6 Data access 70
3.5 Data acquisition scenarios using IBM products. 73

Chapter 4. Populating the ODS from relational sources 91
4.1 Relational data as a source (ODS type A) 92
   4.1.1 The relational replication solution 92
   4.1.2 ODS data transformations. 98
   4.1.3 Near-current data delivery and uptime 100
   4.1.4 Populating the ODS using Data Warehouse Center (DWC). 108
4.2 Relational data as a target (ODS type B) 121
   4.2.1 Managing updates back to data sources 122
   4.2.2 Independent updates 122

Chapter 5. Populating the ODS from non-relational sources 127
5.1 VSAM as an ODS source (ODS type A) 128
   5.1.1 The VSAM issue 128
   5.1.2 Capturing VSAM updates 128
   5.1.3 Populating the ODS using MQSI. 134
   5.1.4 Populating the ODS using the DWC MQ Connector. 153

IBM

International Technical Support Organization

Building the Operational Data Store on DB2 UDB Using IBM Data Replication, WebSphere MQ Family, and DB2 Warehouse Manager

December 2001

SG24-6513-00

Take Note! Before using this information and the product it supports, be sure to read the general information in "Special notices" on page xv.

First Edition (December 2001)

This edition applies to DB2 UDB for z/OS and OS/390 V7, DB2 UDB Extended Enterprise Edition for Solaris and AIX V7.2, DB2 Warehouse Manager V7.2, WebSphere MQ V5.2.1, WebSphere MQ Integrator V2.0.2, DB2 DataPropagator for z/OS V5, DataJoiner V2.1.1, and IMS DataPropagator for z/OS V3.

Comments may be addressed to:
IBM Corporation, International Technical Support Organization
Dept. QXXE Building 80-E2
650 Harry Road
San Jose, California 95120-6099

When you send information to IBM, you grant IBM a non-exclusive right to use or distribute the information in any way it believes appropriate without incurring any obligation to you.

© **Copyright International Business Machines Corporation 2001. All rights reserved.**
Note to U.S Government Users – Documentation related to restricted rights – Use, duplication or disclosure is subject to restrictions set forth in GSA ADP Schedule Contract with IBM Corp.

5.2 Flat files as an ODS source (ODS type A) 165
   5.2.1 Z/OS or OS/390 flat files 165
   5.2.2 UNIX or NT flat files 166
5.3 IMS as an ODS source (ODS type A) 166
   5.3.1 The IMS DataPropagator solution. 166
   5.3.2 Populating ODS using MQ-ASYNC 169
   5.3.3 ODS data transformations. 172
   5.3.4 Performance for near-current data delivery 174
5.4 VSAM and IMS as target databases (ODS type B). 174
   5.4.1 VSAM updates from ODS back to VSAM 175
   5.4.2 IMS updates from ODS back to IMS. 177

Chapter 6. Administration tips for handling rejected records 179
6.1 Business issues. 180
6.2 ODS design considerations. 181
6.3 Real-time user interface characteristics 185
6.4 Back-end processing characteristics. 186
6.5 Data analysis. 187

Chapter 7. Building and managing the ODS population subsystem . . . 189
7.1 Requirements of a population subsystem. 190
   7.1.1 Data conversion project 190
   7.1.2 Populating a data warehouse 190
   7.1.3 Populating an ODS 191
7.2 ODS population subsystem architecture. 191
   7.2.1 Architecture for a population subsystem. 192
   7.2.2 Designing based on the architecture. 193
   7.2.3 Extract component 194
7.3 Automating the population of the ODS 202
   7.3.1 Automating the change capture process. 202
   7.3.2 Implementing and automating the ODS workflows 203
7.4 ODS metadata. 217
   7.4.1 Usage of metadata in the ODS population subsystem 217
7.5 Summary. 227

Chapter 8. Critical success factors for the target ODS servers 229
8.1 DB2 UDB family 230
   8.1.1 Integrating multiple operational sources 230
   8.1.2 ODS data transformations. 232
   8.1.3 Source synchronization. 232
8.2 DB2 UDB EEE. 234
   8.2.1 Level of detail 234
   8.2.2 Near-current data delivery and mixing updates and queries. . . . 237
   8.2.3 Flexible growth path 241

  8.2.4 Uptime 248
  8.2.5 Performance tuning and monitoring 252
  8.2.6 Initial load 255
 8.3 DB2 UDB for z/OS 255
  8.3.1 Level of detail 256
  8.3.2 Near-current data delivery and mixing updates and queries 258
  8.3.3 Flexible growth path 265
  8.3.4 Uptime 267
  8.3.5 Performance tuning and monitoring 270
  8.3.6 Initial load 275

Appendix A. Implementing message flows with MQSI 279
Assumptions 280
 Using the MQSI Control Center 280
Steps required to implement an MQSI flow 281
 Configuring the broker domain and topology 281
 Assigning message flows and sets to the broker 286

Appendix B. Example CICS program 289

Appendix C. Population subsystem: tables; SQL stored procedures . . 293
Example tables 294
 Part source table in DB2 for z/OS 294
 PART source table in Oracle 294
 PART source in VSAM file 295
 DB2 for z/OS PART staging table 295
 Oracle PART staging table 296
 Common changed data table 296
 ODS PART table 297
Stored Procedures 297
 Stored Procedure to process the change records from DB2 for z/OS . . . 297
 Stored Procedure to process the change records from Oracle 302
 Stored Procedure to process the change records from VSAM 307
 Stored Procedure to apply the final change records to the ODS 311

Appendix D. DB2 UDB for z/OS Cross Loader 317

Appendix E. The testing environment 321

Related publications 323
IBM Redbooks 323
 Other resources 324
Referenced Web sites 325
How to get IBM Redbooks 326

IBM Redbooks collections 326
Index 327

Figures

1-1	Positioning the ODS.	9
1-2	Updating/loading of data into ODS and DW	10
1-3	IBM business intelligence architecture.	14
2-1	ODS architecture overview	22
3-1	Consolidated customer portfolio data flow.	35
3-2	Consolidated order maintenance data flow	36
3-3	Consolidated call information data flow	38
3-4	Data flow overview for ODS types A, B, and C	39
3-5	Architecture of ODS types A, B, and C	42
3-6	Architecture of an ODS type A.	44
3-7	Architecture of an ODS type B.	46
3-8	ODS Type B trigger update process	48
3-9	Architecture of an ODS type C.	49
3-10	Selecting the right type of ODS	51
3-11	ERM.	53
3-12	Star schema.	55
3-13	ODS layers.	57
3-14	ODS data source from the operational data	59
3-15	Data acquisition components.	62
3-16	Metadata architecture	65
3-17	Example data access scenario	71
3-18	DB2 DataPropagator Relational and DataJoiner	74
3-19	IMS DataPropagator	75
3-20	DataRefresher and DDU	76
3-21	MQPUT and MQGET.	77
3-22	Writing to a remote queue	78
3-23	DB2 Warehouse Manager	80
3-24	IBM product scenario.	81
3-25	IBM products for an ODS.	83
3-26	ODS type A with relational data.	85
3-27	ODS type B on DB2 UDB for z/OS target with relational data.	86
3-28	ODS type B on DB2 UDB EEE target with relational data.	87
3-29	ODS type A on DB2 UDB for z/OS target with non-relational data	88
3-30	ODS type A on DB2 UDB EEE target with non-relational data	89
3-31	ODS type B on with non-relational data.	90
4-1	UOW table.	93
4-2	Spill file.	94
4-3	Homogeneous replication	95

4-4	Heterogeneous replication with DataJoiner	96
4-5	Apply pull/push modes	103
4-6	Apply tasks	105
4-7	CCD table	107
4-8	Overview of PART replication process	109
4-9	Source databases are registered in the DWC	112
4-10	Define the DB2 replication source and select only replication sources	113
4-11	Define the DB2 replication source: import the source metadata	114
4-12	Selecting sources to be added to the process modeler canvas	115
4-13	Defining a replication step: selecting staging table parameters	116
4-14	Defining a replication step: generating the output table	117
4-15	Defining a replication step: mapping columns to generated table	118
4-16	Defining a replication step: processing options	119
4-17	Defining a replication step: the final workflow	120
4-18	ODS type B: updating back to relational database	123
4-19	MQSI message flows for type B (relational)	124
5-1	Near-real-time updates to the ODS	129
5-2	Synchronous update	130
5-3	Asynchronous update on DB2 UDB for z/OS	131
5-4	Using MQSI to read the MQ queue	132
5-5	Using MQSI on distributed platform	133
5-6	DB2MQ function	134
5-7	Creating an MQSI message flow	136
5-8	Schematic message flow	137
5-9	Deploying the flow to remote machines	138
5-10	MQInput node	139
5-11	MQOutput node	140
5-12	The compute node	141
5-13	Schematic diagram of message flow	143
5-14	Updating the ODS	143
5-15	Multi-broker domain	147
5-16	Simple compute node throughput for Solaris	149
5-17	Database node throughput for Solaris	150
5-18	Simple Compute node throughput for AIX	152
5-19	Database node throughput for AIX	152
5-20	Population process	156
5-21	Using the DWC to create an MQSeries source	157
5-22	MQ-Assist Wizard, selecting the type of read access	158
5-23	MQ-Assist Wizard, naming the UDF	158
5-24	MQ-Assist Wizard, providing the service point name	159
5-25	MQ-Assist Wizard, specifying the message format type	159
5-26	MQ-Assist Wizard, column definition page	160
5-27	Using DWC SQL step to stage MQ messages into a relational table	161

5-28	Workflow to bring orders into the ODS	162
5-29	Synchronous IMS-to-DB2 Propagation	167
5-30	Asynchronous IMS log to DB2 replication	168
5-31	Concept of MQ-ASYNC replication	169
5-32	Near-real-time replication using MQSeries	171
5-33	DB2 UDB EEE as the target ODS from IMS DPROP	172
5-34	IMS DPROP mapping concept	173
5-35	ODS type B flow for non-relational data	175
5-36	MQSI flow to operational database	176
6-1	Reject data analysis for a business unit at ABC Bank	181
6-2	Rejected record not fixed	182
6-3	Rejected record fixed before system of record update	182
6-4	Components for an ODS (type A) reject handling application	184
7-1	The population subsystem reference architecture	192
7-2	High-level view of our PARTs population process	193
7-3	The Extract component of our PARTs ODS	195
7-4	Adding the prepare component to our PARTs ODS	196
7-5	Adding the transform component to our PARTs ODS	198
7-6	Adding the load component to our PARTs ODS	200
7-7	Independently executing units of work	201
7-8	The DB2 replication workflow as seen in the DWC	204
7-9	DWC replication step properties: replication page	205
7-10	DWC replication step properties: parameters page	206
7-11	DWC replication step properties: column mapping page	207
7-12	DWC replication step properties: processing options page	208
7-13	IBM DB2 Stored Procedure Builder	209
7-14	The Oracle replication workflow as seen in the DWC	210
7-15	Schedule of the first step in the Oracle replication workflow	212
7-16	The VSAM PARTs via MQ workflow as seen in the DWC	213
7-17	Schedule of the VSAM MQ Series workflow	214
7-18	The workflow to update the ODS as seen in the DWC	214
7-19	Schedule of the load ODS workflow	215
7-20	The entire ODS population subsystem	216
7-21	Metadata flows using the DWC and the Information Catalog Manager	218
7-22	Metadata execution using the DWC work-in-progress window	220
7-23	Many objects can be defined in the information catalog	221
7-24	Our ODS subjects in the information catalog	222
7-25	Tracing our ODS PART table back to its sources	223
7-26	Starting the publish DWC metadata dialog	224
7-27	Selecting the processes, sources, and targets to publish	225
7-28	Publish metadata processing log	226
7-29	Scheduling future metadata updates to be published automatically	227
8-1	ODS synchronization points	233

8-2	Single partition database compared to a multi-partition database	235
8-3	Sample MPP and SMP configurations	236
8-4	DB2 UDB EEE table partitioning	238
8-5	Three types of collocation	240
8-6	Intra-partition parallelism	243
8-7	Inter-partition parallelism	243
8-8	Combining inter-partition and intra-partition parallelism	244
8-9	SMP scalability with DB2 UDB EE	246
8-10	SMP and MPP scalability with DB2 UDB EEE	247
8-11	DB2 UDB EEE on a large SMP box	248
8-12	Partitioned table granularity	258
8-13	Parallel Sysplex cluster architecture and ODS	266
8-14	Parallel Sysplex with data sharing improves availability	268
A-1	Control center panel	280
A-2	Creating a broker	281
A-3	PART input file	282
A-4	Defining a message set	283
A-5	Defining a message flow	284
A-6	Designing the message flow	285
A-7	Deploying the message flow	287
C-1	Table definition for the PART table in the DB2 for z/OS database	294
C-2	Table definition for the PART table in the Oracle database	294
C-3	Relational view of the MQ queue representing the VSAM PART file	295
C-4	Table used for staging change records from the DB2 PART table	295
C-5	Table used for staging change records from the Oracle PART table	296
C-6	Table used to store the common change records	296
C-7	The final consolidated PART table in the ODS	297
D-1	Cross Loader	318
8-15	Testing environment	322
8-16	Parts-r-Us entity-relationship diagram	322

Tables

1-1	Differences between ODS and DW	13
2-1	Business questions and requirements	18
2-2	Relationships between business requirements and ODS issues	20
3-1	Characteristics for the general ODS types A, B and C	40
3-2	Sample users groups and their requirements	72
4-1	Decrease of connections using subscription sets (part 1)	106
4-2	Minimizing database connections using subscription sets (part 2)	106
D-1	Cross-Loader statistics	319

Special notices

References in this publication to IBM products, programs or services do not imply that IBM intends to make these available in all countries in which IBM operates. Any reference to an IBM product, program, or service is not intended to state or imply that only IBM's product, program, or service may be used. Any functionally equivalent program that does not infringe any of IBM's intellectual property rights may be used instead of the IBM product, program or service.

Information in this book was developed in conjunction with use of the equipment specified, and is limited in application to those specific hardware and software products and levels.

IBM may have patents or pending patent applications covering subject matter in this document. The furnishing of this document does not give you any license to these patents. You can send license inquiries, in writing, to the IBM Director of Licensing, IBM Corporation, North Castle Drive, Armonk, NY 10504-1785.

Licensees of this program who wish to have information about it for the purpose of enabling: (i) the exchange of information between independently created programs and other programs (including this one) and (ii) the mutual use of the information which has been exchanged, should contact IBM Corporation, Dept. 600A, Mail Drop 1329, Somers, NY 10589 USA.

Such information may be available, subject to appropriate terms and conditions, including in some cases, payment of a fee.

The information contained in this document has not been submitted to any formal IBM test and is distributed AS IS. The use of this information or the implementation of any of these techniques is a customer responsibility and depends on the customer's ability to evaluate and integrate them into the customer's operational environment. While each item may have been reviewed by IBM for accuracy in a specific situation, there is no guarantee that the same or similar results will be obtained elsewhere. Customers attempting to adapt these techniques to their own environments do so at their own risk.

Any pointers in this publication to external Web sites are provided for convenience only and do not in any manner serve as an endorsement of these Web sites.

IBM trademarks

The following terms are trademarks of the International Business Machines Corporation in the United States and/or other countries:

e (logo)® @
Redbooks (logo)™

AIX	DB2 Universal Database	Perform
AIX 5L	DRDA	Planet Tivoli
AS/400	Enterprise Storage Server	QMF
Balance	IBM	Redbooks
CICS	IMS	RS/6000
Cross-Site	Information Warehouse	S/390
CS Systems	Informix	Sequent
Current	MQSeries	SP
DataJoiner	MVS	SupportPac
DataPropagator	MVS/ESA	Tivoli
DataRefresher	Netfinity	Tivoli Enterprise
DB2	NetView	TME
DB2 OLAP Server	Notes	Visual Warehouse
	OS/390	WebSphere
	OS/400	Working Together
	Parallel Sysplex	z/OS

Other company trademarks

The following terms are trademarks of other companies:

C-bus is a trademark of Corollary, Inc. in the United States and/or other countries.

Java and all Java-based trademarks and logos are trademarks or registered trademarks of Sun Microsystems, Inc. in the United States and/or other countries.

Microsoft, Windows, Windows NT, and the Windows logo are trademarks of Microsoft Corporation in the United States and/or other countries.

PC Direct is a trademark of Ziff Communications Company in the United States and/or other countries and is used by IBM Corporation under license.

ActionMedia, LANDesk, MMX, Pentium and ProShare are trademarks of Intel Corporation in the United States and/or other countries.

UNIX is a registered trademark in the United States and other countries licensed exclusively through The Open Group.

SET, SET Secure Electronic Transaction, and the SET Logo are trademarks owned by SET Secure Electronic Transaction LLC.

Other company, product, and service names may be trademarks or service marks of others.

Preface

For the past several years many companies have undergone reorganizations and process re-engineering activities to break down their vertical business processes. A more customer-centric and cross functional approach is being taken to increase customer service and reduce costs. The challenge for Information Technology (IT) departments is to integrate and consolidate the required data across many different systems.

This IBM Redbook focuses on how an Operational Data Store (ODS) can be used to satisfy these requirements. We define what an ODS is and the types of business questions it can answer. The ODS is positioned within the Business Intelligence (BI) architecture and specific issues are discussed. Three distinctive business scenarios are used to help explain the ODS architecture.

Using business examples, this book describes the different methods, techniques, and technologies used to implement an ODS:

- IBM Data Replication with DB2 DataPropagator (DB2 DPROP throughout the book), DataJoiner, and IMS DataPropagator (IMS DPROP throughout the book)
- WebSphere MQ (MQSeries throughout the book) and WebSphere MQ Integrator (MQSI throughout the book)
- DB2 Warehouse Manager (DB2 WM throughout the book) and Data Warehouse Center (DWC throughout the book)

These IBM products are used to describe how the ODS is populated. A number of source and target scenarios are used to demonstrate both homogeneous and heterogeneous environments. DB2 Warehouse Manager is also used to manage and control the population of the ODS and both DB2 UDB EEE for UNIX and DB2 UDB for z/OS and OS/390 (respectively termed DB2 EEE and DB2 for z/OS throughout the book) are presented as targets for the ODS.

This book can be used by business decision makers, architects, implementors, DBAs, and data acquisition specialists to gain a better understanding of what an ODS is, how it can be used, and how it should be designed and implemented.

This book makes the assumption that the reader is familiar with many of the issues and characteristics of a data warehouse and its architecture. Using data warehousing terms and techniques, we describe the differences and similarities between the two enterprise data stores: the data warehouse and the ODS.

The team that wrote this redbook

This redbook was produced by a team of specialists from around the world working at the International Technical Support Organization, San Jose Center.

Corinne Baragoin is a Business Intelligence Project Leader with the IBM International Technical Support Organization, San Jose Center. She has over 16 years of experience as an IT specialist on DB2 and related solutions. Before joining the ITSO, she had been working as an IT Specialist for IBM France, assisting customers on DB2 UDB and data warehouse environments.

Marty Marini is a Senior IT Specialist with the Business Intelligence Practice in Toronto, Canada. His main areas of expertise include DB2 UDB EEE, AIX, and RS/6000 SP systems. He is a Data Management Specialist and is a Certified Advanced Technical Expert for DB2 Clusters and a Certified Solutions Expert for DB2 Administration and DB2 Application Development. Marty holds a degree in Computer Science with 14 years of experience in Database and Application Development projects.

Cellan Morgan is a Systems Specialist in the United Kingdom. He has 14 years of experience as a CICS Systems Programmer and two years experience as an MQSeries Systems Programmer and Support Specialist. Cellan provides support for both IBM internal systems and external customers.

Olaf Mueller is an IT Specialist with IBM Global Services, e-Business Integration in Duesseldorf, Germany. He has 13 years of experience as a Database Specialist working in the areas of application development and database administration. He is a Certified Solutions Expert for DB2 Administration and DB2 Application Development. His areas of expertise include Oracle and data modeling.

Andrew Perkins is a Certified Consulting IT Specialist supporting Business Intelligence technical presales activities in the IBM Americas Business Intelligence Solutions Center in Dallas, TX. He has over 20 years of experience in the IT field, concentrating primarily on DB2 and related solutions. He holds a Bachelor of Science degree in Computer Science from the University of Houston. His areas of expertise include DB2 UDB across all platforms, DB2 Warehouse Manager, and DB2 OLAP Server.

Kiho "Henry" Yim is a production DBA at Sterling Forest, NY, IBM Global Services. He joined IBM Korea in 1976 as a Systems Engineer and moved to the United States in 1980. He has held various positions, including DBA and Database Developer for DB2, IDMS, ADABAS, IMS and systems programmer for CICS. He is an IBM certified IT specialist and holds an EE degree from Seoul National University, Korea.

We would like to specially thank Mark Persaud for his contributions in writing some sections of the book:

Mark Persaud is an IT Architect with the Data Warehouse Practice in Toronto, Canada. Mark has 10 years of design and development experience which span data warehouse, ODS, and traditional OLTP system implementations. He worked for more than 6 years in one of Canada's largest banks as a designer and developer of OLTP banking systems. Currently, Mark is focused on working with our clients in the field to define solution architectures for data warehouse and ODS related initiatives.

We would like also to thank Chris Todd and IBM Global Services (IGS) for providing much of the ODS architecture material. The IGS ODS offering was used as a foundation for this redbook.

Thanks to the following people for their contributions to this project:

- By providing their architectural input and/or reviewing this redbook:

    Greg Carroll
    Ted Wong
    Chris Todd
    IBM Canada, Data Warehousing Practice

    John McPherson
    IBM Silicon Valley Lab

- By providing their technical input and/or reviewing this redbook:

    Glen Sheffield
    IBM Toronto Lab

    Julie Jerves
    IBM Silicon Valley Lab

    Rick Long
    IBM Australia

    David Bryant
    Henry Cook
    Simon Harris
    Simon Woodcock
    IBM UK

    John Bell
    IBM Kansas City

    Tom Bauch
    IBM Dallas

    Inderpal Narang
    IBM Almaden Research Center

Geert Van De Putte
Phil Wakelin
Bob Haimowitz
International Technical Support Organization

Notice

This publication is intended to help business users, architects, DBAs, and data acquisition specialists understand the sorts of business issues addressed by an ODS and to help implementors understand the ODS issues. The information in this publication is not intended as the specification of any programming interfaces that are provided by:

- WebSphere MQ and WebSphere MQ Integrator
- DB2 DataPropagator for z/OS
- IMS DataPropagator for z/OS
- DataJoiner
- DB2 Warehouse Manager
- IBM DB2 Universal Database

See the PUBLICATIONS section of the IBM Programming Announcement for the product name(s) above for more information about what publications are considered to be product documentation.

Comments welcome

Your comments are important to us!

We want our IBM Redbooks to be as helpful as possible. Send us your comments about this or other Redbooks in one of the following ways:

- Use the online **Contact us** review redbook form found at:
    ibm.com/redbooks
- Send your comments in an Internet note to:
    redbook@us.ibm.com
- Mail your comments to the address on page ii.

Introduction

Throughout history, successful organizations have managed to consistently evolve with the changing conditions of the business environment. The environment is changing at an exponential rate, causing organizations to continually invent new and innovative ideas at an even more rapid pace. It is a necessity that organizations adapt, evolve, and innovate to stay competitive.

Over the past few years, organizations have routinely used Business Intelligence and Data Warehousing techniques to gather data together into a single integrated view, to store historical data to and to make strategic business decisions by analyzing this data. This used to be a background process.

However, organizations have become more confident in using this type of information. They have seen increasing need to integrate data across business processes, channels, and organizational departments. In the new economy, customers are demanding immediate access to a fully integrated portfolio of products and services. Organizations must quickly satisfy these demands by changing to a more customer-centric infrastructure. In addition, they can see the benefit of doing this in real-time.

In this chapter we introduce the Operational Data Store (ODS) and the business challenges facing organizations in the new marketplace. We then define what an ODS is and compare it to the DW. Finally we position the ODS within the Business Intelligence (BI) architecture.

1.1 Introducing the Operational Data Store

It is addressing business needs that has driven the development of the Operational Data Store (ODS), a data structure designed around a specific set of data — that is, integrated for a specific purpose. The ODS typically contains current data which is dynamically updated in a real-time (or near-real-time) manner. In short, an ODS is an architectural construct containing subject oriented, integrated, volatile, current (or near-current), and detailed operational information.

One of the questions organizations face in deploying an ODS is whether to use their existing DW system to store the real-time updates for the ODS. While this may work in some situations, most clients find that conflicting Service Level Agreements (SLAs) make it more desirable to have the ODS and data warehouse (DW) operate on distinct schemas, or even totally separate environments. Examples of conflicting SLAs include the need to have data in the ODS faster than it can be transformed into the standardized DW format, as well as unresolvable business priority issues between the ODS user and the demands placed on the DW by ad-hoc queries.

> **Note 1:** In May of 2000, IBM Global Services announced the "Operational Data Store" for real-time data access. For more information on this offering visit the business intelligence Internet site at `http://www.ibm.com/BI` and `http://www-4.ibm.com/software/data/bi/consulting/datastore.htm`).

> **Note 2:** The ODS is also a component of the Zero Latency Enterprise (ZLE), a term coined by the Gartner Group for near-real-time integration of operational and information systems for data and business processes. The ZLE solution decreases the time it takes to make business decisions. In effect, there is zero latency between the cause and effect of a business decision. A ZLE with end-to-end quality of service involves heterogeneous and homogeneous replication, one or more near-real-time ODSs, a data warehouse, datamarts, and Business Intelligence applications. The ZLE solution enables analysis across the ODS, the data warehouse, and other sources (for example, weblogs). The ZLE also notifies the business of actionable recommendations (using publication and subscription services), effectively closing the loop on business processes with the operational systems.

1.2 Business questions

The emergence of the Internet and e-commerce have created some unique and interesting opportunities and challenges. We now have the technology to transfer information to anyone anywhere in the world. With this new capability, customers are asking for more and more customized products and services. This has created competitive pressures to get these products and services to the market in shorter and shorter time frames.

Many businesses have undergone a restructuring and reorganization to break down their horizontal functional boundaries. Now the focus is on improving business management and processes across traditional business functions (for example, customer service, campaign management, risk management, inventory, and supply chain management). Unfortunately, users must constantly access multiple applications when dealing with these new processes.

Deploying an ODS is an excellent approach, especially when this challenge cannot be met by the existing operational applications, the DW, or the datamarts. The ODS is not just the data store but the population around it. The front ends and the ODS will provide access to an integrated, consolidated picture of the organization's information and may leverage existing IT investments. This allows organizations to improve or close the loop on business processes.

The technology infrastructure should also be designed for the cooperation and interoperation of processes, in order to automate information flow through the enterprise, enable rapid accommodation to change, and integrate all customer contacts with the organization.

The business requirements may appear to be different across the various industries, but the underlying information requirements are similar — integrated, current, detailed, and immediately accessible. The following business questions in the different industry sectors demonstrate this need:

Insurance

- How can I provide an up-to-date view of insurance products owned by each customer for our Customer Relationship Management (CRM) system?
- How can I consolidate all the information required to solve customer problems?
- How can I decrease the turn-around time for quotes?
- How can I reduce the time it takes to produce claim reports?

Retail

- How can we give suppliers the ability to co-manage our inventory?

- What inventory items should I be adjusting throughout the day?
- How can my customers track their own orders through the Web?
- What are my customers ordering across all subsidiaries?
- What is the buying potential of my customer at the point of sale?

Banking/Finance

- What is the complete credit picture of my customer, so I can grant an immediate increase?
- How can we provide customer service have a consolidated view of all products and transactions?
- How can we detect credit card fraud while the transaction is in progress?
- What is the current consolidated profitability status of a customer?

Telecommunications

- Can we identify what our Web customers are looking for in real-time?
- Which calling cards are being used for fraudulent calls?
- What are the current results of my campaign?
- How can we quickly monitor calling patterns after the merger?

Of course, there are many other possible questions, but most of them can be summarized as follows:

- How do I provide an up-to-date view of cross functional information for a particular business process when the data is spread across several disparate sources?

As with a DW, the ODS should be seen as a journey and not a means to an end. Each business challenge fitting the ODS model should be categorized (by subject area), prioritized (by the business) and then split into manageable projects. Your ODS architecture (along with your entire BI architecture) should be constantly re-evaluated, taking into account the current and future evolutions of the business environment.

1.3 What is an Operational Data Store (ODS)?

In this chapter we introduce the term ODS to get a consistent understanding of what is meant by it. The following topics are described:

- ODS definition
- ODS characteristics
- ODS benefits
- Differences between an ODS and a Data Warehouse (DW)

1.3.1 Definition of an ODS

An ODS is an environment where data from different operational databases is integrated. The purpose is to provide the end user community with an integrated view of enterprise data. It enables the user to address operational challenges that span over more than one business function.

Its principal key differentiators are the update frequency and the direct update paths from applications, compared to the controlled update path of data warehouse or datamart.

1.3.2 Characteristics of an ODS

The following characteristics apply to an ODS:

- **Subject oriented**

    The ODS may be designed not only to fulfill the requirements of the major subjects of a corporation, but also for a specific function or application (for example, risk management, to get a holistic view of a customer).

- **Integrated**

    Legacy systems push their detailed data through a process of transformation into the ODS. This leads to an integrated, corporate-wide understanding of data. This transformation process is quite similar to the transformation process of a DW. When dealing with multiple legacy systems, there are often data identification and conformance issues that must be addressed (for example, customer identification, such as which codes are used to describe the gender of a person).

- **Near current data delivery**

    The data in the ODS is continuously being updated.

    Changing data permanently requires a high frequency update. Changes made to the underlying legacy systems must reach the ODS as fast as needed; that is, velocity is important. Some data is needed directly; other data can come in during a daily update. Thus, update of an ODS has both high frequency and high velocity.

> **Definitions of frequency and velocity:**
>
> *Frequency* is how often the ODS is updated, quite possibly from completely different legacy systems, using distinct population processes, and also takes into account the volume of updates that are occurring.
>
> *Velocity* is the speed with which an update must take place — from the point in time a legacy system change occurs, to the point in time that it must be reflected in the ODS.

- **Current data**

    An ODS reflects the status of its underlying source systems. The data is quite up-to-date. In this book we follow the architectural principle that the ODS should contain little or no history. Usually there is sufficient data to show the current position, and the context of the current position, for example, a recent history of transactions to assist a call center operator. Of course, if there are overriding business requirements, this principle may be altered. If your ODS must contain history, you will have to make sure you have a complete understanding of what history is required and why, and you must consider all the ramifications; for example, sizings, archiving, and performance.

- **Detailed**

    The ODS is designed to serve the operational community and therefore is kept at a detailed level. The definition of "detailed" depends on the business problem that is being solved by the ODS. The granularity of data may or may not be the same as in the source operational system. For example, for an individual source system, the balance of every single account is important; but for the clerk working with the ODS, just the summarized balance of all accounts may be important.

1.3.3 Benefits of an ODS

In this section many of the essential benefits are described that can be achieved by using an ODS:

- The ODS provides improved accessibility to critical operational data.
- With an ODS, organizations have a complete view of their financial metrics and customer transactions. This is useful for better understanding of the customer and to make well-informed business decisions.
- The ODS can provide the ability to request product and service usage data on a real or near real-time basis.
- Operational reports can be generated with an improved performance in comparison to the legacy systems.

- It is the right place to have a central version of reference data that can be shared among different application systems. One way could be that the applications access the data in the ODS directly. Another way is to replicate data changes from the ODS into the databases of the legacy systems.
- The ODS can help to integrate new and existing systems.
- The ODS may shorten the time required to populate a DW, because a part of the integrated data already resides in the ODS.

Attention: Not all ODSs will provide all these benefits.

1.3.4 When to use a separate datastore?

It is worth discussing briefly when to use a separate data store, the ODS — rather than simply extending the use of existing systems; for example, customer master files or a data warehouse.

There is no clear-cut rule for this, and in some cases, it is possible to meet new new real-time requirements by using existing systems.

Many tasks of a system designer or architect involve making trade-offs between conflicting requirements, as well as anticipating how these requirements are likely to change over time. Requirements include response time, throughput, ease of development, cost, service levels, resource utilization, availability, fault tolerance, serviceability, and so on.

An application database that is extended to provide ODS type function is likely to suffer from constraints imposed because it was originally designed as an application specific database. This may limit its performance, or if the ODS is changed to support ODS function, this may adversely impact the original application.

A data warehouse that is used to support more and more ODS style function is likely to become very costly, and you may find it increasingly difficult to meet service level commitments. For example, the DW may have to be "hardened" to make it, or a substantial subset of it, suitable for 24x7 operation.

It is often easier to meet these requirements with a separate dedicated data store, the ODS, albeit at the expense of some data redundancy. The cost of the data redundancy is more than outweighed by other savings in systems cost and development time.

It is also often easier to implement new requirements when an ODS and a DW are used. There is usually an obvious "home" for the requirement: this speeds development and deployment and gets the application to market faster, thus delivering benefit earlier. ODS data is operational and is expected to reliably describe what is happening down to the most detailed level. Mainstream business processes will want to rely upon it, and the update and maintenance procedures should reflect this. The DW, on the other hand, may be targeted more at strategic decision-making, where some degree of imprecision is tolerated, the tolerance and the velocity of the data must be taken into account before making use of it online.

In addition, the workloads for an ODS and DW are usually drastically different. Mixing the two workloads can require more resources, and cost, for a combined system, and can be more difficult to guarantee service levels, than if keeping them apart. The more contention there is between workloads, the more system resources are needed to cope with contention, in addition to coping with each workload.

It is possible to move DWs towards real-time working, that is through trickle feed, but often they cannot also be extended to guarantee fast and assured response times for high volumes of transactions.

1.3.5 Some differences between an ODS and a DW

The ODS may look like a DW, but it is actually quite different. Some of the main differences are described below.

Currency of data

An ODS is a current view of the data. It contains current or near-current data. It may be accurate nearly up-to-the-second, but does not have to meet this standard. That depends on the objectives of the ODS, the user needs, and the business requirements for velocity. For example, a risk management ODS in an investment house may only be updated once to cover off exposures in the overseas markets. If a business condition changes, for example, parts are taken from stock, then the operational data related to that condition quickly changes too. The ODS reflects the current status of a business condition, in this case, the number of parts in stock.

The DW data is quite different. It reflects a more historical view of the business conditions. If there are changes, a new snapshot may be created and put in line with the other snapshots of this business condition. Insertions to the DW (snapshots, events) are usually batched and enter the DW only according to a pre-defined schedule. There is usually a variable elapsed period of time during which the DW is not representative of the current operational situation.

As Figure 1-1 shows, the ODS addresses the tactical operational data needs of an organization by providing current or near-current integrated information, whereas the data warehouse supports the informational or strategic needs of an organization by providing more historical data.

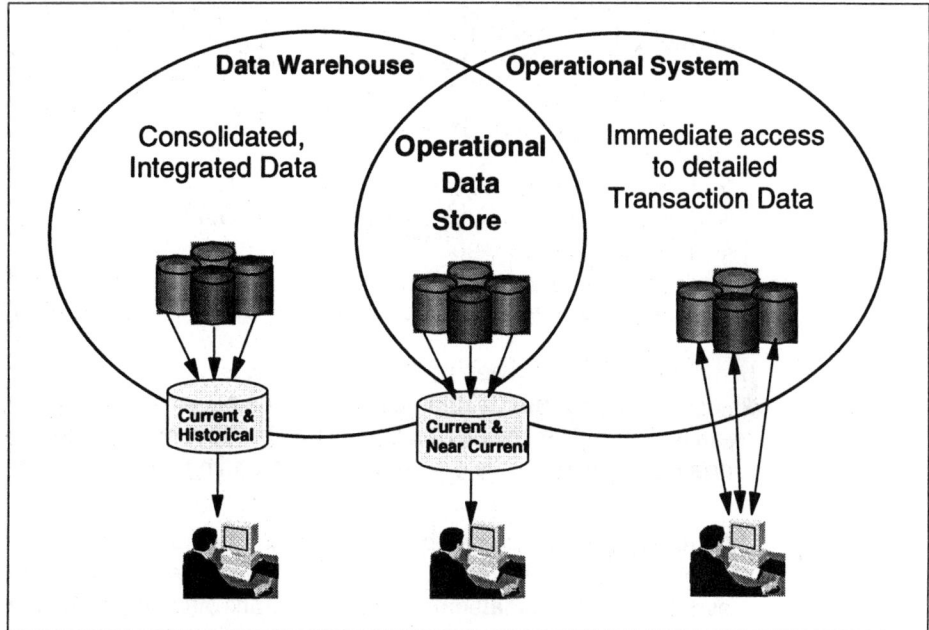

Figure 1-1 Positioning the ODS

Updating/loading data

In an ODS, altering (insert, update, delete) an existing record is a normal and often-used process, because just one status of a business condition is reflected. In the DW, the records are not updated, but a new snapshot or event may be created. This difference is shown in Figure 1-2. Multiple versions of data may exist and this depends on requirements or purpose.

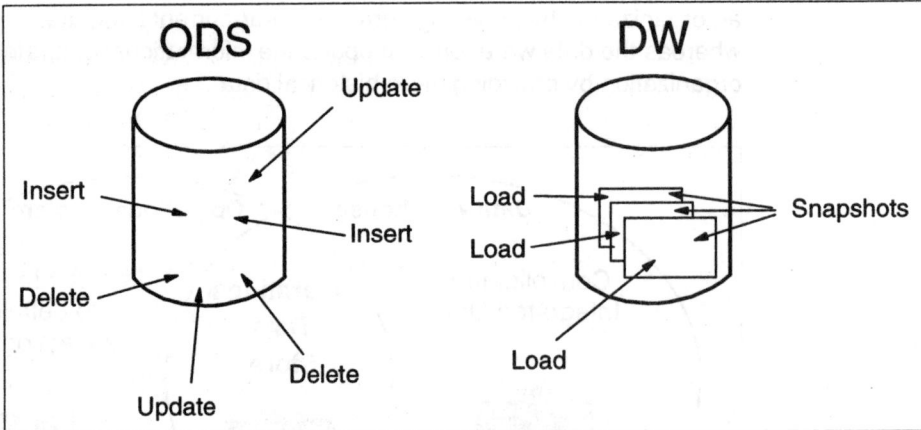

Figure 1-2 Updating/loading of data into ODS and DW

Another difference, when updating the data, is the point in time when the update is done. An ODS needs updates as soon as possible, depending on business requirements. This means there may be the need of a real-time or near real-time update mechanism; this is one of the outstanding characteristics of the ODS.

> **Note:** An ODS is updated based on requirements and not necessarily as soon as possible; that might be once an hour. In fact, an ODS could be updated overnight, but is updated directly from a front-office application such as Siebel.

Updates for a DW are normally collected, and at a predefined point in time, a load is done into the DW.

Summarization of data

The ODS contains primarily detailed data. It may contain summarized data for performance reasons, but this is not its first objective, because it is difficult to keep the summary data current and accurate.

Therefore the summarized data is normally calculated at request. Because of its short effective life it can be called "dynamic summary data". Its value depends on the moment of calculation. For example, consider the collective account balance of a company. This is calculated as a summary of all single accounts of the company. If any of the single accounts changes its value, the summary also changes.

However, certain widely-used summary totals may be maintained in the ODS.

In contrast, the summary data of a DW can be called "static summary data". This is summary data whose result does not depend on the moment of calculation. For example, suppose a manager wants to calculate the total number of cars sold in the year 2000. If he calculates this value in January 2001, he will get the same result as when calculating it in February 2001 (assuming that the December 2000 data has been loaded by January 2001).

Data modeling

The ODS is designed for record level access; a DW or datamart is designed for result set access.

The ODS should support rapid data updates. The DW as a whole is query oriented. It is designed to let people get data out of it according to their business needs, quickly and intuitively. However, individual pieces of the DW (inside the architecture) may not be of this persuasion.

For example, the Business Data Warehouse (as described by Barry Devlin in his book, *Data Warehouse: From Architecture to Implementation*) is the enterprise DW with its normalized data store. It is optimized for inputting data and for data extraction; such DWs are typically implemented with more normalized structures. They are also used for large complex queries that require access to the lowest level of detail and a complete history.

However, Business Information Warehouses (datamart structures) are optimized for getting data out for business purposes. So we typically see star schemas deployed as a physical mechanism for achieving performance. The dimensional model is a natural way that business users look at the data. It is not optimized for long running queries, but for accessing large amounts of data, quickly and easily. It is the physical implementation that gives performance.

As the ODS is usually designed to be application independent, this dictates a 3NF (third normalized form) data model.

The considerations to create a data model for the ODS are described in 3.3, "Data modeling" on page 52.

Transactions compared to queries

Transactions in the ODS are small, use few resources, and have predictable arrival rates. Normally there are a lot of transactions running in parallel. The same transaction is executed frequently during a day.

In the DW, the queries or analytical units of work can be large, use many resources, and may have an unpredictable arrival rate. Some queries or units of work will only be run once during their lifetime.

As an example, an operational transaction might get a list of all accounts of a customer and their balances. A DW unit of work could calculate the difference between the sum of all credits and the sum of all collateral of all customers of a bank.

Usage

The ODS is used for day-to-day operational decisions. For example in an insurance company the agent gets the contracts for a customer to decide which additional products he can offer.

The insurance company uses the DW, in contrast to the ODS, to get strategic and long-term and corporate-wide decisions. For example, the company might decide to start a marketing campaign for certain products that had lower sales last year.

ODS is tactical, whereas DW is strategic.

Users

Because of the different tasks an ODS and a DW fulfill, there are also different working communities that use these systems.

The ODS is used by the *tactical community*. This includes people such as insurance agents who have daily contact with their customers and who need information at their fingertips. The DW is more often used by the *strategic community*. These are people who make decisions — for example, a manager in an insurance company who is responsible for the life insurance branch, and who wants to measure the amount of insurance growth during the last five years.

Data volume

One of the major differences is data volume: the ODS will typically contain less data than the DW:

- The ODS may contain the current value of each customer's balance (by product) to reflect the collective corporate-wide balance of a customer. In contrast, the DW may store historical snapshots of each customer's balance.
- The ODS would contain the details of individual order line items, whereas the DW may have only the order headers.
- The ODS could store the customer contact names for the marketing, accounting, and purchasing departments. The DW may store the history of the customer contact names for the past five years.

Summary

Table 1-1 is a summary of the various differences between the ODS and a DW.

Table 1-1   Differences between ODS and DW

ODS	DW
Data of high quality at detailed level and assured availability	Data may not be perfect, but sufficient for strategic analysts; data does not have to be highly available
Contains current and near-current data	Contains historical data
Real-time and near real-time data loads	Normally batch data loads
Mostly updated at data field level (even if it may be appended)	Data is appended, not updated
Typically detailed data only	Contains summarized and detailed data
Modeled to support rapid data updates (3NF)	Variety of modeling techniques used typically 3NF for DW and dimensional for datamarts to optimize query performance
Transactions similar to an Online Transaction Processing (OLTP) system	Queries process larger volumes of data
Used for detailed decision making and operational reporting	Used for long-term decision making and management reporting
Used at the operational level	Used at the managerial level

1.4 How to position the ODS within the BI architecture

Businesses today are faced with an extremely competitive market place. More and more organizations are relying on Information Technology (IT) to sharpen their competitive edge by adapting to the rapidly changing business conditions. To adapt, they are looking towards business intelligence application solutions.

There have been many successful implementations of data warehousing solutions. The DW supports the informational and strategic needs of an organization by providing historical snapshot data. An ODS, on the other hand, addresses the operational data needs of an organization by providing current, or near-current integrated information which can be directly accessed or updated by the users.

Figure 1-3 shows how the ODS is positioned within the IBM business intelligence architecture. The ODS is an architectural structure that is populated from the operational and external data sources through the integration and transformation programs.

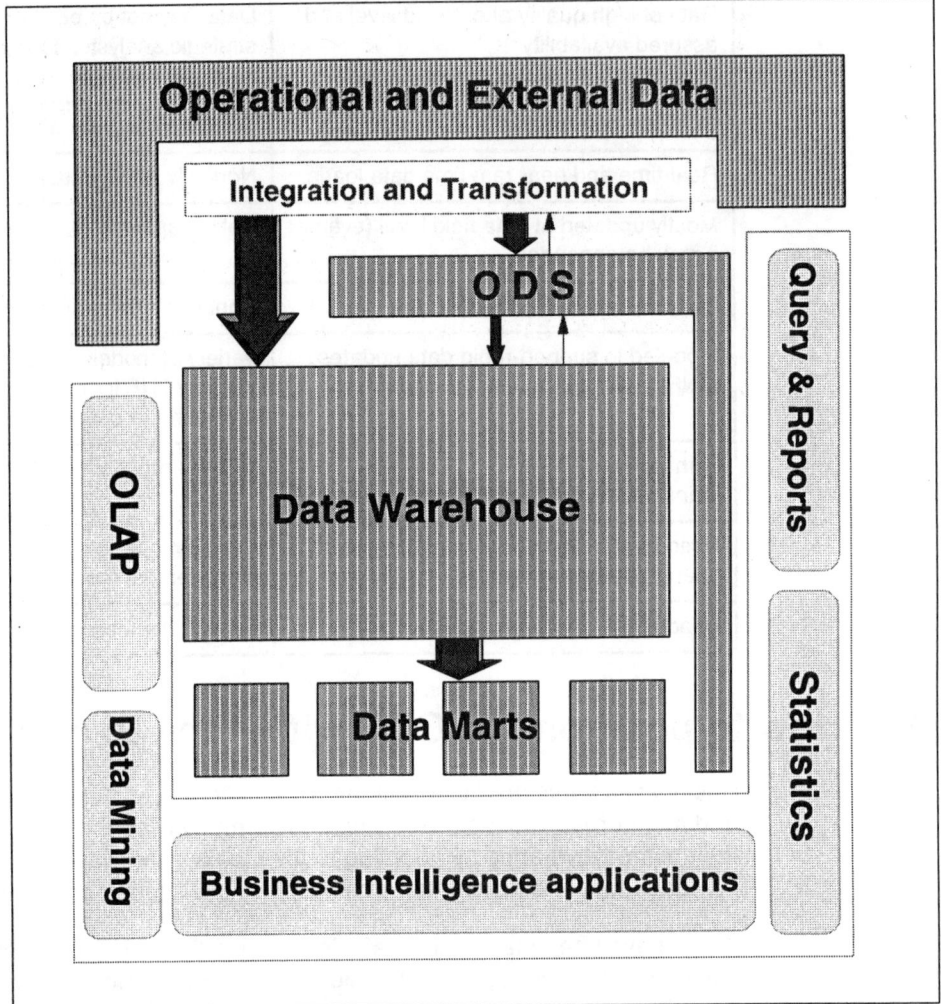

Figure 1-3   IBM business intelligence architecture

When the operational and external data passes through the integration and transformation layer, there will be two different flows, one to the ODS and the other to the DW. These two streams satisfy the different information needs of the various end users across different functions.

The ODS can push data to the DW using normal batch methods. For example, the current value of an integrated data element could be sent to the DW for snapshot, aging, or historical purposes.

Depending on the ODS type, a small amount of data may flow back in a controlled fashion to the ODS from the DW. Even though this flow makes up a very small part of the ODS, the business importance may be significant. For example, when the DW is used to analyze and calculate a competitive interest rate or to alter a production schedule based on the best performing items, the results are passed back to the ODS for the purpose of making corporate-wide operational business decisions.

Depending on the ODS type, updates to the ODS by end-users may trigger data to flow back to the operational data sources. A typical example would be a customer's shipping address. The address will be stored in both the ODS and the data source, however, the address in the ODS may be more up to date. In these cases the ODS should also institute a mechanism in the integration and transformation programs to filter these cyclical updates and stop them from flowing back needlessly to the ODS.

In general, operational access to the ODS will occur through custom interfaces. What we traditionally think of as query tools (QMF, Business Objects, Brio, and so on) are not the main thrust. They might be deployed, but the idea of operational applications must also be considered.

ODS issues

To maximize customer satisfaction and profitability, the ultimate data store would contain all of the organization's operational data. This, of course, is not economical or technically feasible.

To tackle these challenges, an ODS must ultimately be constrained based on business priorities, and the technology is being challenged to step up to these real-time and near-real-time requirements. The existence of these priorities and requirements drives cost and complexity. It is with these constraints in mind that the ODS issues can be properly addressed.

At first glance, it would appear that the ODS presents a paradox. It seems to have the characteristics of an On-Line Transactional Processing (OLTP) system while at the same time accommodating some of the attributes of a data warehouse (for example, integrating and transforming data from multiple sources).

In this chapter we look at many of the issues surrounding an ODS. First, we utilize elements from each business question, as developed in 1.2, "Business questions" on page 3, to apply specific business requirements. We then map these business requirements to their related ODS issues. In the remainder of the chapter we categorize and explore each issue in more detail.

2.1 The business requirements

Each business requirement in Table 2-1 is derived from a sub-component of a particular business question developed in 1.2, "Business questions" on page 3. Many requirements apply to a single business question, however, we have chosen specific business requirements so that a wide range of related ODS issues can be discussed.

Table 2-1 Business questions and requirements

Business question	Business requirements
Insurance: How can I provide an up-to-date view of insurance products owned by each customer for our Customer Relationship Management (CRM) system?	A consolidated view of all our products is needed, by customer, across several heterogeneous operational applications.
Retail: How can we give suppliers the ability to co-manage our inventory?	Consolidation of our three inventory systems (obtained from various mergers and acquisitions) will allow online inventory management by our suppliers.
Insurance: How can I consolidate all the information required to solve customer problems?	The new call center application must have the ability to track the number and type of customer contacts.
Retail: What inventory items should I be adjusting throughout the day?	Inventory management requires a consolidated and consistent view of all product codes and descriptions.
Banking/Finance: What is the complete credit picture of my customer so I can grant an immediate increase?	Our call center requires all account balances for a customer within minutes of an update.
Retail: How can my customers track their own orders through the Web?	Changes to the shipping address using the new on-line Web order maintenance system must also be applied to the legacy order entry system.
Banking/Finance: How can we supply customer service have a consolidated view of all products and transactions?	Customer service requires 30 days of transaction information to solve 99 percent of all customer complaints.
Retail: What are my customers ordering across all subsidiaries?	We need access to invoice line-item information across all of our subsidiary businesses to solve customer problems
Banking/Finance: How can we detect credit card fraud while the transaction is in progress?	The query response time must be five seconds or less during periods of high transaction volumes.

Business question	Business requirements
Insurance: How can I decrease the turn-around time for quotes?	The integration of the legacy applications will be phased in over the next four years.
Telecommunications: Can we identify what our Web customers are looking for in real-time?	Since the new Web application may be accessed in any time zone, the availability must be 24x7.
Telecommunications: Which calling cards are being used for fraudulent calls?	We must have quality data to be successful.
Banking/Finance: What is the current consolidated profitability status of a customer?	We need to know what calculations were used to create the customer profitability number.
Telecommunications: What are the current results of my campaign?	The current status of the data in the ODS must be known at all times.
Insurance: How can we reduce the time it takes to produce claim reports?	We must leverage the infrastructure and standards of our current environments.
Retail: What is the buying potential of my customer at the point of sale?	Our customer services representatives must consistently be able to access the customer information within seconds.
Telecommunications: How can we quickly monitor calling patterns after the merger?	We require access to one accounting period of call information from each source system.

2.2 Mapping the requirements to the ODS issues

Table 2-2 defines the various relationships between the business requirements and the ODS issues. The table also assigns one or more ODS issues to a particular description, these descriptions are used throughout this book.

For this chapter, the issues are further categorized under one of four areas:
- Transferring the data
- Data characteristics
- The ODS environment
- ODS administration and maintenance

Table 2-2 Relationships between business requirements and ODS issues

Business requirements	ODS issues	Description
Transferring the data		
A consolidated view of all our products by customer across several heterogeneous operational applications.	What is the subject area? What are the data source types, locations, and platforms? How can we integrate data from several sources?	Integrating multiple operational sources
Consolidation of our three inventory systems (obtained from various mergers and acquisitions) to allow online inventory management by our suppliers.	Should some or all of the ODS become the single version of the truth or the system of record?	
The new call center application must have the ability to track the number and type of customer contacts.	How to manage user updates to the ODS?	
Inventory management requires a consolidated and consistent view of all product codes and descriptions.	What kind of data transformations are required?	ODS data transformations
Data characteristics		
Our call center requires all account balances for a customer within minutes of an update.	How quickly must the ODS be populated after an operational transaction completes (for example, seconds or minutes)?	near-current data update (velocity)
Changes to the shipping address using the new on-line Web order maintenance system must also be applied to the legacy order entry system.	How to automate the synchronization of the ODS and legacy systems?	Source synchronization
Customer service requires 30 days of transaction information to solve 99 percent of all customer complaints.	What are the current and near-current data requirements?	Current data delivery
We need access to invoice line-item information across all of our subsidiary businesses to solve customer problems	What is the level of detail required?	Level of detail

Business requirements	ODS issues	Description
The ODS environment		
The query response time must be five seconds or less during periods of high transaction volumes.	How to control concurrent updates and queries? How to handle intensive transaction rates?	Mixing updates and queries
The integration of the legacy applications will be phased in over the next four years.	How to handle the growth of the ODS (network and server)?	Flexible growth path
Since the new Web application may be accessed in any time zone, the availability must be 7X24.	What are the availability requirements and how do we satisfy them?	Uptime
ODS administration and maintenance		
We must have quality data for this project to be successful.	Who owns the various data elements in the ODS?	Administration
We need to know what calculations were used to create the customer profitability number.	How do we know what data is in the ODS and what it can be used for?	
The current status of the data in the ODS must be known at all times.	How do we control the population of the ODS?	
We must leverage the infrastructure and standards of our current environments.	How can we leverage the current infrastructure and enterprise standards?	
Our customer services representatives must consistently be able to access the customer information within seconds.	How can we maintain the performance of the ODS?	Performance tuning and monitoring
We require access to one accounting period of call information from each source system.	How do we initially load the ODS?	Initial load

The remaining sections of this chapter expand on each ODS issue.

2.3 Transferring the data

Populating data into the ODS is arguably the most complex activity of an ODS system. Adding to this complexity is the potential for some of the ODS data to be transferred back to the source systems.

As shown in Figure 2-1, the ODS architecture is split into three layers. The operational and external data sources required to populate the ODS are found in the *data sources layer*. The *data acquisition layer* extracts from the data sources, integrates, consolidates, and transforms the data into the target format and loads the data into the ODS. The *enterprise data layer* includes the target ODS database. The entire ODS system is built on a foundation based on the administration and maintenance layers. Chapter 3, "ODS architectures" on page 33, expands on this architecture by adding more layers and adding more details for these.

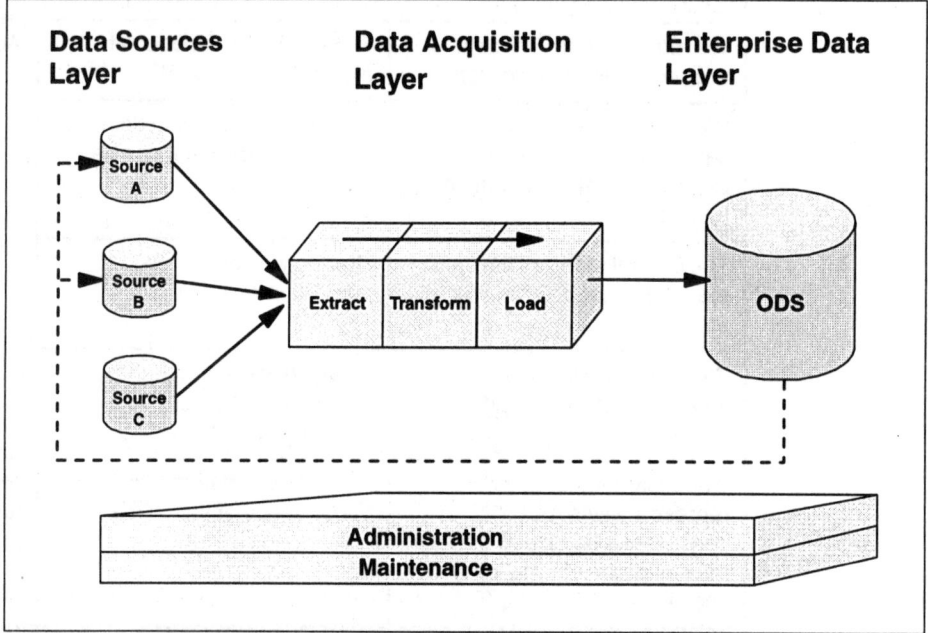

Figure 2-1 ODS architecture overview

We now discuss the two primary tasks involved in moving the data from the data sources to the ODS:

- Integrating multiple operational sources
- ODS data transformations

2.3.1 Integrating multiple operational sources

In this section we discuss the data integration issues surrounding the population of the ODS. We cover the following topics:

- What data to put in the ODS
- What data *not* to put in the ODS
- Integrating multiple heterogeneous data sources
- The ODS as the system of record
- User updates to the ODS

The data elements in an ODS should be limited to the specific subject area required to support the cross functional business process we are modeling. For example, if the ODS is to facilitate customer service, then it should contain customer order information and not financial accounting data.

Ideally, an enterprise data model exists and is used to define the scope of the subject area. Multiple ODSs may be built based on different subject areas, however, to maintain integrity overlapping data must be minimized by using the enterprise data model. The amount of integration, if any, between multiple ODS should be based on the enterprise-wide business requirements.

Do not place data in the ODS just because it may be required by the data warehouse. Also avoid placing data in the ODS just because it exists. This extra data will add to the complexity of the project and may determine its success or failure. You should attempt to simplify the ODS structure while fulfilling the business requirements.

As with a data warehouse, the first function of an ODS is to integrate and consolidate data from multiple disparate data sources. This integration has many of the same issues as the data warehouse. For example, how do we match data from two different systems; how do we extract from two different platforms; and which data source is the system of record? Middleware can be used to connect the heterogeneous environments including relational and non-relational data (such as VSAM, IMS or flat files).

You should also decide carefully whether the entire ODS (or some part of it) will become the system of record and/or the "single version of the truth". Both have major implications on the complexity of the ODS. If the ODS is to become a system of record, then all affected legacy applications and possibly the data warehouse will have to be modified appropriately — a potentially huge undertaking.

> **Note:** We have defined the terms: *system of record* and *single version of the truth* as follows:
>
> ► System of record: Multiple data stores may hold the same data elements, such as customer name and status code. Each data store may update the data elements without any synchronization between them. What version of the data is to be considered the correct version in two different systems systems? The data store with the most trusted value for the data element (as defined by the business) is called the system of record for that element.
>
> ► Single version of the truth: One and only one data store contains the data elements. All applications wishing to make changes to the data element must use the defined data store. (Note that *multiple read-only* copies of the data may exist in other data stores for performance reasons.)

Careful planning is required for the user update portion of the ODS. It should be based on new data requirements not existing in the current legacy applications. One purpose for users writing to the ODS is to update the data warehouse, for example, with a call resolution status code. An example of data existing in both the legacy system and the ODS would be contact information, such as address and telephone number.

The data may originally come from the legacy system; however, in the ODS, it is updated by the users of the call center. The call center applications use the ODS as their authoritative source and want to keep it up to date. If these changes are not applied back to the legacy system, then the transformation layer will require a rule for these fields. For example, you may want to block temporary future updates coming from the legacy system.

Allowing the ODS to become inconsistent with the legacy systems will compound the current data integration problems. If an overriding business requirement must update a common data element, then you should consider a mechanism to feed these changes back to the operational source. In this case, the transformation layer can filter any cyclical data so that it does not replicate back to the ODS.

That is an enterprise view. However, the ODS could also be built to support a particular business area that needs to feed back changes; for example, the ODS might be built to support a call center.

2.3.2 ODS data transformations

After the data has been sourced and extracted, we must apply any transformations required by the business. These transformations give the final touches to the integrated data, eliminating any last remnants of the operational application silos.

Many of the types of transformations for a data warehouse are also included in an ODS. The only limitation as to what transformations can be performed is the latency constraint, that is, how quickly the data must be updated. The amount of transformations that can be done is inversely related to the latency, that is the more near-real-time the update requirements are, the fewer transformations can be done.

> **Note:** An ODS is not necessarily near-real-time. It is definitely more volatile — in terms of frequency and velocity. But daily updates might meet the business need especially in companies where monthly DW updates are the norm.

Transformations include:

- Cleansing
- Conversions
- Some summarization
- Decoding/encoding
- Reformatting
- Converting physical structures

The extent and type of transformations are dependent on the ODS data delivery timing requirements. These requirements may be at odds with the transformation requirements, and trade-offs may have to be made. In a real-time environment, much of the data coming from the legacy systems may arrive "as-is" and should be documented accordingly.

An Extract Transform Move Load (ETML) tool with the capability of handling high update volumes should be considered. Some of this analysis may have already been done for those companies that have functioning data warehouses. The method of representing gender or status, for example, may have already been decided upon, and some of the transformation rules may have already been defined.

The transformation tool or tools used to populate the ODS will have to be able to handle a heterogeneous environment. Most often, the legacy environment will have data sources on many different platforms. The ODS itself may be on a distinct platform, depending on the requirements of your situation. The tool must be able to handle a wide range of data formats and structures. It must handle many data types and the conversions between them. You should also choose a tool which is constantly adding new sources and targets.

The ODS can be populated in real-time at the same instant as the operational data. This can be an expensive strategy for the refreshment of the ODS. Another method is to feed the ODS incremental changes from the operational data. Capturing the changes can be performed by the source systems, requiring modifications to the operational applications. The journal or log files of the online transaction manager or database management system provide another way to capture data changes.

2.4 Data characteristics

Once the data requirements have been defined and the data sources have been located, we can concentrate on the following data characteristics:

- Near-current data delivery: How often should the ODS be updated?
- Source synchronization: How do we keep the ODS and the legacy system synchronized?
- Current data: How much history is required, if any?
- Level of detail: What level of data granularity is required?

2.4.1 Near-current data delivery

We next look at the timing issues for updating the ODS. This will depend on your business requirements, since timing must be considered along with the transformations. For example, if the data is to be delivered within seconds, you may not be able to execute a complex profitability calculation.

2.4.2 Source synchronization

The data coming from the legacy systems must not only arrive in a timely manner, but all changes must have guaranteed pickup and delivery. The delivery mechanism must insure that the ODS is consistent with the legacy applications. The integrity of the related data elements must not be compromised.

2.4.3 Current data

The ODS should contain current and/or near-current information. If the business process requires more than one accounting period of history, the question of why must be raised. Some other system (for example, the data warehouse or a datamart) could possibly fulfill this request. If the ODS contains unnecessary data, the performance will degrade and the management complexity will increase. If the ODS does include some limited historical requirements, then an efficient method must be chosen for purging the data, archiving the data (if needed), or moving the data to the data warehouse.

2.4.4 Level of detail

The information in the ODS must be detailed enough to support the business process we are modelling. For example, a customer service application may require detailed transactions whereas a financial analysis application may only require the latest balance. Typically the ODS will contain a high level of granularity which may result in large data volumes.

> **Note:** The current constraint is likely to limit the size of an ODS: The volumes are in tens and hundreds of gigabytes. They are not in terabytes.

Some techniques can be used to decrease the amount of data such as aggregation and summarization. As with data integration and transformation the amount of data you combine should be weighed with the data currency requirements. The ODS will be smaller than the data warehouse but may still contain huge amounts of data. As the data volumes grow, so do the costs of managing the ODS.

2.5 The ODS environment

In this section we look at some of the issues surrounding the ODS environment:

- Mixing updates and queries, what loads must the ODS handle?
- Flexible growth path, how do we cope with the growth of the ODS?
- Uptime, what are the availability requirements?

2.5.1 Mixing updates and queries

The ODS structure must take into account the mixed workload of transactional updates, tactical queries, and some analytics. The data access requirements must be well defined and understood so that an appropriate data structure design may be created. Typically the data accessed in the ODS will be transactional in nature, using customized front-end applications and/or custom built applications. At the same time, the design must be able to handle an update intensive workload from the various data sources.

Because of the large number of updates and the data integration issues, an ODS transaction must be accurately defined. These are some questions to ask: Should we insert a new record into the ODS when a record is created in the legacy application? Should we replace the current record if it exists? Should we only update the modified fields, accumulate the fields, or accumulate multiple records? Transactions should also be kept as small as possible to decrease locking.

2.5.2 Flexible growth path

For an ODS to be successful, you are advised to take an iterative approach, both when building and rolling it out to users. Invariably this will require changes to the ODS data structure, data sources, and transformations. The environment's components should be designed to take in account the ODS growth: centralized or distributed data structures, tables sizes, update capabilities.

The platform chosen needs to be flexible. It must handle greater volumes of data and higher numbers of users as it grows and becomes more popular. There are two types of scalability:

- You can choose a platform which allows you to upgrade the hardware (for example, CPU, memory, disk). Unfortunately, once you reach the limits of the machine's upgrade path, it must be replaced.
- Another option is an architecture which allows you to add more hardware as required (for example, to add another physical machine). You may wish to consider Symmetric Multi Processing (SMP) and Massively Parallel Processing (MPP) hardware architectures. There are some platforms today which will handle a combination of both.

2.5.3 Uptime

As with any operational system, the ODS will be used to run the day-to-day operations of your organization and will therefore require a service level agreement (SLA) for availability. Depending on the business requirements this will include some level of built-in redundancy. Examples include a hot-swap database, mirroring, RAID technology, and High Availability Cluster Multi-Processing (HACMP). The Parallel Sysplex cluster technology with DB2 UDB for z/OS data sharing is another example. Batch window limitations and update scheduling considerations should also be weighed when considering your ODS platform.

2.6 ODS administration and maintenance

There are numerous issues related to the administration and maintenance of an ODS. Most issues are the same as with the data warehouse, and in fact, are the same as with most systems. In this section we cover the following topics:

- Administration
    - Data ownership: Who owns the data?
    - Rejected records: How do we handle such records?
    - Information catalog: How do we know what data is in the ODS, and what it can be used for?
    - Flow control: How do we control the population of the ODS?
    - Leveraging current infrastructure and standards: How can we use the current infrastructure?
- Performance tuning and monitoring: What methods can be employed to maintain the required level of performance?
- Initial loads: How do we initialize the ODS?

2.6.1 Administration

As with the data warehouse, deciding who owns which data elements in the ODS is very important. The ideal situation is to have the owners of the legacy data also own the corresponding data in the ODS. You should also assign an overall data steward to the ODS. Someone must be accountable for the data quality of each data element. When the data from the source systems is particularly "dirty" (for example account data sent from external sources) and the business requirements place a high priority on data quality, you will have to consider a reject handling mechanism.

Handling rejected records is something projects should not overlook and not ignore as an issue. Chapter 6, "Administration tips for handling rejected records" on page 179 outlines a process and a sample application solution for managing the rejecting, reporting investigation, fixing and reprocessing of this "dirty" data.

The information catalog is also an important component of the ODS just as it is in the data warehouse.

With regard to business metadata, most access to the ODS is through custom interfaces. It is not analytical and query oriented in general. Users are generally operational troops who are working over and over with the same screens. They do not need to understand data structure, even from a business view. They are not constructing ad hoc queries and not running reports.

Now business metadata is still going to be needed. But the people most likely to be using it are not the operational staff, but rather, the supervisors or managers behind the scenes.

The information catalog allows users to navigate the consolidated picture and must answer questions such as these:

- What data is in the ODS?
- What was the source of the data?
- How was the data transformed?
- How are different data elements related to each other?

To increase the success of a metadata strategy, the various tools chosen to populate and access the ODS should generate and/or incorporate metadata from multiple sources.

The ODS should be populated in a managed and controlled manner. Usually this is accomplished using a tool which has the ability to control the flow of data and to notify operators when something is wrong. This can also be a good place for gathering and integrating metadata for the information catalog.

When the ODS supports the information requirements across enterprise-wide functions, corporate standards should be used during all project phases. As technology changes and more and more heterogeneous source and target platforms participate in the ODS, there will be an increasing need to share data throughout the various parts of the organization. Using an enterprise-wide standard will help alleviate some of the complexity inherent in this type of environment.

Note: The ODS may support just one business area (such as a call center) and is not necessarily enterprise-wide.

To minimize development and maintenance costs, the ODS should leverage the current corporate standards and infrastructure. Much of the data warehouse infrastructure may also be leveraged: the ODS could be the system of record for the DW to reduce duplicating ETML. If you build the DW first and then the ODS, then you are potentially creating two interfaces. Note that the DW and/or ODS can be developed in either order. Building the data warehouse before the ODS decreases temptation to use the ODS as a staging area.

2.6.2 Performance tuning and monitoring

The data access requirements of an ODS will push your system resources to their limit. The ODS design should include components for reducing resource usage, for example, limiting transaction processing during peak periods. Other techniques, such as constraining the data model, optimizing the data structures, tuning the database design, and reducing input/output (I/O), should also be employed.

Physical data base tuning examples include creating appropriate indexes, running reorganizations and statistics, and disabling logging when recovery is not an issue. Performance must be constantly monitored: Be prepared to "tweak" the ODS in order to optimize the use of the system resources. Performance monitoring and prioritization tools should also be investigated.

2.6.3 Initial loads

The ODS must be configured and populated before the on-going transaction and delta processing can be started.

The initial loads for both the ODS and the data warehouse share many of the same issues. The current or near-current data characteristics of an ODS should produce smaller data volumes compared to the data warehouse, however, the volumes may still be significant due to the data granularity. A bulk load utility and log disabling should be considered under these circumstances.

> **Tip:** As shown in Figure 2-1 on page 22 the data acquisition layer contains four components: *extract*, *transform*, *move*, and *load*.
>
> The data integration and data transformation processes should be designed to use at least these four components. Using this building block approach, we can then reuse some of the same components for the initial load and the on-going process (for example, they could both use the extract component; whereas the initial load could take advantage of a bulk load utility). On-going support and maintenance will also be improved. This type of design is dependent on the compatibility of the on-going and initial load transformation requirements.
>
> The latency challenge can sometimes be addressed with this component based approach when the requirement is not so close to real-time.

3

ODS architectures

This chapter describes what we need to keep in mind when designing an ODS. We have identified four major steps to build the architectures:

- Analyzing the business requirements
- Defining the ODS type needed
- Data modeling
- Defining and describing the different ODS layers

In section 3.1, "Business scenarios" on page 34, we describe three business scenarios with different requirements that can be solved with an ODS architecture.

Referring to these scenarios, in section 3.2, "ODS types" on page 38 we detail three different types of ODS architectures. We also provide guidelines to help you decide what architecture type should be used in what situation.

In section 3.3, "Data modeling" on page 52 we discuss what kind of data modeling technique makes sense for what type of ODS. We discuss the strengths and weaknesses of several techniques, and offer hints to help you choose the best technique to be used.

Finally, section 3.4, "ODS layers" on page 57, explains the different layers that an ODS consists of. For every layer we describe what technique and what products are needed to fulfill the architectural requirements.

3.1 Business scenarios

We now introduce three business scenarios to better illustrate how the ODS architecture fits together. Each example contains unique requirements which call for a different type of ODS.

The business scenarios were created from the following three business questions:

- Banking/finance: What is my customer's entire product portfolio?
- Retail: How can my customers track their own orders through the Web?
- Telecommunications: Which calling cards are being used for fraudulent calls?

3.1.1 Consolidated customer and product information

The General Manager of Consumer Banking at ABC Bank would like to have a consolidated view of each customer's product portfolio. This customer view would be accessed by the branch relationship managers and the call center. The integrated product information should include products the customer currently holds and is in the process of applying for. This would allow for additional cross-product selling and increased customer service.

ABC Bank's legacy systems were designed and built in the early years of IT development and followed the standard evolutionary process. The product applications are divided across several heterogeneous platforms, all of which have to be accessed to facilitate a holistic view of a customer's portfolio.

The relationship managers and the call center require immediate access to a current customer view. Due to time and budget constraints the legacy systems will continue to be used in their current capacity for all customer and product changes. The only new data requirements consist of customer contact tracking information.

A new application will be created to be used by the relationship managers and the call center. This application will be transactional in nature. Ninety percent of all data access will be on a specific customer or all products for a customer. There will be minimal updates on the customer record for contact tracking.

Limited decision support reporting will be required to extend ABC Banks current data warehouse (the data warehouse is only loaded monthly). This reporting is for a small number of users who require up-to-date campaign results and will leverage one of the current data warehouse data access tools.

Figure 3-1 demonstrates a sample data flow for this business scenario. Data is integrated and transformed from multiple heterogeneous data sources and used to populate the customer portfolio ODS. A custom application is used by the relationship managers and call center users to read and write to and from the ODS. The campaign management users have direct query access to the ODS through an existing decision support tool.

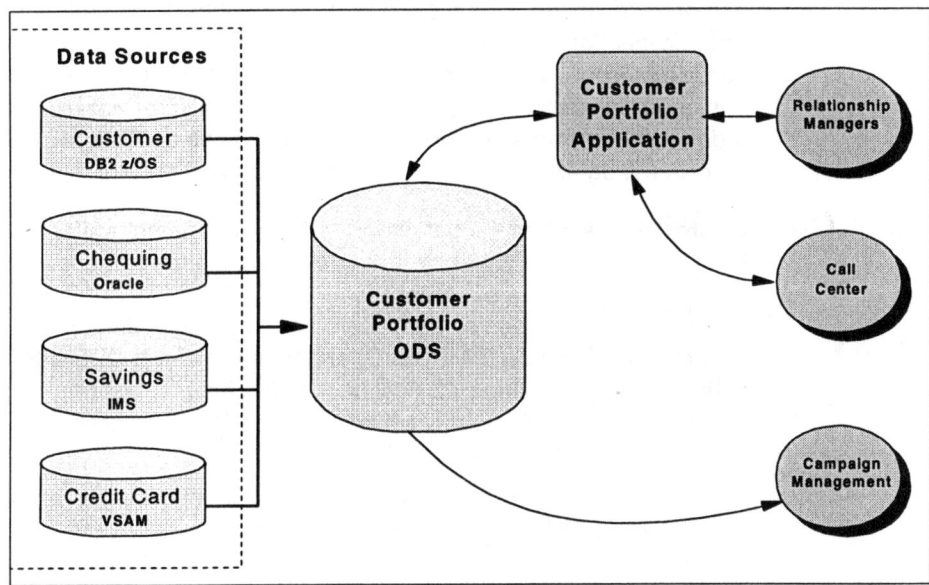

Figure 3-1   Consolidated customer portfolio data flow

3.1.2 Consolidated customer and order information

The CEO of Parts-r-Us, a parts manufacturer, has received several requests from her larger customers for a facility which would allow them to track and maintain their own orders over the Web. The CEO is feeling some pressure, as other parts manufacturers in the same market segment are already working on similar solutions.

This will require an integration of data from several legacy systems, including accounts receivable (customer), warehouse logistics, inventory, and order entry. The data is located on two separate platforms and uses four different database or storage technologies.

The new ODS data structure will be updated directly instead of using the legacy applications. This will support a simplified front-end application (a single source and target) and will support future integration projects. Due to the urgency of the first phase of the project, the online order maintenance feature will be limited.

This will facilitate a simplified feedback to the legacy systems. For example, the customer will be able to update the "quantity ordered" and "ship to" fields (until the order enters a "filled" status), but regular channels would be used to enter the order. After discussing these issue with her customers, the CEO concluded that this would be acceptable.

A new Web application will be written to allow customers to access their orders and provide limited update capability. Data will be accessed at the customer and order levels (for example, all orders for a particular customer or details of a particular order). The existing online legacy applications will denote when data has been updated by a customer using a special ID. The customer service and order entry functions will also have access to this application. Inventory control reports will be executed at timed intervals throughout the day.

Figure 3-2 describes the data flow for the order maintenance business scenario. Data is integrated and transformed from multiple heterogeneous data sources and used to populate the order maintenance ODS. An order maintenance application will be used by both customers and the customer service department to access and update the ODS. Changes made to the ODS through the order maintenance application will flow back to the source systems using a trigger and apply mechanism. Regularly scheduled reports will be created for the inventory management department.

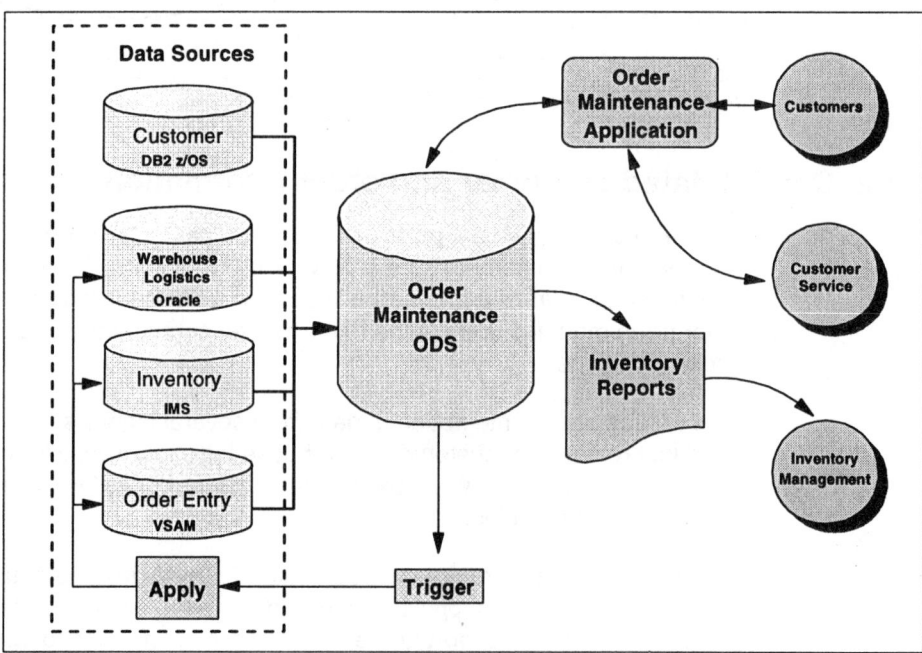

Figure 3-2 Consolidated order maintenance data flow

3.1.3 Detect calling card fraud while the call is in progress

MNM Canada is a national telecommunications company that focuses on providing long-distance service to both corporate and private customers. Lately the number of incidences of calling card fraud have been on the rise, and despite the fact that MNM is absorbing many of these long-distance charges, customers are becoming concerned. Long-distance fraud is prevalent in airports, where bystanders observe callers making long distance calls and note the numbers dialed. The customer service manager would like to figure out a way to quickly verify that the person using the calling card is really the person who owns it.

The servers recording call information are decentralized in different parts of the world. Calls from various locations are recorded on local servers or backup servers during high traffic periods. Data is then aggregated weekly for billing purposes.

MNM Canada requires central up-to-the second access to all phone call transactions that the customers make and needs to have these transactions tightly integrated with other legacy systems.

The integrated information will be accessed by both the legacy applications and the various reporting functions. Data will be updated on a per-call basis, whereas most queries will be by customer/calling card for a particular time period.

Figure 3-3 represents the data flow for the consolidated call information scenario. Data is integrated and transformed from multiple homogeneous data sources and used to populate the calling transaction ODS. This data flow into the ODS is real-time. A custom-built fraud application will be used to verify calls and trigger customer service when a suspect call is identified. The existing customer service and billing applications will be migrated to the ODS, eliminating their data stores. A follow-on phase will eliminate the customer data store.

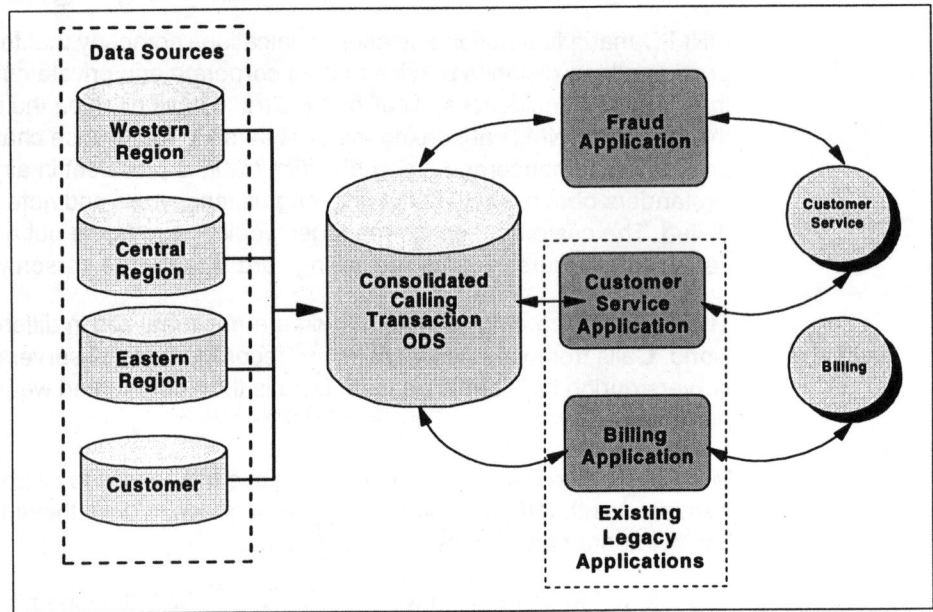

Figure 3-3 Consolidated call information data flow

3.2 ODS types

There are three general types of ODS architectures. They are differentiated by the level of integration between the operational systems and the ODS. In practice, a hybrid will most likely be used. Figure 3-4 demonstrates the data flow for the three ODS types.

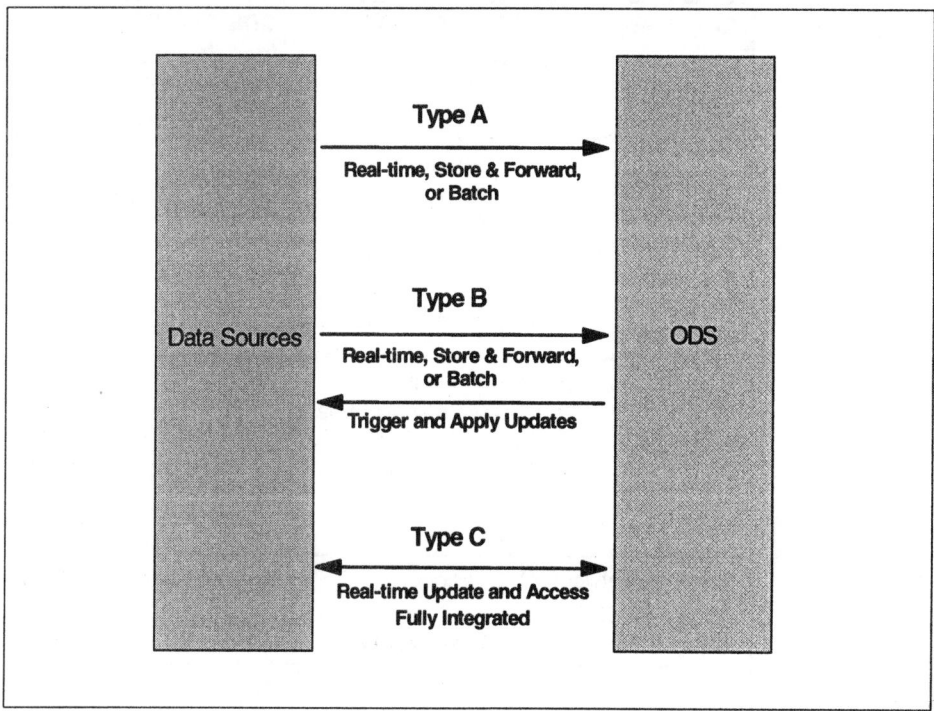

Figure 3-4   Data flow overview for ODS types A, B, and C

An ODS *type A* includes real-time (or near-real-time) legacy data access and localized updates (data modifications are not fed back to the legacy systems). The localized updates would typically include new data not currently captured in the operational systems.

An ODS *type B* includes the characteristics of an ODS type A along with a trigger and apply mechanism to feed data back to the operational systems. Typically these feedback requirements would be very specific to minimize conflicts.

An ODS *type C* is either fully integrated with the legacy applications or uses real-time update and access. Table 3-1 cross-references the various characteristics of each ODS type.

Table 3-1 Characteristics for the general ODS types A, B and C

Characteristics	ODS Type A (real-time data access/localized update)	ODS Type B (update transaction trigger)	ODS Type C (fully integrated)
Data source	Operational and other	Operational and other	Operational and other
Real-time update of ODS (potential) by front-end applications	Yes	Yes	Yes
Direct access from front-end applications	Read/write (the tendency might be to read more than write, because of the perceived out-of-sync issues)	Read/write	Read/write
Data flow between operational system and ODS	One way	Both ways	Both ways
Timing of operational system updates (where applicable)	N/A	Asynchronous Triggers (for example, batch)	Real-time

The three business scenarios, as described in 3.1, "Business scenarios" on page 34, can be mapped to the three ODS types:

- The customer portfolio ODS fits the description of an ODS type A, since it does not contain any data flowing back to the data sources.
- The order maintenance ODS matches an ODS type B, as it has some limited data flowing back to the data sources.
- The calling transaction ODS is an integrated ODS type C solution.

Also, please refer to Figure 3-1 on page 35, Figure 3-2 on page 36, and Figure 3-3 on page 38 for each scenario.

The following key characteristics are common to all three ODS types:

- The ODS can be directly updated by front-end applications (such as Campaign Management, Customer Service, Call Center) or by the user directly through an application interface (such as a new Web application).
- The ODS can be a source of data for the warehouse. Batch processes will be used to populate the data warehouse.
- The ODS complements or extends the operational systems. It is not intended to replace them.
- Although most sources will be used to populate both the ODS and the data warehouse, two data acquisition streams will probably exist due to the temporal differences in the data required. For example, the data warehouse may require a monthly inventory snapshot whereas the ODS may require an up to the minute inventory status.

Figure 3-5 contains an overview of the three ODS types and how they fit within the logical BI architecture. The scope of the ODS is limited to the shaded region in the lower half of the figure. The diagram is split vertically by the six layers of the BI architecture, as labelled across the top.

The data enhancement and datamart layers only apply to the data warehouse; all other layers apply to both the ODS and the data warehouse. The data acquisition layer that applies to both ODS and DW takes on a different form due to the temporal differences in population. The dotted circles denote the three types of ODSs and are described in the next three sections of this chapter.

Attention: Data is either populated into the ODS (and then to the DW) or to the DW, not both, to answer to one of the key design principles — that is, *single source population*.

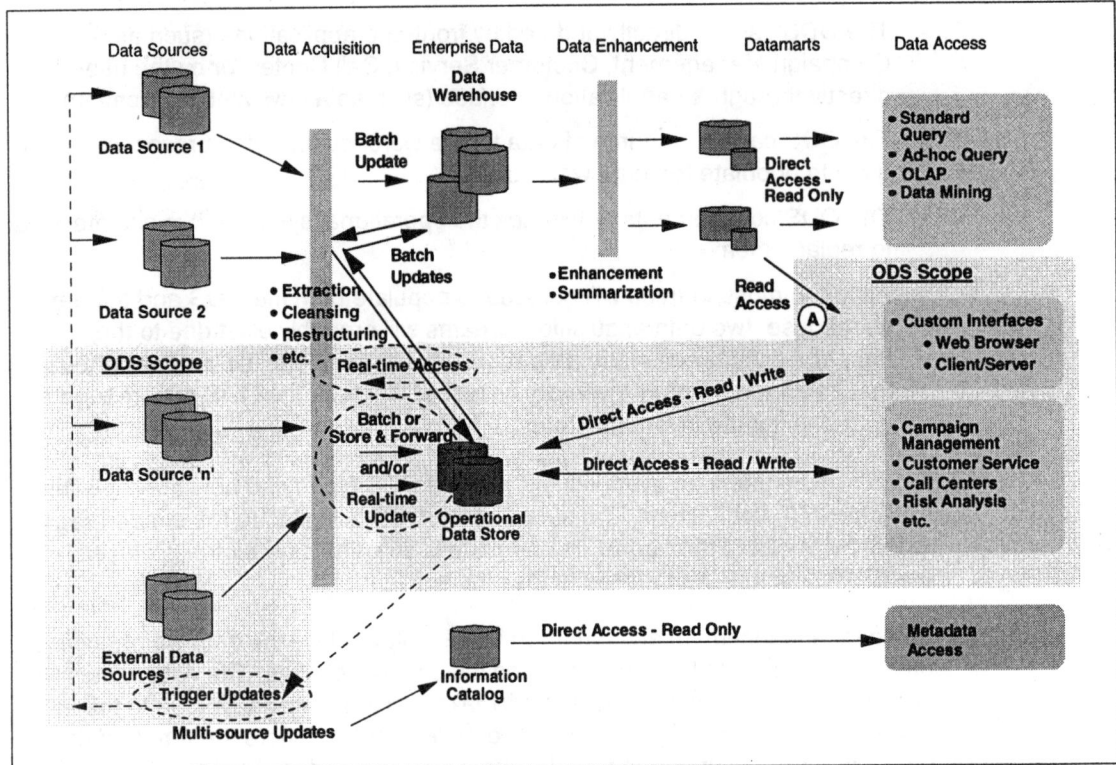

Figure 3-5   Architecture of ODS types A, B, and C

As shown in the data sources layer, the ODS can have internal and/or external sources. Some of the sources may be shared with the data warehouse while others may not.

The source data flows through the data acquisition layer much as it does in the data warehouse (although some of the issues are quite different). This layer integrates and transforms the data. Because of the different data delivery timing requirements, the ODS and the data warehouse will probably have two separate acquisition streams.

The enterprise data layer contains the ODS, the data warehouse, and the information catalog. An ODS does not use the data enhancement or datamart layers. The information catalog must integrate the ODS and data warehouse metadata.

The users have read and write access to the ODS using the data access layer. This layer uses custom built applications or customized off-the-shelf products to access the ODS. Some applications may access the ODS and the datamarts at the same time (note in Figure 3-5 the arrow labelled 'A' pointing from the datamarts to the data access layer).

Data flowing from the ODS to the data warehouse and vice versa use batch update processing like any other data source. These two data flows must go through the data acquisition layer as shown in the diagram.

The dotted circles distinguish the three different ODS types. The ODS type A uses a batch/store and forward or a real-time update process to populate the ODS. The ODS type B uses a trigger update mechanism to send data back to the data sources. The ODS type C ODS is fully integrated or uses real-time access to send data back to the legacy applications. Note that an ODS type C only uses the real-time update for data coming from the legacy applications.

3.2.1 ODS type A: real-time data access/localized update

Data flows from the operational systems to the ODS through the data acquisition layer. Updates to the ODS can be real-time, store and forward, and/or batch. In a real-time environment changes are applied to the ODS immediately, for example, using the same operational application. A store and forward scheme may use tools such as replication or messaging to populate the ODS. Changes which are only required daily, for example, could use a normal batch process. Operational systems are not updated from an ODS type A. Figure 3-6 describes the architecture of an ODS type A.

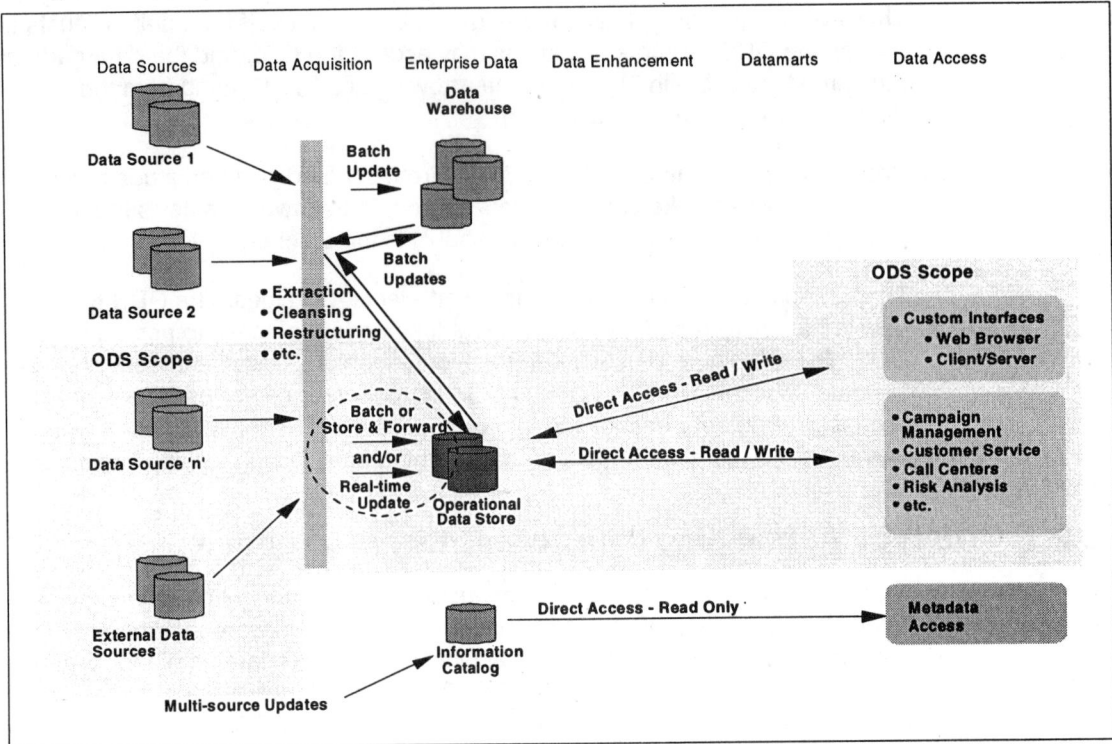

Figure 3-6   Architecture of an ODS type A

The ODS type A receives updates from data sources that are of two principal classes — internal (for example, enterprise applications) and external (for example, purchased demographics data). Internal data is fed into the ODS in a real-time or near real-time fashion on a individual record basis. Updates received from external sources and the data warehouse may be done in batch during off-peak periods, depending on business requirements.

The data warehouse may receive data snapshots from the ODS for historical analysis. At the same time, data may also flow from the data warehouse to the ODS (for example, the ODS may require a profitability calculation based on twelve months of history). Both data flows will use batch processes on a regularly scheduled basis as if the ODS and data warehouse were normal operational applications.

Business users gain entry to the ODS and have read and write privileges. Pre-packaged front-end applications or custom built applications are used for access. Here are some examples:

- A vendor-supplied campaign management tool
- A custom-built call management system for the call center
- An online customer-support Web application.

Changes to the ODS are not reflected back to the data sources. Typically the requirements for writing to the ODS would contain new data elements not currently stored in the operational systems. For example, customer interaction and contact tracking information for a call center application. There are some situations where updates to data elements in the ODS type A are also in the legacy applications. These situations requires careful consideration with the understanding that this data will not always be synchronized with the legacy systems. For example, you might update the ODS immediately (knowing it will be rewritten later) to handle multiple interactions with the customer during an exposure window.

You should also consider user updates to the ODS as a data source for the data warehouse. If strategic analysis is required for this data, then extracts or snapshots should be taken and stored in the data warehouse using its regular data acquisition services. The ODS should be treated the same as any other data warehouse data source and vice versa.

The data elements flowing to the ODS must be carefully constrained to simplify the design and increase the chances of a successful implementation. Do not use the ODS as a staging area for the data warehouse. Only populate the ODS with data required by the modeled subject area and dictated by business requirements. Also resist the urge to populate the ODS with data just because it exists.

This type of ODS is the least complex since it does not send updates made to itself back to the data sources. Most ODS projects will start with this type, depending on requirements and needs

Our first business scenario, the consolidated customer portfolio, fits nicely into an ODS type A architecture. Figure 3-1 on page 35 shows data flowing from multiple heterogeneous source systems to the ODS with no requirements for synchronization back to the source systems. The example also shows a custom built customer portfolio application which will allow the two user groups to read and write to the ODS.

3.2.2 ODS type B: update transaction trigger

The ODS type B includes the characteristics of an ODS type A plus the additional feature of an asynchronous triggering mechanism. This triggering mechanism is used to send ODS changes back to the operational systems. Figure 3-7 describes the architecture of an ODS type B.

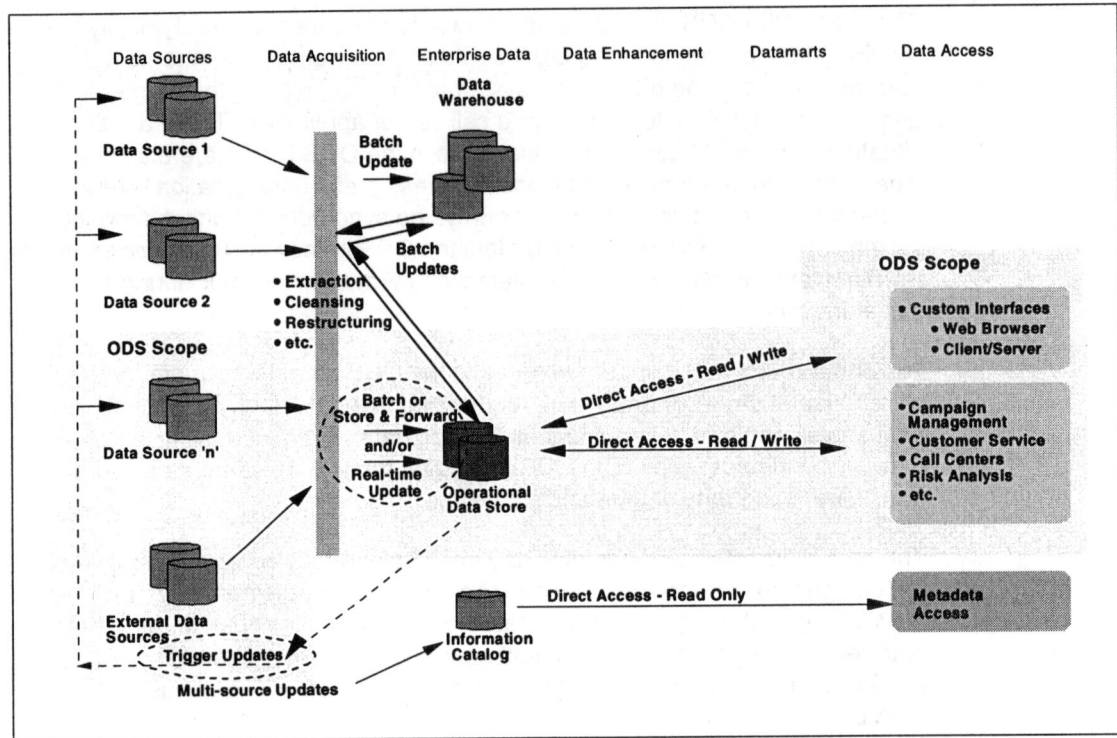

Figure 3-7 Architecture of an ODS type B

Business users gain access to the ODS with read and write privileges. Changes made to the ODS by an end-user may trigger an update to the data sources. For this reason there is a loose integration between the legacy applications and the ODS environment.

The data feedback to the legacy systems will have to be well defined — all possible inconsistencies have to be considered and appropriate designs have to be put in place. For example, it is unlikely that an update to an address using an online legacy application will coincide with a customer updating the same address through the call center. The business requirements are very important and need to be understood by all parties. Remember, only data that has a business need should be sent back the data sources.

For some data elements (such as address) the business may decide that the ODS will become the system of record. In these cases business rules will have be defined for updates to the ODS not initiated by an ODS end-user. These rules will decide which data should overwrite the ODS system of record. If the ODS is not the system of record, then the same types of business rules will have to be developed for the trigger mechanism. In this case some of the data sources may be the system of record.

From the architecture diagram it would appear that a cyclical data update could occur in an ODS type B. The following examples describe various methods for stopping this type of update:

- Most legacy systems have an audit ID field for the person or application making changes to a record. The ODS could be given a unique ID which becomes part of the data flowing to and from the data sources. The extract or load layer could then use this information to bypass the synchronized records. We can also add a timestamp in the update record.
- By placing audit information in the ODS this type of processing could also be placed in the trigger mechanism. Since the ODS is technically an operational system the typical auditing requirements would apply.

As Figure 3-8 shows, the trigger update mechanism of an ODS type B contains a trigger component and an apply component. Middleware may be considered to off load the work and act as a data storage area. The trigger component must accommodate:

- Multiple platforms
- Exception handling during errors in the apply component
- Capturing changes by time or event
- Mask the technical complexities of different networks and protocols
- Manage the quality of the data

The design of the apply component must have minimal impact on the operational applications. If possible it should be developed on the target environment's technologies and accommodate:

- Exception handling when the ODS or data sources are unavailable
- Data integrity between the data sources and the ODS

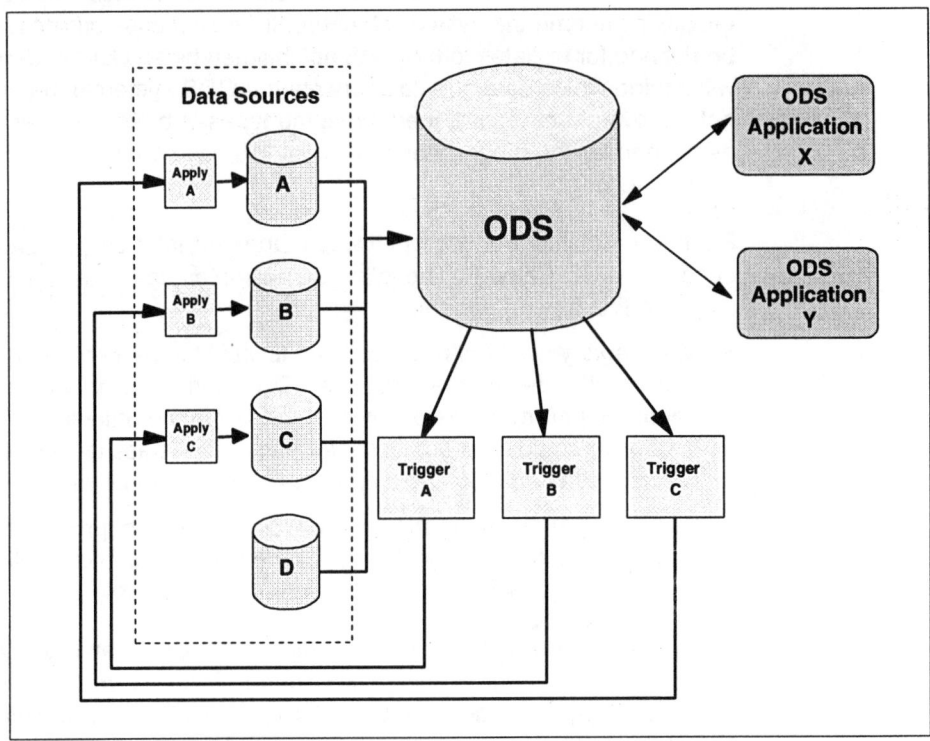

Figure 3-8   ODS Type B trigger update process

A separate trigger component should be created for each target data source requiring updates from the ODS. This will provide maximum flexibility for handling current and future business requirements. For example, in Figure 3-8, if application X updates an ODS data element also stored in data sources A and C, then triggers A and C can be used to capture the change. Later, if the business requirements change, trigger B could be used if the same change should be applied to data source B.

The second business scenario, the order maintenance ODS, conforms to an ODS type B architecture. As Figure 3-2 on page 36 demonstrates, data flows from multiple heterogeneous source systems to the ODS with limited synchronization back to the source systems. The scenario also shows a custom built order maintenance application which allows the two user groups to read and write to the ODS. Some of these writes to the ODS will trigger updates back to a particular data source.

It is important to stress that only a limited number of data elements should flow back to the data sources in an ODS type B. This data must not change often and the volumes should be relatively small. If you find that a large amount of data is being sent back to the data sources, then an ODS type C should be considered instead, in regards of integration requirements as well.

3.2.3 ODS type C: fully integrated

Data flows back and forth between the data sources and the ODS through the data acquisition layer on a real-time basis. The ODS becomes the single source for much of the corporation's key operational data. Figure 3-9 describes the architecture for an ODS type C.

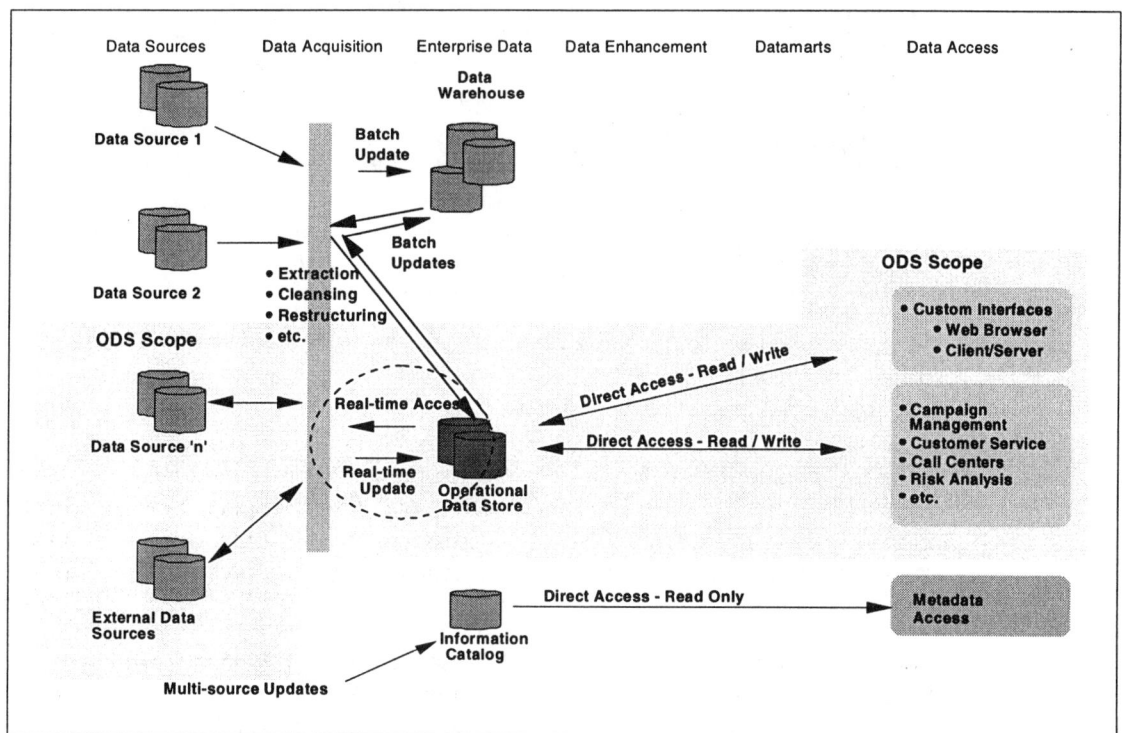

Figure 3-9   Architecture of an ODS type C

What differentiates an ODS type C from an ODS type A and an ODS type B is that the stored information is common across applications and lines of business. This provides the benefit of seamless integration across mutual data, applications, and business functions. The ODS type C receives updates from the end-users through a messaging system on a real-time basis enabling the ODS to become the single source for much of the corporation's key operational data.

There are many restrictions for using this type of ODS. It works best in a homogeneous environment so that native synchronization tools can be used. The whole issue of conflicts will have to be dealt with in great detail. There is the added complexity of trying to synchronize with multiple legacy systems. Transformations in the data acquisition layer must work both ways. For example, if the ODS uses M and F for male and female whereas the legacy system uses 0 and 1 then the updates back to the legacy systems would have to 'reverse' this transformation.

One method of implementing an ODS type C is to have it become the "single version of the truth" for all applications. In this scenario there is one and only one copy of each data element and it is stored in the ODS.

> **Note:** There is an inherent latency in replication. Multiple physical copies of the ODS means propagation, transmission, and delay. You would still need a concept of an official mother copy with as many shadow copies as was required to meet performance requirements. In theory with a message broker based hub and spoke approach you could distribute updates to multiple physical databases and have them all update concurrently and in parallel. That would be one complex beast though. If you ever got out of synchronization (and Murphy says it will happen) it becomes difficult to know know which of the multiple single truths was the real truth.

All applications would have to access the ODS to get at this "single version of the truth". This could be accomplished by slowly migrating the legacy applications to use the ODS and retiring their current data stores.

An ODS type C could also be implemented using an update anywhere strategy (using replication for example). In this scenario more than one copy of each data element would exist, but they would always be synchronized. Of course there are a number of issues surrounding this type of implementation. The number of data sources would have to be restricted. There would have to be a one to one mapping between the data structures of the ODS and the data sources. A homogeneous environment would also be required (for example, DB2 to DB2).

The third business scenario, the call transaction ODS, suits an ODS type C architecture. Figure 3-3 on page 38 shows data flowing from multiple homogeneous source systems to the ODS with the requirement for maximum integration with the source systems. The data flow shows a custom built fraud application which will allow customer service to read and write to the ODS. The diagram also shows that the two existing applications (customer service and billing) have been migrated to use the ODS as their data store.

3.2.4 Selecting the right type of ODS

Business requirements dictate the right type of ODS. Asking the correct questions can help you choose the right type of ODS for your situation. First, ask yourself if you require an ODS or a data warehouse/datamart solution. When real-time access to current and integrated operational data is required then an ODS is the right solution. Then you must decide how tightly you would like to integrate your ODS with the operational systems. If you do not require any updates, choose an ODS type A; if you require some updates, choose an ODS type B; if you require a single version of the truth, then choose an ODS type C. Figure 3-10 demonstrates a flow chart of the selection criteria.

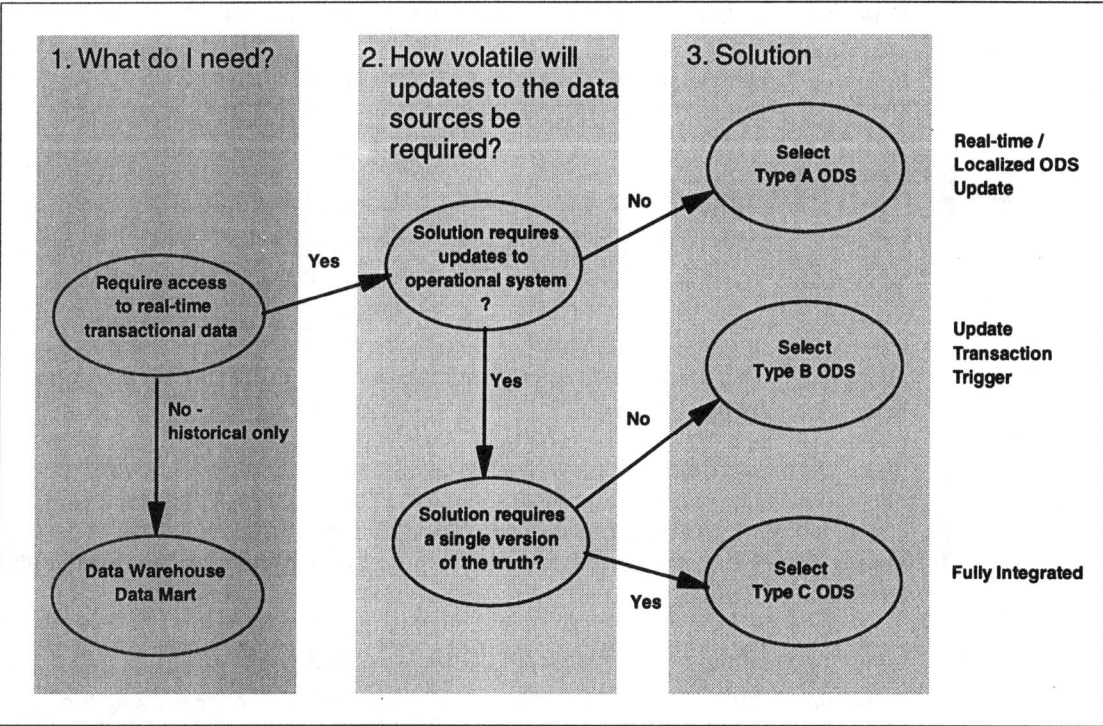

Figure 3-10 Selecting the right type of ODS

We can apply this selection criteria to our three business scenarios as follows:

- What do I need?
    - None of the scenarios require historical access.
    - All three scenarios require real-time or near real-time transactional data.

- How often will updates to the data sources be required?
    - Customer portfolio ODS: No updates to the data sources, choose type A.
    - Order maintenance ODS: Limited updates to the data sources, choose type B.
    - Calling card transaction ODS: Single version of the truth is required, choose type C.

We have restricted our discussion by using project scenarios with ideal conditions. This has allowed us to demonstrate the differences between the ODS types but in reality you will be constrained by other factors such as budget and time, business requirements that inconveniently don't conform to our idealized architecture models. All of these restrictions will have an affect on your choice, in fact your design will probably contain a mixture of the different ODS types.

3.3 Data modeling

This task is one of the most difficult in the ODS context, because the ODS plays two different roles. It has characteristics of an operational system as well as of a decision support system (DSS). The DSS characteristics are defined through its integration and subject orientation. The operational characteristics are its high availability and fast response times, and therefore the ODS can act as a basis of mission-critical applications.

The ODS data model can be derived from an enterprise data model, when one exists. The enterprise data model describes all data which is needed for corporate information purposes. The ODS data model is a subset of the enterprise data model. Only those parts which are really needed are taken for the ODS data model.

> **Note:** More frequently the data model is built from the functional/departmental level up. Using this approach, it is much more difficult to anticipate all the requirements across the enterprise. And even if it is not enterprise in the purist sense, a business unit can still get substantial benefit from it.

There are two different approaches of data modeling which can fulfill the needs of the ODS:

- Entity Relationship Model (ERM)
- Dimensional modeling

We describe the two approaches and give some hints about when to use them.

3.3.1 ERM modeling

The ERM is an abstraction tool because it can be used to understand and simplify the ambiguous data relationships in the business world and complex systems environments. A simple ERM is shown in Figure 3-11. ERM modeling produces a data model of the specific area of interest, using two basic concepts:

- Entities
- Relationships between those entities

Entity

An entity is defined to be a person, place, thing, or event of interest to the business or the organization — for example, "Product", as shown in Figure 3-11. An entity represents a class of objects, which are things in the real world that can be observed and classified by their properties and characteristics.

Relationship

A relationship depicts the structural interaction and association among the entities in a model. It shows the dependencies of the entities from each other — for example, the arrow pointing from "Product" to "Order" in Figure 3-11. The numbers at each end of the arrows define the cardinality of the relationship, in this case 1 to n (or 1 to many).

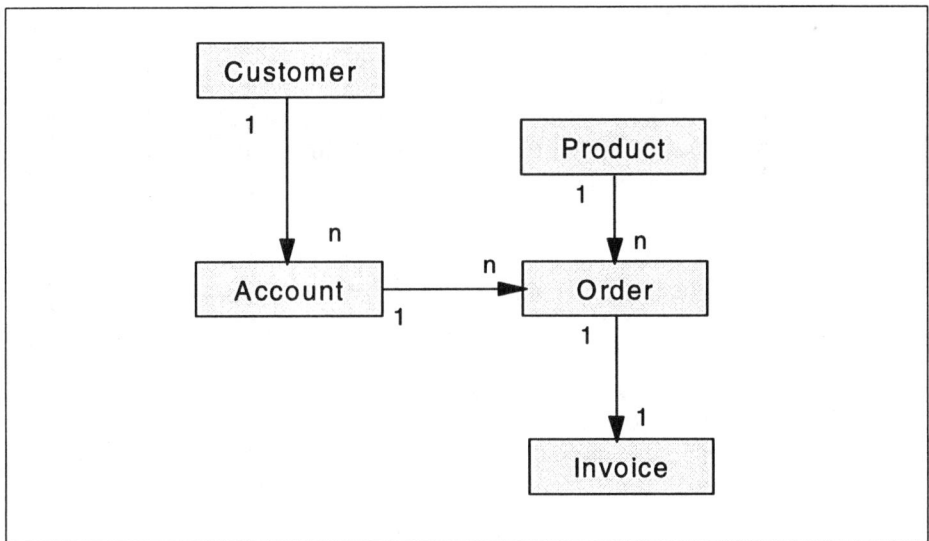

Figure 3-11   ERM

Most ODSs are implementing a 3NF model. This type of model was originally designed to minimize data redundancy, as such models minimize the amount of updates required in a database when values change. This capability explains its value to OLTP databases and its value in updating ODS databases now.

3.3.2 Dimensional modeling

Dimensional modeling is a technique for conceptualizing and visualizing data models as a set of measures that are described by common aspects of the business. It is especially useful for summarizing and rearranging the data and presenting views of the data to support data analysis. Dimensional modeling focuses on numeric data, such as values, counts, weights, balances, and occurrences. The basic concepts of a dimensional model are:

- Facts
- Dimensions
- Measures (variables)

Fact

A fact is a collection of related data items, consisting of measures and context data. Each fact typically represents a business item, a business transaction, or an event that can be used in analyzing the business or business processes.

Dimension

A dimension is a collection of members or units that describe the fact data from a particular point of view. In a diagram, a dimension is usually represented by an axis. In a dimensional model every data point in the fact table is associated with only one member from each of the multiple dimensions. The dimensions determine the contextual background for the facts.

Measure

A measure is a numeric attribute of a fact, representing the performance or behavior of the business relative to the dimensions. The actual members are called variables. For example, measures are the sales in money, the sales volume, the quantity supplied and so forth. A measure is determined by combinations of the members of the dimensions and is located on facts.

Basic model

The basic model for dimension modeling is the star model as shown in Figure 3-12. It typically has one large central table (fact table) and a set of smaller tables (dimension tables) arranged in a radial pattern around the fact table.

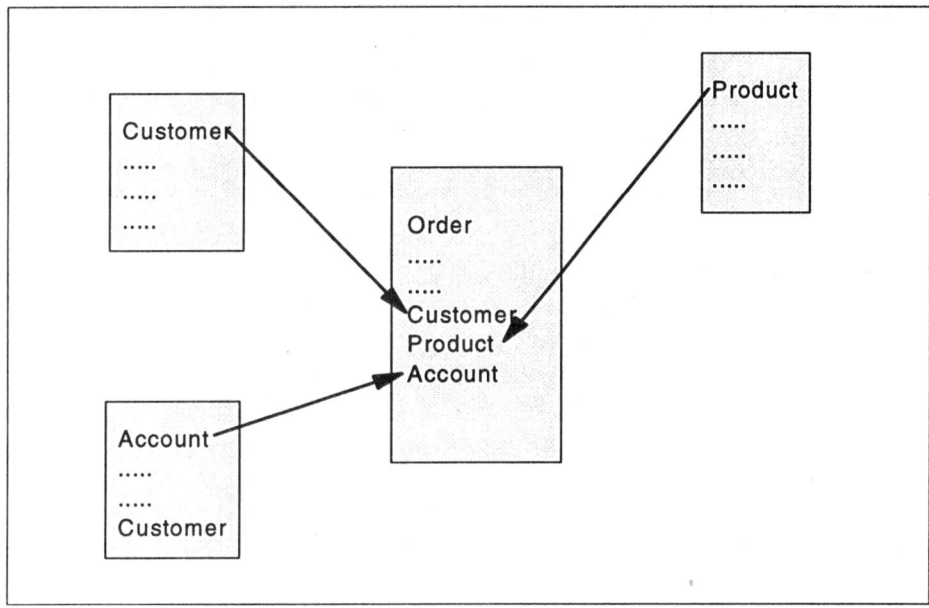

Figure 3-12 Star schema

3.3.3 Deciding on the modeling technique

In our experience it is best to take a pragmatic rather than a purist approach to choosing the modeling technique. Both approaches can be of benefit when used appropriately and many ODSs will be a mix of the two.

The two techniques for data modeling sometimes look very different from each other, but they have many similarities. Dimensional modeling can use the same notation, such as entity, relationship, attribute, and primary key. And, in general, you can say that a fact is just an entity in which the primary key is a combination of foreign keys, and the foreign keys reference the dimensions.

Therefore, we can say that dimensional modeling is a special form of ERM modeling. Whereas the traditional ERM has an even and balanced style of entities and complex relationships among entities, the dimensional model is very asymmetric.

The preferred technique depends on the purpose of the ODS; but mainly, if the ODS is used as a pure operational system, the ERM technique is preferred. In an operational system we normally have only requests for a small amount of data for very specific tasks. These tasks are often represented by entities of the ERM. In an operational system you need data very fast, also from the source systems.

Because there is no data or just a small amount of redundant data in the ERM, you can make updates from the source systems or through the application very fast. Another reason for the fast update capability is that the legacy systems are also often designed with an ERM. So the need for transformations during the update process may be very small.

If the ODS is more used as a data access system, then the dimension modeling approach may be preferred. In this case you normally have scheduled your data updates. While updating the data, many transformations can be done, and the data can be arranged to fulfill the needs of the data access application. This implies also a higher redundancy of data to make the complex queries for the analysis run faster.

We might use dimensional modeling because:

- The type of analysis lends itself to it.
- The query tool being used requires it or can benefit from it.
- Users prefer to think dimensionally.
- Data is being loaded from a dimensional data store (for example, a datamart).
- The access required for analysis is more efficient for high volume access with dimensions. (Many relational database management systems have implemented in their engines optimizations for star schemas and can process them very efficiently.)

The basis for a successful data model is a very precise analysis of your business requirements. Depending on your business issues, there are many intermediate forms of modeling which could be expected. If your ODS fulfills more than one purpose, you have to decide which technique to use for each of these purposes.

Regarding the physical database design of the ODS, there are no special techniques needed. All known techniques can be used, such as merging tables physically, using indexes, or defining purge criteria to get data out of the ODS.

3.4 ODS layers

In this section we introduce the different ODS layers that define the whole process to get the data from the legacy systems to the ODS end-user community. First, you have to define the data sources for the ODS. Then you have to find a way to get the data from the legacy systems to the ODS. In this case, you must have the workload of the ODS in mind and think about how to maintain your information catalog.

Another important point involves the systems management requirements of your whole system. Finally, you must prepare the data access to the ODS for the end-user community. An overview of how the different layers are connected to each another is given in Figure 3-13.

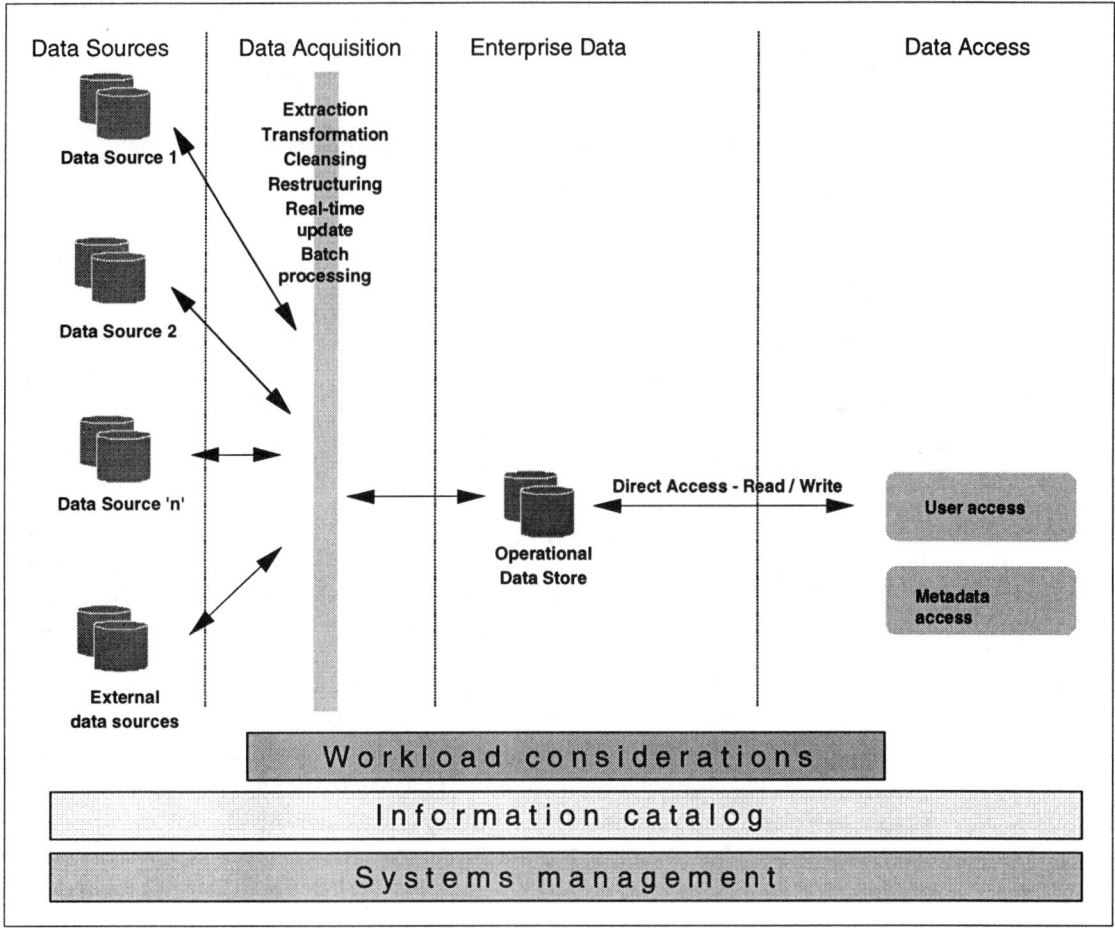

Figure 3-13   ODS layers

3.4.1 Defining the operational data needed

Most organizations show that there has been a progressive enhancement of the data warehouse and ODS to integrate corporate data from the original islands of application. The legacy data applications were created and added to the existing application inventories. Then interfaces between applications of islands were created, and extract files were needed to interface with other applications along with countless reports.

Organizations desiring to integrate large amounts of complex and fragmented operational data need to capture the source data to populate the ODS in order to meet their business objectives. Although there are many characteristics with ODS, we are mainly interested in the ODS characteristics of data that is subject oriented, integrated with multiple operational sources, current valued, and detailed, in selecting operational data for the ODS deployment. Here is a useful approach in defining the operational data sources prior to an ODS deployment:

1. Identify the business requirements that can be used as the base to begin the process and data modeling.
2. Synchronize the ODS data model to the corporate-wide data model.
3. Develop ODS scope and methodology to design an ODS to satisfy the business requirements.
4. Develop ODS high level design as a prototype to verify the scope and methodology deployed.
5. Outline solution strategies using the high level design as a blueprint that should identify all necessary components.
6. Determine costs, benefits, and sizing using the blueprint above.
7. Assess solution impacts using the prototype and blueprint with all representatives from the ODS development team.
8. Confirm solution definition with all responsible parties for the ODS development.
9. Identify system records and determine which is the single version of truth for each.
10. Identify the operational sources for ODS.

The identified source data of an ODS may be across all operational data and external data. However, the data volume of ODS can be much smaller than the data warehouse, and volumes of each entity in ODS will differ a lot as with the operational data. For example, the data volume of a CUSTOMER_ORDER entity would be considerably bigger than the volume of a VENDOR_SUPPLIER entity.

The operational data source will depend on the ODS design and scope of the business requirements. The initial data source for an ODS from the operational data is likely to be defined as those needing to populate a vertical slice through the model by a business subject. For example, the initial ODS design might be concentrating on the Customer subjects for the enterprise or Order Fulfillment subject, which will require a vertical column of the subject related data from the operational data. Until you progress to the ODS type C, your ODS is likely to be a subset of the whole operational data.

A concept of the ODS data source from the legacy operational data is depicted in Figure 3-14. The ODS architect should avoid the temptation to place unjustified data, such as the historical data in the data warehouse, into the ODS. Let us look at the possible ODS sources and considerations necessary to populate an ODS from the operational and external data.

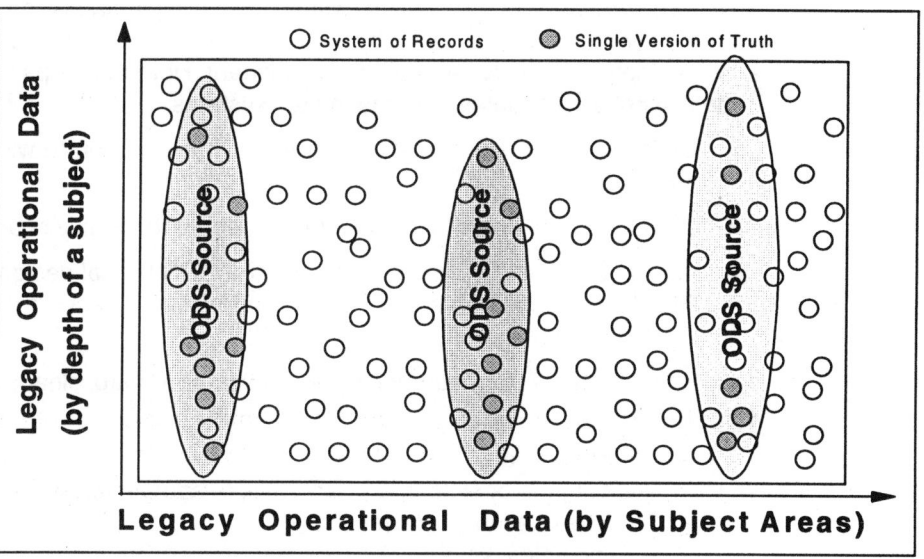

Figure 3-14 ODS data source from the operational data

Considerations on sourcing from legacy systems

An ODS is built to integrate legacy application data transforming into a cohesive and collective form. Most large IT organizations keep the operational data in multiple products running on different platforms. Therefore, the data sources could be on the DB2 UDB family, IMS, DL/I, Informix, Oracle, Microsoft SQL Server, Sybase, Teradata, VSAM, and other linear files on z/OS or OS/390, VM, VSE, i-series or OS/400, p-series or AIX, UNIX (such as Solaris), Windows NT/2000/XP, and Linux. Legacy systems were written at different times by different people using different hardware and software and to different objectives. It should come as no surprise that they do not easily integrate together.

Today's heterogeneous environments do present challenges to acquire and integrate data from various sources.

IBM products include:

- IBM Data Replication products such as DB2 DataPropagator, DataJoiner, and IMS DataPropagator
- WebSphere MQ family products such as WebSphere MQ (formerly MQSeries), WebSphere MQ Integrator (formerly MQSeries Integrator)
- DB2 Warehouse Manager and Data Warehouse Center to aid populating an ODS.

The detailed data acquisition products and considerations are discussed in Chapter 3.5, "Data acquisition scenarios using IBM products" on page 73.

No one can start to build an ODS without preparation and planning. Some tasks might have already been done by the customer for DW purposes. Many of these issues may be already handled to some extent. Here are steps to consider when identifying ODS sources from the legacy systems:

- ODS sourcing should be synchronized with the corporate-wide data model and standards.
- ODS logical design should provide a blueprint to identify sources.
- Identify operational sources based on the ODS logical design, and classify the sources based on the usage, characteristics, size, volume, subject, replication method, and targets.
- Choose the ETML methodology — extract, sort, map, cleanse, rollup, and transform:
    - Converting data
    - Deciding the best source when multiple sources exist
    - Code translation or conversion
    - Altering fields, keys
    - Reformatting data
    - Aggregating or recalculating data
    - Sampling data
- Identify data sources for initial loads.
- Classify data sources for the refresh timing/lagging.
- Identify critical transactions to update the ODS immediately from source data.
- Calculate the source data volume to be inserted to the ODS.
- Find massive load methods, time, and performance for a large volume of sources.

- Determine the scheduling of source slicing by batch window allocations, and the scheduling of ODS updates.
- Determine the sourcing integrity by rolling back all related sourcing transactions if one or more fail.
- Filter the turn-around replication back to the ODS for the changes (cyclical data) made by ODS users in the ODS, and that flows back to the source(s).
- Identify a management tool, such as DB2 Warehouse Manager, to control the replication process flows.
- Determine the level of audit trails of sourcing, such as record counts from sources and targets. Since the replication process are asynchronous, it may be a good idea to keep the records counts by source, target, and record type on any given day or period which deemed to be appropriate by ODS designer. These counts can be used to verify the integrity of the complex ODS population processes.

Other data sources to ODS
ODS may need to integrate data from other data sources, including the popular software packages such as SAP, PeopleSoft, BAAN, JD Edwards, Oracle, Siebel, and other commercial packages. There will frequently be data sources from e-business solutions, such as Web traffic data. There could be some other external sources that may be passed from other organizations as interface files or even purchased data.

There are a variety of tools that can be used to extract data from the commercial packages such as SAP. Also, the middleware, such as MQSeries, can be used to populate an ODS from commercial packages such as Siebel. We introduce these tools in the following section, which describes the data acquisition layer.

3.4.2 Data acquisition

Once the data requirements for the ODS have been defined, we can start creating the architecture for the data acquisition layer; see Figure 3-13 on page 57. This layer extracts the required ODS data by capturing the changes made to the data sources. The data is then passed through an integration and transformation process, and is loaded into the ODS. The consistency of the entire environment must be maintained by this layer.

As shown in Figure 3-15, the following components are included in the data acquisition layer:

- Extract and/or capture
- Build and/or transform
- Trigger updates (for ODS type B only)

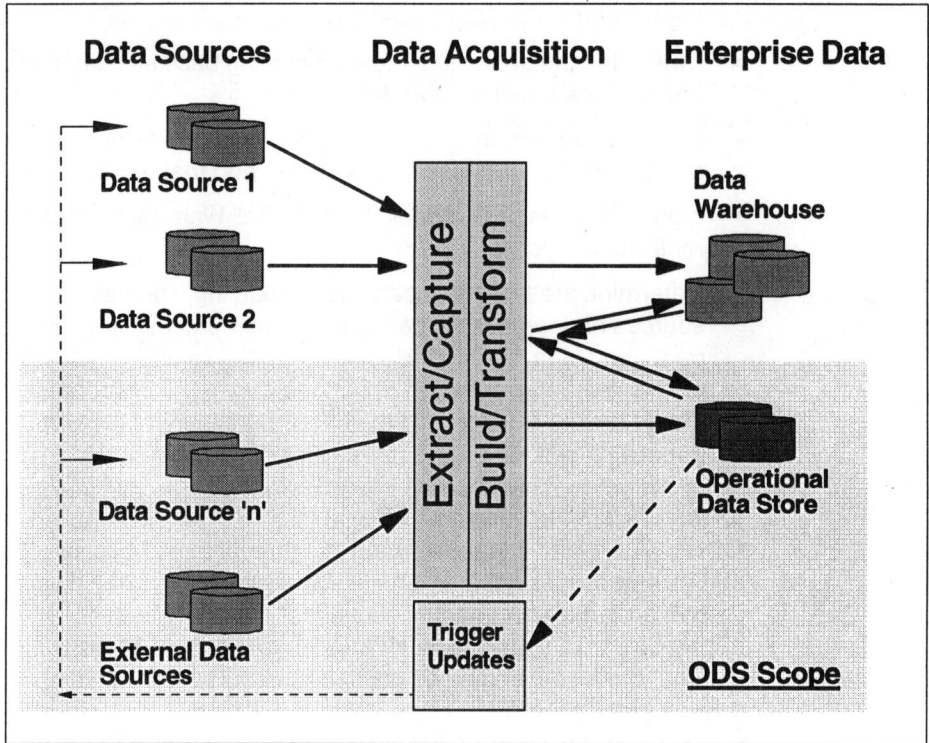

Figure 3-15 Data acquisition components

The extract/capture component must have minimal impact on the design and architecture of the data sources. Because of the operational nature of an ODS, this component must be highly reliable and be able to scale in size. Many different methods can be used to retrieve the deltas from the data sources, for example, reading from a change log, capturing the changes between the client and server, and capturing the changes after they are applied to the data source. This component must also be capable of bulk extracts for initial load and re-synchronization.

The build/transform component is responsible for preparing the extracted data for populating the ODS. This component executes data transformations such as cleansing, aggregating, denormalizing, reconciling, consolidating, formatting or a combination of these functions in real-time or near real-time. The transformation requirements will have to take into account the data delivery requirements. The number and type of transformations may be limited depending on the timing of the updates to the ODS. Because this component calls for the detailed integration and transformation requirements, it will require the most time to scope and develop.

The trigger update component only applies to an ODS type B. This component builds the transactions that ensure specific changes in the ODS are reflected back to the desired data sources. These transactions must support a well defined business process. The ODS type B represents a loose form of integration (in contrast to an ODS type C) with the advantage of propagating some changes back to the data sources.

Section 3.5, "Data acquisition scenarios using IBM products" on page 73 provides several detailed examples of data acquisition solutions.

3.4.3 ODS workload considerations

The ODS workload considerations are necessary to prevent the ODS from being a performance bottleneck. There are three major factors that affect the ODS workload:

1. The rate at which updates from the legacy systems occur, and the kind of transformations that have to be applied to the loaded data
2. The rate of large analytical requests to the ODS from the end-users
3. The rate of small transactions or tactical queries with a fast response time needed by the end-users

The goal concerning the *first* workload factor is to reduce the frequency of updates to the ODS. There are several ways to achieve this goal:

- Update only data directly that really needs to be updated, otherwise collect data for scheduled loads.
- Process transformations on data not in the ODS itself, but where possible before entering the ODS.
- Schedule data loads during off-peak hours where possible.

The *second* workload factor requires considerable resources, since we are analyzing a large amount of data in the ODS. To reduce the impact on performance, the number of these queries should be limited, and they should run during off-peak hours where possible.

If these limits are too restrictive to the end-users, there are two other possible solutions, as described in 3.3, "Data modeling" on page 52. The data model should be designed to fulfill these requirements.

> **Note:** Large ad-hoc queries or analytical requests from the end-users should be run in the DW instead of running them in the ODS. When there is a need to analyze current operational data in a multidimensional fashion, operational datamarts could be created.

For the *third* workload factor, you must keep two important things in mind — first, the arrival rate of such transactions; and second, what resources are used by these transactions. To achieve a fast response time, you need to optimize the physical data model for these kind of transactions, because it is very important to reduce the amount of I/O. It may also help to prevent updates on the data during runtime of these queries, as described for the first workload factor.

3.4.4 Information catalog

The ODS information catalog contains data about the data (known as metadata), which describes the data in the ODS environment.

There are three types of metadata that exist within the ODS environment:
- Build-time metadata
- Control metadata
- Usage metadata

Each type of metadata contains business and technical components, and each has a specific purpose.

- **Build-time metadata**

    Build-time metadata is created and used in the process of building the ODS applications (for example, transformation development), as well as query and database design and construction. It is the source for most control and usage metadata used within the ODS environment.

- **Control metadata**

    Control metadata is actively used to control and manage the operations of the ODS environment. There are two general kinds of control metadata: metadata used during the execution of the population processes, and metadata created and used in the management of the ODS. The former consists of the physical structures of the data sources and the cleansing and transformation rules that define how the target sources get populated from the data sources. The latter consists of currency and utilization metadata.

- **Usage metadata**

    Usage metadata (also called business metadata) is another key metadata type of the ODS environment. It will be accessed by business users to gain understanding of the business data, what data exists, where it has come from from, and for what purposes it can be used. Most access to the ODS is through custom interfaces. It is not analytical and query oriented in general.

Users are generally operational troops who are continually working with the same screens, and they do not always need to understand data structure, even from a business view. They are not constructing ad hoc queries and are not running reports. Usage metadata is still going to be needed, but the people who will be using it are not the operational staff, but rather, the supervisors or managers behind the scenes.

The dependencies between these different types of metadata are shown in Figure 3-16.

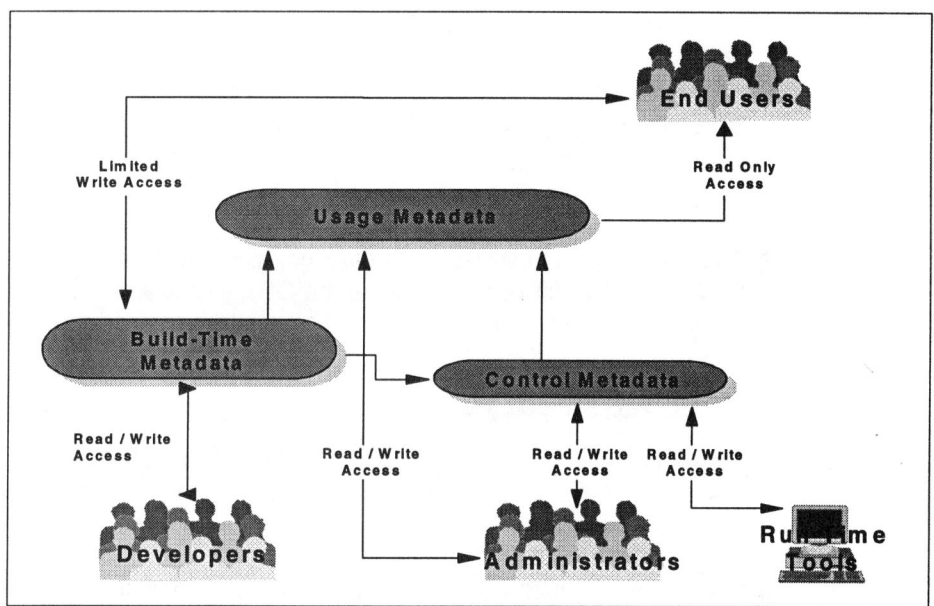

Figure 3-16   Metadata architecture

Purpose

The primary role of the ODS information catalog is to help users find out what data is available and what that data means in terms they can understand. The secondary purpose to assist in the data management process by documenting information concerning the data environment such as the rules for the data acquisition processes. The ODS information catalog is primarily oriented toward the search and display of metadata by the users and hence supports the use of the information within the ODS environment.

Design principles

The following design principles should be kept in mind while building the information catalog:

- All required types of metadata are developed and maintained based on a defined metadata model; for example, a data model representing all the metadata the organization wishes to maintain.
- All metadata should be centrally located and administered.
- Ownership of the metadata should be assigned to the owners of the data content with which the metadata is associated.
- The administration tool and the information catalog should be very tightly integrated to other vendor supplied components such as query tools and ETML tools. We recommend using the Information Catalog Manager that is part of DB2 WM.
- If possible, try to leverage the existing data warehouse information catalog.

The information catalog for your ODS can be maintained by DB2 WM. In Chapter 7, "Building and managing the ODS population subsystem" on page 189, we describe how DB2 WM can fulfill the requirements described.

3.4.5 System management requirements

After an ODS is built, the on-going system administration for the ODS environment is quite challenging. It involves system management of the ODS population processes, including scheduling, pruning, regular maintenance (backup and reorganization, including the replication control tables), performance monitoring, and validating the ODS design for the iterative ODS development.

The ODS environment is imbedded with the transaction processing (high-volume and real-time performance), batch loads, bundled processing of a small batch queues, bursts of insert/update/delete and few resource consuming DSS processing and end-user queries.

In order to successfully manage the ODS, an intelligent and delicate trade-off must be made to accommodate the disparate types of processing. Optimal management of one type of processing may not be optimal for another type of processing, and even may have a negative impact on it.

The result is that the on-going management of the ODS environment requires a delicate balance based on acquired knowledge from the constant monitoring of the ODS performance and activity. We introduce the major components of the ODS system management below.

Managing the ODS population process

When designing the ODS, we define a set of sources, a set of target tables, and a number of process steps mapping the source data to the target tables. These process steps typically include staging the data into an ODS work area; some steps to transform the data into a format acceptable for the final ODS tables; and still other steps that actually insert, update, or delete data from the ODS.

As this population process is very critical to the overall success of the ODS, we need to be able to manage and monitor the entire process. It is very important to understand and visualize the data flows and the process flows, to automate the execution of these process steps. We must be able to see what is happening in our population process in terms of steps that are scheduled, executing, or finished, and to gather execution statistics to identify any potential bottlenecks.

Data pruning

The ODS reflects the current status of our business operations and contains primarily detailed data as in the operational systems. As we capture data changes (inserts/deletes/updates), from the operational systems and apply these to the ODS, the detailed data is mostly self-maintaining, meaning that we need not be overly concerned about pruning history from the ODS.

> **Note:** You will need to develop a method to *delete* the data once it exceeds some set of criteria (based on business requirements).

There is usually a limited amount of history maintained in the ODS. Normally, you do not archive data from the ODS. That is, once you take data out, you do not intend to bring it back. If there are requirements for seeing longer term history for different subject areas, then that is what the data warehouse (DW) is for.

However, there are times when we need to keep more history than the operational systems; for example, the ODS will keep order transactions for a longer period than in the original operational system. Or, we may wish to create some summary tables to ease the query load; for example, to create daily sales summaries. As we introduce data that is not strictly current into the ODS, we have to develop some strategies for purging that history when it is no longer relevant to the business issues being answered by our ODS. The types of data pruning and the techniques used will depend on:

- The data requirements of our business
- The design of our ODS
- Whether the ODS feeds the data warehouse
- The technologies of the products and tools we have in our ODS toolkit

Maintenance

The regular maintenance for ODS includes the usual activities for any objects in DB2 system. We exclude the DB2 system maintenance itself here. The ODS recovery procedure is critical in order to avoid costly losses of data. You should develop procedures to backup and recover from a hardware or power failure or unexpected operating system failure:

- Backup strategy for all ODS tables, including the disaster recovery:
    - Quiesce
        - Point of consistency
        - Coordinated quiesce points for related subjects coming into ODS as a bundled unit of work)
    - Full image copy
        - Point-in-time or point of consistency for ODS
        - Individual copy of table(s) as required)
    - Incremental image copy
    - Local and remote copies
    - Disaster recovery (DR) strategy and DR tests
- Reorganization (on-line or off-line).
- Runstats to keep the catalog statistics current.
- Modify Recovery to clean up Image Copies catalog entries.
- Space extents report and monitoring.

Not only we need to run the maintenance for all ODS objects, but also we should not forget to run the maintenance for those control tables (ASN.IBMSNAP_*) of the replication itself. Most of the time, the source and target tables are being maintained, but replication control tables are often overlooked. Although they are functioning as control tables for the replication, they are just like any other ODS tables with many inserts and deletes, as seen by a DB2 system.

Most ODS populations depend on the replication, and it is also important to have a proper backups, reorganization, and run statistics for the recovery and better performance of the apply and capture process, especially for the Unit Of Work and Change Data tables.

Without well-planned backup schedules with control tables, you will be forced to do more full refreshes to guarantee data integrity when unexpected problem occurs.

For details of backup and recovery, please refer to *DB2 UDB for z/OS and z/OS V7 Administration Guide,* SC26-9931, *and DB2 UDB for OS/390 and z/OS V7 Utility Guide and Reference,* SC26-9945.

For the distributed platforms, please refer to *DB2 UDB Administration Guide: Planning,* SC09-2943, and *DB2 UDB Administration Guide: Implementation,* SC09-2944.

Performance monitoring

Performance monitoring for the ODS is just as important as for any other DB2 applications. But there is one more complexity to overcome in the ODS monitoring. You need to monitor all the replication processes (apply/capture) to confirm that everything is working as registered and subscribed. It is likely that you will institute a procedure for the replication audit/control purpose by using record counts and timestamps, but it could still be your initial challenge to monitor your replication processes to confirm that all is well. That is only one factor of the ODS monitoring, and surely there are more.

Due to the dynamism of the ODS environment, the ODS can easily get out of balance without constant adjustments through a continual monitoring. The ODS environment is constantly changing — the data itself, data size, dormant data, number of ODS users, deletion or additions to the sources, or changes in system records. Each change may require adjustments to be made to the ODS.

However, most of the adjustments necessary should be brought forward systematically to the system management triggered by a continual monitoring to respond to any changes made, such as the following:

- Hardware utilization
    - CPU utilization by hourly, daily, weekly, and monthly
    - Disk spaces
    - Memory, buffer utilization
    - Network

- Throughput monitoring
    - Response time
    - Granularity of the data and transactions
    - Balance between the batch and online processing
    - Peak load
    - Profiling of workloads
    - Distribution and scheduling of workloads

- External activity monitoring
    - Profiling of user activities:
        - End user query patrol
        - Resource usage pattern
        - Change requirements
        - Problem analysis
    - Environmental changes

End-users will access the information in the ODS in two general categories: static applications and dynamic reports. Static applications are usually a known quantity from a performance viewpoint and would typically include operational-like transactions that read and update the ODS or applications that produce some type of tactical operational report. In this way, typical operational performance monitoring and tuning techniques apply. However, the other personality of the ODS is that it is a DSS system. This typically means that users are dynamically creating reports for analysis purposes. Users in this category could easily create a report that could scan a 100,000,000 row table and bring your ODS to a grinding halt.

To control this, we need a system that can intercept these type of requests, evaluate the impact and, for long queries, either automatically reschedule them for the off shift or reject the request altogether. It should do this proactive before the query gets to the database system. For detail performance issues, please refer to 8.2.5, "Performance tuning and monitoring" on page 252 and 8.3.5, "Performance tuning and monitoring" on page 270.

Validating the ODS design

The ODS management system should include the acquiring knowledge process to enhance the iterative ODS development to respond to the changing environment. An acquired knowledge must be organized into a well defined category based on the adjustment made from the monitoring the ODS system. It may be integrated with the change and problem management to provide the necessary feedback to enhance the future ODS management and iterative development.

3.4.6 Data access

The data access layer enables the business users to query and manipulate the ODS. The architecture of this layer depends heavily on the data access requirements.

Figure 3-17 shows a sample architecture where the ODS is accessed by three groups of users using two different applications:

- In the first application, a customer portfolio application is used by the customer relationship managers and the call center users to access the customer's consolidated product portfolio. These two user groups can also write contact tracking information back to the ODS through the application.

- The second application is an OLAP tool used by the campaign management users to make strategic decisions regarding current campaigns.

All user groups will require access to the metadata in the information catalog.

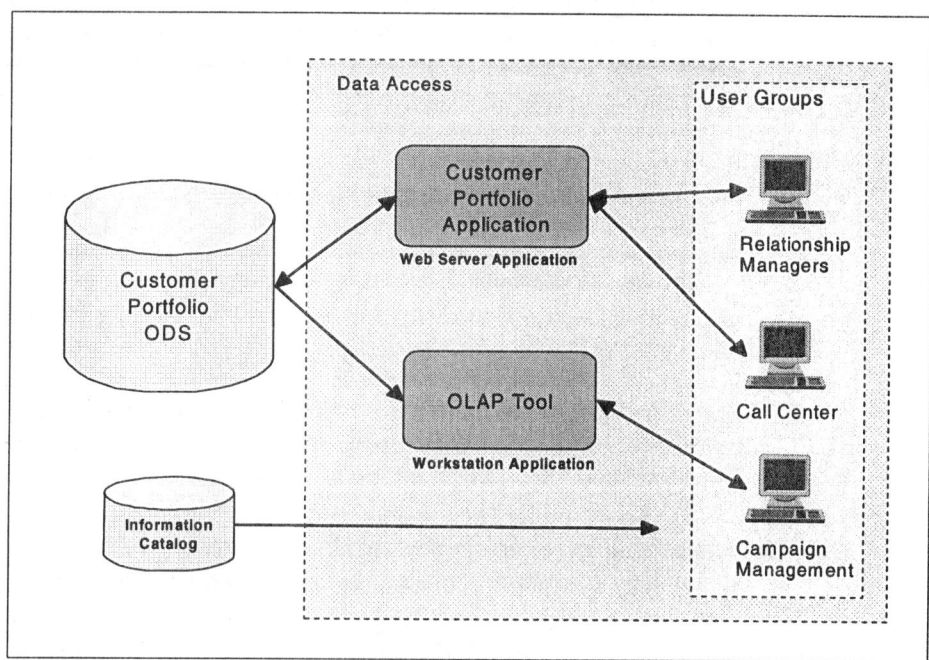

Figure 3-17 Example data access scenario

The components of the data access layer comprise the client workstations, the applications, and the communication standards. It further includes the hardware and software for any data access middleware requirements. This layer should provide high availability, be reliable, and be scalable. Security services should be built into this layer. Consideration should also be given to groupware and e-mail access.

To construct the architecture for this layer you require a clear definition of the user groups, their category types, and their requirements. Table 3-2 documents a few sample user groups and their high level access requirements. In reality, the user group definition should include much more detail, for example, number of users, geography, and performance requirements.

Table 3-2 Sample users groups and their requirements

User Group	Type	Access requirements
Call center	Customer service representatives	Query by customer and update contact tracking information.
	Customer service managers	Query all customers by problem resolution codes
Campaign Management	Campaign managers	Query customers and products by campaign
	Strategic power users	Query customer, product and campaign information using statistical algorithms

The ODS data access layer should be based on the current and future project requirements, project constraints, current infrastructure, and user definitions. The access layer can employ traditional client server applications, Internet technology, mainframe based software, or a combination, as in these examples:

- A world-wide external user group may require Internet technology.
- A world-wide internal user group may require intranet technology.
- A high performance read/write requirement may necessitate the ODS and the application to be on the same platform
- An overtaxed mainframe may require a middleware solution to minimize the workload.

Purpose
The data access layer must provide the connectivity, translation, location, transport, and delivery of the ODS data. Access can be through the intranet, Internet, Wide Area Network (WAN), and/or Local Area Network (LAN). Business users will require an interface to the ODS that facilitates read and write access and supports their query requirements. This layer should also provide access to the information catalog.

Design principles
Keep the following principles in mind when designing the data access layer:

- Leverage the skills within the organization and the established standards from the data warehouse and operational applications.
- Strive to use common communication standards and protocols such as Transmission Control Protocol/Internet Protocol (TCP/IP) and Open Database Connectivity (ODBC).

- For performance reasons, when possible, connect natively to the ODS database.
- Make sure the design accommodates users writing back to the ODS.
- Consider the following in the context of the business objectives when selecting a client access tool or application:
    - Support for a mixed workload environment with operational analysis and transactional capabilities
    - Compatibility with the current environment
    - Thin or wide client
    - Middleware requirements
    - Complexity of building a desktop tool compared to customizing a packaged front-end application
    - End-user involvement in the tool selection process
- Enable an interface to the ODS Information Catalogue

The type of client access may be very different for the three types of ODS implementations. The ODS type A and ODS type B will have similar issues when implementing a front-end tool and the business objectives can guide the tool selection. The sophistication of an ODS type C will require attention to the technical capabilities of the tool as well as the business objectives.

3.5 Data acquisition scenarios using IBM products

This section describes different solutions for the data acquisition Extract, Transformation, Move, and Load process (ETML). This process moves the data from the operational legacy systems (or external data sources) to the ODS.

At first we introduce several IBM products and products of IBM partners. Then we develop several architectures to establish different types of ODSs based on the IBM products to show how powerful these products are to build an ODS.

As target systems for the ODS, in our examples we use either DB2 UDB EEE or DB2 UDB for z/OS because they fulfill the requirements of an ODS as described in Chapter 8, "Critical success factors for the target ODS servers" on page 229.

IBM Data Replication products

IBM Data Replication products include DB2 DataPropagator, which is a feature delivered automatically in DB2 UDB on UNIX and Windows NT/2000 platforms, or which can be purchased as an additional feature to DB2 for z/OS. IBM Data Replication products also include DataJoiner to access non -DB2 databases and IMS DataPropagator to replicate data from IMS to DB2 for z/OS or vice-versa.

DB2 DataPropagator

This product is used to replicate data from DB2 source systems into DB2 target systems. DB2 DPROP consists of a *Capture* component to grab changes from the DB2 log files and put them into staging tables or Change Data (CD) tables. The *Apply* component then applies the data from the CD tables to the target system. This process flow is shown in Figure 3-18 (steps 1 and 4). During the apply process transformations can be made to the data.

DB2 DPROP components as *Capture*, *Apply* are delivered with DB2 UDB for the MS Windows NT/2000 and UNIX environments. For the z/OS and OS/390 platform it is sold as a separate product that can include *Capture*, *Apply* or both.

DataJoiner

This product, when used in conjunction with DB2 DataPropagator, gives transparent access to non-DB2 relational data sources, like Informix, Oracle, Microsoft SQL Server.

It is a separate product, that is available on the AIX, Solaris and Windows NT platform. As shown in Figure 3-18 (steps 2 to 4), DataJoiner creates triggers in the heterogeneous sources to collect the changed data into the CD tables. Then the *Apply program* accesses the data from the CD tables through DataJoiner and applies it to the target DB2 system.

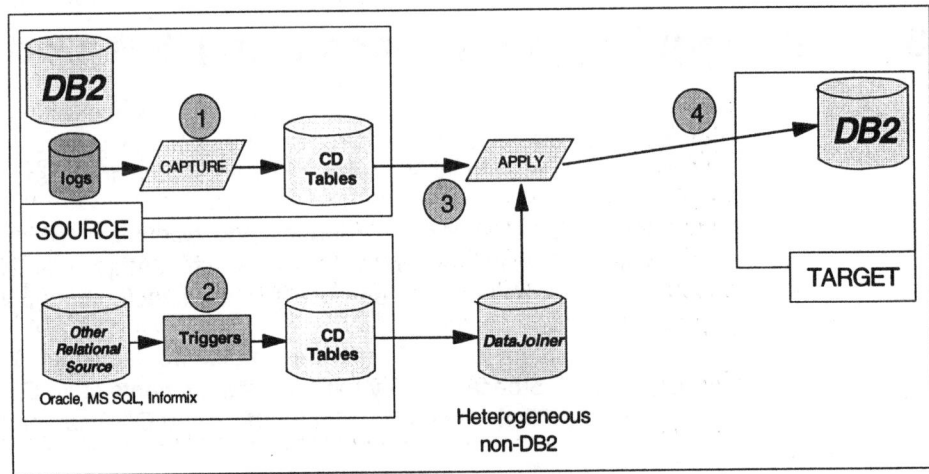

Figure 3-18   DB2 DataPropagator Relational and DataJoiner

IMS DataPropagator

This product is used to replicate data from IMS legacy sources to DB2. It is only available on the z/OS and OS/390 platform and supports only DB2 UDB for OS/390 as target system. Through an user exit in the DL/I update call you are able to copy the database changes into a MQSeries queue. The data is sent by MQSeries to another queue which is read by the apply process to insert the data into a DB2 table. This process is shown in Figure 3-19.

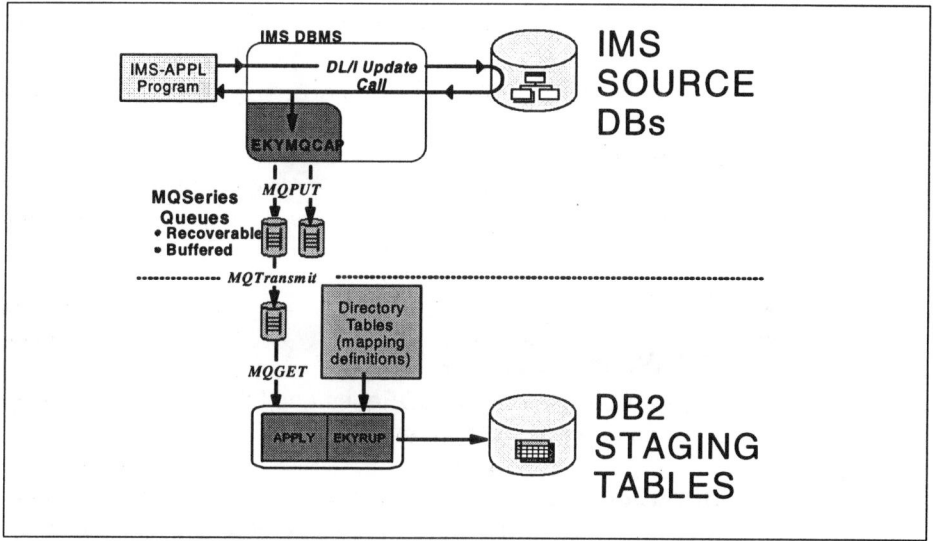

Figure 3-19   IMS DataPropagator

DataRefresher

This is a product, that gives you access to all kind of files on z/OS or OS/390 platforms, for example VSAM. It makes a copy of the file and with the Data Difference Utility (DDU) you can compare two versions of the same file and produce an output file that shows the differences. See the README file that accompanies the DDU for details. The difference file then can be used to populate the ODS with these changes. The data flow is shown in Figure 3-20.

The DDU is available on the Web site under:

ftp://ftp.software.ibm.com/ps/products/datapropagator/fixes/

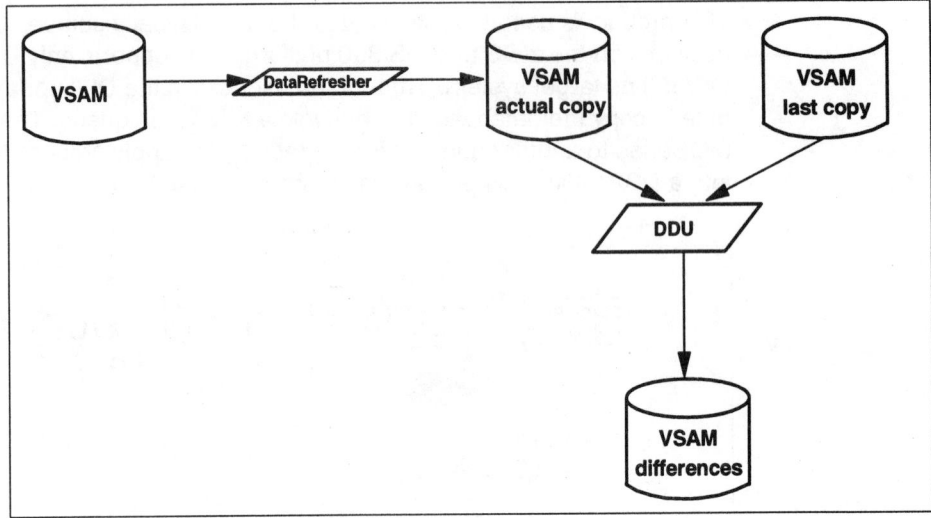

Figure 3-20   DataRefresher and DDU

IBM WebSphere MQ family

In this part, we introduce MQSeries and MQSeries Integrator (MQSI), both of which can also be used for building an ODS.

Introduction to MQSeries

MQSeries is an IBM software product that allows application programs to communicate with each other using messages placed on queues. It provides once-only assured delivery of messages. It allows programs to send messages and then to continue processing without having to wait for a response from the receiver. If the receiver happens to be unavailable then the message will be delivered at a later time.

The programs that comprise an MQSeries application could be running on several different computers with different operating systems and different locations. These applications are written using a common programming interface known as the Message Queue Interface (MQI), so that applications developed on one platform can easily be transported to another. Currently MQSeries can run on over 35 platforms including OS/390, Linux, Windows NT, Sun Solaris, HP-UX, Java, AIX and AS/400. For a complete list, look at the Web site:

http://www-4.ibm.com/software/ts/mqseries/platforms

Queues are managed by a component called a queue manager. The queue manager ensures that messages are put on the correct queue or are forwarded on to another queue manager. When two application programs communicate with each other they use the following mechanism, where one program writes to a queue (*MQPUT*) and the other gets the message from the queue (*MQGET*) as shown in Figure 3-21.

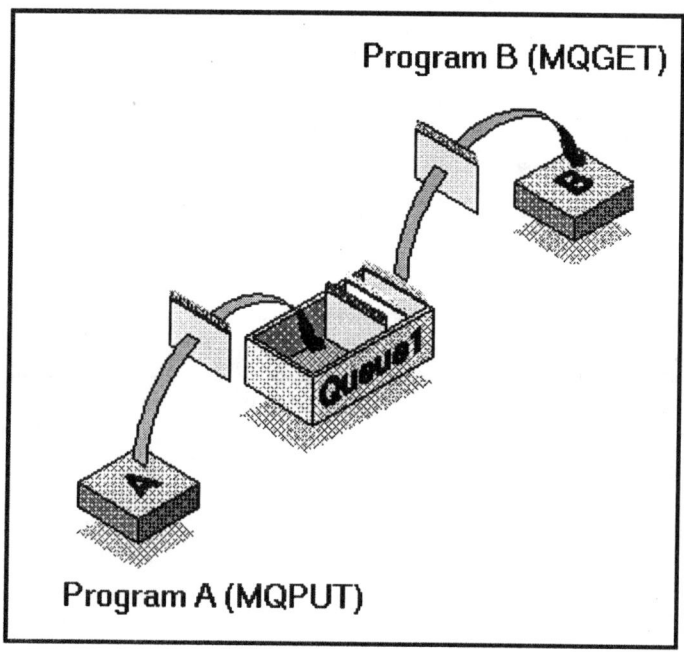

Figure 3-21   MQPUT and MQGET

In this example, both programs happen to reside in the same machine and the same queue manager.

Program A needs first of all to connect to the queue manager, using the MQ verb MQCONN, then open the queue using the command MQOPEN and finally issue the MQPUT.

Program B can either be started independently or, more typically, will have been triggered by the writing of a message to Queue1. This program too needs to issue MQCONN, MQOPEN and then to get the message uses the command MQGET. In MQSeries V5.2 messages of up to 100MB can be handled.

Using more than one queue manager

More typically both programs will not be running on the same machine, and therefore two different queue managers are involved, connected by message channels as shown in Figure 3-22.

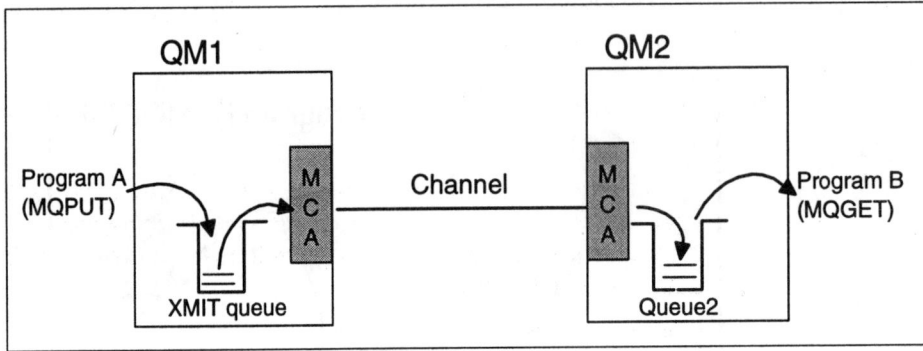

Figure 3-22   Writing to a remote queue

In this situation, Queue1 is defined as a remote queue residing on queue manager 2. The message is placed on a transmission queue which is then sent across the channel using the Message Channel Agent (MCA). Finally the message is placed on Queue2 for retrieval by Program B.

DB2 UDB V7.2 has some new MQSeries functionality that can be used to treat an MQSeries queue as a DB2 table. This feature can be used to populate an ODS. This is described more fully in 5.1.4, "Populating the ODS using the DWC MQ Connector" on page 153.

Another method is to use the powerful message handling facilities of MQSI in conjunction with MQSeries to read and transform data and to write it into an ODS. This subject is dealt with in 5.1.3, "Populating the ODS using MQSI" on page 134.

WebSphere MQ Integrator

WebSphere MQ Integrator (MQSI) is a powerful information broker that selects and distributes information to the applications, databases and people who need it. Users can implement application-to-application message transformation and intelligent message routing quickly and easily.

It uses user-defined rules to enable the business intelligence of an enterprise to be implemented and applied to business events. These rules can be designed and manipulated by business analysts without the need for detailed product knowledge. GUI tools are used to design and implement a message flow which describes the business requirement.

Using MQSeries to deliver messages, MQSI establishes a hub through which they pass. It simplifies connections between applications, integrates information from databases and other sources, applies enterprise-defined business rules, dynamically directs the flow of information and transforms and reformats the data to suit the recipients. Please refer to 5.1.3, "Populating the ODS using MQSI" on page 134 for more technical detail on how MQSI carries out the data transformations functions.

The main components in an MQSI environment are:

▶ **Configuration manager**

The configuration manager is the main component of the MQSI runtime environment. It maintains configuration details in the configuration repository, manages the initialization and deployment of the broker and checks the authority of defined userid.

▶ **One or more brokers**

A broker is a named resource that hosts and controls your business processes, which you define as message flows. Applications send new messages to the message flow and receive processed messages from the message flow. The broker may reside in the local NT environment or may be remote as in our ODS on the Sun server. A pair of sender and receiver channels need to be defined in the queue manager to communicate with each broker defined in the broker domain. Please see 5.3.3, "ODS data transformations" on page 172 for more detail on this.

▶ **Control center**

The control center is used to configure and control the broker domain. This works in association with the Configuration Manager, passing messages back and forth (via MQSeries) as information is requested and making updates to the components.

▶ **User name server**

An optional resource and not required if publish/subscribe is not used.

▶ **MQSeries queue manager**

As described in "Introduction to MQSeries" on page 76, a single MQSeries queue manager can only host one broker. When a message flow is deployed to that broker, the queues referred to in that flow must be defined in the queue manager. Note that MQSeries is the transport layer used to store and deliver messages between queue managers. MQSI can monitor and intercept messages arriving at a queue and apply rules to the message, transform it and route it to the required destination.

▶ **Message repository manager**

This is involved in defining message structure and parsing messages.

DB2 Warehouse Manager (DB2 WM)

The DB2 Warehouse Manager provides a distributed, heterogeneous infrastructure for designing, building, maintaining, governing, and accessing highly scalable, robust DB2 data warehouses and ODSs. You can move data directly from source-to-target and control the servers on which transformations take place with distributed warehouse agents, and you can speed warehouse and ODS deployment with commonly used, pre-built data cleansing and statistical transformations. These capabilities can be expanded by adding your own user-defined transformation functions or by integrating products from other vendors, like ETI*EXTRACT or Vality Integrity.

The different components of DB2 WM are shown in Figure 3-23. There you can also see what components are already part of DB2 UDB. The capabilities of DB2 WM and how it can be used in an ODS environment are described in much more detail in Chapter 7, "Building and managing the ODS population subsystem" on page 189.

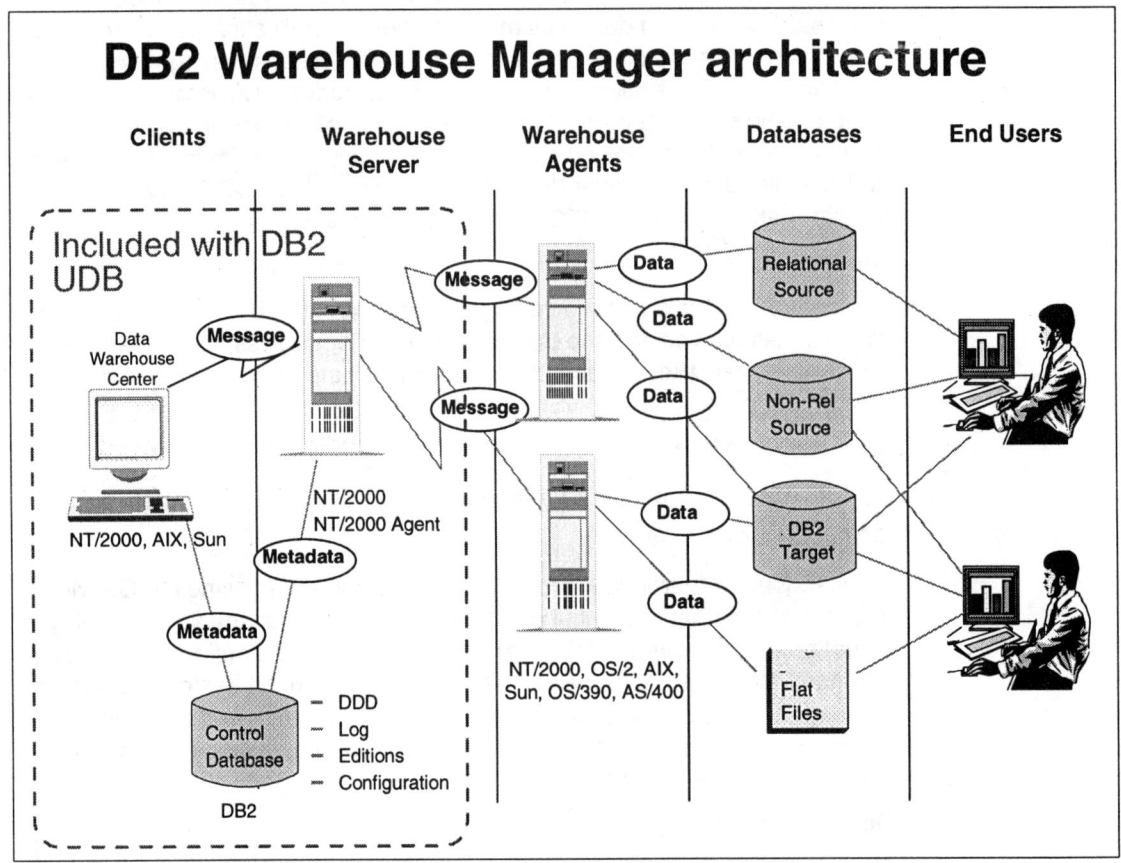

Figure 3-23 DB2 Warehouse Manager

Additional IBM partner products

The main focus of this book is to introduce ODS architectures with IBM products. However, where the capabilities of these products are not sufficient, we expect you to use additional IBM partner products. These products are introduced in this section with a short description of their strengths and in what cases they might be helpful. We also reference to these products, where necessary, in the following chapters. Figure 3-24 shows what products are available, and how they fit together with the IBM products.

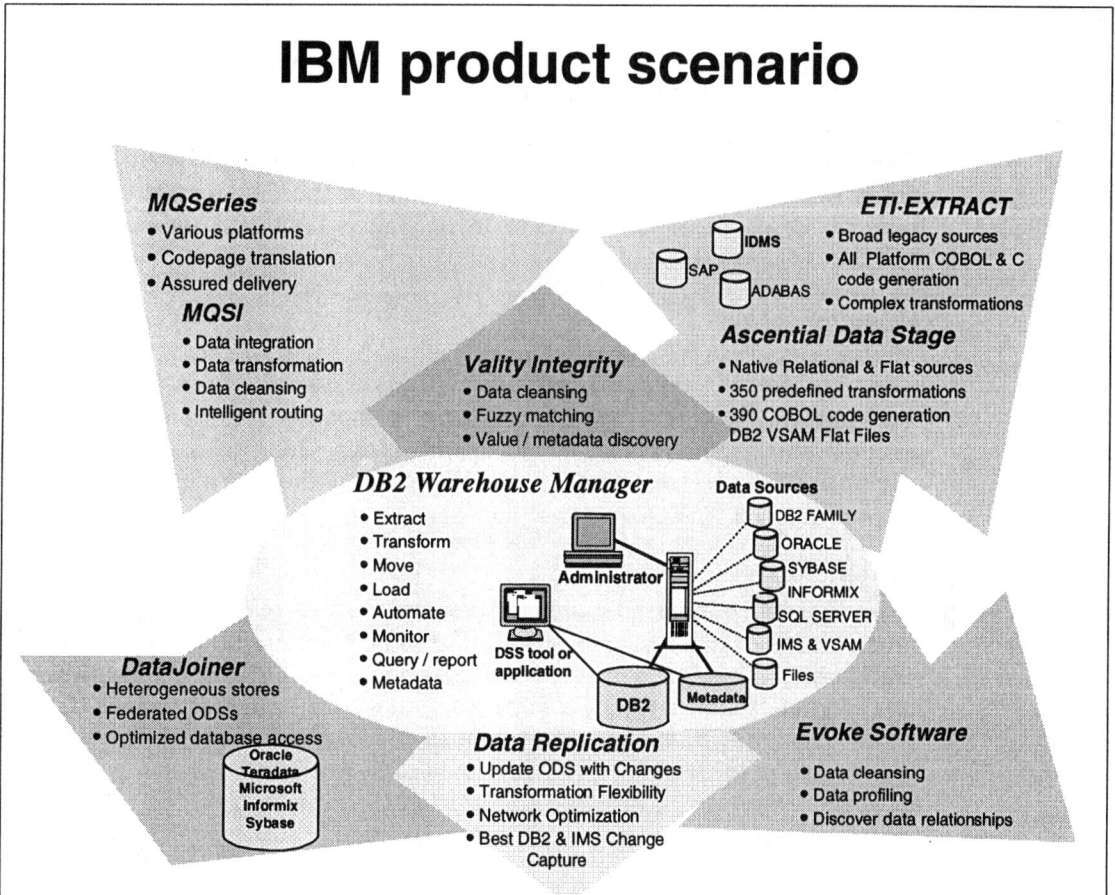

Figure 3-24 IBM product scenario

DataStage for DB2 WM

This is a transformation engine essential to data migration projects where implementation of complex transformations is a must. It is also an optional code generator for deploying JCL and COBOL Extract Transform Move Load (ETML) processes on the IBM z/OS and OS/390 platforms sourcing VSAM and DB2. You can use it as a development environment for designing, debugging, executing and maintaining ETML sequences. All these tasks can be managed from DB2 WM. This product is very useful when the complexity of the ETML process for the ODS cannot be handled by IBM products.

ETI*EXTRACT

This product covers the whole ETML process. It generates 3GL programs (COBOL, C and ABAP/4) to extract data from source systems, transform these data and load the data into the target systems. There is an interface to transfer the metadata to DB2 WM in order to schedule the ETI programs. There is also an interface to MQSeries. With this product you can support more source heterogeneous operating systems to get data into a DB2 ODS, for example, ADABAS systems.

Vality Integrity

This tool is specialized on data cleansing and focus on data content. It provides support to increase the data quality, for example consolidating address data and finding similarities. It has data analysis and investigation, conditioning, and unique probabilistic and fuzzy matching capabilities. This product can be called from DB2 WM to enhance the data cleansing capabilities of the IBM products for the population of your ODS, if needed.

Evoke

Evoke Software's Product Suite automates the analysis of corporate data structures residing in disparate systems across the enterprise. It discovers data relationships and dependencies. It identifies data quality issues, inconsistencies between data sources, legacy systems, and new target systems such as data warehousing or ODS implementations. It also provides accurate maps and transformation specifications that drive subsequent ETML processes or application integration between e-Business applications and existing back-end operational systems.

The Evoke Software Product Suite provides the capability to extract data from source systems and prepare it to be imported through Evoke import adapters into Evoke Software Repository, profile the data content in three dimensions (for example: down columns, across rows and between tables), map the source data to the target database, and create the Data Definition Language (DDL) to implement the target database.

DB2 WM can leverage the information insights derived from Evoke's Repository. This product may be useful during the analysis phase of your ODS, especially as a support during data modeling. The generated DDL, and the defined process to get the data, can then be used by the IBM products to implement the ETML process and the ODS database.

Building an ODS with IBM products

In this section we introduce different architectures to build an ODS type A and an ODS type B, using and combining IBM products. Figure 3-25 shows the products used for the specific ODS layers.

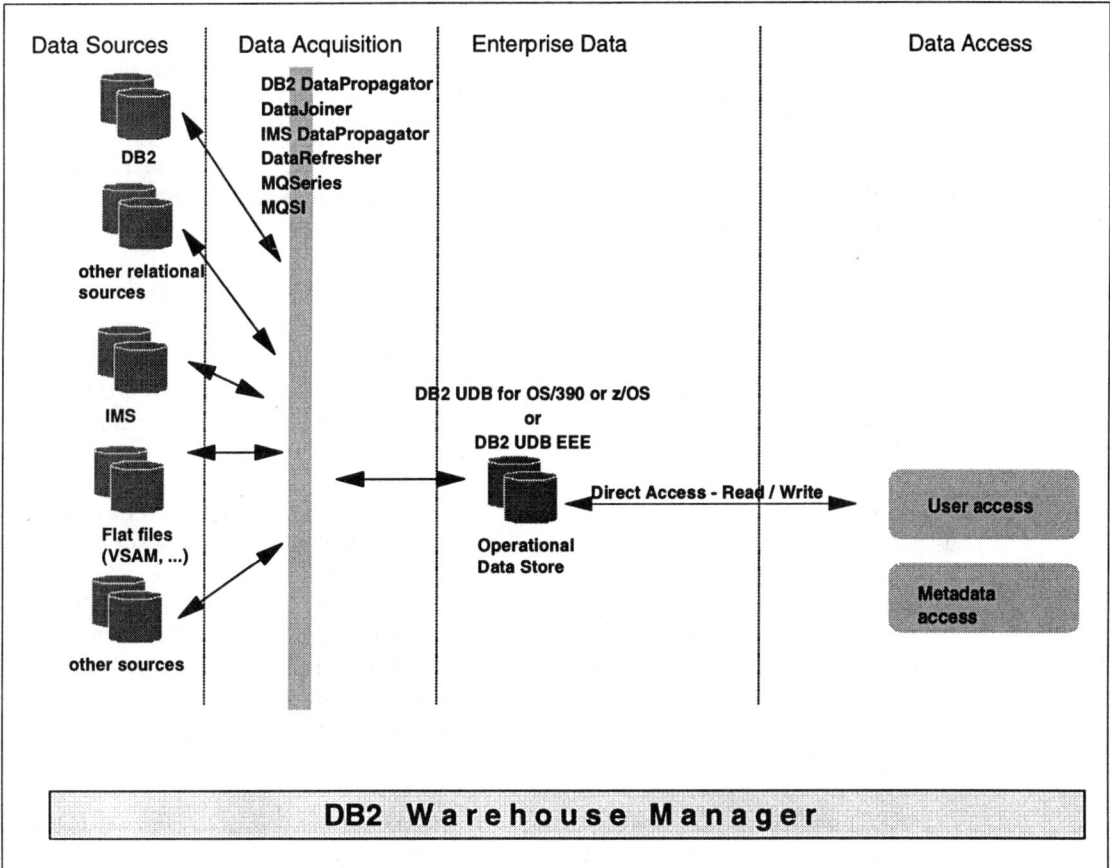

Figure 3-25 IBM products for an ODS

First we describe architectures to get data from relational data sources for both ODS type A and ODS type B. Details are provided in Chapter 4, "**Populating the ODS from relational sources**" on page 91.

Later on, we describe architectures to get data from non-relational data sources for both types. Details are provided in Chapter 5, "**Populating the ODS from non-relational sources**" on page 127.

These architectures should be taken as a guideline to implement an ODS using IBM products. For your own ODS, please analyze the requirements very carefully and use the combination of IBM products that fits best for your environment.

In all the architectures you find DB2 WM as a global tool to control the whole acquisition process. It is used for example to schedule tasks and storing the metadata. The details about using DB2 WM in this context are provided in 4.1.4, "Populating the ODS using Data Warehouse Center (DWC)" on page 108, in 5.1.4, "Populating the ODS using the DWC MQ Connector" on page 153 and in Chapter 7, "Building and managing the ODS population subsystem" on page 189.

Acquisition from relational data sources for an ODS type A

First we have to know whether the relational data sources are DB2 systems or non-DB2 systems. In the case of DB2 systems, we use DB2 DataPropagator to replicate the data into our ODS. On the source system, the *Capture* program is running; and on the ODS, the Apply program replicates the captured data from the source system.

The performance reasons to run the Apply program on the ODS are described later on in 4.1, "Relational data as a source (ODS type A)" on page 92.

Because the *Capture* program is not available on non-DB2 relational systems, we use DataJoiner to enable replication from non-DB2 systems. Through DataJoiner, DB2 DataPropagator is able to replicate data from non-DB2 systems. On the source systems, capture triggers are running; and the Apply program running on the ODS replicates the captured data through the DataJoiner database.

DB2 DataPropagator is able to replicate the data into DB2 UDB EEE and DB2 UDB for z/OS. The whole process can be scheduled via Data Warehouse Center. In Figure 3-26 we show a possible high-level architecture for an ODS type A.

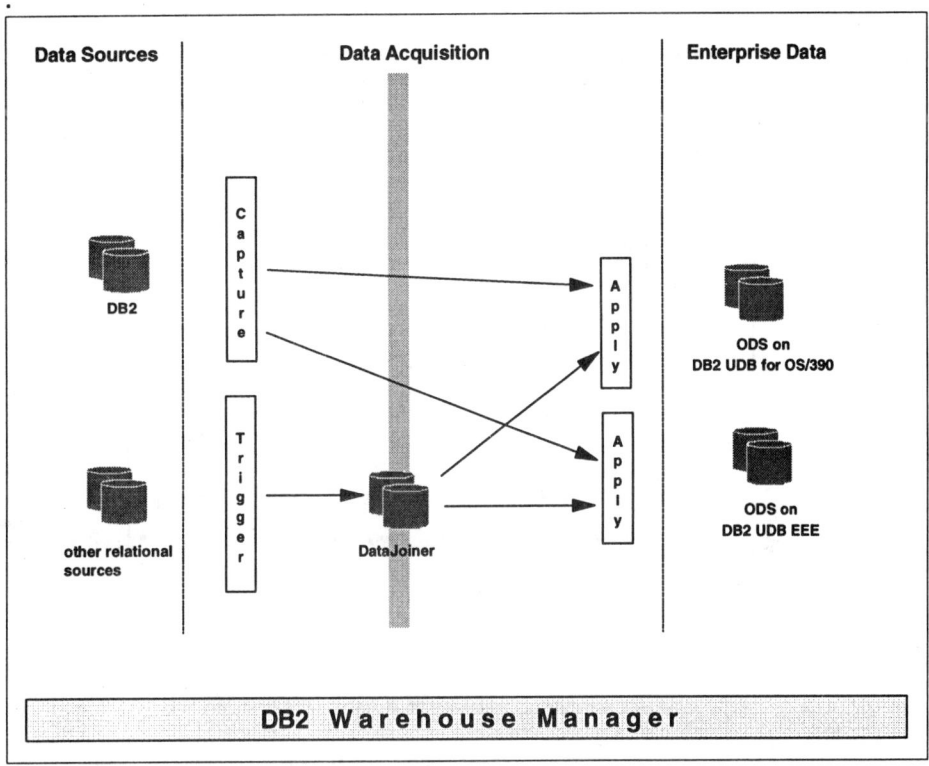

Figure 3-26   ODS type A with relational data

Restriction: At the moment, it is only possible to replicate data **from** a DB2 UDB EEE system under very special circumstances. The *Capture* program of DB2 DataPropagator is not yet able to capture data from log files on different nodes of the database. So your source table must be on one partition. This partition must be the catalog partition of your database. Because it can degrade the performance of your database when you store operational data on the catalog partition, we presently recommend *not* to use DB2 UDB EEE as a replication source. For further information, read the *IBM DB2 UDB Replication Guide and Reference* that is delivered with DB2 UDB.

Acquisition from relational data sources for an ODS type B

For an ODS type B, it is important to know if it is implemented on DB2 UDB for z/OS or on DB2 UDB EEE. If it is implemented on DB2 UDB for z/OS, then we can use the same IBM products to replicate the data back into the source databases. This is shown in Figure 3-27.

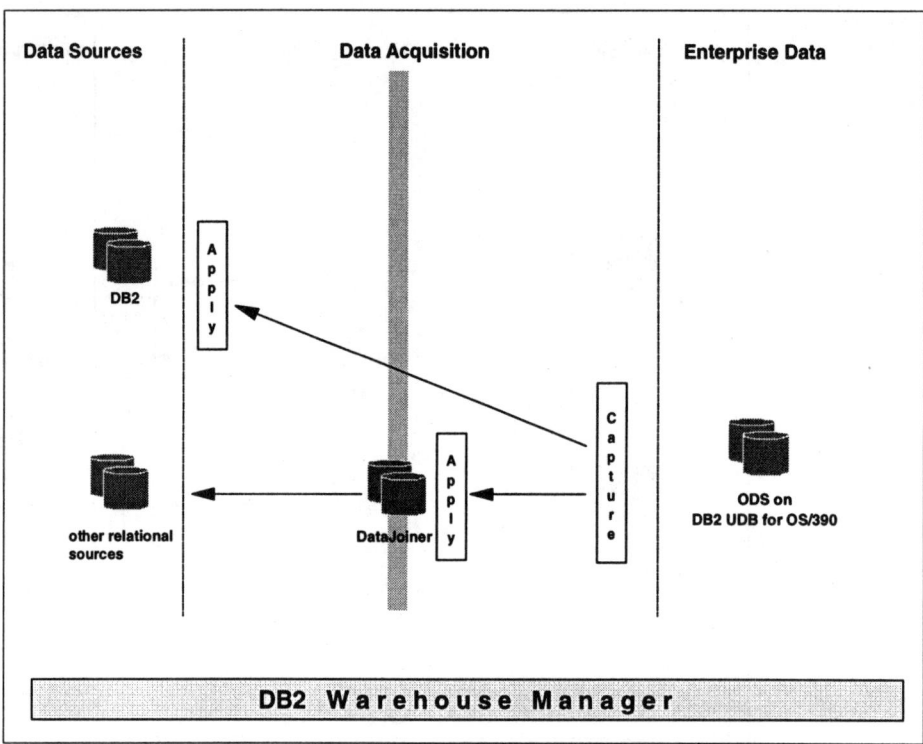

Figure 3-27   ODS type B on DB2 UDB for z/OS target with relational data

Now the *Capture* program is started on the ODS and we have the *Apply* programs running on the operational systems. Because the *Apply* program is not available on non-DB2 systems, it resides on the system where DataJoiner is running and pushes from there the data into the non-DB2 systems. The whole process can be scheduled again via DB2 WM.

As mentioned above, we cannot yet use DB2 replication to replicate data back to the source systems when the ODS is implemented on DB2 UDB EEE. Therefore, we must develop another solution. To get the data back into the source systems, we use MQSeries in connection with MQSI. To avoid a performance impact on the ODS, we recommend that the user applications updating the ODS, write directly in parallel into a MQSeries queue.

Otherwise, you would have to implement triggers on the updated tables. These triggers would also be fired when updates from the source systems occur. This data then would also be replicated back to the source system, which is not our goal. This is discussed in more detail in 4.2, "Relational data as a target (ODS type B)" on page 121. Figure 3-28 shows our solution for DB2 UDB EEE.

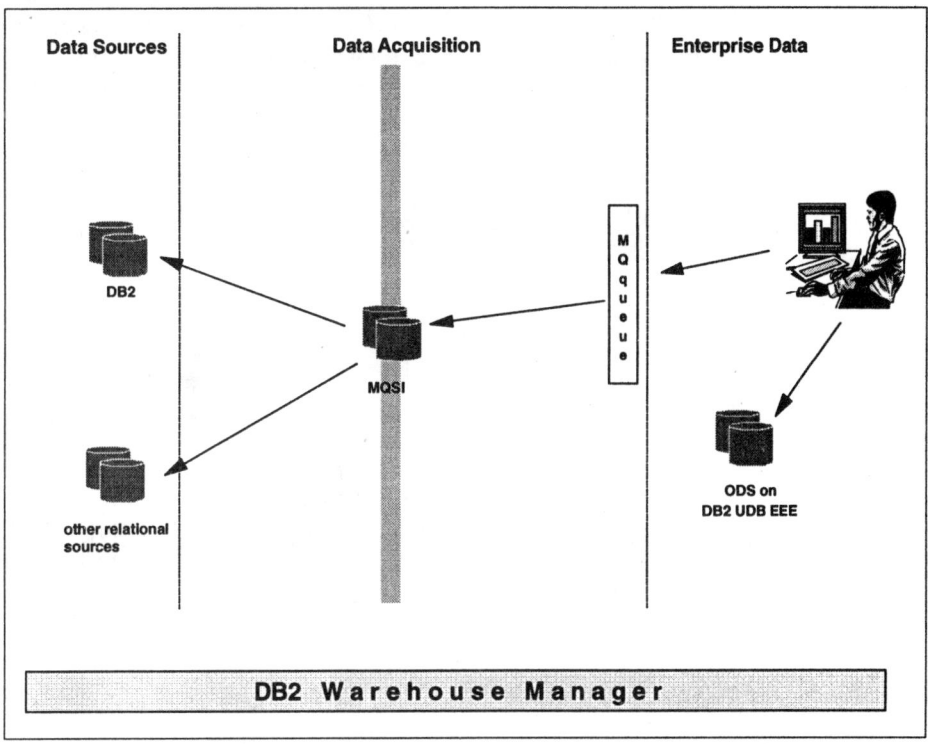

Figure 3-28 ODS type B on DB2 UDB EEE target with relational data

Acquisition from non-relational data sources for an ODS type A
In our example we want to replicate data from VSAM and IMS. First we look for a solution for an ODS type A on DB2 UDB for z/OS.

For VSAM files we use DataRefresher in connection with the Data Difference Utility (DDU) to get a file which contains the differences between two points of time. The DDU is delivered with DB2. A CICS program takes the data from this file and put it into a MQSeries queue. This queue is read by MQSI that replicates the data into the ODS.

For IMS data sources we use IMS DataPropagator to get data into the ODS. The *Capture* component of IMS DataPropagator runs on the IMS system writing the changed data into a MQSeries queue. MQSeries transports the data to another queue residing on the ODS system. Then the *Apply* component replicates the data from this queue into the ODS. This is a proprietary process because the MQSeries message format for this process is not published.

These processes are shown in Figure 3-29 and are discussed in more detail in 5.1, "VSAM as an ODS source (ODS type A)" on page 128. There we also discuss the reasons to choose this architecture for VSAM.

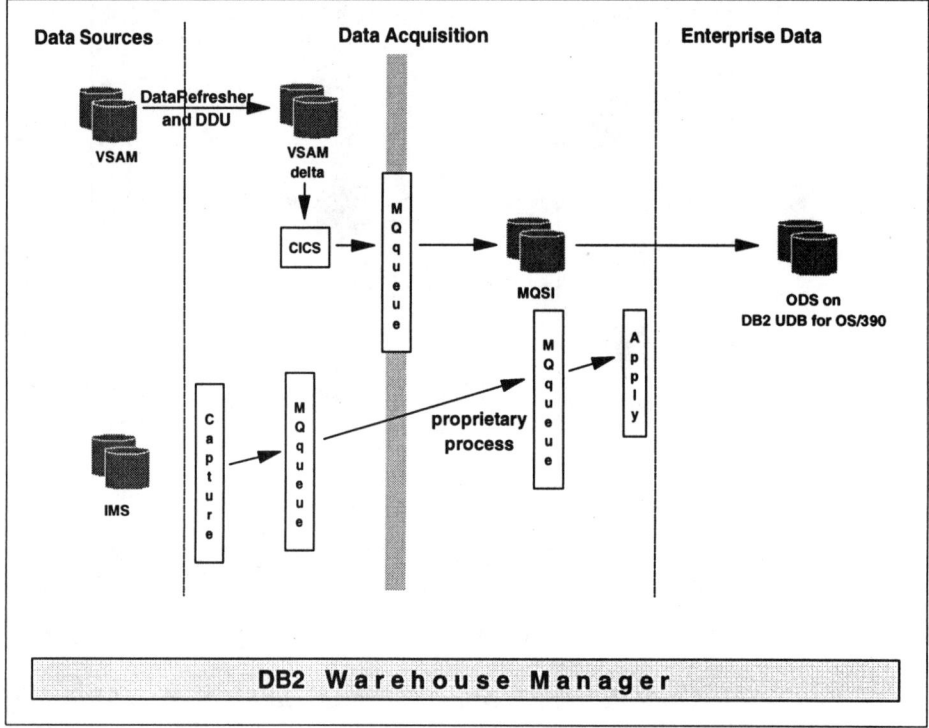

Figure 3-29   ODS type A on DB2 UDB for z/OS target with non-relational data

To replicate from VSAM to DB2 UDB EEE, we use the same method as for an ODS on DB2 UDB for z/OS. Figure 3-30 shows the alternatives for an ODS on DB2 UDB EEE with non-relational data sources.

If your ODS resides on DB2 UDB EEE, you have two different alternatives. For the first one, we need a database on DB2 UDB for z/OS to get data from IMS using IMS DataPropagator. Then the data is replicated with DB2 DataPropagator from DB2 UDB for z/OS to DB2 UDB EEE. This is shown as method number 1 in Figure 3-30.

The other alternative is to change the IMS applications, so that the changed data is also written into a MQSeries queue defined by you, and then sent via MQSI to your DB2 UDB EEE system. The first method has less effort than the second one, but you need a database on DB2 UDB for z/OS. So the costs of the two alternatives must be compared precisely to get the right decision for your ODS.

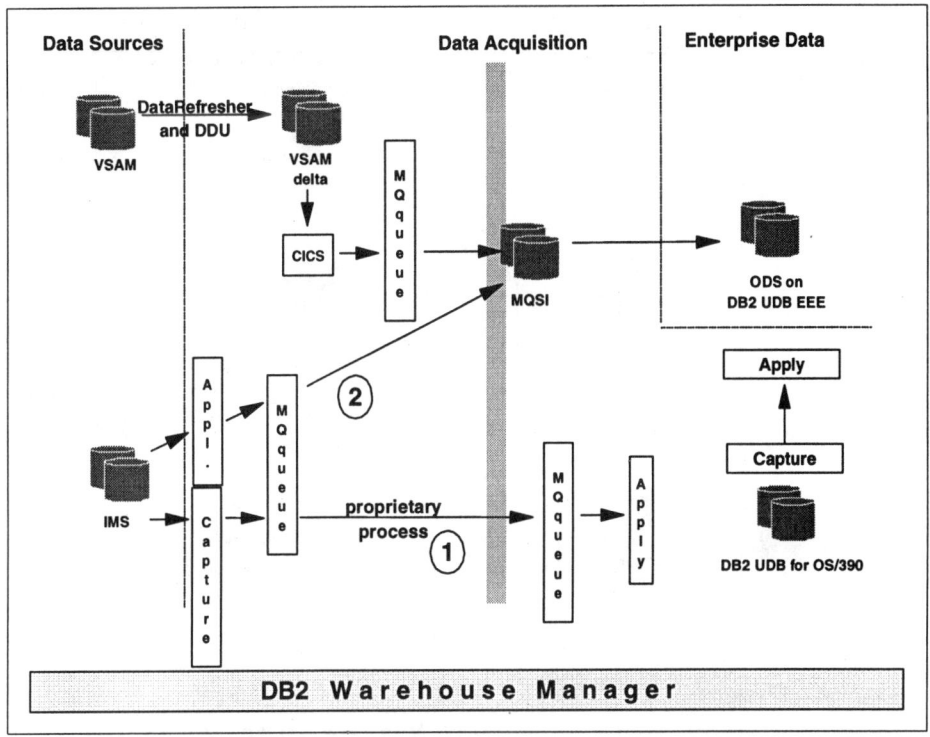

Figure 3-30   ODS type A on DB2 UDB EEE target with non-relational data

Acquisition from non-relational data sources for an ODS type B

In this situation we have the same scenario for an ODS type B on DB2 UDB for z/OS and on DB2 UDB EEE.

For VSAM and IMS, we use the same way back to replicate the data to the source systems. With IMS DataPropagator there is a method to replicate data from DB2 UDB for z/OS into IMS. But this method has a great impact on the performance of our ODS. This replication works synchronous. So the ODS application has to wait until the data is stored in IMS. Therefore, in both cases we use MQSeries and MQSI to replicate data back. DataRefresher is not needed in this context because we need no difference file on our way back. As described in "Acquisition from relational data sources for an ODS type B" on page 85, we recommend that the user applications updating the ODS should write directly in parallel into a MQSeries queue to avoid a performance impact on the ODS.

The architecture is shown in Figure 3-31.

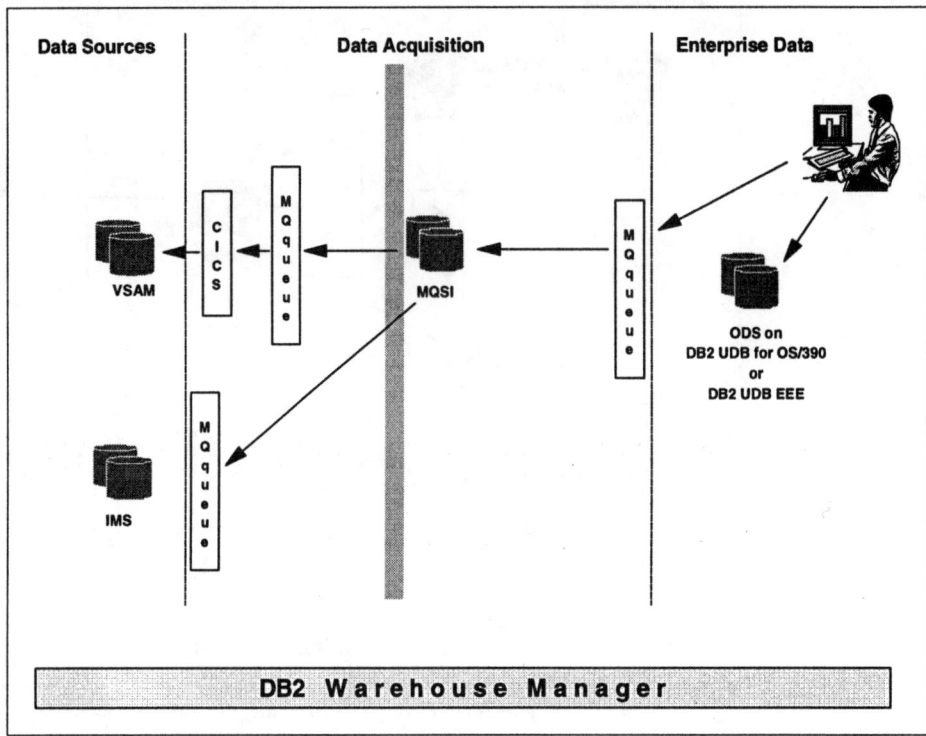

Figure 3-31   ODS type B on with non-relational data

Populating the ODS from relational sources

In this chapter we discuss how the ODS issues, which we have described in Chapter 2, "ODS issues" on page 17, can be solved by the IBM Data Replication and/or MQSeries products of IBM. We focus on an ODS type A and an ODS type B with data from relational data sources.

In section 4.1, "Relational data as a source (ODS type A)" on page 92, we discuss the capabilities of DB2 DataPropagator, DataJoiner and DB2 WM to solve ODS issues.

In section 4.2, "Relational data as a target (ODS type B)" on page 121, we discuss the specific issues that have to be solved when we try to replicate data back to the operational sources and describe possible solutions. One issue is how to decide what data should be transferred back to the operational systems and how it can be identified. The other issue is that the data transferred to the operational systems will come back to the ODS through the normal replication process.

4.1 Relational data as a source (ODS type A)

When we need to transfer data from any relational source to a DB2 UDB source, DB2 DPROP is the best suitable tool to use, as it takes into account code page resolution, data consolidation from several relational sources, aggregation requirements, and relational data access optimization. Also, it has been built to minimize the impact on the online transaction processing which is taking place on the operational systems.

In the scenario to replicate data from different relational sources into the ODS, for DB2 sources we use DB2 DataPropagator and for the non-DB2 relational sources we use DB2 DataPropagator in combination with DataJoiner. If you need more technical information on how to plan, design, and implement a relational replication solution and on how to administrate it using the DataJoiner Administration Tool (DJRA), please refer to the IBM redbook *My Mother Thinks I'm a DBA!*, SG24-5463-00 *or The DB2 Replication Certification Guide*, SC09-2802-00.

In this section we focus on the four main ODS issues that can be solved by using DB2 DPROP and DataJoiner. First we describe the IBM relational replication and how the data integration can be done with these products. Then we discuss the data transformation capabilities. Next we explain how the IBM data replication products can help you to obtain high performance through near-current data delivery and uptime during the population process of the ODS. Finally we describe how the DB2 WM and Data Warehouse Center can be used to integrate DB2 DataPropagator and DataJoiner to administer your whole population process.

4.1.1 The relational replication solution

First we define some very important expressions that are necessary to understand the replication process using DB2 DataPropagator and DataJoiner before defining data sources, subject area, and integration criteria.

Definitions
The main terms to use when defining a replication process are:

- Subscription
- Subscription set
- Unit of work
- Spill file
- Control server
- Nickname

Subscription

Subscription is the process of establishing the relationship between a registered replication source and the target table. While defining the subscription, you specify the target table and its structure, the source tables for the target table, and the schedule for the replication. Each such definition is called a subscription member.

Subscription set

If your subscription consists of more than one subscription member, it is called a subscription set. The *Apply* program processes all the subscription members within a set in one commit scope. This allows related tables to be copied with application integrity by ensuring that the changes to multiple source tables are applied to the target tables in the same unit of work.

Unit-Of-Work (UOW) table

This a table used by the *Apply* program to identify the changes in the change data (CD) table that are committed. This table is needed because the *Capture* program writes any changes from the DB2 logs into the CD tables even if they are not committed. If they are committed, an entry in the UOW table is made. The process is shown in Figure 4-1.

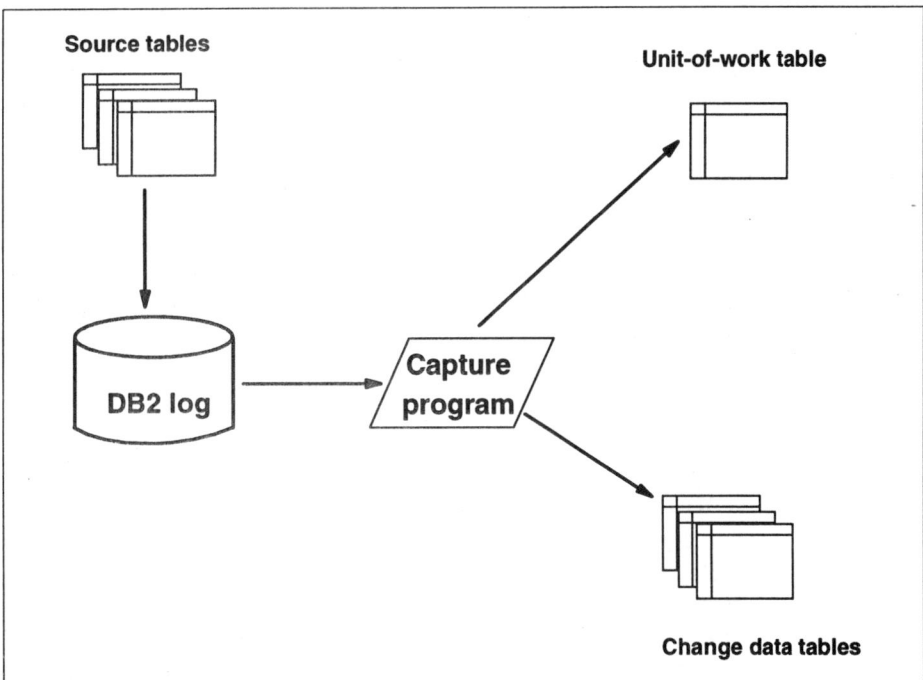

Figure 4-1 UOW table

Spill file

The *Apply* component uses work files called spill files when it fetches the data from either the source tables or the staging tables. This is a file (could be more than one) on the target system where the *Apply* program stores the fetched rows from the source system. From this file the data is applied into the target table, one row at a time. This process is shown in Figure 4-2.

> **Note:** *Apply* on DB2 for z/OS provides the option to create the spill file in memory rather than on disk. That can be useful if the replication cycles are short and the amount of data not too big.

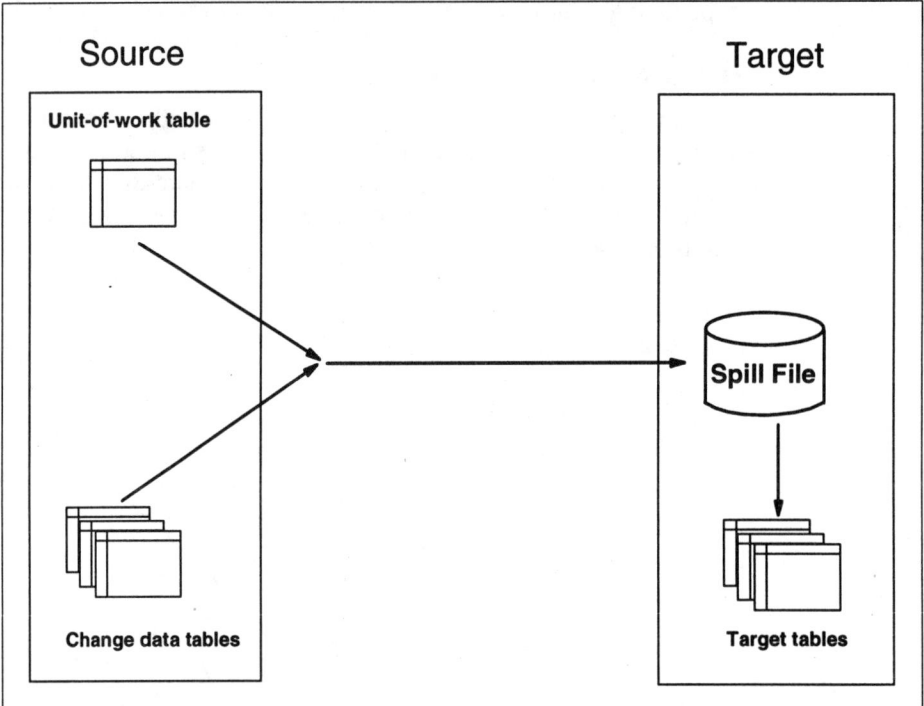

Figure 4-2   Spill file

Control server

The control server is the database server or database that contains the replication subscription control tables used by the *Apply* program. For better performance, the control server should be located at the server where the *Apply* program runs, because the control tables are frequently read by the *Apply* program.

Nickname

A nickname is similar to a synonym or table alias, with the important distinction that it refers to the physical database object (such as a table, a view, or a stored procedure) stored in the remote non-DB2 data source. The nickname is created in the DataJoiner database. The nickname appears to applications connected to DataJoiner as a local table or view or stored procedure and can be accessed with SQL.

Define data sources

Now we shall describe what data sources are supported by the IBM replication products and explain how the data needed from these sources can be defined and selected. This issue is normally an architectural task. During the database and system design, you decide what data from what system is needed in the ODS. We just describe what type of data sources can be accessed, and how: either homogeneous (DB2) and heterogeneous (non-DB2) data sources.

Homogeneous data sources

These are data sources on DB2 UDB tables. With DB2 DataPropagator you can replicate data from these sources into an ODS on DB2 UDB EEE or into an ODS on DB2 UDB for z/OS. DB2 DataPropagator is already part of the DB2 UDB on UNIX/NT platforms and is an additional feature to purchase on z/OS and OS/390 to be used with DB2 UDB for z/OS.

On every source system, a program called the *Capture* program must be running. This program reads the DB2 logs to get the defined data changes, which are stored in separate tables: Change Data (CD) tables, or staging tables. These CD tables are read by another program, the *Apply* program. This program applies the changes read from the CD tables to the target tables. The *Apply* program normally runs on the target system because of performance reasons described later in 4.1.4, "Populating the ODS using Data Warehouse Center (DWC)" on page 108. The whole process is shown in Figure 4-3.

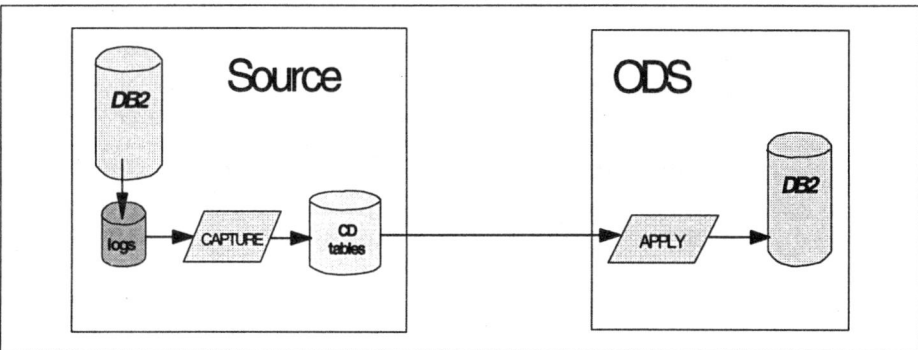

Figure 4-3 Homogeneous replication

Heterogeneous data sources

These are data sources on non-DB2 relational systems. Because the *Capture* program of DB2 DataPropagator is not available on these systems, we need another solution to enable DB2 DataPropagator to replicate data from these systems. Therefore we use an additional product called DataJoiner.

DataJoiner has the ability to emulate a *Capture* program on the source system by defining triggers on the source tables, using the administration tool DJRA. These triggers copy the changed data into the CD tables residing on the source system. These CD tables are also created by DataJoiner. Then the DB2 *Apply* program is able to read the data from the CD tables through DataJoiner. Therefore, within the DataJoiner database, nicknames are created that reference to physical database objects such as the CD tables that are stored on the non-DB2 systems to simulate that the non-DB2 tables are DB2 tables. DataJoiner then handles optimizing and passing the SQL to the downstream data source for execution. This process is shown in Figure 4-4.

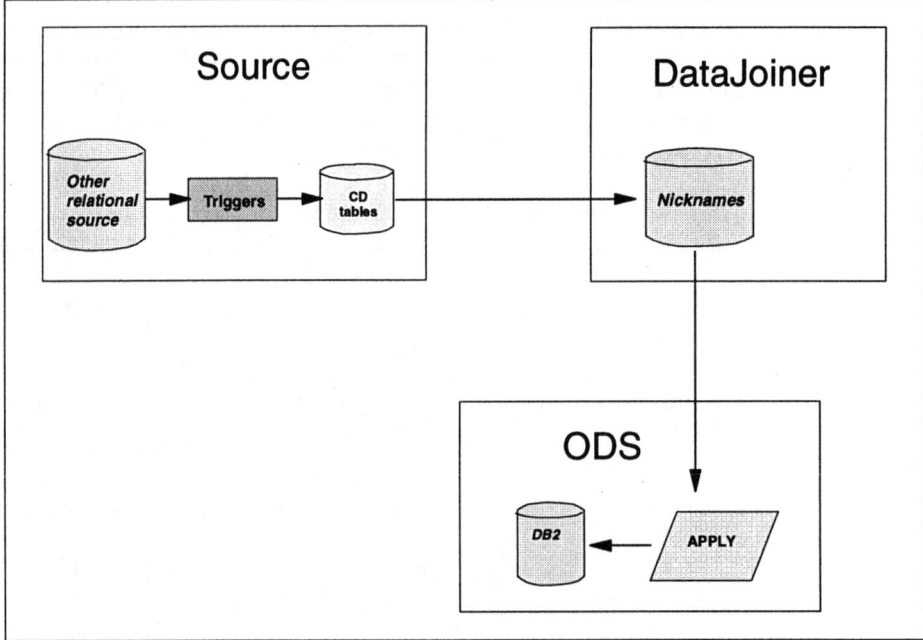

Figure 4-4 Heterogeneous replication with DataJoiner

These are some relational non-DB2 data sources supported by DataJoiner:

- Oracle
- Informix
- Sybase
- Microsoft SQL Server

Because we need a separate database for DataJoiner, we have to decide where to put it. There are three possible scenarios:

- DataJoiner resides on one of the source systems.
- DataJoiner resides on the ODS system.
- DataJoiner resides on a separate system.

DataJoiner on the source system

DataJoiner can reside only on AIX, SUN, and Windows NT platforms. Normally your source system is tuned for your operational applications, so that it can be difficult to add another database. On the other hand the data from this source where DataJoiner resides is transported just once across the network, because the part of getting the data to DataJoiner is local.

DataJoiner on the target system

DataJoiner can reside only on the target system when you use DB2 UDB EE or EEE on AIX or SUN as your ODS platform. DataJoiner is not available on the OS/390 or z/OS platform and you cannot run two different DB2 versions on Windows NT. So for these platforms, you need a separate system for DataJoiner, or you can put DataJoiner on one of your source systems. Normally your target system is tuned for your ODS, so that it can be difficult to add another database. On the other hand, the data is transported just once across the network, because getting the data from DataJoiner to the ODS is local.

DataJoiner on a separate system

This solution gives you the possibility to tune your system perfectly for DataJoiner's needs. On the other hand, the data is transported twice over the network — once from the source systems to DataJoiner, and then from DataJoiner to your ODS.

Define subject area

This is also more of an architectural task, but we describe how the capabilities of DB2 DataPropagator and DataJoiner can be used to get just the data you want.

As mentioned in "Define data sources" on page 95, DB2 DataPropagator is capable of replicating changes from the source tables to the defined target tables. To get just the data you need in your ODS, you can refine the access to your source tables. For the *Capture* program, you can define which columns you need from a table and which rows you want to replicate. So, only the desired data is replicated.

Integration criteria

In the context of two business requirements, we now describe the capability of DB2 DataPropagator to insure data integrity, and the capability to join data from different source tables into one ODS table.

Data integrity

Data integrity refers to the case in which data from different tables belongs together. So if data is replicated from one table, you have to ensure that the corresponding data from the other table is also replicated.

For example, consider a bank transaction transferring money from one account type to another. These two account types are stored in different tables. If an amount of money is transferred from the first account to the second, this must be done in one unit of work to insure data integrity. Therefore, both tables have to be replicated at the same time to ensure the data integrity in the ODS. This can be done by defining a subscription set that contains the subscriptions of the both tables. The *Apply* program processes all the subscription members within a set in one commit scope.

Joining source tables

When your ODS table needs to contain columns from different tables of your source system, DB2 DataPropagator provides the ability to define a replication source that is a view. Views can be based upon multiple replication source tables and can be used to denormalize your data in the ODS. Just the data from the view is replicated to the ODS by the *Apply* program.

4.1.2 ODS data transformations

You will need to carefully analyze what transformations must be done to your data, and determine whether these transformations can be done by the *Apply* program or not. If you have data from very different data sources, relational and non-relational, and very different data structures, it might be useful to create a staging area. In this staging area, all the incoming data is collected and then comprehensive transformations over all data are made, for example, data cleansing. In this case, DB2 WM may be used as described in Chapter 7, "Building and managing the ODS population subsystem" on page 189.

In this section we describe the capabilities of DB2 DataPropagator to transform the data on its way from the source systems into the ODS.

Business requirements

Due to business requirements, considerable changes in the data might be necessary while replicating the data to the ODS system. Following is a list of possible business requirements that must be resolved by a transformation tool:

- Table and column names are different in the source and in the target system.
- Data value conversion (for example, the possible values for a column for type of gender are changed from 'm' and 'f' to '0' and '1').
- Data type conversion (for example, a customer number is converted from a column of type INTEGER into a column of type CHARACTER)
- Data summarization (for example, only the sum of changes to the value of a bank account is needed in the ODS)
- Data decoding/encoding (for example, a gender column is decoded from the values 'm' and 'f' to the values 'male' and 'female')
- Data format (for example, a column for street values is extended from 25 to 50 characters or reduced from 50 to 25 characters)
- Data structure (for example, columns from different source tables are now stored in one ODS table)
- ASCII/EBCDIC conversion
- Data cleansing (for example, it must be evaluated whether a ZIP code for a town is valid or not)

DB2 DataPropagator transformation capabilities

DB2 DataPropagator is capable of most transformations that can be expressed in SQL; such as using stored procedures, or scalar functions. In 4.1.4, "Populating the ODS using Data Warehouse Center (DWC)" on page 108 we show how to set up a stored procedure with DB2 WM.

In the following sections we show how these transformation issues can be solved with DB2 DataPropagator.

Changing table or column names

While building the relation between source and target table you define what source table with which columns is replicated to what target table. You also can add new columns to the target tables. The table and column names are not important; just the right definition of the relation between the source and the target tables.

Executing SQL statements or stored procedures
While defining the replication process, you can tell the system to run SQL statements or stored procedures before the *Apply* program or afterwards. This capability can be used to solve the following business requirements:

- Data cleansing (when no data from other sources is needed)
- Data value conversion
- Data decoding/encoding

Using SQL functions
During the definition of the columns of the target table you can tell the replication process what SQL functions to use to convert data into this column. These functions can be scalar functions like CHAR (converts an INTEGER value into a CHARACTER value), or column functions like SUM (summarizes all values of a column), or AVG (calculates the average value of a column). With these functions you can solve the following business requirements:

- Data type conversion (for example, CHAR; several other functions available)
- Data summarization (for example, SUM; several other functions available)
- Data format (for example, SUBSTR; several other functions available)

Changes to the data structure
Therefore we can use the view capability as described in "Joining source tables" on page 98.

ASCII/EBCDIC conversion
This feature is already implemented in DB2. If you connect from the ODS to remote data sources, this conversion is automatically done where needed.

4.1.3 Near-current data delivery and uptime

In this section we show you how to configure DB2 DataPropagator and DataJoiner to prevent performance problems while using these products. We concentrate on two important requests for performance during the replication process:

- Near-current data delivery
- Uptime

For further information, please use the IBM Redbook, *My Mother Thinks I'm a DBA!*, SG24-5463; or the *IBM DB2 UDB Replication Guide and Reference*, SC26-9920, which is delivered with DB2 UDB.

Near-current data delivery

In this section we need to distinguish between near-real-time updates of the ODS and massive updates (when scheduling updates on a daily basis, for example). For both cases, we discuss the tuning capabilities of the IBM replication products.

Near-real-time updates

Here we are describing the capabilities of realizing a near-real-time scenario. This means that the data changes have to be replicated to the ODS as fast as possible. Therefore, we have to tune the *Capture* and the *Apply* parts of the replication process.

However, tuning these two programs is just one aspect of getting the data in near-real-time. Your ODS architecture must also support very fast updates to your ODS. For example, if you have numerous transformation functions implemented and your ODS data model has a totally different structure than your source systems it is quite difficult to get your data within seconds into your ODS. So, you need to take care that your design suits your performance requirements.

For the *Capture* program, we must distinguish between DB2 and non-DB2 sources. In non-DB2 sources we cannot tune the *Capture* part, because it is realized through database triggers. This means that the data is written to the CD tables in the same moment as it is written to the source tables, and it is also committed in the same transaction.

We shall now describe the possibilities for tuning the *Capture* program on DB2 sources for near-real-time updates:

- **Set commit interval**

  For the *Capture* program, a tuning parameter called COMMIT_INTERVAL tells the *Capture* program after what time to issue a commit statement on the CD table. The default value is set to 30 seconds. The *Apply* program only copies records to the target table that are committed. So if you need your data copied very fast to the ODS and you have a high rate of change to your source table, you should decrease this value.

- **Set pruning on/off**

  You have the option to start the *Capture* program in pruning or non-pruning mode. We recommend to start the *Capture* program with the NOPRUNE option, because otherwise, pruning will automatically interrupt the change capture activity on a regular basis. The default is 300 seconds. Pruning the CD tables should be launched during off-peak hours so that the *Capture* program is not influenced by the pruning process.

- **Capture program priority**

    In operating systems where you are able to influence the priority of programs, you should use this instrument to tune the *Capture* program. The faster you need your data on the target system, the higher should be the priority of the *Capture* program. But you will need to find a good average for all applications running on your system.

Next we describe the possibilities to tune the *Apply* program for near-real-time updates. We introduce some of the major tuning factors for this process:

- **Index usage on CD tables**

    Be sure to create the index generated for the CD tables and the UOW table as a unique index. To guarantee optimal performance, one (and only one) CD table index should be on the columns IBMSNAP_UOWID and IBMSNAP_INTENTSEQ, and for the UOW table, it should be on the columns IBMSNAP_COMMITSEQ, IBMSNAP_UOWID and IBMSNAP_LOGMARKER.

    The CD tables contents and the UOW table contents are varying in size from the initial zero rows to the maximum size right before the *Capture* program prunes the CD tables. This means that the timing of RUNSTATS is critical. RUNSTATS must be run at a time when the CD tables contain sufficient data so that the carefully chosen indexes on CD tables and on the UOW table will be used by the *Apply* program and the *Capture* program. It is not necessary to update the statistics again, once the catalog tables show that there is an advantage using the indexes.

- **Pull mode**

    Pull mode means that the *Apply* program is running at the target server, fetching data from the replication source server. When all the data has been pulled, the *Apply* program connects to the target database and applies all the fetched changes into the target tables.

    In push mode, the *Apply* program is normally running at the source server. Once the changes are retrieved locally, the *Apply* program then connects to the remote target database and pushes the changes one-by-one into the target tables.

    These two configurations are shown in Figure 4-5. From a performance perspective, it is better to design and configure your replication system so that it uses pull mode, because *Apply* will be able to make use of DB2/DRDA block fetch in these cases. Selecting data from a remote site over a network using block fetch capability is *much* faster than inserting data over a network without the possibility of blocking multiple inserts together.

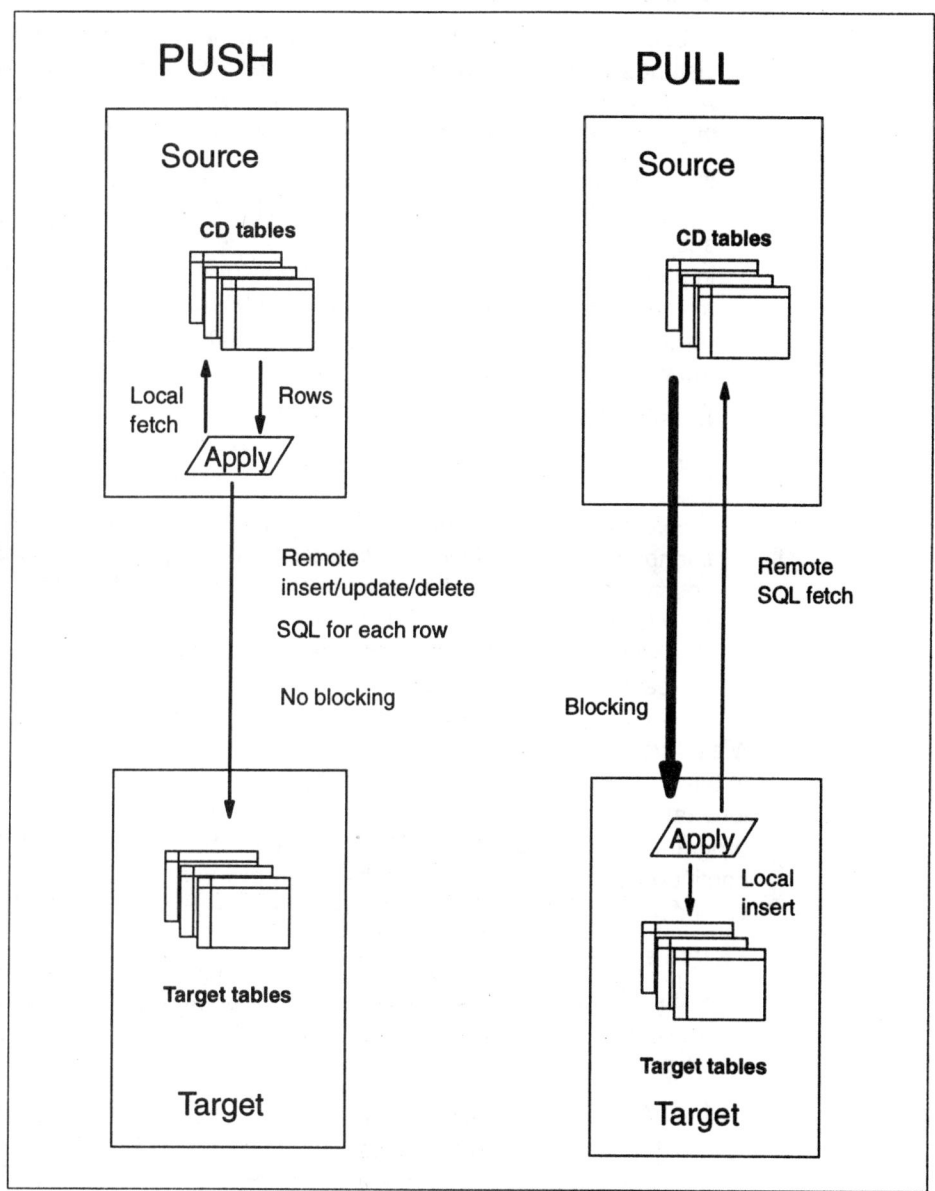

Figure 4-5   Apply pull/push modes

- **Using multiple Apply programs**

    In DB2 DataPropagator you can define multiple *Apply qualifiers*. One *Apply* instance is started for each *Apply qualifier*. When *Apply* is started for one *Apply qualifier*, it immediately calculates, based on the subscription timing that you defined, if subscription sets need to be serviced.

    If several subscription sets are awaiting replication, *Apply* always services the most overdue one first. That means, a single *Apply* program always services subscription sets sequentially. If you want to have subscription sets serviced in parallel, choose to have multiple *Apply qualifiers*. For each *Apply qualifier*, a single *Apply* program can be started subsequently. Multiple *Apply* programs obviously can be advantageous from a performance perspective, because the work is done in parallel.

- **Event-triggered Apply**

    The *Apply* program can be run scheduled or event-triggered. Wherever possible, use the event-triggered mode when you need your data fast. The problem is that the events must be created by the source application and cannot be created by the *Capture* program. So you have to change your source applications. If this is not possible, you have to run the *Apply* program as scheduled (minimum value is 1 minute) or continuously. These means that *Apply* connects to the source system again after it has finished copying data, to see if new data arrived.

Massive updates

In this section, are described the mechanisms to use with a large update volume, for example, when updating the ODS on a daily basis. In this case, the *Capture* program has no influence on the performance because the data is captured continuously to the point of time the *Apply* program runs. The following factors can influence the performance of the replication process:

- **Use subscription sets**

    Subscription sets provide a huge performance advantage compared to replicating every table separately. To show this, let us take a closer look at what happens when the *Apply* program services a subscription set.

    Figure 4-6 shows that the *Apply* program performs several single tasks during a subscription cycle. Some tasks are executed at the replication control server, others are executed at the replication source server, and finally others at the replication target server. Of course, the *Apply* program needs database connections in order to perform the tasks at the different databases.

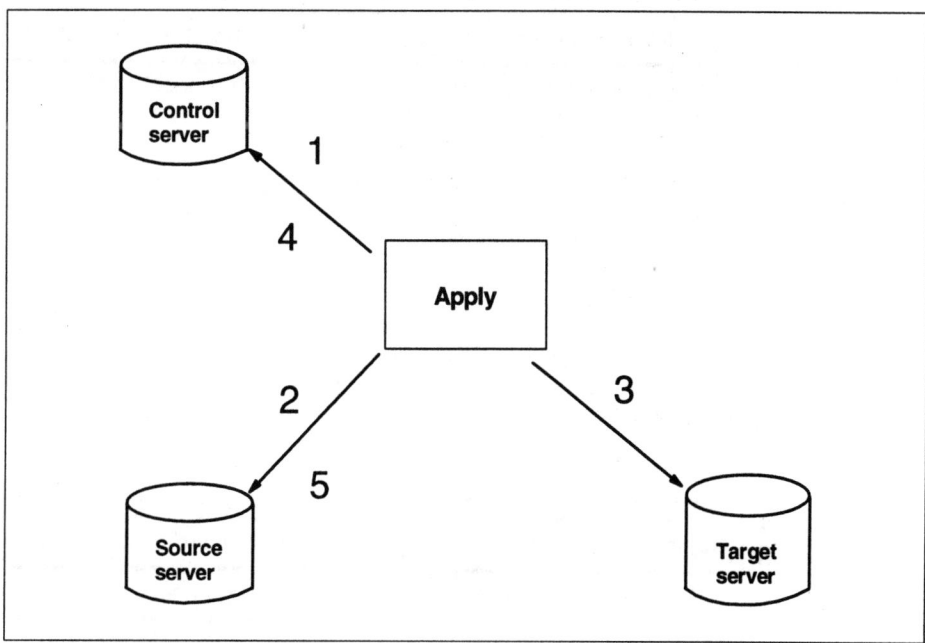

Figure 4-6   Apply tasks

We can identify at least the following *Apply* tasks, which execute in the following sequence:

- Look for work on the control server (**1**).
- Fetch changes from CD tables into the spill file on the source server (**2**).
- Apply changes from the spill file to target tables on the target server (**3**).
- Update subscription statistics on the control server (**4**).
- Advance pruning control syncpoint to enable pruning on source server (**5**).

All these tasks need database connections and are executed at subscription set level. The number of database connections (established one at a time) that are needed to replicate a given number of tables can be dramatically reduced by grouping the target tables together in subscription sets. Table 4-1 shows alternatives for replicating 100 tables.

Table 4-1   Decrease of connections using subscription sets (part 1)

Number of subscription sets	Number of connections
100 sets / 1 member per set	500 connections
50 sets / 2 members per set	250 connections
10 sets / 10 members per set	50 connections
2 sets / 50 members per set	10 connections
1 set / 100 members in the set	5 connections

Even if the control server is identical with the target server, you can reduce the number of connections remarkably by using subscription sets. This is shown in Table 4-2. In this case, you have still 4 connections per set because you can just join the steps 3 and 4 together.

Table 4-2   Minimizing database connections using subscription sets (part 2)

Number of subscription sets	Number of connections
100 sets / 1 member per set	400 connections
50 sets / 2 members per set	200 connections
10 sets / 10 members per set	40 connections
2 sets / 50 members per set	8 connections
1 set / 100 members in the set	4 connections

The only impact of having big subscription sets is that the transactions needed to replicate data into the target tables can become quite large (all changes within one subscription set are applied within one transaction). Be sure to allocate enough log space and enough space for the spill file.

- **Using CCD tables**

    Normally, in a replication environment, the *Capture* program captures the changes from the logs and inserts them into the CD tables and the related transaction information into the UOW table. The *Apply* program determines the committed changes by joining the CD table and the UOW table and then applies these changes to the target tables.

    But it is even more efficient to define a staging table as the join of the CD table and the UOW table. This staging table is called the Committed Change Data (CCD) table. In this case the *Apply* program on the target system can read the CCD table without needing to join the tables at each subscription cycle.

This process is shown in Figure 4-7. The CCD table can reside on the source (local) or on the target (remote) system. The remote CCD table should be used, for example, when the source data is replicated to different tables on the target system. Then the data is copied only once over the network into the CCD table and then applied to the target tables. Otherwise, the data has to replicated over the network for each target table where it is needed.

The CCD table can be registered automatically as a replication source and can be used for another subscription.

CCD tables can be run in condensed mode. This means that the CCD table contains only the newest version of a source table row. This is useful when your system performs multiple updates to a row between two *Apply* program cycles. Normally every update would be applied to the target table. When using a condensed CCD table, only the last update would be applied. This can reduce network traffic remarkably.

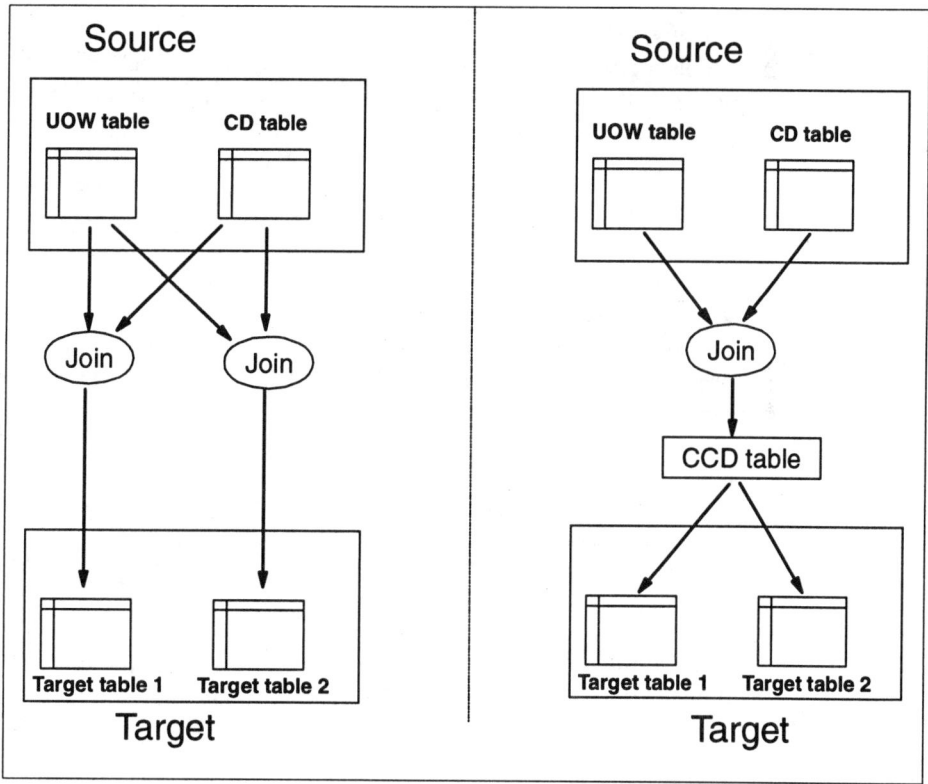

Figure 4-7 CCD table

> **Attention:** CCD tables are not automatically pruned like CD tables. Subscriptions that maintain CCD tables can be made to prune the CCD tables using SQL-after DELETE statements attached to the subscription.

4.1.4 Populating the ODS using Data Warehouse Center (DWC)

As you see in the previous section, you can accomplish quite a bit using just the DB2 replication technology. However, integrating the DB2 replication technology along with the warehouse management capability provided by the Data Warehouse Center (DWC), we have a very powerful solution for designing and implementing an ODS.

In this section, we will discuss how DB2 replication technology is integrated into the DWC and how to design and define a replication scenario with DWC.

Overview of DWC replication integration

As discussed in this chapter, there are two basic processes in a replication solution, the capture of changed data by the DB2 *Capture* program at the source DB2 and the update of a target table by the DB2 *Apply* program at the ODS DB2. In the case of heterogeneous replication, the *Capture* function is accomplished by methods particular to the non-DB2 source, such as via triggers in an Oracle database. Those changes are captured into a CD table in that source database. The *Apply* component accesses the CD table via DataJoiner.

When using the DWC to manage the population process, replication basically works the same, except that we use the DWC to define and automate the *Apply* process at the target database, in this case our ODS. Definition of the capture process is the same and is done outside the DWC, either interfacing directly with the source database or via the DB2 Control Center. The replication subscription is accomplished by defining a replication step via the DWC, and the *Apply* scheduling is defined using the DWC scheduling capabilities. In addition, once the changes have been propagated to our ODS environment, we have available the capabilities of the DWC to transform the data, integrate and combine the data with data from other sources before updating the ODS.

See Chapter 7, "Building and managing the ODS population subsystem" on page 189 to see an example of integrating replicated relational data with data from a VSAM source that is delivered to the ODS via MQ Series.

This is the basic process to define a replication scenario in the DWC:

1. Import metadata into the DWC about source tables that are registered as replication sources.
2. Select the appropriate replication step and connect the input source table.
3. Fill in the appropriate parameters.
4. Either connect the replication step to an output table or have the DWC generate an output table based on the replication step.
5. Define the appropriate scheduling for the step, whether time-based or dependency-based.

Design

In this example, we are bringing PART information into our ODS from two replication sources, one in DB2 and one in Oracle. The setup of the *Capture* component is independent of how we set up the DWC *Apply* component. From a DWC perspective, we only see replication sources; and whether it is a DB2 replication source or a Oracle replication source is immaterial to how we define the apply step within DWC.

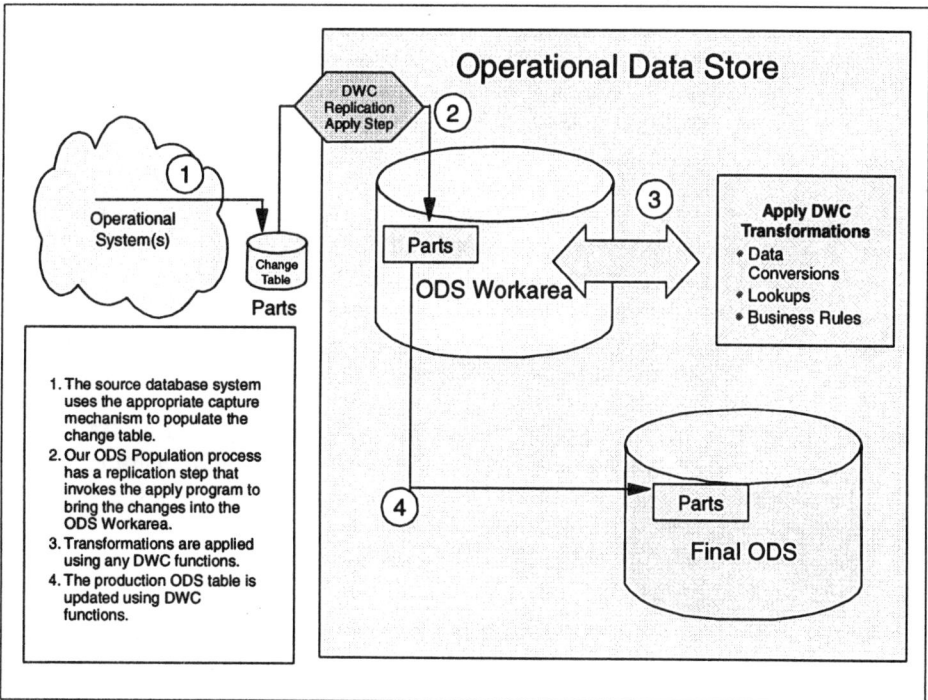

Figure 4-8 Overview of PART replication process

When designing a replication scenario in the DWC, we have to decide what type of replication step we need. DWC supports five types of replication:

1. **User Copy:** This is a complete, condensed copy of the replication source table which must have a primary key. This table will be maintained as an exact duplicate of the original table.

2. **Point-In-Time:** This is a complete, condensed copy of the replication source table which must have a primary key and has timestamp columns added to indicate when a transaction occurred.

3. **Base Aggregate:** This is a history table in which new rows are appended during each subscription cycle and uses the result of a SQL column function calculation against the source table data.

4. **Change Aggregate:** This is a history table in which a new row is appended for each changed row in the replication source table using the result of a SQL column function calculation against only recently changed data.

5. **Staging Table:** A staging table, also known as a Consistent Change Data (CCD) table, can have many purposes, but it originated to provide a staging area for the purpose of replicating data to multiple target tables without each target accessing the original source. There are many options in configuring a CCD table, but in an ODS environment, we want to use a complete, condensed CCD which captures each change made to the source table as a individual row with an indication of the type of change, Insert/Update/Delete. We will capture the data after the change was made but could also capture the data before it was changed. This is the type of replication table that is most useful in our ODS and is the type that we use in our examples.

So, in our example, we will use a staging table to capture a row for each change in our two PART databases with the data column values after the change and an indication of the change type, Insert/Update/Delete. We will process transformations against these change records as needed to prepare the data for our ODS and then process the changes as appropriate for the type of change based on our business requirements.

For more information about DB2 Replication, see the IBM *Replication Guide and Reference* and the *Data Warehouse Center Administration Guide,* SC26-9920.

Defining the population process

As we have seen, DWC is not concerned with exactly how the source records are captured or how the replication source is defined. Rather, we are concerned about the fact that the replication source exists in our source database.

Our problem is how to take those change records, apply whatever transformations our business requires, and then update the ODS. Using the DWC, this is relatively simple. In general, when using the DWC, our first step would be to "stage" our source changes into a common storage format, which in our case would be DB2 relational tables.

> **Note:** The time available to stage the data is dependent on the data delivery timing requirements.

This applies to any source, whether it be flat files, any relational source, replication sources, Web sources, IMS, VSAM, and so forth. Once we have staged our data into relational tables, we can now use the full power of DB2 UDB and the DWC to apply our transformations and update the ODS. We can therefore integrate and consolidate data from many sources into our ODS.

See Chapter 7, "Building and managing the ODS population subsystem" on page 189 for more information about architecture of the population process.

In this replication scenario, we will be bringing change records from two different replication sources in different source systems. There will be one replication source with its associated changed data table in our DB2 source system and one replication source with its associated changed data table in Oracle, which we will access via DataJoiner.

As with any source to the DWC, we must register our source databases (see Figure 4-9) and import the metadata for the replication sources to the DWC.

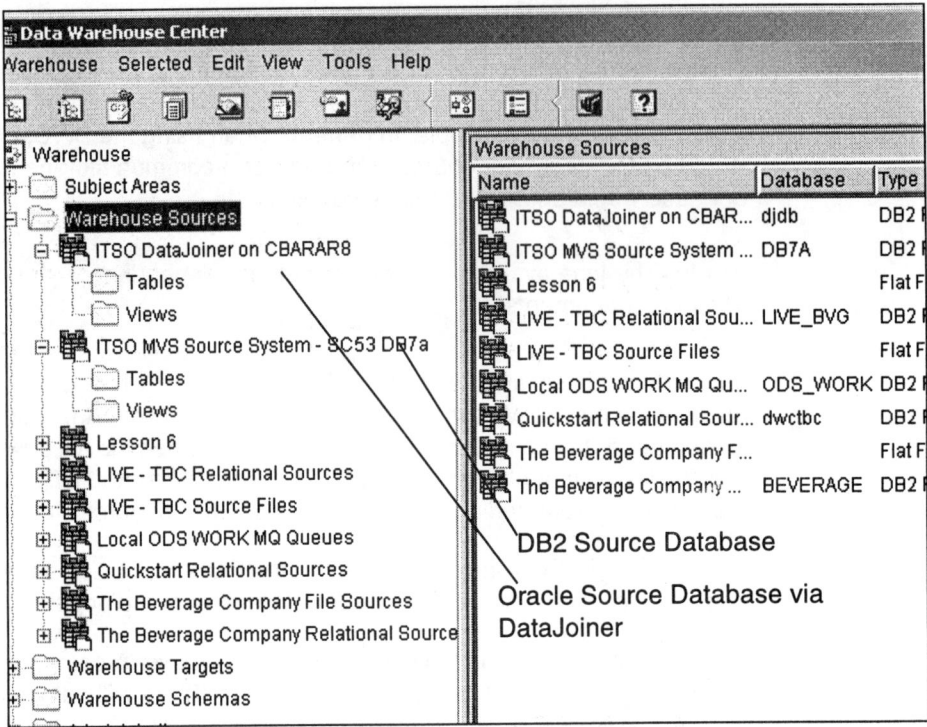

Figure 4-9   Source databases are registered in the DWC

Once our source databases are registered in the DWC, we can get a list of all replication sources for a database and import the table metadata. Once a source table is registered, it is now available to use in any DWC process.

Figure 4-10 and Figure 4-11 are screen captures showing the selection of a DB2 replication source and the importing of its metadata. The steps are the same for registering the Oracle replication source to the DWC.

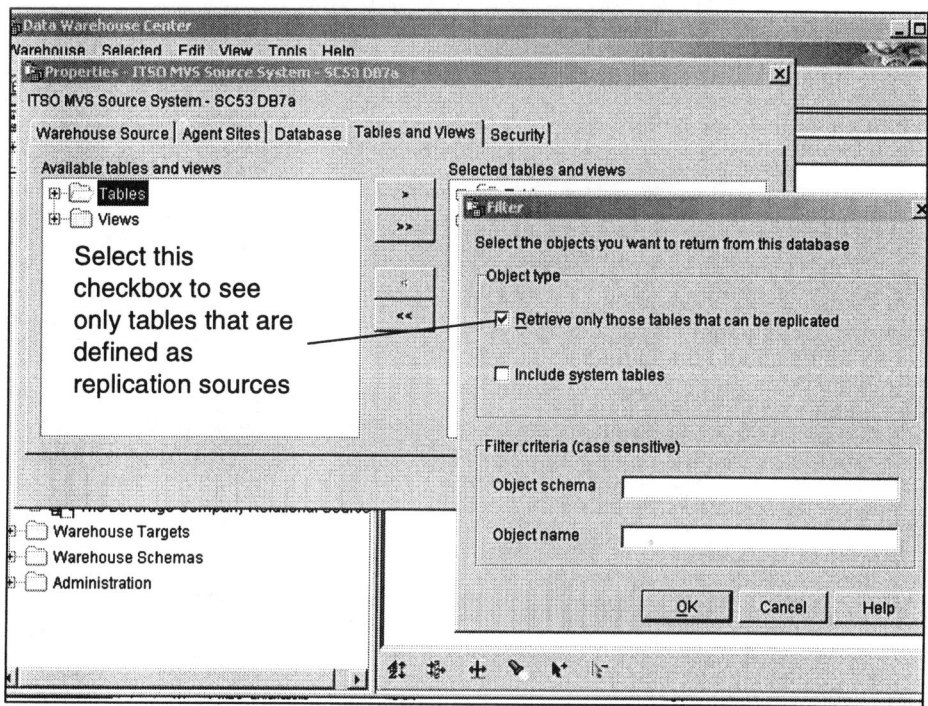

Figure 4-10   Define the DB2 replication source and select only replication sources

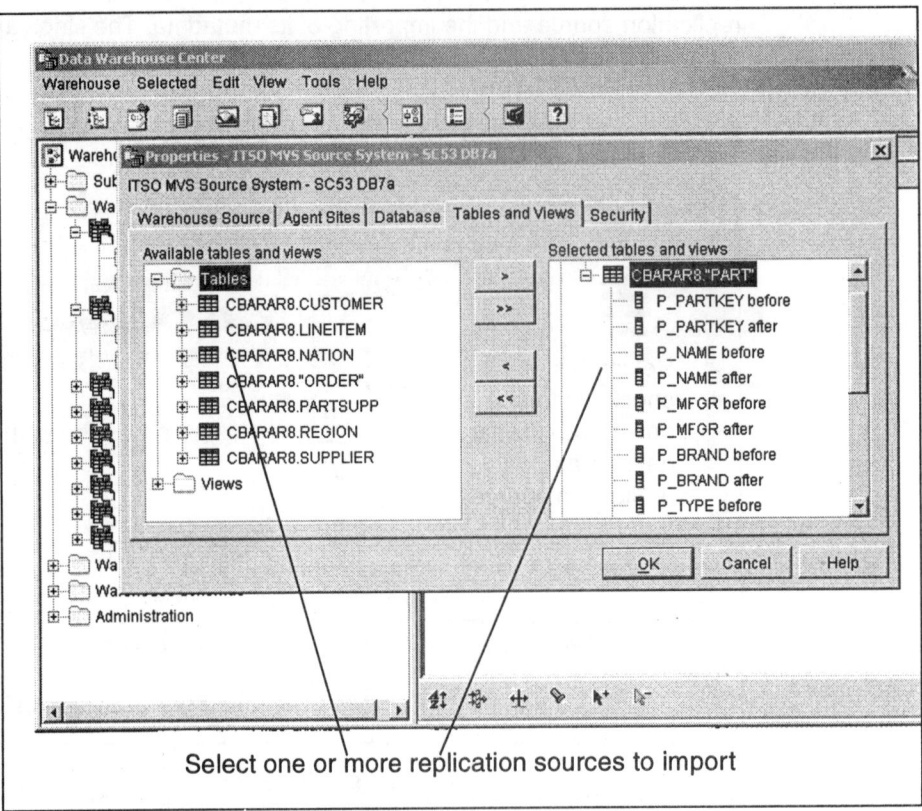

Figure 4-11 Define the DB2 replication source: import the source metadata

Now that we have registered both of our replication sources to the DWC, we can use these in any DWC process. We create a process, select our replication sources, and add them to the process modeler canvas as shown in Figure 4-12.

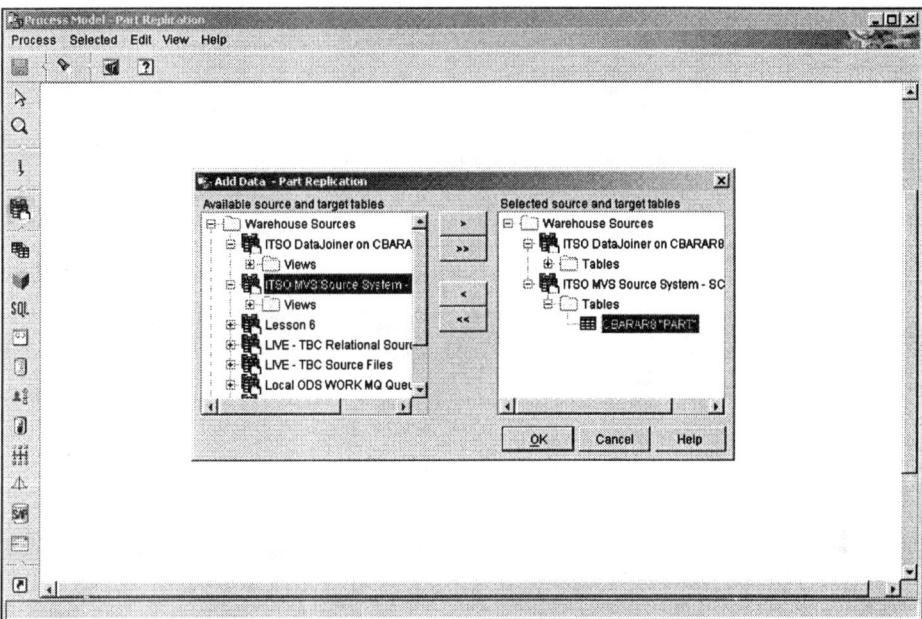

Figure 4-12   Selecting sources to be added to the process modeler canvas

After adding the replication sources as icons on the process modeler canvas, we select the Replication Step menu and select the type of replication step we want, in this case, a Staging Table. We do this once for each replication source and connect each source to its replication step with a data connection arrow, which is a visual programming way to indicate that the source is the input to the replication step.

For each step, we open the properties dialog and define the metadata needed to execute this replication. There will be a tabbed page, the Parameters Page, to select the columns that we want to replicate from the selection of before and/or after images as defined in the Replication Source. We can add calculated columns and even filter with a where clause. We also can select various characteristics of our staging table. The mapping page allows us to map our selected input columns to the output table columns. We can even have the output table definition and column mapping generated.

(The various menus in defining a replication step are shown in Figure 4-13 through Figure 4-17).

Defining a replication step and selecting staging table parameters is shown in Figure 4-13.

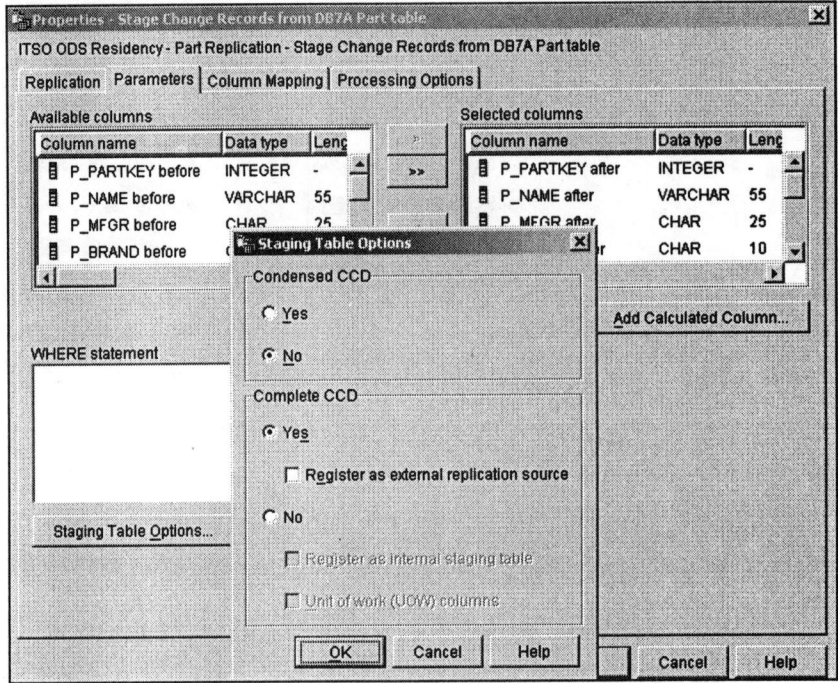

Figure 4-13 Defining a replication step: selecting staging table parameters

Defining a replication step and generating the output table is shown in Figure 4-14.

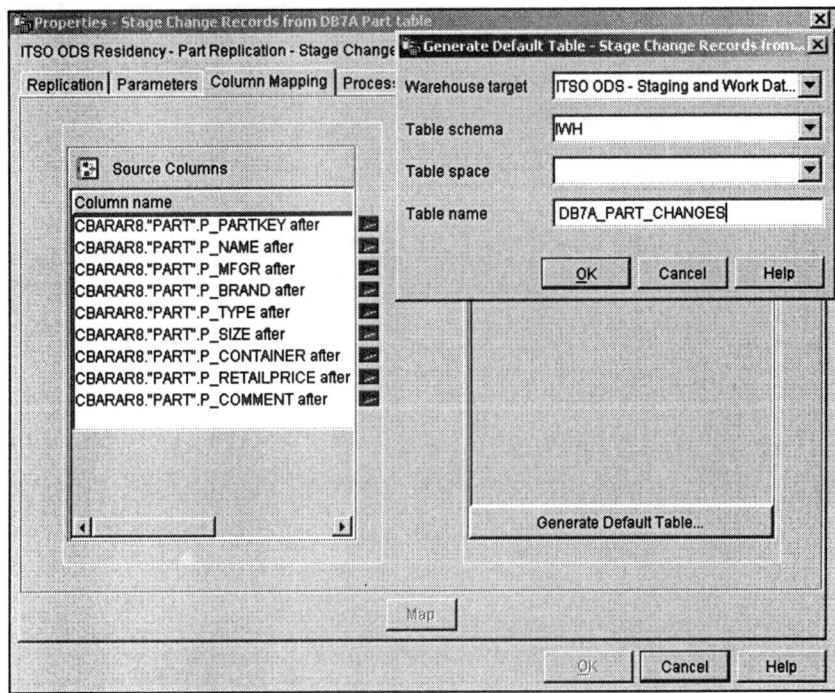

Figure 4-14   Defining a replication step: generating the output table

Defining a replication step and mapping columns to generated table is shown in Figure 4-15.

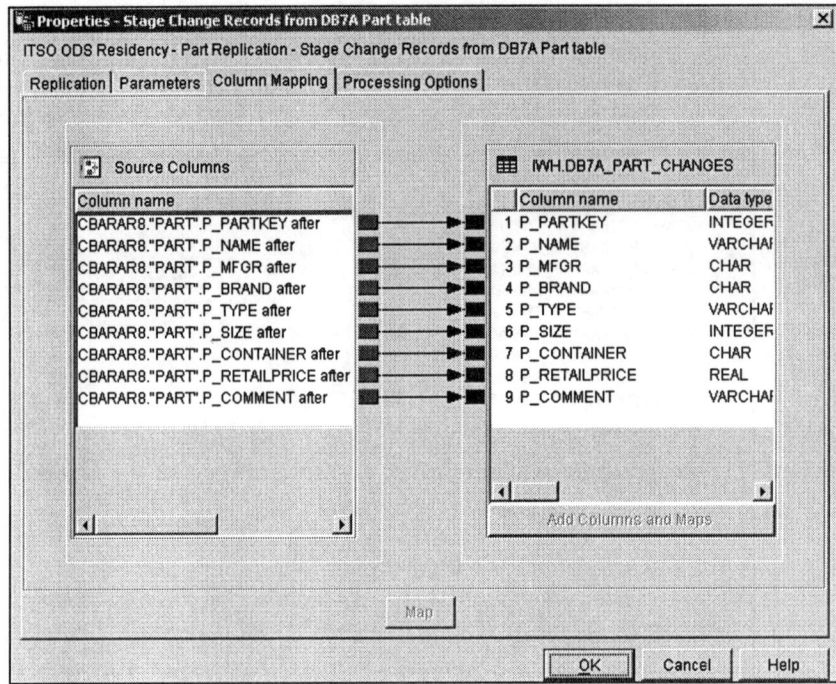

Figure 4-15 Defining a replication step: mapping columns to generated table

Finally, on the Processing Options page, we provide information that influences the execution of the replication step and the location of the replication control tables (see Figure 4-16).

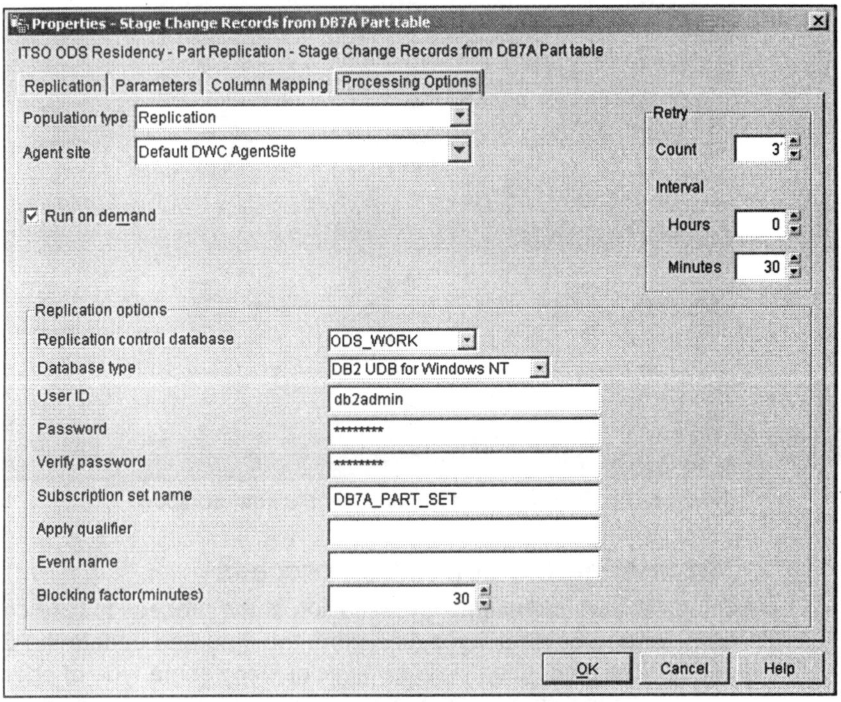

Figure 4-16 Defining a replication step: processing options

We have defined a step that when executed will take the change records from the changed data table at the source DB2 database and insert them into a staging table in our ODS. We use exactly the same steps to define the replication from the Oracle source which isolates us from the fact that our original source is Oracle. Now that we have change records from both sources in DB2 tables within our ODS workarea, we can use the power of DB2 and the DWC to perform our transformation process and update the ODS tables.

Our final workflow for the replication looks like Figure 4-17.

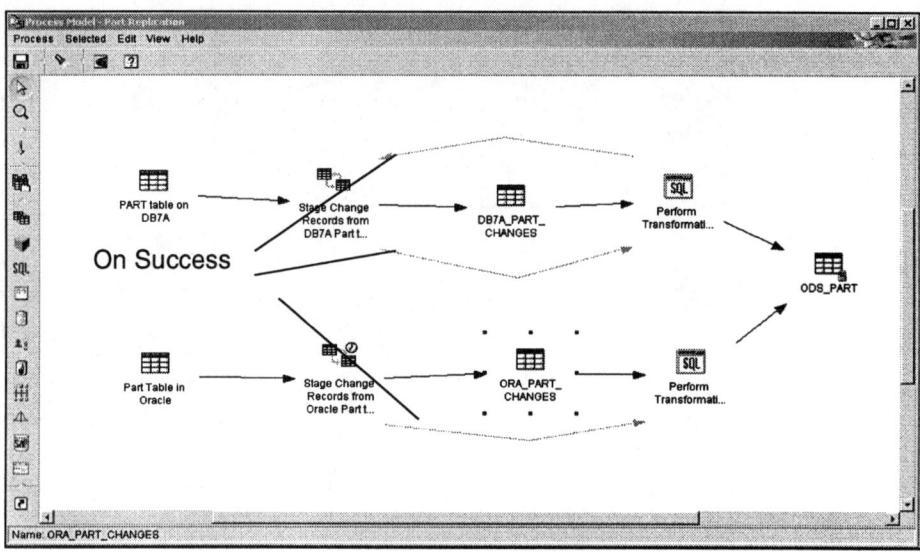

Figure 4-17 Defining a replication step: the final workflow

Automating the population process

Once we have completed the definition of the process to take change records from our source databases, transform the data and update the ODS, we have to put this into production. This involves defining some type of operational workflow which links together steps based on execution dependencies resulting in a number of separate independent workflows. For each workflow, we need to determine how to invoke the first step in the workflow. Also, we have to be able to monitor what is going on in our ODS population process. The DWC provides all of these capabilities. We will illustrate specifically on scheduling issues by using our example replication process.

In this example, we can easily see two independent workflows, one for the DB2 PARTs source and one for the Oracle PARTs source. We see that in each workflow, we have two steps, one to stage the change records into the ODS workarea and one to do the transformations and update the ODS table. These two steps must execute serially and, obviously, we must stage the changes before we can transform the data, so we have a dependency in both of the workflows. We can reflect this scheduling dependency by drawing a green process flow arrow from the staging step to the transform step which tells the warehouse server that, after successful completing the staging step, execute the transformation step. We connect the execution dependencies resulting in our two independent workflows.

The issue we must now decide is how to start the execution of the first step of each workflow and how do we keep repeating the workflows? There are several methods that we could use. We could simply have the first step start executing based on some time schedule, perhaps every five minutes as we have done in the Oracle workflow. Notice the little clock icon on the Oracle replication step. Every five minutes, the warehouse server will execute this replication step and when it completes successfully, the green arrow tells the warehouse server to execute the transformation step and once it finishes, there is no more work in this workflow. This entire process will be repeated every five minutes.

A second method to get a step started is to manually start the process. An ODS operator would use DWC facilities to manually start the execution of the DB2 replication step and when it finishes we see that the transformation step executes. However, when the transformation step completes, we don't want to simply stop, but instead, we want to go back and get the next bundle of change records. Hence, the second green arrow leading from the transformation step back to the DB2 replication step resulting in a nice little loop that will execute either one of the steps fails or we stop the automatic execution of step by taking one of them out of production.

There is a third way to start the execution of the first step in a workflow which is to have a process outside of the warehouse server environment invoke the external trigger mechanism to execute the first step. Perhaps we are dependent on a process in our operational system completing before we start our workflow. A process on the operational system can invoke the external trigger which communicates with the warehouse server to start the step. See 5.1.4, "Populating the ODS using the DWC MQ Connector" on page 153 for an example of using an external trigger.

4.2 Relational data as a target (ODS type B)

In an ODS type B, we consider the situation where a user can make an update directly to the ODS. This update then gets propagated towards the operational database, in other words we are updating in the opposite direction to that which we have discussed up till now. Typically more than 99 percent of updates to the ODS will consist of changes that had been made to the operational database, but there may be occasions where the flow may need to be in the other direction. An example of this may be where the customer may be accessing his own personal details via the Web and needs to make a change, say a change of address.

4.2.1 Managing updates back to data sources

The simplest method for allowing a user to update the ODS is to let the user update the operational data directly, and then wait for that data to be propagated to the ODS. This is, of course, the type A scenario.

However, there are a number of issues with doing things this way, not the least of which is that the customer is allowed direct access to the operational data. Also, it may take a minute for the update to be reflected in the ODS and this may be unacceptable.

Given that a type B scenario proves necessary, we may ask, what methods are there of getting the update back to the operational database?

Triggering stored procedures

One method that could be used is to create a trigger on the ODS table so that every time a row in the table has an update, insert or delete done to it, an action is triggered. This action will consist of one or more SQL statements, one of which could be an EXEC SQL CALL to a stored procedure. This stored procedure would be written to use MQ verbs that will write to a queue on the local queue manager. From here on, the situation is the exact reverse of the situation described in the type A scenario. That is, MQSeries and MQSI are used to transform and transport the data back towards the operational database.

The difficulty with this method however, is that for 99 percent of updates, that is, those that have originated from the operational data, you do not want any form of triggering to occur. Although the stored procedure can be written to ignore updates that have arrived from the operational database, it still means that much unnecessary triggering and calling of stored procedures is occurring, and this is likely to be an unacceptable overhead.

4.2.2 Independent updates

A better method is for the user's update to be written to ODS and the operational database at the same time. In this scenario the user accessing the appropriate Web page from a browser changes his personal details. The update code on the Web server is written so that it updates the ODS using SQL and using MQSI commands puts the record to a queue on a MQSeries queue manager residing on that server. For more information on MQSeries and MQSI, refer to the introductory sections in 3.5, "Data acquisition scenarios using IBM products" on page 73 and Section , "ODS data transformations" on page 139.

This queue is defined as a queue-remote (QR) pointing to a queue on our NT server which is monitored by MQSI. In our example this queue is called CUST_IN. From here on, the process is analogous to the reverse of the type A update. MQSI gets the data from CUST_IN, transforms the data, and writes it to the operational database, as shown in Figure 4-18.

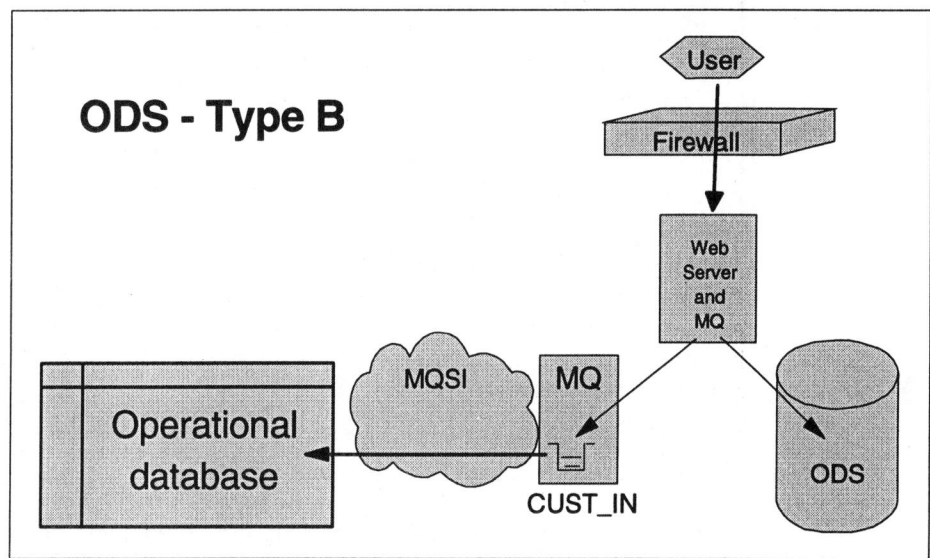

Figure 4-18   ODS type B: updating back to relational database

The WebSphere MQ Integrator (MQSI) message flows are shown in Figure 4-19.

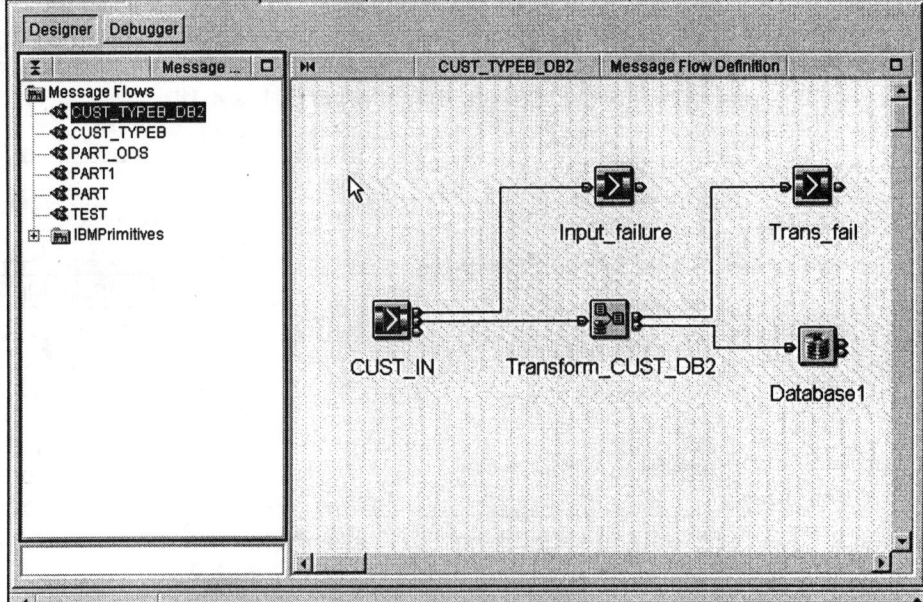

Figure 4-19 MQSI message flows for type B (relational)

The flows show that if the message arriving from the server fails to map properly it is routed to a queue defined in the *Input_failure* node. If the message maps correctly but the data transformation step fails then the message is sent to another queue as specified in the *Trans_fail* node. If all is well, then the data is written to the operational table on z/OS as defined in the Database1 node.

Integrity controls

Now that we have updated the operational table, we have to confront the fact that this update will again be picked up as a change and propagated towards the ODS. There are two potential problems with this double update:

- Synchronization of data
- Performance

A method on how to prevent this double update could be defined, as described in the following sections.

Synchronization of data
If the user makes two updates to the same bit of data, then there exists a window of time where his second update to the ODS will have been overwritten by his first update being propagated to the ODS. This will soon be corrected by the arrival of the second update, but if this situation proves unacceptable, then a means must be found to prevent it from happening.

Performance
This merely refers to the fact that the ODS is updated twice with exactly the same data and therefore is an unnecessary overhead. In a real environment when only one percent of the updates to the ODS are made by the user, then this is unlikely to be a problem, but again, it might be desirable to prevent the double update from happening.

How to prevent the double update
A filter process could be added to the data acquisition layer to prevent a double update from occurring. This process would look at each transaction coming from the data sources and when it is recognizes that the record has been updated by the ODS the record would be thrown out. For example, the ODS can be given a specific user identification to use when updating the data source; this identification would then be captured as part of the data acquisition process.

Populating the ODS from non-relational sources

In many organizations, business data is not held exclusively on relational databases. Quite frequently, a significant proportion of the data is kept on files, such as a VSAM file or flat files or in IMS. In this chapter we discuss how this data can be extracted from the operational database, integrated with other data, transformed, and then used to populate an ODS, using mainly WebSphere MQ Integrator (MQSI) message flows.

5.1 VSAM as an ODS source (ODS type A)

In this section we discuss ODS scenarios where the operational data resides in VSAM files and how to solve the ODS issues.

We address:

- The VSAM issue
- How to capture the VSAM updates
- How to apply updates using WebSphere MQ Integrator (MQSI)
- How to apply updates using DB2 UDB V7.2 MQ connector

5.1.1 The VSAM issue

Many companies hold much of their business data in files. For this data to be incorporated into an ODS, we must first find a way of capturing updates made to the operational files and then apply them to the ODS.

5.1.2 Capturing VSAM updates

There is no straightforward way of capturing these updates; however, there are several products in the marketplace that can take a "delta" of successive copies of the operational data. That is, the current data can be compared with the previous copy of the data and the changed data can then be written to a VSAM file. With this method, it would be difficult to generate near-real-time updates to the ODS as the process would have to be carried out many times a day and would likely prove too unwieldy.

However, it would be reasonable to carry out this process on a less frequent basis, such as once a day. If it is acceptable to have an ODS containing day-old data, then this is a good method of capturing updates. It also has the advantage that not as much data needs to be sent to the ODS. This is because a record may be changed several times during the day, but only the latest version is sent to the ODS.

If it is necessary to have near-real-time data in the ODS, then a more realistic method is to change the application code so that as it updates the operational data, it also writes the changed record to a VSAM file. In fact, this method could also be used to update a z/OS or OS/390 flat file if any operational data resides there.

We propose to use a CICS transaction to read this file, propagate the updates towards the ODS, and then to delete the changed or delta data as soon as the unit of work is complete.

Here, an update transaction (UPDT) has been rewritten so that it not only updates the operational database, but also writes the new record to the VSAM delta file. Using CICS Interval Control, the PART transaction can be scheduled to run at particular times or at regular intervals, as required.

This transaction reads each record in the delta file and then propagates it towards the ODS. When the whole file has been read, the records are deleted from the file.

The PART transaction then reschedules itself to run at some pre-specified interval or time. (See Figure 5-1.)

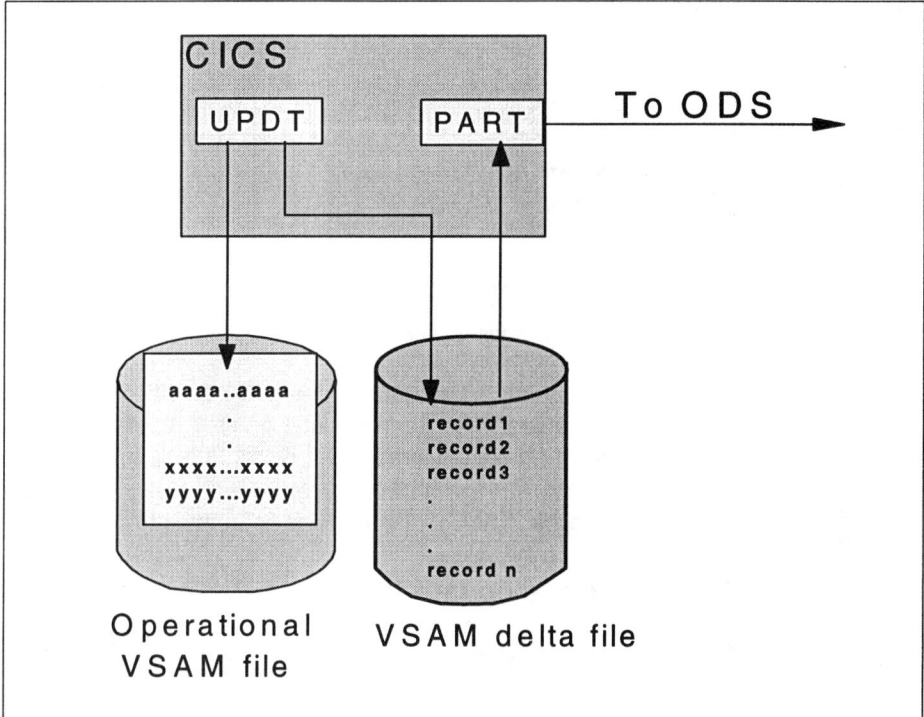

Figure 5-1   Near-real-time updates to the ODS

Whether the updates to the ODS are near-real-time or on a daily basis, the process from here is essentially the same in that we take updates from a VSAM delta file and propagate them towards the ODS.

There are three scenarios that we consider here:

- Synchronous update to ODS on DB2 UDB for z/OS
- Asynchronous update to ODS on DB2 UDB for z/OS
- Asynchronous update to ODS on DB2 UDB EEE

Synchronous update to ODS on DB2 UDB for z/OS

In this method the PART transaction is written to communicate with a remote CICS system. A synchronous conversation with the target CICS transaction is initiated in which the remote transaction receives the record and uses an EXEC SQL statement to write it directly to DB2 UDB, as shown in Figure 5-2.

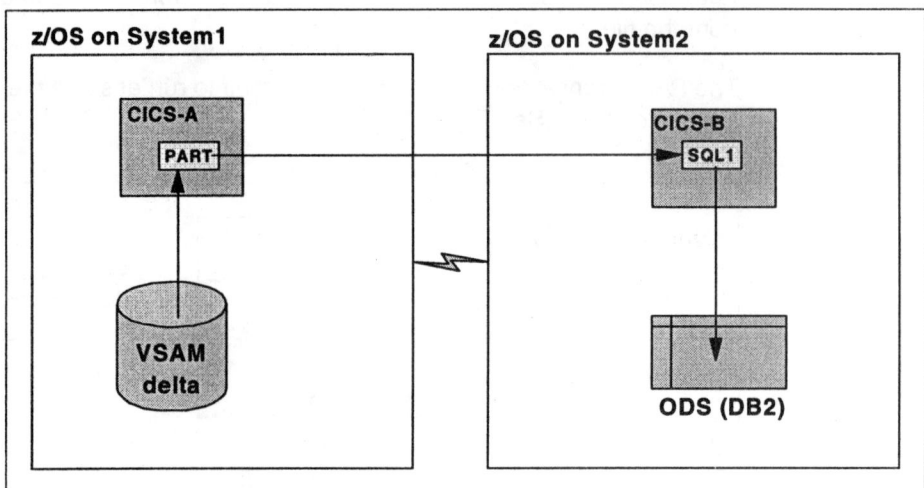

Figure 5-2 Synchronous update

The difficulty in using this method is due to the number of resources locked out at any given time and the length of the unit of work. In processing terms, this is going to be less efficient than asynchronous update. It also fails to make any use of the data transformation facilities of MQSeries Integrator (MQSI) and the Data Warehouse Center (DWC), discussed later in this chapter.

Asynchronous update to ODS on DB2 UDB for z/OS

In this example we use MQSeries in conjunction with CICS to move the data towards the ODS. MQSeries flows and components are described in "IBM WebSphere MQ family" on page 76.

The PART transaction has been written to issue an MQOPEN on the queue PART.QUEUE.

> **Note:** MQCONN is basically not required with CICS, that can only connect to one queue manager, that is the one to which CICS is connected

Now the program successively reads the records from the VSAM delta file and writes the record to PART.QUEUE using an MQPUT. This continues until the end of the file. The records then are all deleted from the file. For the PL/I source of this program, see Appendix B, "Example CICS program" on page 289.

In order to send a record to a remote system, the target queue PART.QUEUE2 on QM2 must be defined in QM1 as a remote queue. So in our example PART.QUEUE is defined in QM1 as a queue-remote (QR). In this definition PART.QUEUE2 is defined as existing on QM2. The process is shown in Figure 5-3.

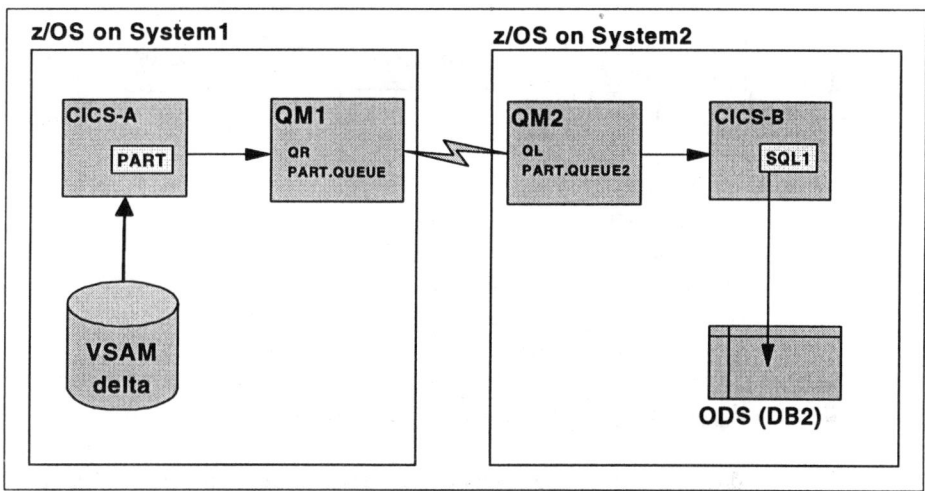

Figure 5-3 Asynchronous update on DB2 UDB for z/OS

On the target queue manager (QM2), the queue has to be defined as a queue-local (QL) that can be triggered. This definition points to a process that will be started when the trigger conditions are met. In our example the process is a CICS transaction called SQL1.

This transaction has been written to read the queue PART.QUEUE2 and to write the message using EXEC SQL statements into DB2 UDB.

Although the process is asynchronous, in fact, there is negligible delay in performing the update using this method. It has the added advantage that if there is a problem with connectivity or System2 is down for some reason, then the updates are queued up on QM1, and as soon as the remote system is available again, the updates will be written.

In this solution MQSeries can be used as a means of transporting the data from one machine to another. However, MQSI as well as MQSeries can provide a great deal of functionality and flexibility with the way messages are routed, transformed and handled. The schema is shown in Figure 5-4.

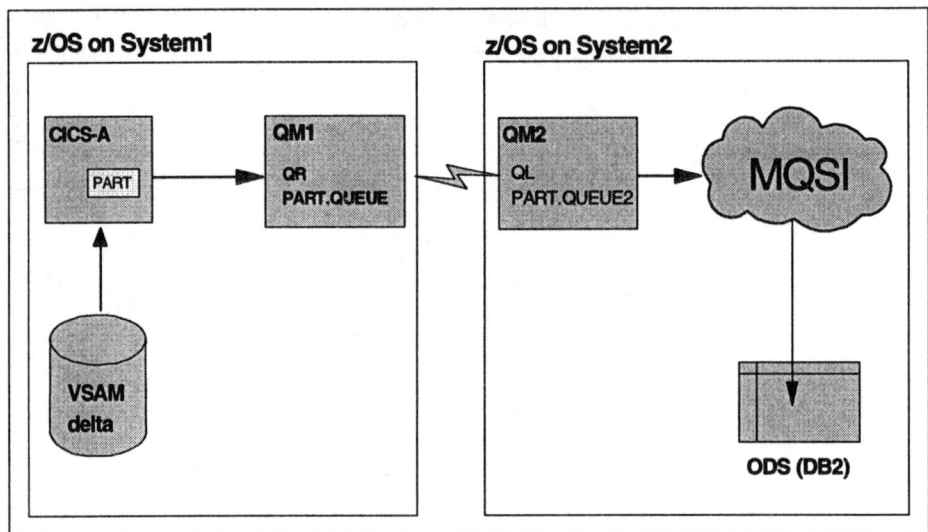

Figure 5-4 Using MQSI to read the MQ queue

This implementation will be discussed in section 5.1.3, "Populating the ODS using MQSI" on page 134 where instead of using CICS to read the MQ messages from the target queue, we use MQSI.

Asynchronous update to ODS on DB2 UDB EEE

This method is similar to the asynchronous updates to DB2 UDB on z/OS, where we use MQSI to populate the ODS. This is discussed in more detail in the section 5.1.3, "Populating the ODS using MQSI" on page 134.

The process we are concerned with here is shown in Figure 5-5.

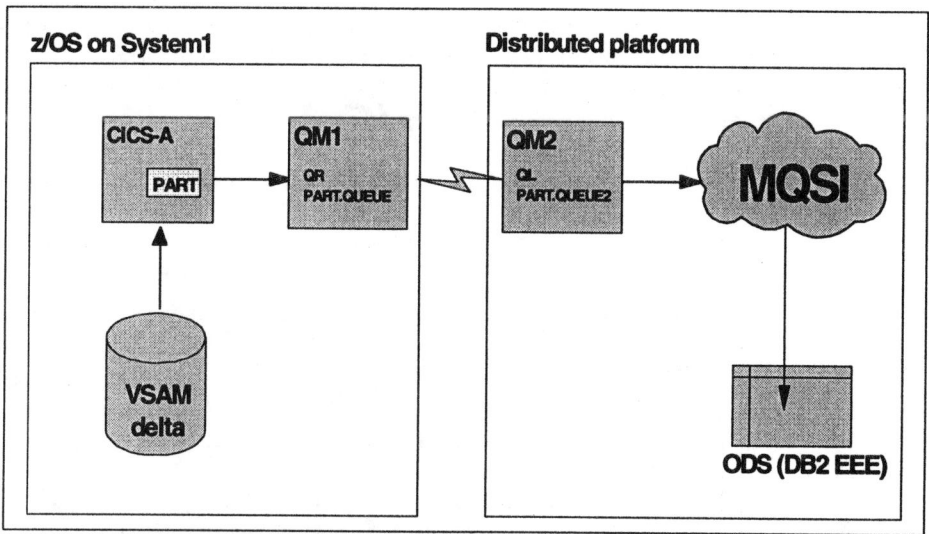

Figure 5-5   Using MQSI on distributed platform

Another method that can be used is to use a new feature of DB2 UDB EE/EEE V7.2 which allows an MQSeries queue to be treated as a DB2 UDB table and as a result any message written to the target queue (PART.QUEUE2) can be inserted directly into DB2 UDB using the new DB2MQ commands. (Refer to Figure 5-6.)

For example, the equivalent of an SQL insert would be:

DB2MQ.MQSEND ('P_PARTKEY','P_NAME')

There is more information on how to do this in 5.1.4, "Populating the ODS using the DWC MQ Connector" on page 153.

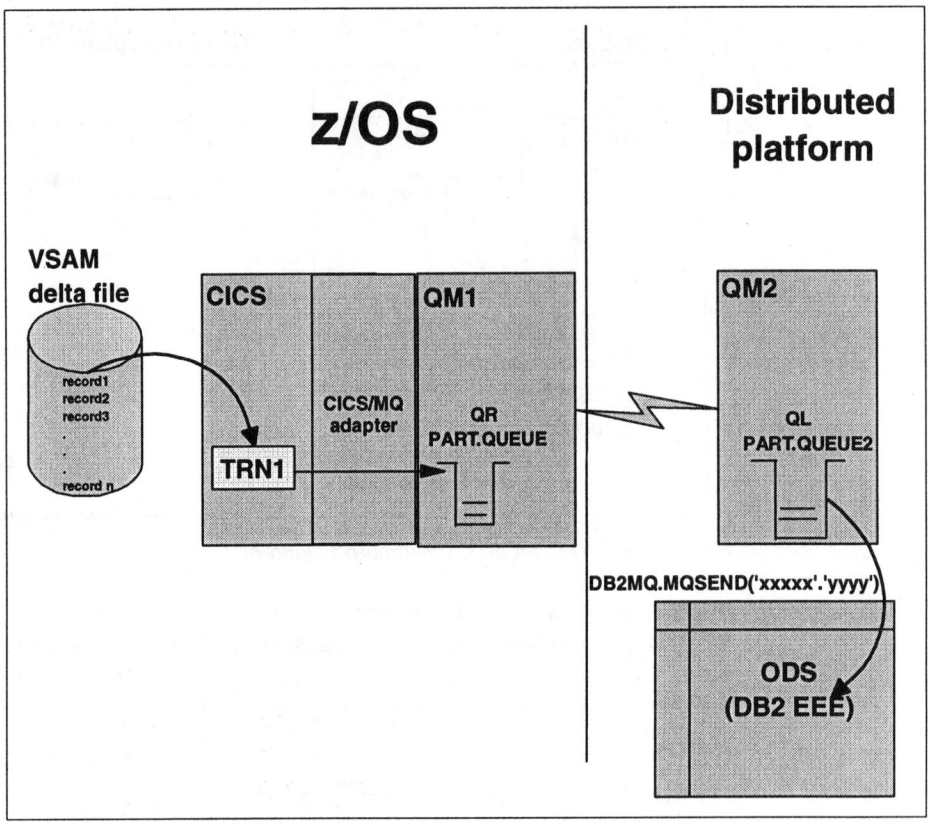

Figure 5-6   DB2MQ function

5.1.3 Populating the ODS using MQSI

In this section, we explain how ODS population can be achieved by MQSeries and MQSI.

Using MQSeries to transport and deliver messages, MQSI establishes a hub through which they pass. It simplifies connections between applications, integrates information from databases and other sources, applies enterprise-defined business rules, dynamically directs the flow of information and transforms and reformats the data to suit the recipients. For the ODS, it facilitates the update on the DB2 target and may take care of some data transformations required by the ODS.

In the examples used in this section, we consider a VSAM file containing part information in the format given by the C structure shown here. Example 5-1 shows our input structure.

Example 5-1   PART input structure

```
typedef struct tagINPUT_FORMAT {
   char P_PARTKEY(12);
   char P_NAME(55);
   char P_MFGR(25);
   char P_BRAND(10);
   char P_TYPE(25);
   char P_SIZE(12);
   char P_CONTAINER(10);
   char P_RETAILPRICE(12);
   char P_COMMENT(23);
} INPUT_FORMAT;
```

This input structure needs to be converted into an MQSI message set. There is an explanation in Appendix A, "Implementing message flows with MQSI" on page 279 on how to do this.

Design flow

Defining message flows is made easy by using the GUI Control Center on an NT platform. When defining message flows, you make use of *nodes*. MQInput nodes, Compute nodes, MQOutput and Database nodes are defined in the following sections. These are predefined (they are known as IBM Primitives) and can be dragged onto your workspace and connected together.

An example of creating an MQSI message flow is given in Figure 5-7.

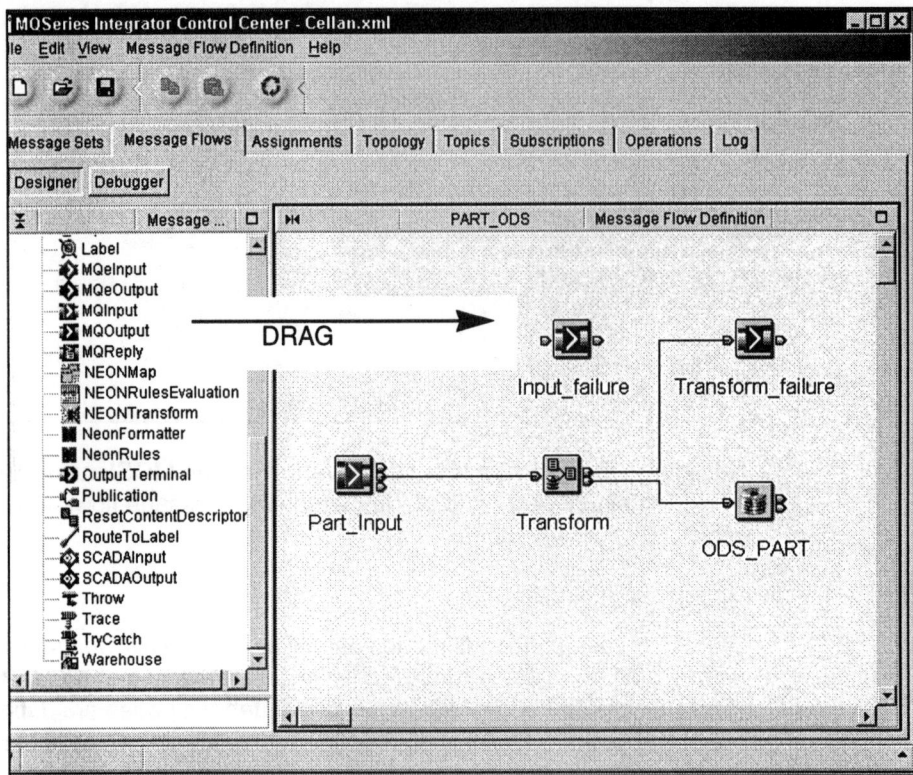

Figure 5-7 Creating an MQSI message flow

Again, for more details, refer to Appendix A, "Implementing message flows with MQSI" on page 279, which shows you how to do this.

Figure 5-8 gives this message flow again, showing how MQSI interfaces with MQSeries and a relational database.

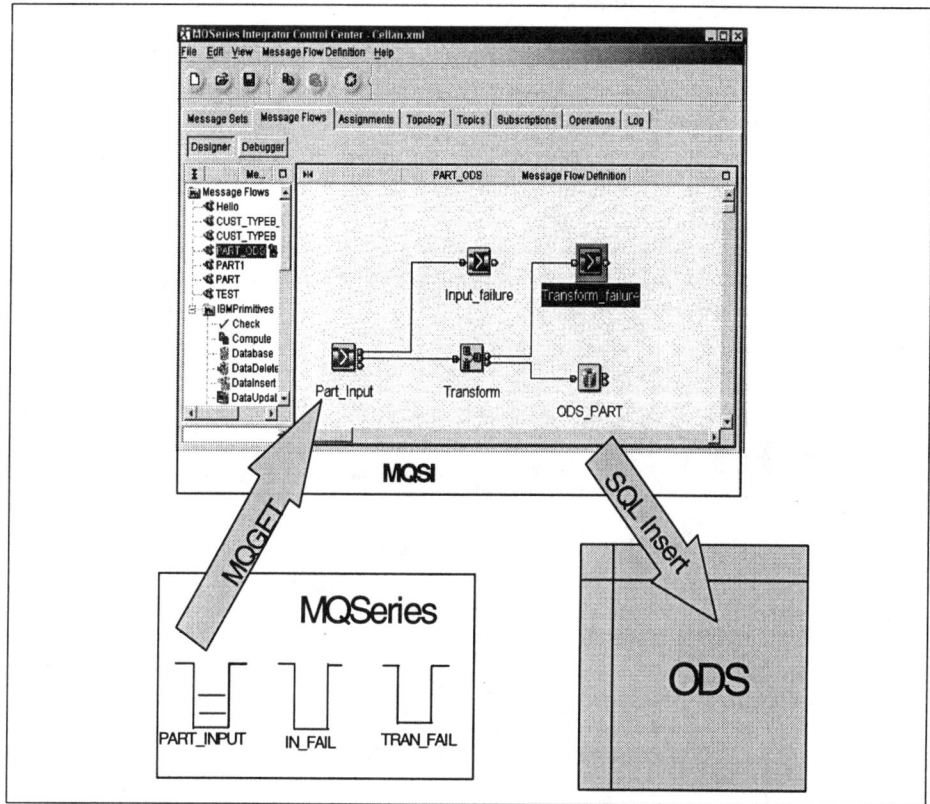

Figure 5-8 Schematic message flow

This message flow, when created, needs to be deployed. A message flow (and a message set) is deployed to a defined broker, but never to the machine that runs the Control Center. It can happen that the Control Center and the broker run on the same box (as in our test environment).

> **Note:** We can have multiple Control Center users connected to the unique Configuration Manager, that manages configuration information for the whole MQSI domain. A MQSI domain can contain several brokers: It is the broker that does the work.

The MQ queue-remote on the source machine will therefore need to point to the MQinput node on the target machine.

In Figure 5-9 we show how a message flow designed on the control center is deployed on various brokers perhaps residing on different machines. How to do this is explained in detail in Appendix A, "Implementing message flows with MQSI" on page 279.

In Section 5.3.4, "Performance for near-current data delivery" on page 174, we describe how we may decide to use a multi-broker domain to help improve throughput to an ODS. It is in the brokers where the execution-time routing, transformation, and writing of messages to the ODS occurs. In the example in Figure 5-9, each of the three brokers could be used to write to the same ODS.

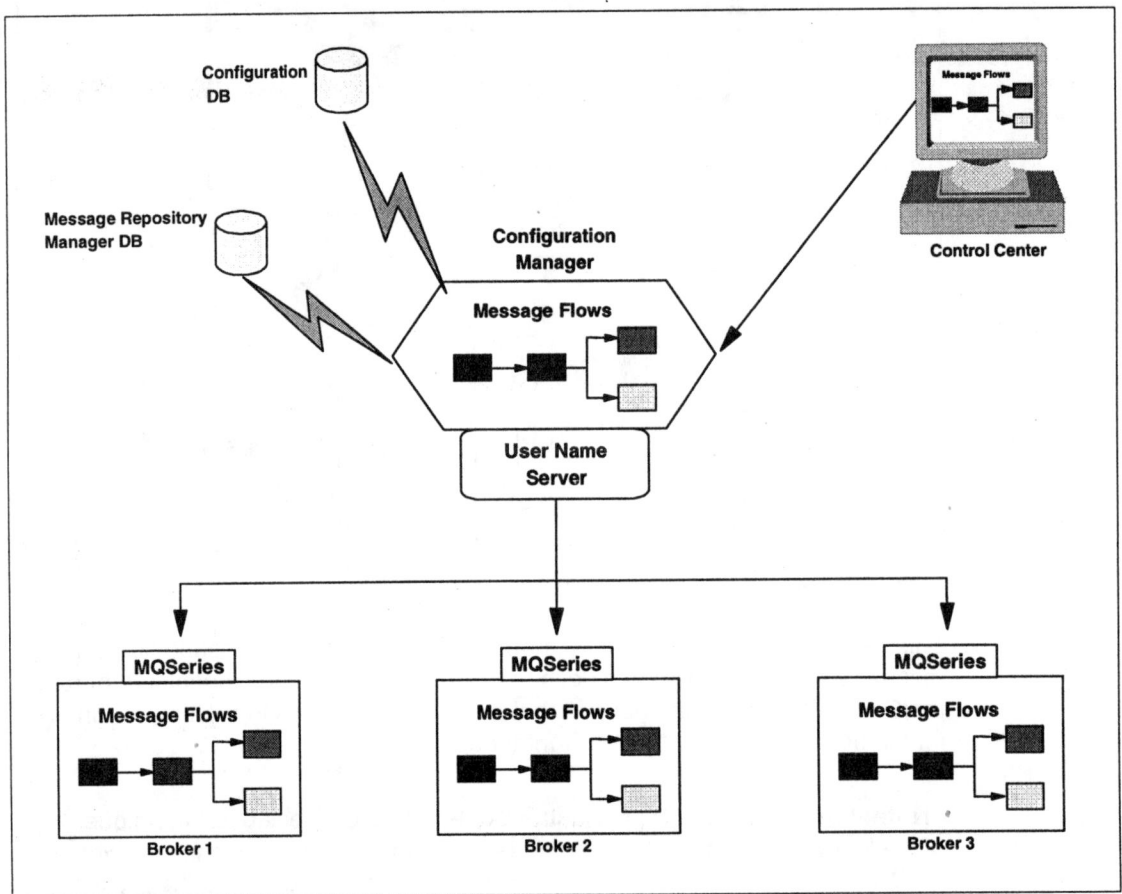

Figure 5-9 Deploying the flow to remote machines

ODS data transformations

MQSI is a tool with very powerful data transformations capabilities. Messages can be manipulated, translated, reassembled in nearly any way you like. Data transformations in MQSI takes place within certain MQSI nodes. The MQSI nodes that we have used in our scenario are explained below.

MQInput node

The MQInput node maps to an MQSeries queue on your local system which will receive your input messages. In fact, the MQInput node is an encapsulation of an MQGET command. In the MQInput node you need to specify the name of the local queue that MQSI is to monitor.

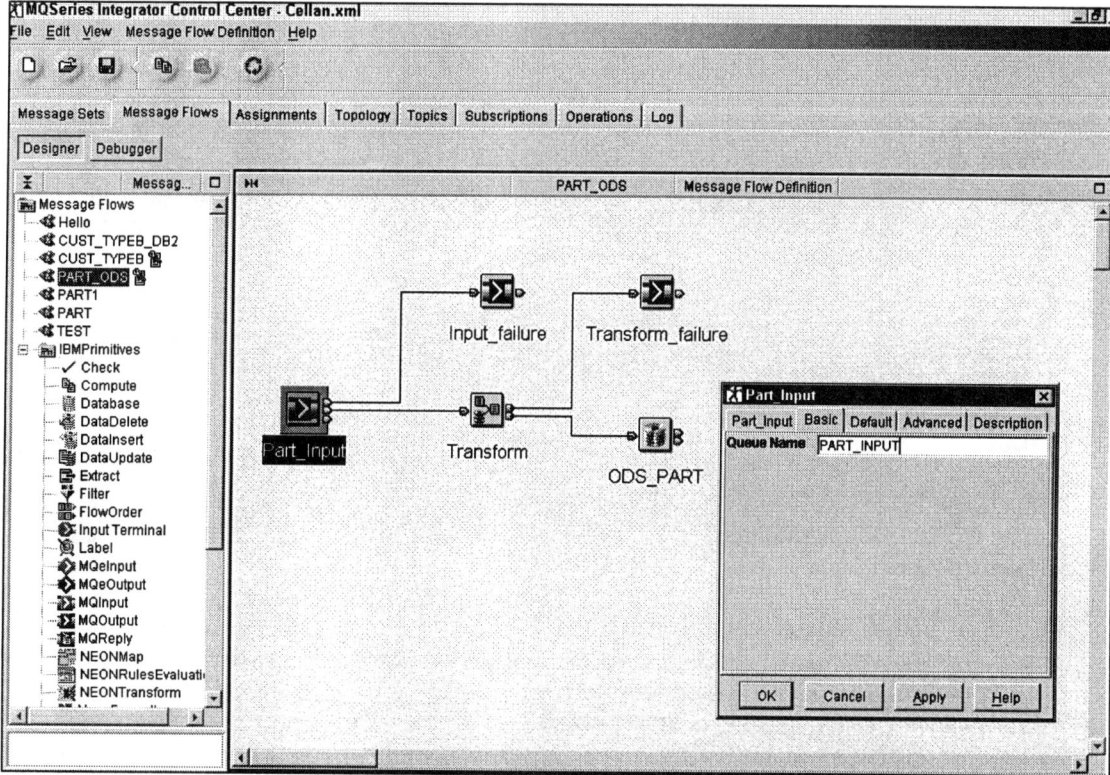

Figure 5-10 MQInput node

MQOutput node

The MQOutput is an encapsulation of an MQPUT command. When a message arrives at the input terminal of this node, MQSI will direct the message to the queue name and queue manager specified in this definition.

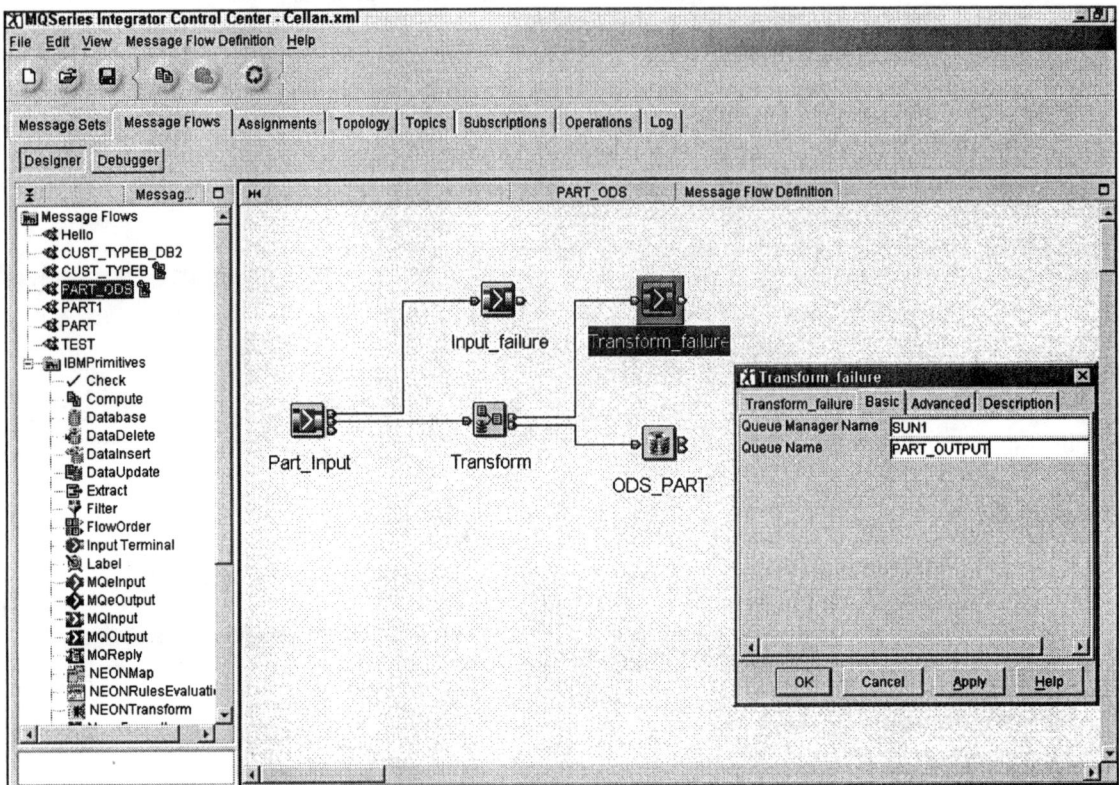

Figure 5-11   MQOutput node

Compute node

The *compute node* in the middle of the flow provides the capability to transform messages. It is this node which MQSI uses to transform input data and write this newly transformed data to the ODS. This data transformation is done using Extended SQL (ESQL). An example of a compute node is shown in Figure 5-12.

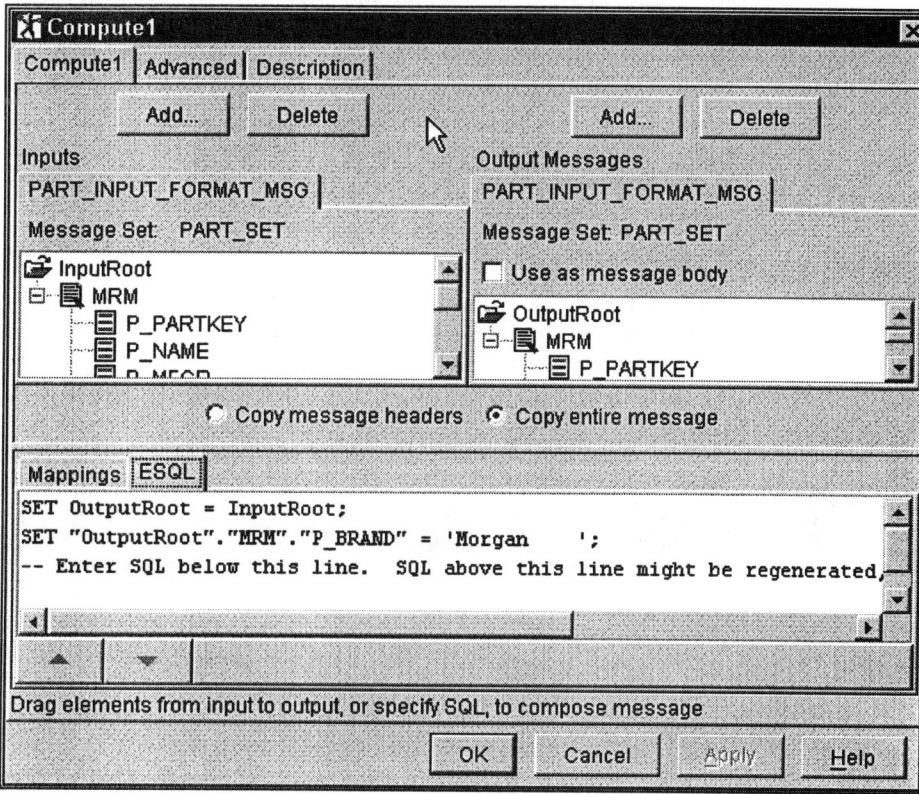

Figure 5-12 The compute node

In this simple example, the ESQL copies the message directly to the output node but changes the Brand name field to "Morgan".

Here we have created an input message and an output message in the message set that manages a set of messages types. In effect, the input message is the data format that has been received from the queue manager on the z/OS system. The output message defines the data as it is to be written into the ODS.

Note that we are receiving data in EBCDIC and the output could be in EBCDIC (if written to DB2 UDB for z/OS) or ASCII (if written to, say, DB2 UDB EEE). This code page conversion is handled by MQSeries as follows. On the source queue manager we must define the sender channel to our target system as Conversion(Y). The MQ Message Descriptor (MQMD) in the PART transaction is coded an MQFMT_STRING. Please read *MQSeries Application Programming Guide,* SC33-0807, for more details, or reference the PARTQ1 program in Appendix B, "Example CICS program" on page 289.

If the data in the message contains not only characters (string), but float and integer fields, then MQSeries cannot translate the message on its own, as it has no knowledge of the various fields in the message. However, with MQSI it is easy to get around this problem. Because you have defined the message sets, all that has to be done is to ensure that every message is properly translated when sent from one queue to another. The ESQL required to do this is shown in Example 5-2.

Example 5-2   Float and integer fields translation

```
DECLARE I INTEGER;
SET I = 1;
WHILE I < CARDINALITY(InputRoot.*[]) DO
    SET OutputRoot.*[I] = InputRoot.*[I];
    SET I=I+1;
END WHILE;
-- The lines of code above this line are generated by MQSI and updates to it
will be lost. Enter SQL below this line.
SET OutputRoot.MQMD.Encoding = 546;
SET OutputRoot.MQMD.CodedCharSetId = 437;
```

In this example, notice the statement:

-- The lines of code above this line are generated by MQSI and updates to it will be lost. Enter SQL below this line.

This is given to indicate that the lines of code above the comment are generated by MQSI when radio buttons are chosen, or as the result of drag-and drop-operations, so updates will be lost.

Database node

In order to write to the ODS directly, instead of using an MQOutput node, we could use what is known as a *database node*.

The database node allows a database operation in the form of an ESQL statement to be applied to the specified ODBC data source. Note that the syntax of the statements that can be used by the database node is a subset of those that can be used by the compute node. Unlike the compute node, the *database node* propagates the message that it receives at its input terminal to its output terminal unchanged.

You can carry out these tasks using message sets defined in the Control Center or by using self-defining XML messages that do not require a message set.

The message flow is shown schematically in Figure 5-13.

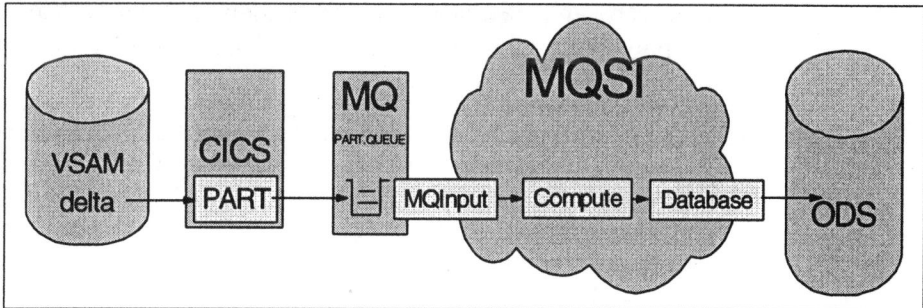

Figure 5-13 Schematic diagram of message flow

The message flow within the MQSI "cloud" is shown in Figure 5-14.

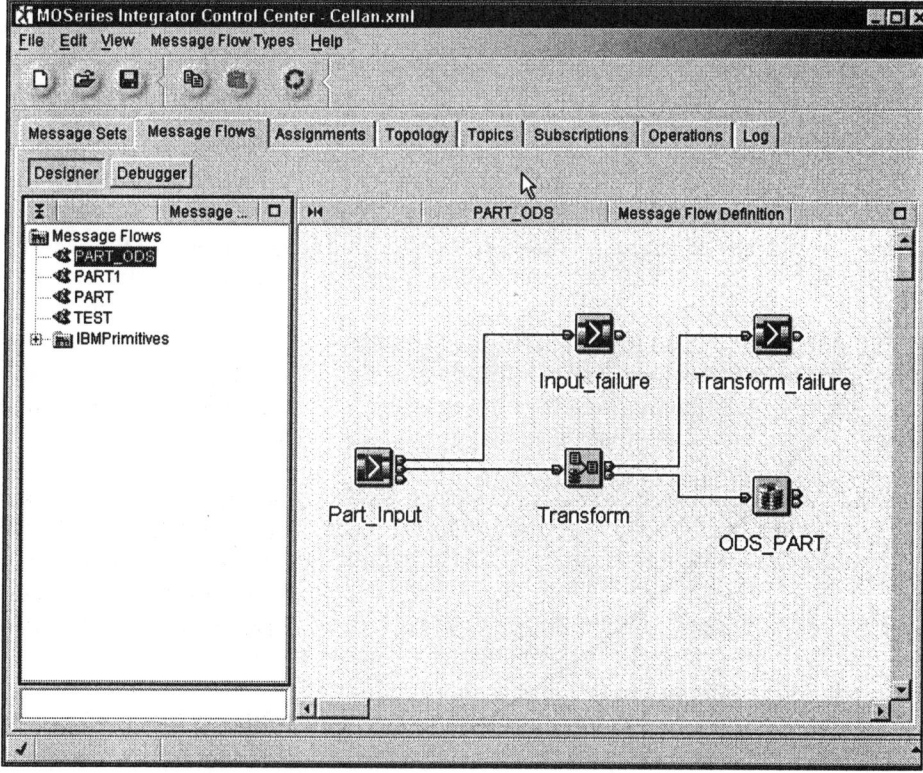

Figure 5-14 Updating the ODS

Other nodes

If a message arrives on the PART_INPUT queue which the MQSI parser decides does not conform to the expected message type as defined in the input message set, then the message is routed to the *Input_failure node* (this could be another queue in MQSeries).

If there is some sort of error when executing the ESQL in the compute node, then the message in this instance will be routed to the *Transform_failure node* here. Again, this may well be another MQSeries queue. In a real production scenario, we could expect the logic of the message flow to be a little more complex than the examples shown above.

We could introduce *filter node* which will route a message according to message content using a boolean filter expression specified in ESQL. The filter expression can include elements of the input message or message properties. It can also use data held in an external database. The output terminal to which the message is routed depends on whether the expression is evaluated to true, false, or unknown. You can use this method in order to cleanse the data before writing it to the ODS by excluding messages that fail to confirm to the specified criteria.

Also, SQL select statements in the compute node can be used to read data from a table on a relational database. Using this facility you can do some data integration. The way this would work is for the ESQL in the compute node to examine the data that has arrived from VSAM via the MQInput node. The ESQL, based on the contents of the input message, issues SQL statements against your DB2 UDB table which you will have defined in MQSI as a database node. Data received from the SQL select can be incorporated into the output message and used to update the ODS. Integration of data from non-relational sources, such as two VSAM files could be carried out within the PART CICS transaction and the two messages merged using a new output structure. The merged message would then be sent to MQSI for transformation.

MQSeries and MQSI therefore provide a great deal of function and flexibility when it comes to data parsing, transformation, and cleansing of data before writing to the target ODS. Code page translation is done for you and many platforms are supported. Message delivery is assured and the asynchronous method of delivery allows faster throughput of data by ensuring that there are no long units of work which can tie up system resources.

Performance considerations for near-current data delivery

In the following sections we consider various factors that affect the rate of processing of messages through MQSeries and MQSI:

Message persistence

MQSeries considers a message to be either persistent or non-persistent. Persistent messages are to be recoverable in the event of a problem, non-persistent messages are messages that do not survive a system/queue manager restart (normal and abnormal restarts). A queue can be defined with an attribute called *default persistence* (DEFPSIST). If DEFPSIST is YES, then messages written to that queue will be recoverable, unless the application writing the messages specifically requests it not to be. Persistent messages have to be logged and this takes up more CPU cycles and system I/O. Non-persistent messages therefore have a considerably faster throughput in MQSeries. However, in our Part data scenario, given the importance of the data, we will use only persistent messages.

Near-current data delivery or daily updates?

Near-current data delivery by nature involves applying all the updates to the operational database to the ODS as they happen.

If, on the other hand, we apply the differences between today's file and yesterday's file, there will be fewer updates to the ODS, as intermediate changes to a record do not get sent. As a result, there is a trade-off between the currency of the ODS and the volume of updates.

Complexity

The examples of message flows that we have shown have been relatively simple. The power and flexibility of MQSI allows you to create much more complex message flows than this, consisting perhaps of various compute nodes chained together. However, there is a measurable performance impact in doing this, and therefore it is best to keep the logic simple if possible. A simple data transformation for a compute node would include:

- Changing the length of a field
- Changing a CHARACTER to an INTEGER
- Changing date format
- Changing the order of the fields in a message, analogous to changing column positions in a table

If the data needs to be heavily manipulated, then this will take significantly longer; and if we require a very complex compute node, then message throughput can take twice or three times as long. For more information on this, see the SupportPac:

http://www-4.ibm.com/software/ts/mqseries/txppacs/supportpacs/ip64.html

Parallel processing/scalability

Up until now, we have only mentioned the case where the broker domain, the configuration manager, and the queue manager are on the same platform (Windows NT in our test environment). From here we have directed our messages via the MQSI database node using ODBC to an ODS on a remote machine.

Although this is the simplest configuration, it is by no means the only one (see Figure 5-9 on page 138). In fact, it is typical to have the Control Center on the NT platform, but to have the broker deployed on the target/ODS machine. The configuration manager does not absolutely need to be on the target/ODS machine. The configuration manager is a development server, while the broker is the runtime server. When a message flow is deployed, the broker has everything it needs and can process messages without a running configuration manager.

Moreover, in the target machine, you are not limited to having just one queue manager and one broker processing the messages; you may have several.

Also, within each broker, you may have more than one execution group (this is described in Appendix A, "Implementing message flows with MQSI" on page 279). Essentially, it means that for every queue manager, you may have messages written to more than one instance of an input queue and therefore you have parallelism within a single queue manager.

Indeed, you could have a combination of these two methods, that is, a multi-broker with a multi-execution group scenario. In Figure 5-15, we have two MQSeries queue managers (QM1 and QM2), and each has two execution groups. This broker/execution group configuration can exist on any platform including z/OS and OS/390. It is merely the means to increase throughput by making a one-lane road into a four-lane highway.

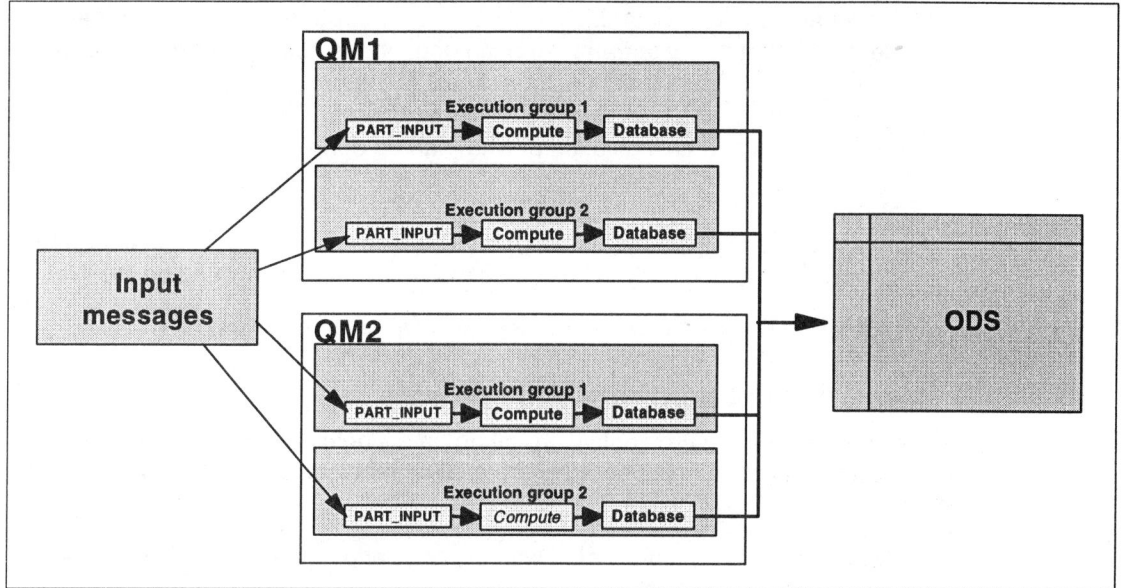

Figure 5-15 Multi-broker domain

Considerations

Although parallel processing will improve throughput, there are two important considerations.

First of all, unless the amount of traffic arriving at the ODS is very large indeed, say more than 10 per second around the clock, it is unlikely that you will require more than one queue manager and one broker. A multi-broker domain may prove to be unnecessarily complex. However, see the Section , "Performance measurements" on page 148 section below on the improved throughput of a parallel process.

The second and more serious consideration is that as the process stands you cannot guarantee that updates will arrive at the ODS in the correct order. Since this is an important issue in our ODS environment, the problem needs to be addressed.

One method may be to separate the messages by row key (this could be done at the application level), therefore each execution group would handle messages with a certain range of keys. So the PART transaction in the scenario we have used would write the message to a different target queue depending on what range the key of the record was in. Each of these target queues is handled by a different MQSI thread and therefore updates cannot get out of sequence. The messages being kept separate would lead to less contention in the ODS table.

Performance measurements

Our scenario consists of an MQInput node, a compute node, and a database node. Given that the data transformation done in the compute node is not very complex, we anticipate that the slowest part of the process is likely to be in the database node, which executes the SQL statements. The following measurements give an indication of what can be done.

Solaris Server

Here are some measurements taken on a Solaris server for a simple compute node and a database node. These measurements are to be found on the Web at:

http://www-4.ibm.com/software/ts/mqseries/txppacs/supportpacs/ip64v11.pdf

Measurement hardware and software

All throughput measurements were taken on a single server machine driven by MQSeries clients running on a separate client machine connected by a 100 Mb Ethernet link.

MQSeries Clients communicated with the MQSeries queue manager on the server machine using an MQI channel.

Server machine

The server machine hardware consisted of:

- A Solaris E450 with 4 * 400 MHz processors
- Eight 4.2 GB SCSI hard drives and three 9.0 GB SCSI hard drives
- 1GB RAM
- 100 Mb Ethernet Card

The server machine software consisted of:

- Solaris 2.7
- MQSeries V5.2
- MQSI for Sun Solaris V2.0.2
- DB2 UDB for Solaris V7.1

Client machine:

The client machine hardware consisted of:

- An IBM Netfinity 5500 M20 with 4 * 550Mhz Pentium III Xeon processors
- Six 8.0 GB SCSI hard drives formatted to use NTFS
- 1GB RAM
- 100 Mb Ethernet Card

The client machine software consisted of:

- Microsoft Windows NT V4.0 with Service Pack 6a
- MQSeries V5.2

Network configuration

The client and server machines were connected on a full duplex 1 Gigabit Ethernet LAN with a single hub.

Note the column on the right-hand side in Figure 5-16. A message of 1024 bytes, rather larger than our sample ODS data of 190 bytes, takes about 20 milliseconds to be processed by the compute node.

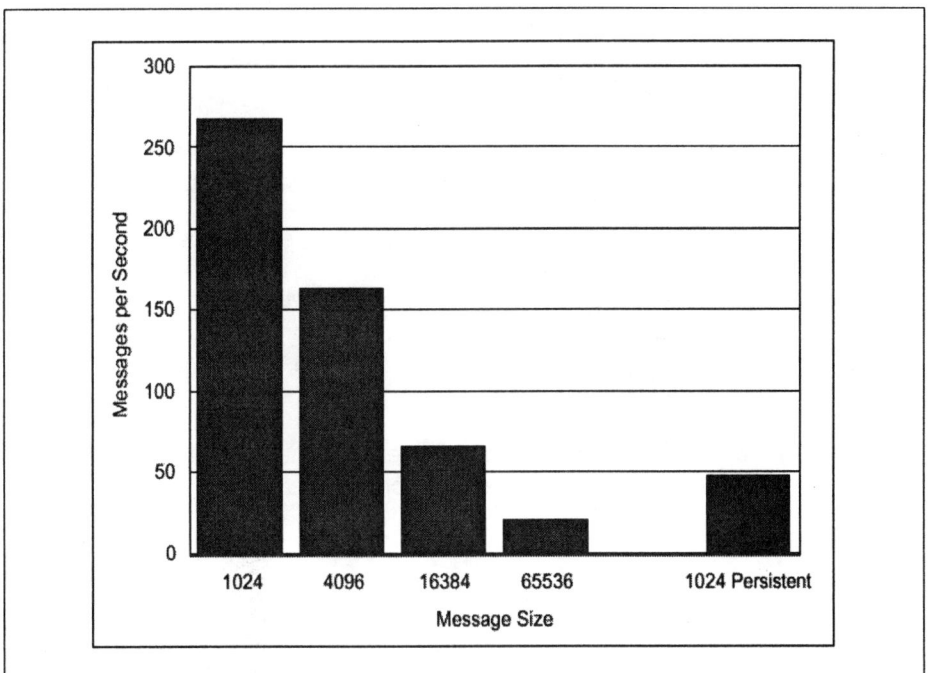

Figure 5-16 Simple compute node throughput for Solaris

Again, note the column on the right-hand side on Figure 5-17. Roughly 23 inserts and deletes per second were achieved by the database node.

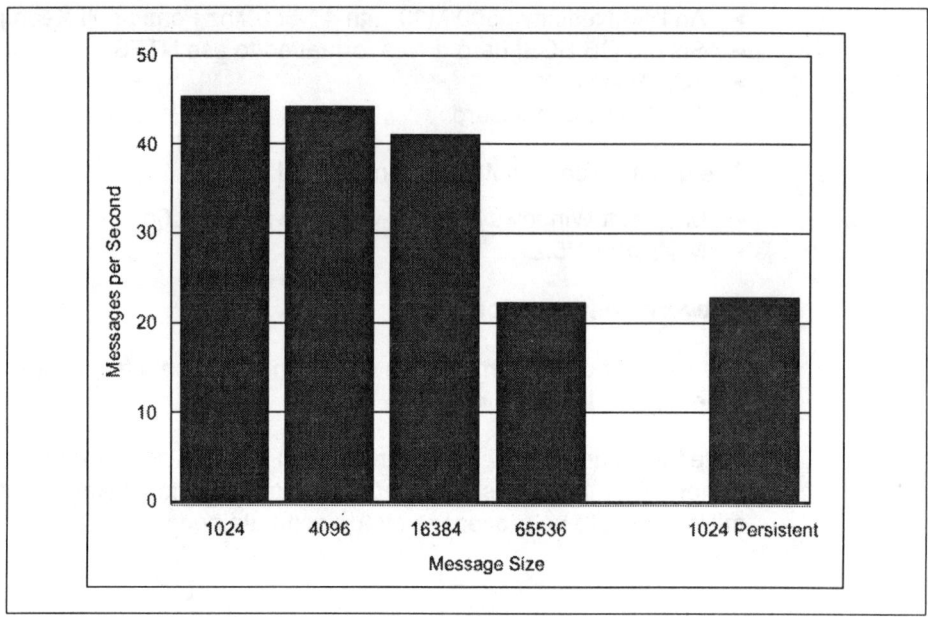

Figure 5-17 Database node throughput for Solaris

AIX server

Here are some measurements taken on an AIX server for a simple compute node and a database node. These measurements are to be found on the Web at:

http://www-4.ibm.com/software/ts/mqseries/txppacs/supportpacs/ip63v11.pdf

Measurement hardware and software

All throughput measurements were taken on a single server machine driven by MQSeries clients running on a separate client machine connected by a 100 Mb Ethernet link.

MQSeries Clients communicated with the MQSeries queue manager on the server machine using an MQI channel.

Server machine

The server machine hardware consisted of:

- An IBM 44P Model 270 with 4 * 375MHz POWER3-II Processors
- Three 8.0 GB SCSI hard drives
- 1GB RAM
- 100 Mb Ethernet Card
- 16 * 9.1 GB SSA disks with fast write nonvolatile cache

The server machine software consisted of:

- IBM AIX 4.3.3.0
- MQSeries V5.2
- MQSI for AIX V2.0.2
- DB2 UDB for AIX V7.1

The client machine

The client machine hardware consisted of:

- An IBM Netfinity 5500 M20 with 4 * 550Mhz Pentium III Xeon processors
- Six 8.0 GB SCSI hard drives formatted to use NTFS
- 1GB RAM
- 100 Mb Ethernet Card

The client machine software consisted of:

- Microsoft Windows NT V4.0 with Service Pack 5
- MQSeries V5.2

Network configuration

The client and server machines were connected on a full duplex 1 Gigabit Ethernet LAN with a single hub.

- An IBM 44P Model 270 with 4 * 375MHz POWER3-II Processors
- Three 8.0 GB SCSI hard drives
- 1GB RAM
- 100 Mb Ethernet Card
- 16 * 9.1 GB SSA disks with fast write nonvolatile cache

Again, note the right-hand column on Figure 5-18 and Figure 5-19, where the rate of delivery to the database is about 150 per second.

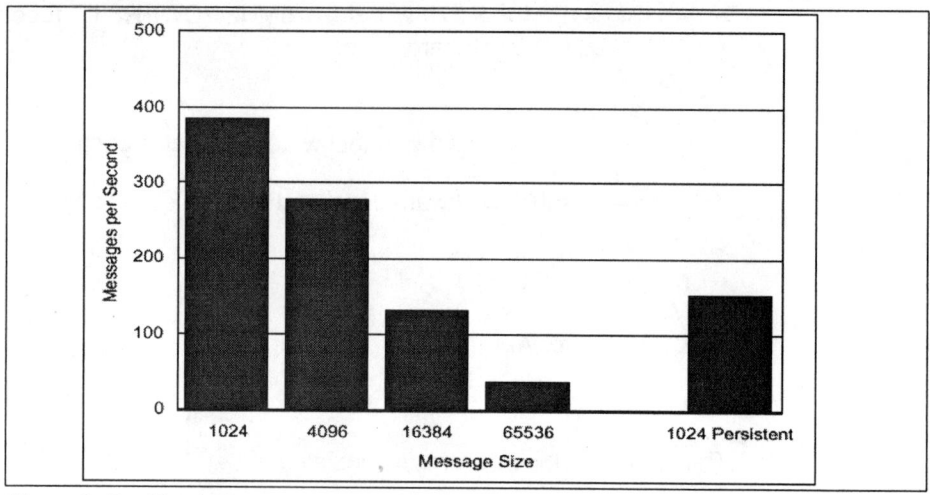

Figure 5-18   Simple Compute node throughput for AIX

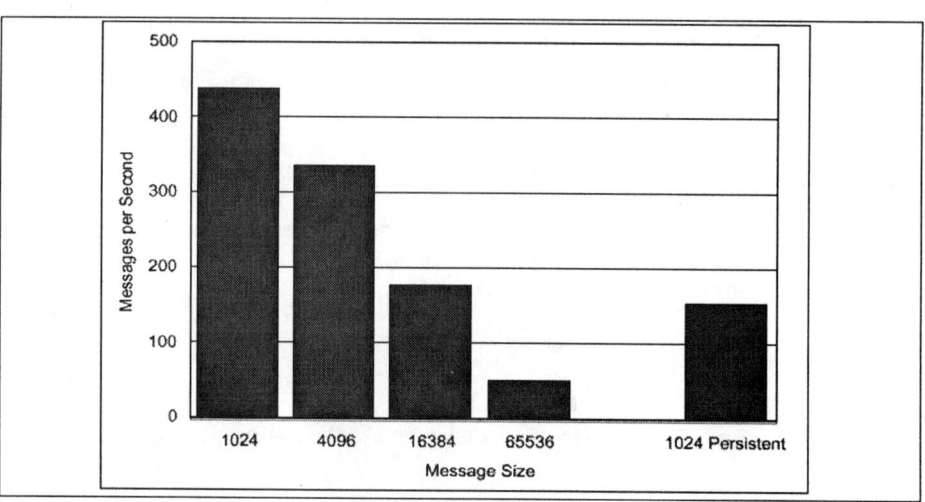

Figure 5-19   Database node throughput for AIX

In a busy production environment, where hundreds of updates may be occurring every second, it is possible that the performance described above would not be sufficient to cope with the volume of data arriving. If this is the case, then we may need to increase the throughput by adding more database nodes, faster CPUs, faster disks, or to adopt the daily method of extracting data, which would reduce the amount of data to be sent to the ODS.

This would sacrifice currency to gain performance. Also we may need to make the process more parallel in the method described in the previous section. There are some performance measurements for parallelism in the redbook, *Business Integration Solutions with MQSeries Integrator,* SG24-6154. However, note that for these figures, the target is a queue, rather than a database node that we have in our environment. Nevertheless, it is worthwhile to mention that there are real improvements to be gained from a parallel process using a multi-broker solution. There are also some more moderate performance improvements to be gained by increasing parallelism using a multi-execution group solution.

For more information on how to increase throughput in MQSI by making message flow design more efficient, look at the SupportPac on:

http://www-4.ibm.com/software/ts/mqseries/txppacs/supportpacs/ip04.pdf

Summary
In conclusion, MQSI will be able to handle the volumes of data in all but the busiest of operational environments. However, if there are performance issues, then there are several actions that can be taken as described above, such as daily updates, parallelism, and better message flow design, which will help improve throughput. In a type B scenario where volumes are less, MQSI will easily be able to handle the volumes of data involved.

5.1.4 Populating the ODS using the DWC MQ Connector

In this section we will discuss, by means of a simple example, how we might use the MQSeries support in the DWC to provide a near-real-time update of an ODS. We will show how to design and define an MQSeries scenario and explain how this solution addresses some of the issues found with deploying an ODS.

Of course, this is not the only way to utilize these functions, but this example may help spark ideas for other solutions. Also see Chapter 7, "Building and managing the ODS population subsystem" on page 189 for another example of using MQSeries functions to integrate MQ messages along with relational data obtained with replication technology.

DB2 UDB and DWC MQSeries integration overview

With the release of DB2 UDB V7.2 in the Windows and UNIX environments, we now have easy access to the world of distributed heterogeneous asynchronous messaging that is provided by MQSeries. There are two levels of MQSeries support:

1. **DB2 User Defined Functions (UDFs)** are provided that allow us to read messages from and write messages to MQSeries queues from within SQL statements. They support a variety of messaging models, including:
   - Simple one-way messages
   - Request/reply messages
   - Publish/subscribe messages

A DB2 MQ UDF is shown in Example 5-3.

Example 5-3 Examples of using the DB2 MQ UDFs

```
Simple message send:
    values DB2MQ.MQSEND('a test')

Simple message receive:
    values DB2MQ.MQSEND('a test')

Message send via a specific queue:
    VALUES DB2MQ.MQSEND('ODS_Input', 'simple message')

Sending messages based on the content of a table:
    SELECT DB2MQ.MQSEND(LASTNAME || ' ' || FIRSTNAME || ' ' || DEPARTMENT)
      FROM EMPLOYEE
        WHERE DEPARTMENT = '5LGA'

Return just the message portion of all messages in the queue
    SELECT t.MSG FROM table (DB2MQ.MQREADALL()) t
```

For more examples, see the *IBM DB2 UDB Release Notes for V7.2*.

These functions can be used via the command line interface, in application programs, or in stored procedures, including SQL Stored Procedures.

2. **DB2 relational views** can be created over MQSeries queues so that semi-structured messages appear as a typical relational rows. These views are defined using the new MQ-Assist Wizard in which you define the specification for the message as either a delimited string or fixed-length columns. The MQ Assist Wizard then creates a table function utilizing the DB2 MQSeries UDFs and creates a view over that table function. The resulting view can then be accessed as any other relational view.

The DB2 UDB Data Warehouse Center (DWC) allows the user to invoke the MQ_Assist Wizard to define an MQSeries queue as a data warehouse source. The resulting view is then used in the Process Modeler to integrate MQSeries messages with other corporate data into an ODS or data warehouse.

In addition, MQSeries messages that are XML documents can also be used as a warehouse source. See the *DB2 V7.2 Release Notes* for more information about XML formatted messages.

Design flow

In this example (see Figure 5-20), we will be bringing Part information into our ODS. The original source is VSAM and PART information is put onto a MQ queue within our operational system, as noted in 5.1.2, "Capturing VSAM updates" on page 128. From an ODS perspective, it is of no concern to us how the data was put into the queue. We are concerned primarily with the format of the message on the queue. This gives us a certain amount of independence from the operational system. In fact, the operational system could change and, as long as the format of the message on the queue does not change, we are isolated from that change. There could even be multiple systems putting data onto the queue and we still maintain our independence.

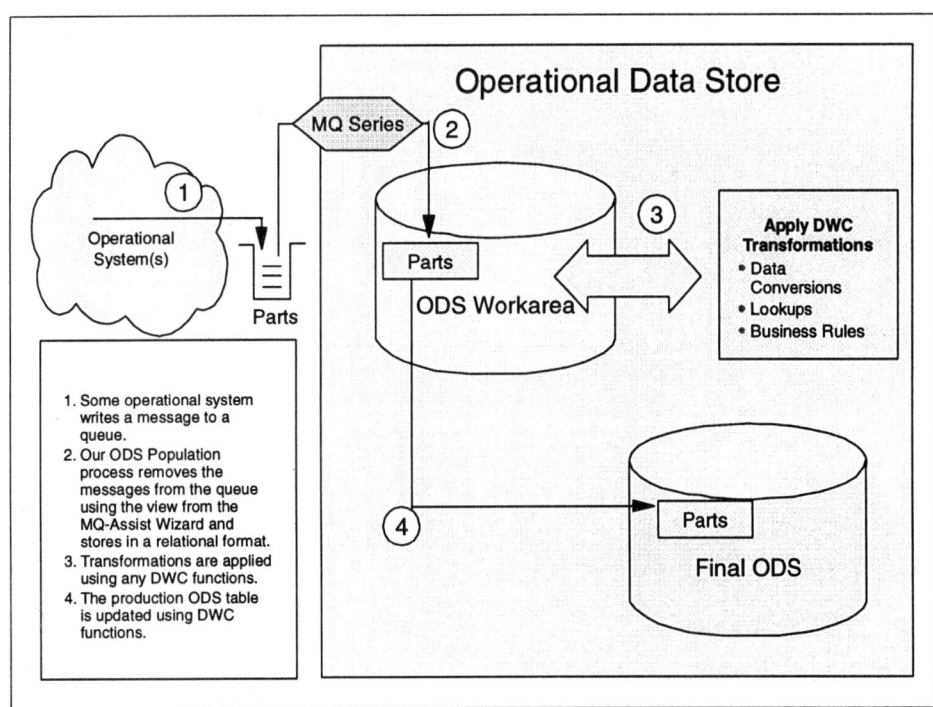

Figure 5-20   Population process

Data transformation

As you see in our design, we are not concerned with how the messages are put into the queue. Our problem is how to take the messages out of the queue, apply whatever transformations our business requires and then update the ODS. Using the DWC, this is relatively simple. In general, when using the DWC, our first step would be to "stage" our source data into a common storage format which, in our case, would be DB2 UDB relational tables. This applies to any source, whether it be flat files, any relational source, replication sources, Web sources, IMS, VSAM, and so forth.

Once we have staged our data into relational tables, we can now use the full power of DB2 UDB and the DWC to apply our transformations and update the ODS. We can therefore integrate and consolidate data from many sources into our ODS. See Chapter 7, "Building and managing the ODS population subsystem" on page 189 for more information about architecting the population process.

In this scenario, we are bringing in messages from a MQ queue that was populated from a VSAM source. We will use the DWC to register our MQSeries queue as a source (Figure 5-21) which, in turn, invokes the MQ-Assist Wizard, resulting in a relational view defined over our queue.

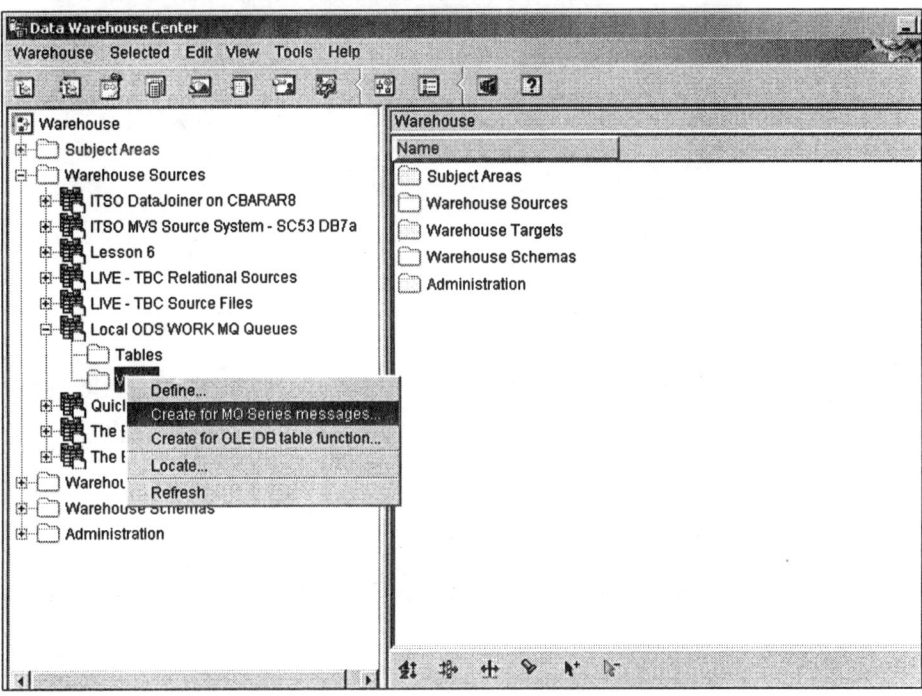

Figure 5-21   Using the DWC to create an MQSeries source

We provide to the MQ-Assist Wizard some MQSeries information such as the type of read (destructive or not), MQ Service Point (which points to the proper queue and queue manager), the message format (delimited or fixed-column) and the mapping of the message fields to columns. This information is used by the MQ-Assist Wizard to first create a DB2 Table Function to interface with the MQSeries UDFs, and a DB2 View to provide the relational look-and-feel. This view is automatically registered as a source view within the DWC.

On the first page, shown in Figure 5-22, we select the type of message retrieval we want to use. We can choose a destructive read, or retrieve, where the message is automatically deleted after we read it, or a read where the message is not deleted, or both.

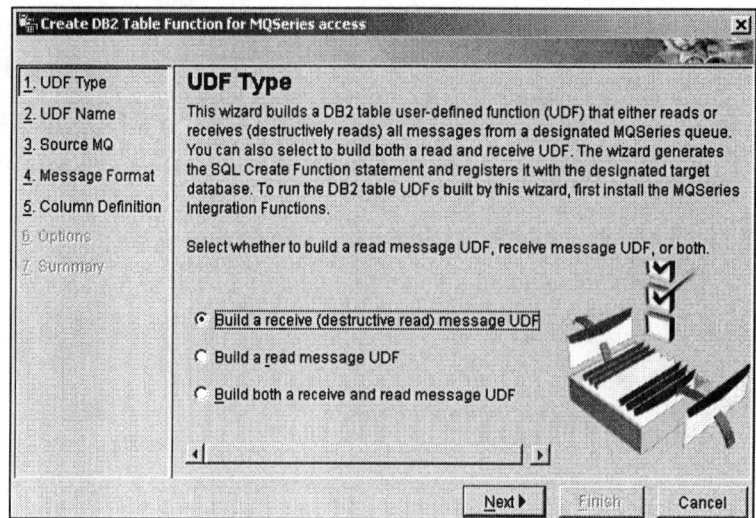

Figure 5-22   MQ-Assist Wizard, selecting the type of read access

On the second page, shown in Figure 5-23, we simply give the UDF a name.

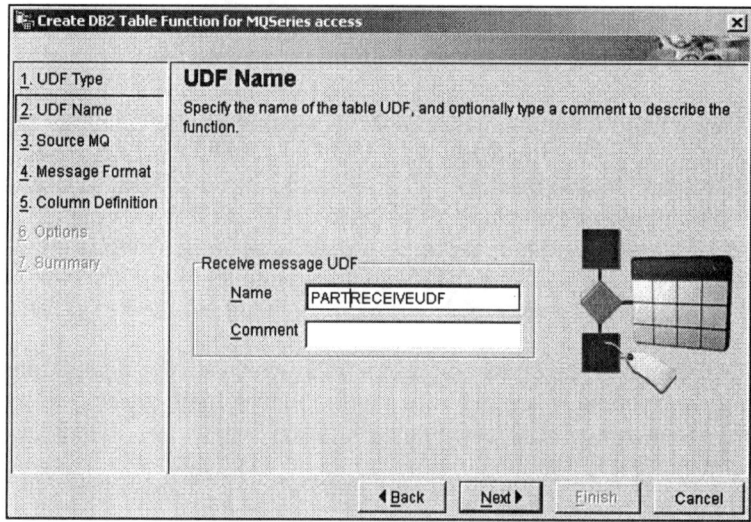

Figure 5-23   MQ-Assist Wizard, naming the UDF

On the third page of the MQ-Assist Wizard, shown in Figure 5-24, we provide the MQ Application Messaging Interface (AMI) Service Point name which provides the linkage to the source MQSeries queue manager and queue.

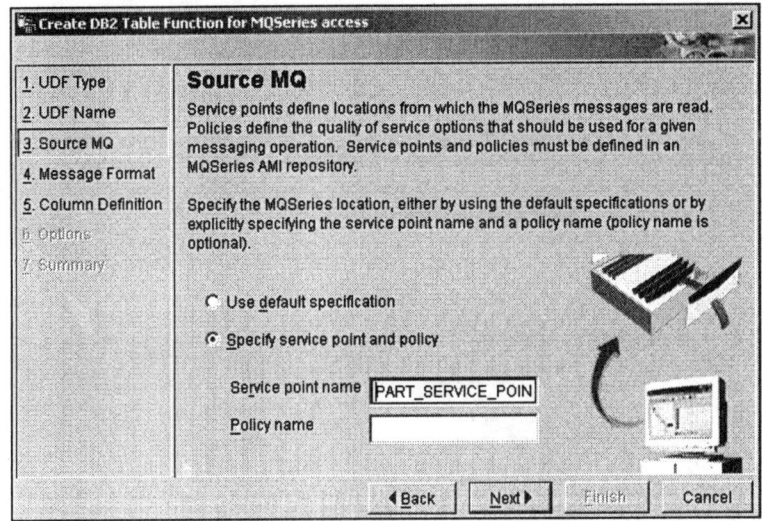

Figure 5-24 MQ-Assist Wizard, providing the service point name

Now, we get to the heart of the definition, mapping the message layout to the view column definitions. The format type of the message can be delimited fields or fixed column fields. We can also use a previously saved column definition file to define the message format (see Figure 5-25).

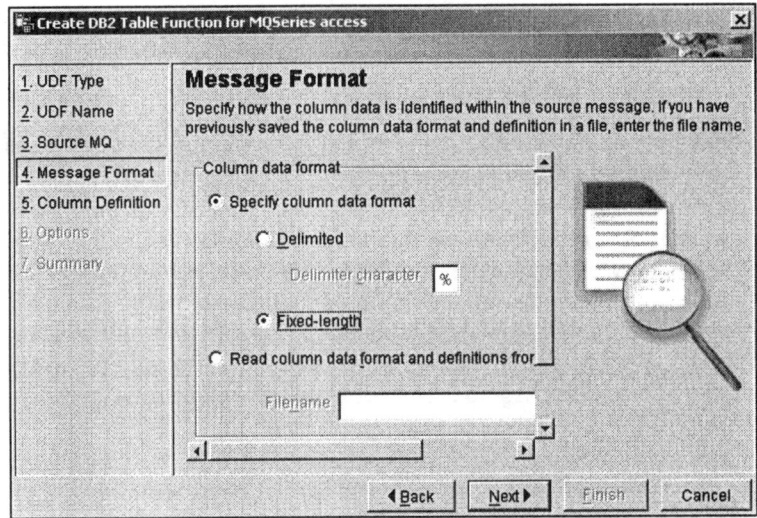

Figure 5-25 MQ-Assist Wizard, specifying the message format type

The column definition page (see Figure 5-26) is where we define the layout of the various fields in the message. These columns will be the columns defined in our resulting view. This implies that our messages must have some sort of structure which can be mapped to view columns.

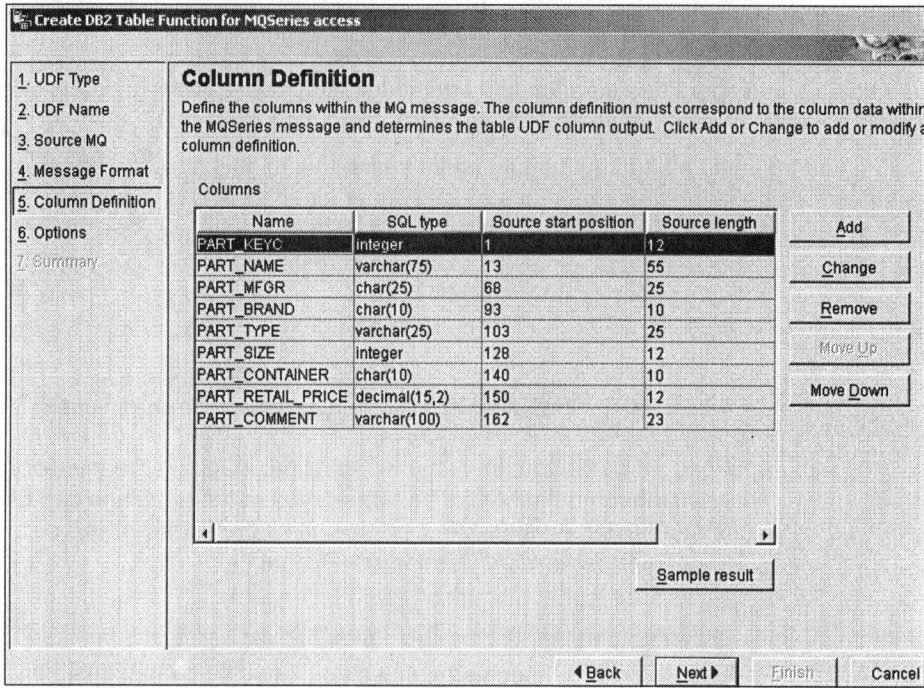

Figure 5-26   MQ-Assist Wizard, column definition page

Now that we have the MQ queue registered to the DWC as a relational view, we can use it as a source within the DWC Process Modeler and can be used by a variety of DWC step types that can accept a relational view as input, including the SQL Step. Typically, this SQL Step is used to stage the data into a relational table in a work area within the ODS, as shown in Figure 5-27.

Our data from the MQ messages is now in a very common data storage, the relational table, which allows us to manipulate the data using common relational techniques. This staging table would be the input to one or more steps that would prepare the data in the proper format for the updating of the ODS. This may include data consolidation with data from other systems that has been staged into a relational data store, data enhancement, data cleansing, or application of specific business rules. We have at our disposal the full range of capabilities of the DWC and the SQL language.

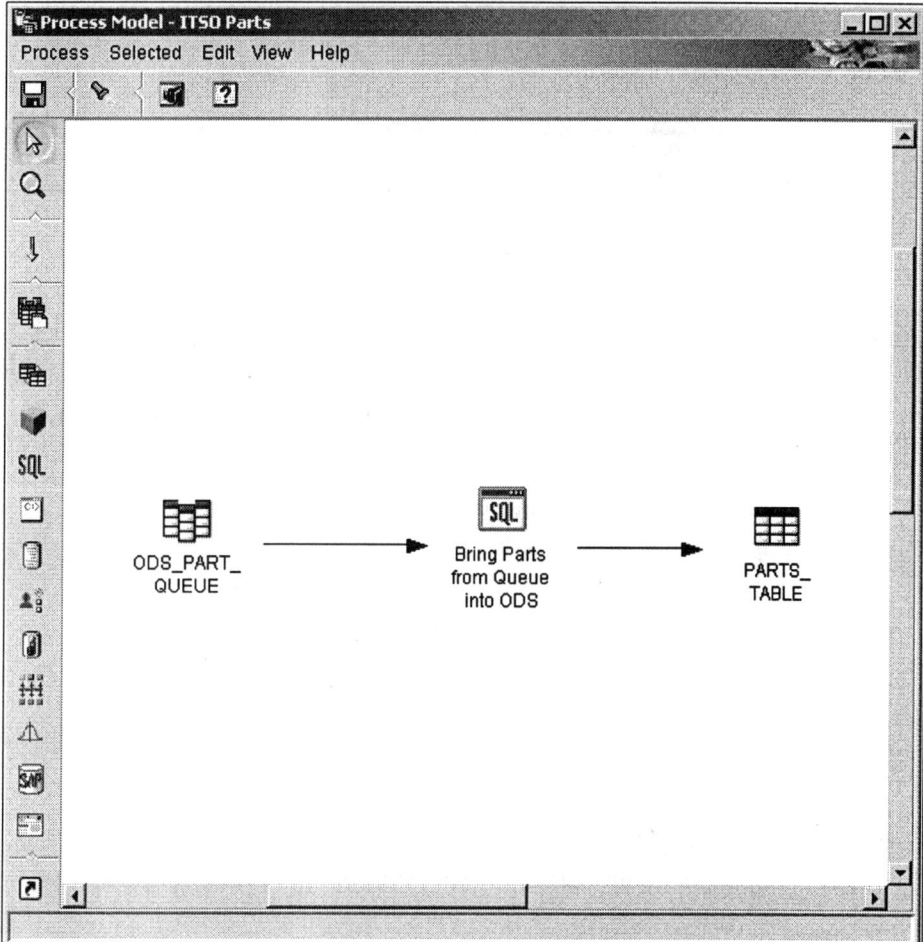

Figure 5-27 Using DWC SQL step to stage MQ messages into a relational table

Automating the population process

Once we have defined the process to take messages off of the MQ queue, transform the data, and update the ODS, we have to put this into production. This involves defining some type of operational workflow which links together steps based on execution dependencies resulting in a number of separate independent workflows. For each workflow, we need to determine how to invoke the first step in the workflow. Also, we have to be able to monitor what is going on in our ODS population process. The DWC provides all of these capabilities. We will illustrate specifically on scheduling issues related to using MQSeries queues as a source to an ODS, using an example to discuss one solution for putting into production a workflow using an MQSeries queue source.

In the example in Figure 5-28, we have an operational order system that somehow puts order information onto an MQSeries queue. We want to capture that information in our ODS and provide a current count of orders in the system.

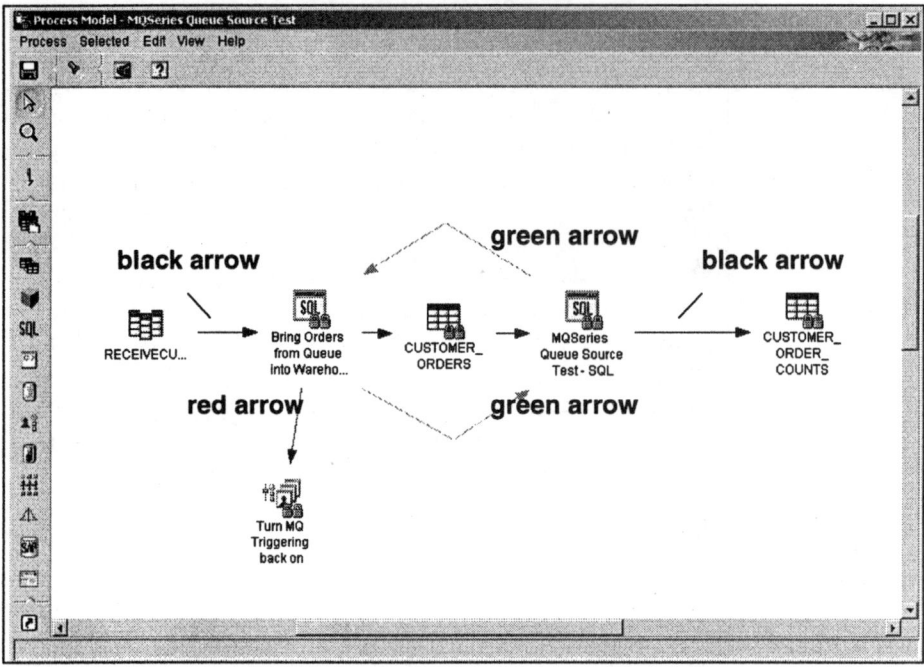

Figure 5-28   Workflow to bring orders into the ODS

As you can see, we have as input to our workflow a view that represents our input queue. Black arrows represent data flows and green arrows represent process flows. We then have two steps which are DWC SQL Steps:

1. Step 1 retrieves the messages from the queue using the view that was created using the MQ-Assist Wizard. This is a destructive read in that after we read a message from the queue, it is deleted from the queue. This step then appends these new Orders to the CUSTOMER_ORDERS table in our ODS.

2. Step 2 will then use the updated CUSTOMER_ORDERS table to count the Orders by the specified criteria. This step has a dependency on Step 1 which is represented the green arrow leading from Step 1 to Step 2.

Our basic process, then, is this:

1. Read all of the current order messages from the queue and insert into the CUSTOMER_ORDERS table.
2. Update the counts in the summary table.
3. Go back Step 1 as long as there are messages on the queue.

We see in the basic process that we simply continue looping and processing small batches of messages as long as there are messages on the queue. However, there are some issues that we need to address. First, how do we automatically start this workflow? Second, what do we do when there are no messages on the queue?

As it happens, we can use a combination of MQSeries and DWC capabilities to address both of these issues. MQSeries can monitor a queue, and when there are some defined number of messages on the queue, it can invoke some type of external program. DWC has the capability to have a step invoked from outside the Warehouse Server. Combining these two capabilities, allows MQSeries to invoke our DWC Step 1 when there are a defined number of messages in the queue. When this MQSeries trigger is fired, it is no longer in effect. At this point, our workflow takes over and continues to process its loop until there are no messages in the queue and then it fails. DWC has the ability to execute a new step when the current step fails, as represented by the red arrow in our workflow. Upon failure, we can use a DWC User Defined Program to execute an MQSeries command line utility to turn back on the MQ trigger monitoring.

So, our process flow is now like this:

1. MQSeries monitors the queue until it reaches a certain depth and then will then invoke our Step 1.
2. The Step 1 --> Step 2 loop executes until there are no messages on the queue and Step 1 fails.
3. Step 3 then turns on the MQSeries monitor, which again waits until it reaches a certain depth.

Once we have gotten our source data into a relational format within our ODS, we can use the full power of the DWC to transform the data to whatever format is required for our ODS data model. Due to the near-real-time nature of an ODS, we typically cannot afford to have very extensive data transformations as in a data warehouse. In an ODS population subsystem, we would find field transformations such as data type conversions, algorithmic conversions such as US measurements to metric, simple code conversions such as (s,m,l) to (small, medium, large), assigning surrogate keys for new data, lookup functions to find the surrogate key for an existing operational key, and more. There are SQL functions and DWC functions to handle these types of conversions.

Other types of transformations we may find in an ODS include separation or concatenation of data during the reconstruction of textual information, as well as normalizing or denormalizing of data structures to match the ODS structure and enrichment functions that add new data fields such as profit calculations based on other fields. Again, the rich DB2 UDB SQL language in conjunction with other DWC provided functions provides this support.

Performance

Here we describe factors concerning the performance of the MQ Connector.

Near-current data, current data and level of detail

A number of these issues are mostly ODS design issues, but the chosen tool must be able to support the design. The DWC does not limit you to any particular design point. Assuming that the underlying DB2 UDB server, hardware and network can support the processing requirements, there is nothing inherent in the DWC to limit the design. The issues of how often you update the ODS, how much history do you keep, and the granularity of the data, are all business decisions that have to be made. The amount of time that any one workflow takes to move data from the source to the ODS is dependent upon the complexity of the transformations that have to take place.

Mixed workload, flexible growth path, uptime

Again, these issues are addressed by correct database and process design, but the chosen tool must be able to support the design. The DWC and the overall architecture of the DB2 WM agents provide you the flexibility to design the proper balance of a mixed workload and the needed scalability, both of which help maintain ODS availability.

To address a mixed workload, the DWC allows you the flexibility to design a workflow that can update the ODS with smaller bundles of updates and do them more often. To be able to handle a fairly constant update stream, at the same time users are running queries, requires some very careful design work. A carefully thought-out architecture for the population subsystem is key to balancing this mixed workload.

You should consider segmenting or partitioning your ODS updates and only having one update process handling all updates to a particular segment or partition. With this architecture, you could parallelize processing updates to separate segments or partitions. Careful planning of commit scope to balance how long update locks are held versus user query processing must be done. The DWC has various ways in which to control how after data is committed to the database such as a commit count in the SQL step or, if you need ultimate control over commit scope, a Stored Procedure can be written.

If you have a situation where you have a very intensive transaction rate that must be reflected in your ODS very quickly, there are basically two design issues to resolve:

- First, the amount and complexity of the transformation process will have a great impact on how fast you can move data from source. Shortening that path will allow you to process a larger transaction rate.
- Second, consider where you might be able to parallelize the workflows. One way would be to use several source queues to provide the data to your ODS workflows. This will allow separate workflows to concurrently process each queue.

As you look at your overall ODS system, you must design an architecture that allows you to take advantage of opportunities to parallelize workflows, move workloads around, increase hardware scalability, manage and control your mixed workloads, and automate the processes.

5.2 Flat files as an ODS source (ODS type A)

Occasionally operational data will reside on flat files such as z/OS or OS/390 flat files or UNIX or NT flat files.

5.2.1 Z/OS or OS/390 flat files

Typically data residing on a sequential QSAM file is likely to be control or reference data but it still may be required to be incorporated as part of an ODS. In fact, this can be done using methods already described in previous sections of this document.

One method would be to use a DB2 UDB load utility to load the data into a DB2 UDB table. The process from here on is the same as 4.1, "Relational data as a source (ODS type A)" on page 92.

Another method could be to use the same process that is used for VSAM files. That is, the update transaction could be written so that every time an update is made to the flat file, it is also written to a "delta" file which can be read by CICS and propagated to the ODS, as with the VSAM process described in the previous section.

5.2.2 UNIX or NT flat files

Flat files on UNIX and NT can be loaded directly in the staging area described in 5.1.4, "Populating the ODS using the DWC MQ Connector" on page 153, by using the flat file source access provided by DWC.

It can also be loaded using the DB2 load or import utilities in a DB2 UDB table on UNIX or NT, and that table will be replicated to populate the ODS target on DB2 UDB.

5.3 IMS as an ODS source (ODS type A)

There are still very large volumes of data in IMS databases throughout the world. The data in IMS databases could be a source for an ODS. The IMS DataPropagator (IMS DPROP) solution provides a near-real-time asynchronous feature based on MQSeries that can be used to populate ODS in DB2 UDB.

We describe the IMS DPROP solution with its three different technologies:

1. Synchronous replication
2. Asynchronous replication
3. Near-real-time asynchronous replication

We then provide details on using the near-real-time feature (MQ-ASYNC) to solve the ODS issues.

5.3.1 The IMS DataPropagator solution

We can populate IMS hierarchical data to the relational data using IMS DPROP in different ways.

Synchronous IMS-to-DB2 population

This is a method to capture the changes from the source in a real time basis in a synchronous way within the same unit of work (UOW), as shown in Figure 5-29. This requires changes to the existing applications, and you will increase the size of UOW to include instruction sets and I/Os for DB2 UDB operations along with IMS workloads in the same UOW. With high volume and sub-second response time of IMS transactions, it may preclude this from being the recommended way to populate ODS from IMS operational data.

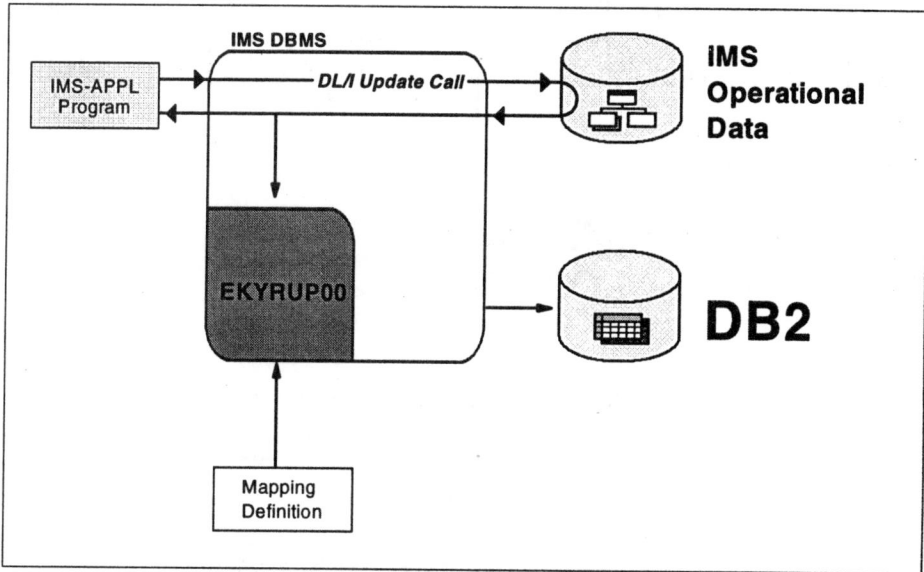

Figure 5-29   Synchronous IMS-to-DB2 Propagation

Log asynchronous population

This has been widely used to populate relational data from IMS data base to capture the changes from the IMS log and apply them to DB2 UDB target tables through the mapping definition and apply process. Figure 5-30 depicts the asynchronous replication using the IMS log.

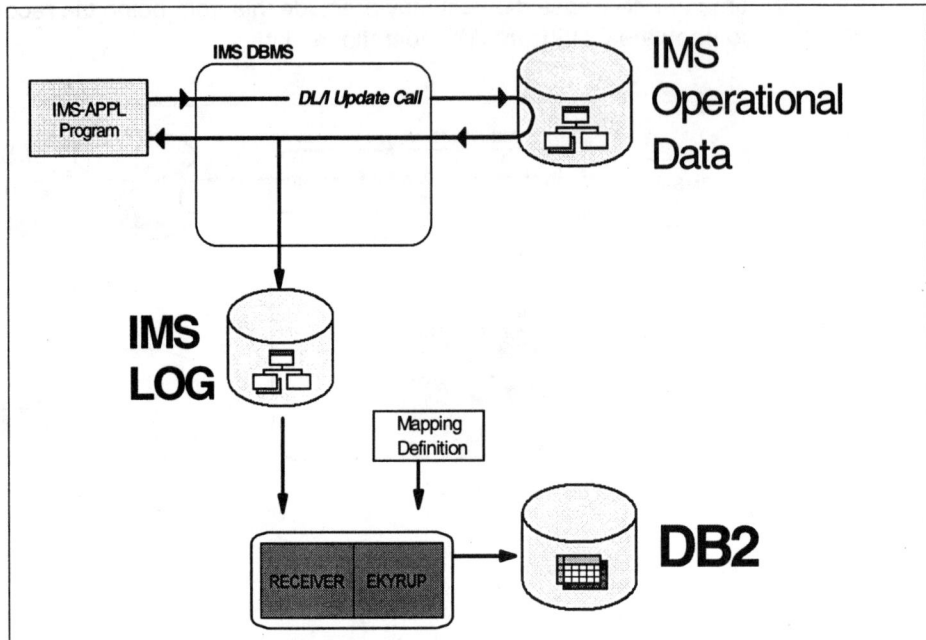

Figure 5-30 Asynchronous IMS log to DB2 replication

Near-real-time asynchronous replication using MQSeries

This is a new IMS feature using the MQSeries to support the near-real-time replication. As we can see in Figure 5-31, updates made to IMS can be captured and placed into MQSeries queues, then those MQSeries queues can be propagated to an ODS in the DB2 UDB for z/OS. This is a beneficial method to populate a near-current ODS without a significant effort or changes in the legacy applications. (The specific way to use MQSeries is IMS DPROP proprietary.)

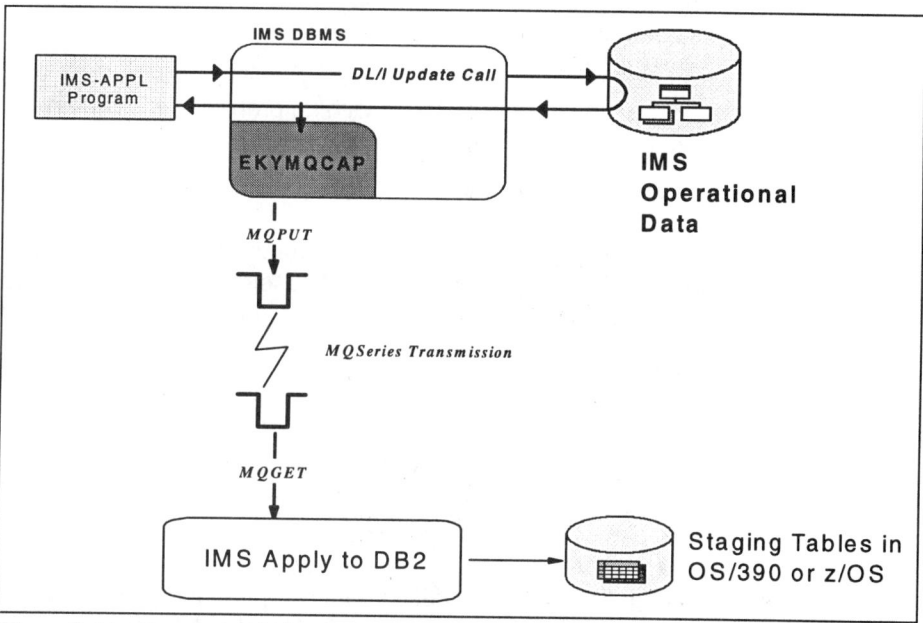

Figure 5-31   Concept of MQ-ASYNC replication

5.3.2 Populating ODS using MQ-ASYNC

To populate an ODS from IMS data, where near-current data delivery may be an issue, the new IMS enhancement using the MQSeries fits very nicely to the ODS architecture. As we can see in Figure 5-32, updates made to IMS can be captured and placed into MQSeries queues, then those MQSeries queues can be propagated to an ODS in the DB2 UDB for z/OS.

This is a beneficial method to populate a near-current ODS without a significant effort or changes in the legacy applications. Please note that the target ODS resides on z/OS or OS/390 because a certain function of IMS DataPropagator is a mainframe-only program that runs in z/OS or OS/390. If the target ODS resides on anything other than z/OS, then the data has to be propagated from DB2 UDB for z/OS to the ODS in other platforms.

Overview of MQ-ASYNC propagation

Next we detail the MQ-ASYNC propagation to capture IMS updates and propagate them to DB2 UDB ODS. The following list describes how it works and how it can be used to populate an ODS:

1. When an IMS application changes data to be propagated, IMS DPROP captures the update using the EKYMQCAP exit routine.

2. The MQCapture exit routine builds an MQSeries message containing the changes and places this message on an MQSeries message queue. MQSeries queues are reliable and high performance, and this should process very quickly.

3. If all the processing performs with no problems, the IMS data is committed and the UOW is complete.

4. MQSeries transmits asynchronously the message to another MQSeries queue where the target ODS resides. Note that the queue format is not externalized which means that the queue format is an internal format to IMS DPROP and you are not advised to use the queue by your program. The queue format can be changed in the future for other improvements as it is deemed necessary.

5. The IMS DPROP Apply program retrieves the message from the queue and passes it to the IMS DPROP Relational Update Program (RUP).

6. The RUP queries the mapping definitions that describe how the IMS changes data "maps" to the target DB2 UDB table and make updates the target tables accordingly. This is the mainframe-only program, and therefore the target table must reside on DB2 UDB for z/OS. Please note that MQ-ASYNC propagation does not preserve the scope of the IMS UOW, which means that more than one update in different DB2 UDB UOWs can be made for an IMS UOW.

With the reliability and high performance of MQSeries and IMS DPROP, we can deliver IMS changes to DB2 UDB tables in a near-current timing, in a matter of seconds.

Target ODS on z/OS

If the target ODS is to reside on DB2 UDB for z/OS, we can populate the ODS directly using IMS DataPropagator MQ-ASYNC as you see in Figure 5-32. There is no need to have a staging table when you have the target ODS in DB2 UDB for z/OS.

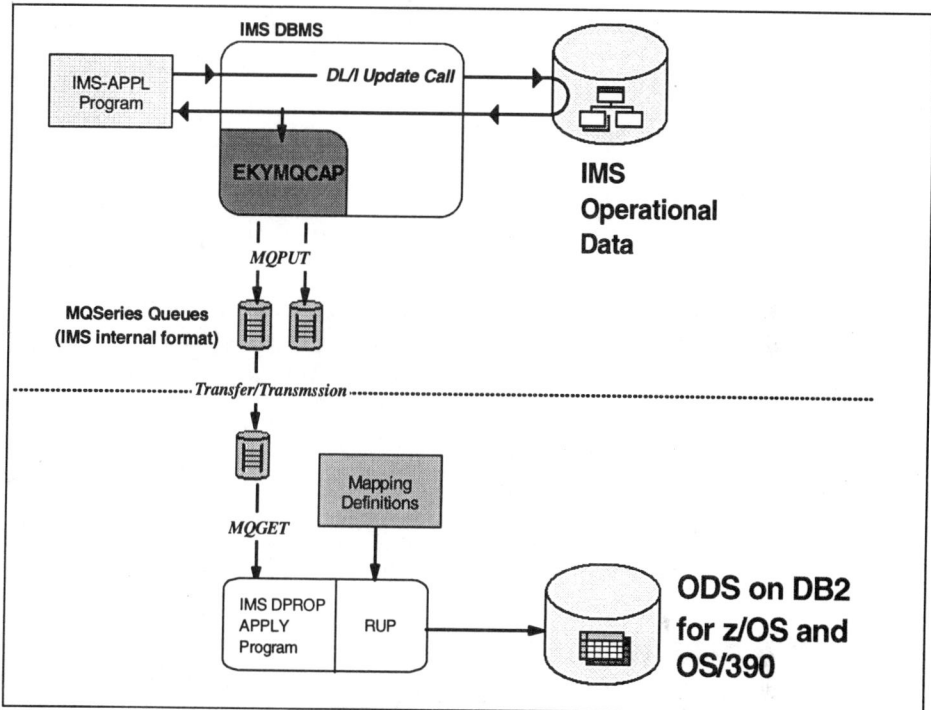

Figure 5-32 Near-real-time replication using MQSeries

Target ODS on DB2 UDB EEE

Once we captured data and applied it to the DB2 UDB target tables, then we may also replicate it to other targets in different platforms, like DB2 UDB EEE in UNIX or NT, using DB2 DPROP.

If the target ODS is not on DB2 UDB for z/OS, then a staging table in DB2 UDB for z/OS has to be populated before it is replicated to the UDB EEE, as shown in Figure 5-33. There is no function provided by IMS DPROP to directly populate an ODS on UDB EEE, as the target since the apply program can only run on z/OS or OS/390.

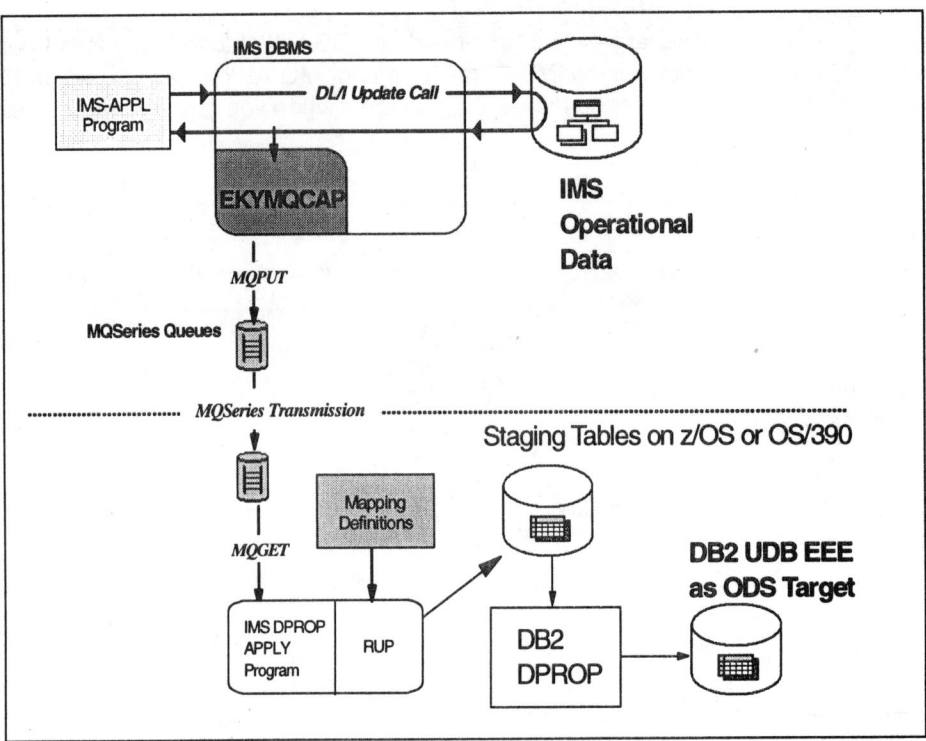

Figure 5-33 DB2 UDB EEE as the target ODS from IMS DPROP

5.3.3 ODS data transformations

There is one extra layer in the transformation for the IMS source. The ODS data acquisition layer to integrate and translate sources to the integrated ODS target is present, just like other source acquisitions. There is also one additional transformation to map the IMS data to a DB2 UDB table.

For the ODS data acquisition layer, IMS DPROP provides a place as an user exit that you can add some transformation logic, such as '0' to 'M' or '1' to 'F' in the DPROP field exit in RUP before you push the data to the ODS. You can add the transformation and integration logic in the user exit. You can also perform the collective form of an integration to the ODS after you map the IMS data into the DB2 UDB columns before you apply data to the DB2 UDB table in the ODS.

Due to the fact that IMS DPROP needs to map the hierarchical data to the relational data in the ODS target tables, you need to define the mappings:

- Identify mapping requirements.
- Select IMS segments and data fields that are to be propagated.
- Identify DB2 UDB tables and columns.
- Determine the mapping case or design your own mapping.

To reformat the hierarchical IMS data to the DB2 UDB table columns, IMS DPROP has to understand how it maps IMS fields in segments to the DB2 UDB column in a same key. The concept of the mapping is shown in Figure 5-34.

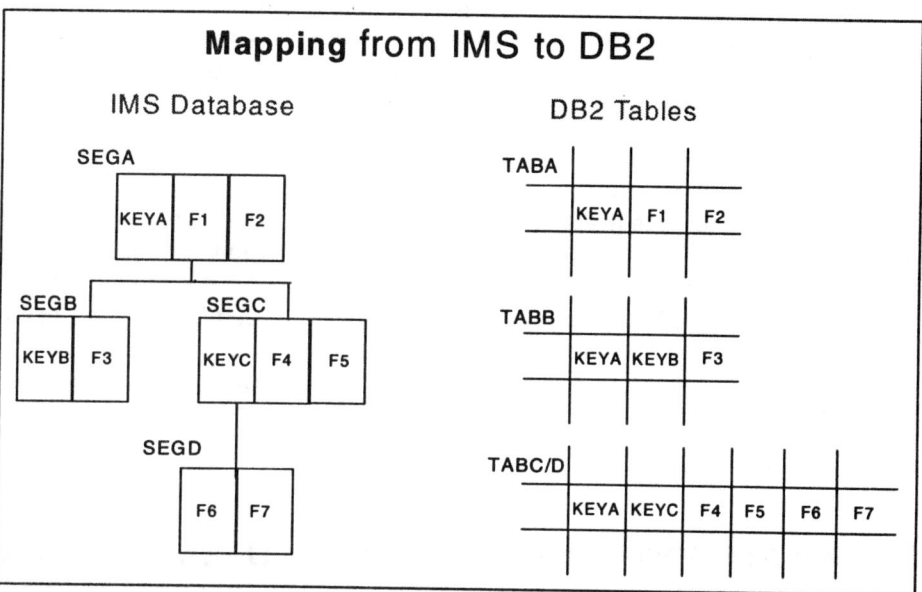

Figure 5-34 IMS DPROP mapping concept

With the mapping definitions, rules, and field conversion to the DB2 UDB format, IMS DPROP is able to replicate the IMS data to DB2 UDB ODS. The ODS may require more than field conversions or simple transformation to collectively integrate into a subject data from IMS data; then you might need to use the staging tables and use DWC to integrate the staging tables into the ODS.

You also may need to preserve the staging tables in case you want to run the integrity verification program to synchronize data between IMS and DB2 UDB if you find any violating data. Otherwise, it might be a challenging matter to run the integrity verification program against the ODS which has been already consolidated or integrated.

5.3.4 Performance for near-current data delivery

The first tests from the development indicated that IMS DPROP with MQ-ASYN could achieve few seconds latency of the replication for the IMS workloads of 1,000 - 2,000 transactions/second.

When the source and target systems are on different z/OS systems, the network between the two systems will affect the performance. If there are high volumes of changes from the source IMS with high performance and high volume transactions, the target DB2 UDB should be tuned to perform fast as well. Provided that we do not have any bottlenecks from the participating parties, the latency should be a matter of seconds between the updates of IMS source and DB2 UDB target tables using the new feature, MQ-ASYN replication, whereas the latency of the replication using the IMS log asynchronously could be in the range of minutes, for example.

It is possible to run multiple occurrences of the Apply program in parallel, and we can also take advantage of DB2 UDB parallelism to improve the throughput and decrease the latency of the propagation if there are high rate of changes from the source. Multiple queues can be used to propagate to different targets if you choose to have a distributed ODS. There is a caution to remind you that multiple Apply/RUP occurrences are not synchronized in the scope of the source IMS UOWs, which means that there is no guarantee to populate the target ODS in the exact same update sequence as with the IMS source. For details of MQ-ASYNC, please refer to the *Administrator's Guide for MQSeries Asynchronous Propagation*, SC27-1217.

5.4 VSAM and IMS as target databases (ODS type B)

In this section we discuss the update of the ODS by an user and the propagation of that update back to the non-relational operational database. We propose the same "independent update" method described in 4.2.2, "Independent updates" on page 122.

5.4.1 VSAM updates from ODS back to VSAM

In this section we explain how an update to the ODS is reflected back to the VSAM operational file, by using a Web access scenario.

Independent update

In this scenario, the user accessing the appropriate Web page from a browser changes his personal details. The update code on the Web server is written so that it updates the ODS using SQL, and using MQSI commands, it puts the record to a queue on an MQSeries queue manager residing on that server.

This queue is defined as a queue-remote (QR) pointing to a queue on the NT server monitored by MQSI. In the example this queue is called CUST_IN. From here on, the process is analogous to the reverse of the type A update. MQSI gets the record from the CUST_IN queue, and does any data transformation that is required. Then, instead of writing the record to a database node as in the type A example, it instead writes it to an MQOutput queue called CUST_OUT on the z/OS machine. This is shown in Figure 5-35.

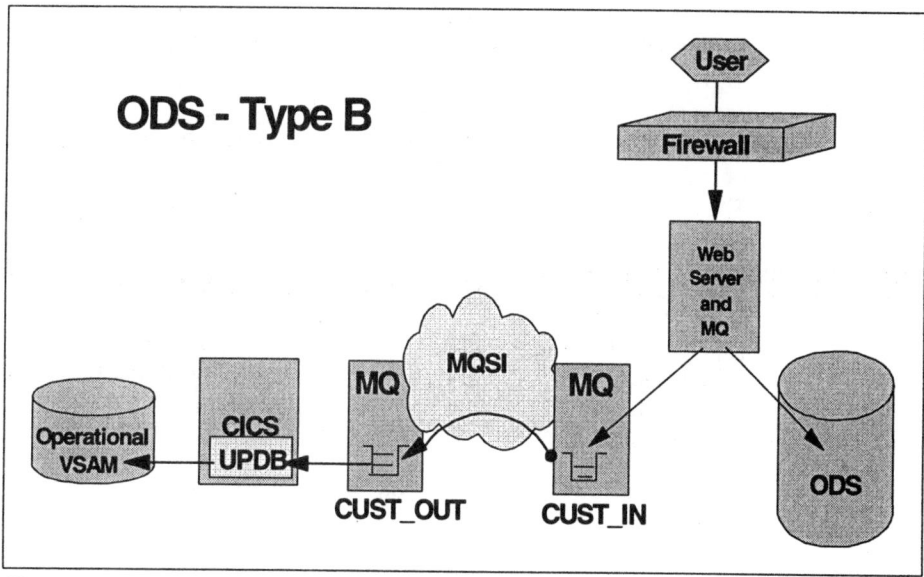

Figure 5-35   ODS type B flow for non-relational data

The WebSphere MQ Integrator (MQSI) part of this message flow is shown in Figure 5-36.

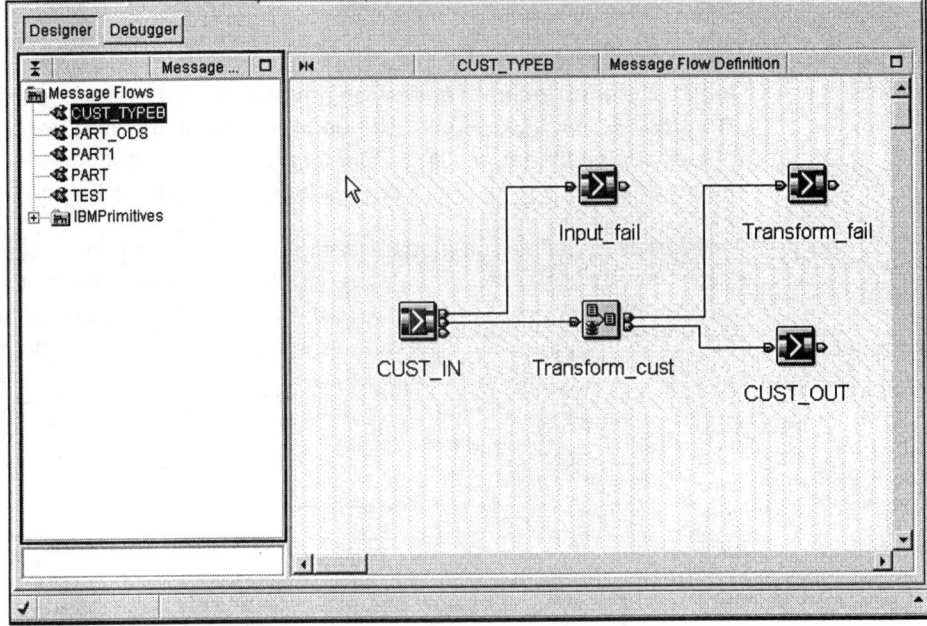

Figure 5-36 MQSI flow to operational database

The CUST_OUT queue is triggered so that every time a record is written to it, a process is triggered. In this case, the process that is triggered is a CICS transaction called UPDB. This transaction is written to read the data from CUST_OUT and to write it into the operational VSAM file.

So the update to the ODS has now been reflected in the operational data. Note that the UPDB transaction does not write to a delta file, so we do not have to consider the situation where the update will again be propagated to the ODS, as in the relational database scenario which is described in Chapter 4, "Populating the ODS from relational sources" on page 91.

5.4.2 IMS updates from ODS back to IMS

In the ODS type B, there might be a very small data to flow back to the IMS operational source if there is a critical business needs for it. There should be a special IMS transaction assigned to selected ODS users to execute them in a very controlled way for two reasons:

1. To prevent the cyclical replication back to the ODS; the replication to the ODS from IMS sources should have a mechanism to exclude those changes that were originated from the ODS itself.

2. To minimize the number of the transactions with costs of updates for both ODS and IMS in the same UOW, since the IMS-to-DB2 only works synchronously.

We can use the two-way propagation provided by IMS DPROP to flow the ODS data back to the IMS operational source. This works in the reverse order as compared to the synchronous IMS-to-DB2. The transaction to flow the ODS data back to the IMS is all in the same UOW and the updates in ODS wait until the IMS update is complete. Of course, if the IMS update fails, the DB2 UDB update is backed out. The bigger the UOW, the longer the response time. Therefore we must be careful to review the performance and frequency of using these kinds of transactions to flow the ODS data back to IMS source — they should be used in exceptional situations, for small update rates.

We recommend using MQSeries flows for larger volumes of data to minimize the impact on performance, as described in 3.5, "Data acquisition scenarios using IBM products" on page 73.

Administration tips for handling rejected records

It is possible for some of the data transferred from data sources through the data acquisition layer to be "dirty" (for example, it might contain invalid or non-existent dates). To deal with this situation, business requirements may demand a process for rejecting, reporting, investigating, fixing, and reprocessing "dirty" records, especially when "clean" data in the ODS is a high priority.

The chapter explains the issues surrounding the process for handling rejected records. We discuss the issues and solutions using the ODS type A business scenario that was presented in 3.1, "Business scenarios" on page 34. In this scenario, the General Manager of Consumer Banking at ABC Bank wants a consolidated view of each customer's product portfolio. This customer-centric view will be accessible by the branch relationship managers and the call center. The operational business units will use the reject handling application to manage the correction and reintroduction of rejected change data records.

We first describe the business issues and the ODS design considerations, then walk you through the design of a real-time user interface and the required back-end processing. Finally, we discuss the process and characteristics of analyzing the data for reject scenarios.

6.1 Business issues

When determining data ownership, we have recommended that the operational business units be responsible for the quality of the data destined for the ODS. In this case, the Reject Handling Application can be rolled out to each business unit to manage their own data.

The operational data sent to the ODS must be validated, as this information resides in the data sources layer which is typically comprised of legacy systems. These systems do an excellent job of storing and retrieving large volumes of transactional data but a poor job of enforcing data quality. More often than not, these systems contain dirty or invalid data, which manifests itself through the following types of errors during change data validation processing in the ODS:

- Inappropriate values:
    - Invalid dates
    - Blank dates
    - Missing values
    - Out-of-range values
    - Invalid domain values for coded fields
    - Dirty source data, such as numeric data in a person's name
- Interface record out-of-alignment (for example, expected blanks in fillers have values other than blank).
- Operational system key errors (for example, an operational system key has an invalid format or is different from the key used to create the original record on the ODS).
- Data integrity errors (the ODS and the system of record could become out of synchronization and no longer share the same value for a given field).

As an early warning system, some architectures include a data integrity check in the data acquisition layer. A "before" value for each field to be updated in the ODS is sent by the operational system and compared to the "current" value of this field in the ODS. This ensures that the ODS and source operational systems are synchronized. For the purpose of preserving synchronization, it is necessary to fix and reprocess the rejected record before applying a fix to the corresponding field in the system of record.

This is very important, as the invalid data has the potential to corrupt both the ODS database and its consuming applications, such as the Customer Portfolio Application and Campaign Management system.

6.2 ODS design considerations

This section discusses two very important design considerations for the ODS.

1. **The ODS must have a supporting infrastructure which facilitates the reprocessing of records that were rejected during ODS validation processing.**

To keep the ODS and system of record synchronized, the record that was rejected must be manually investigated and corrected by a user through a user interface (UI). The record is then reprocessed (see Figure 6-1 for examples of reject scenarios and handling approaches for ABC Bank's XYZ business unit).

#	FIELD NAME	Validation Rule(s)	Risk Level By ABC Source			ABC System Fix	ODS FIX	
			ABC	Tape	Internet		Reint.	L.-Del
1	Firstname	- Reject if field is spaces	None	Medium	None	Input first name in ABC system same as that input through UI for reprocessed record. This will keep ODS and ABC in sync.	Yes	-
2	Lastname	- Reject if field is spaces	None	High	None	Input last name in ABC system same as that input through UI for reprocessed record. This will keep ODS and ABC in sync.	Yes	-
3	Gender Code	- Reject if field is other then domain values	None	Medium	None	Update ODS Domain Table with missing code and flag rejected record for reprocessing via UI	Yes	-
4	Marital Status Code	- Reject if field is not populated with 'U'	High	None	None	This field is not available in ABC so they default to 'U', if it is somehow passed incorrectly, fix rejected record through UI and fix bug in Data Acquisition module(s)	Yes	-
5	Preferred Language Code	- Reject if field is other than domain values	None	None	High	If this is an incorrect language code, correct the rejected record using the UI and fix the code on the source record to keep ABC and the ODS in sync.	Yes	-
6	Contract Effective Date	- Reject if date is invalid format	Medium	High	None	This date is given for initial record *create* and, if invalid, the entire set of rejected *create* records should be deleted through the UI. The source system will then delete the original contract on ABC and add a new contract which will spawn the relevant *create* records	-	Yes

Figure 6-1 Reject data analysis for a business unit at ABC Bank

The next example is intended to illustrate why this is so important. In Figure 6-2, we see that there was a change at 9:00 AM to the Gender Code field in ABC, the system of record. This field was changed from a value of blank to 'X'. During ODS validation of the change data record at 9:01 AM, it was determined that 'X' is not a valid domain code, and the record is rejected.

At 12:00 PM, without fixing the original record, the business unit identified the problem and applied the correct code, 'M', to ABC, which generated a new change data record. As you can see, when the change data record was generated at 12:01 PM, it was determined by the ODS synchronization check that the "before" value for this field in ABC does not match the current value of this field in the ODS, which is still blank, due to the original rejection. This second record will also be rejected. Both systems, the ODS and ABC, will be out of synchronization.

Source	Field	Before	After	Time	Comments
ABC	Gender Code	Blank	X	09:00	Gender code updated in ABC from blank to 'X'
ODS	Gender Code	Blank	Failed Validation	09:01	Change data record is rejected because 'X' is invalid code
ABC	Gender Code	X	M	12:00	Business unit identifies problem and changes Gender Code in ABC to 'M'
ODS	Gender Code	Blank	Failed Validation	12:01	Change data record is rejected because 'before' values don't match (out of sync error)

Figure 6-2 Rejected record not fixed

However, as Figure 6-3 illustrates, if the original rejected record was instead corrected and reprocessed at 12:00 PM before ABC was manually corrected, we could achieve synchronization. After ABC was updated at 12:30 PM, the resulting change record would have a unique signature which could allow the record to be identified and logically deleted. That is, the "before" value in this particular change record would already match the current value in the ODS, given the update that previously occurred through the reprocessed record.

Source	Field	Before	After	Time	Comments
ABC	Gender Code	Blank	X	09:00	Gender code updated in ABC from blank to 'X'
ODS	Gender Code	Blank	Failed Validation	09:01	Change data record is rejected because 'X' is invalid code
ODS	Gender Code	Blank	M	12:00	Business unit identifies problem, changes value to 'M' in rejected record and reprocess
ABC	Gender Code	X	M	12:30	Business unit duplicates change in ABC to maintain synchronization
ODS	Gender Code	M	Failed Synchronization Check and Logically Deleted	12:31	Resulting change data record logically deleted during ODS processing as 'after' or new value from ABC already matches 'before' or current value in ODS. Systems now in sync.

Figure 6-3 Rejected record fixed before system of record update

2. **The reject handling process must also be able to delete a rejected record in situations where the solution may require correcting the problem in the operational system.**

For example, if the create records for an invalid operational system account were rejected during ODS validation processing, the business unit would probably want to delete the rejected records and add a valid new account in the operational system to replace it. The creation of this new account will generate create transactions through the Change Capture tool, and new create records would be generated for processing in the ODS.

One source where such an invalid account may have been generated is through tape transfers from external client systems. Sometimes, vital information is missing or invalid after external tape data has been converted and added to a company's operational system.

Figure 6-4 depicts the design for a reject handling application for ABC Bank's type A ODS. All data change capture and propagation processes occur in near real-time. A change capture tool gathers the changes (as they occur) in the operational systems and propagates them as interface records and are validated in the first ODS processing step. As our purpose here is to explore the subject of reject handling, the overall ODS architecture has been somewhat simplified, with many processes omitted, so that those components relevant to reject handling can be highlighted.

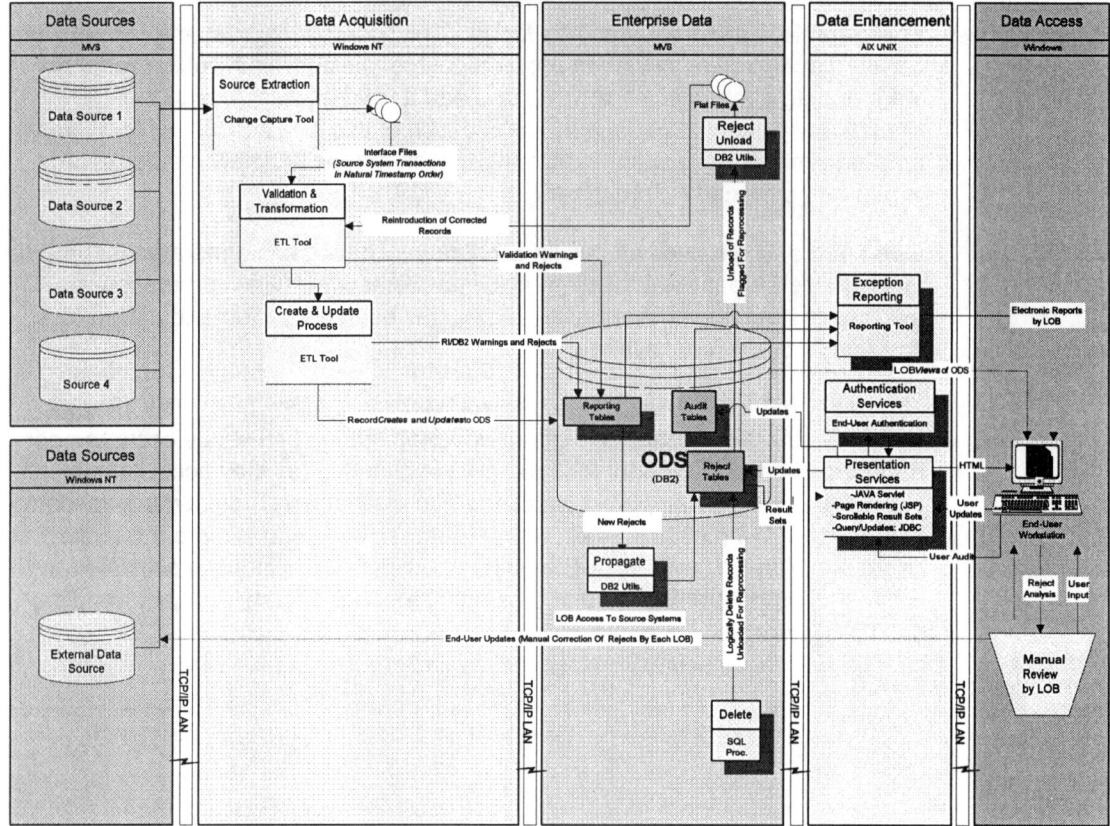

Figure 6-4 Components for an ODS (type A) reject handling application

Typically, it is best to validate change data records being fed into the ODS for create, update, delete, or key change transactions early in the process. For this reason, *the validation and transformation* process and the *create and update* process were designed. These processes reside in the data acquisition layer. They validate the records, flag the rejected records, and produce the associated reject messages:

▶ **Validation and transformation process:**

– This process executes validation rules (for example, out of range, invalid character, and invalid date) and makes sure the coded fields match those found in a central code domain table.

– If any change data record fails validation on a mandatory field, the entire record, with all associated changes, will be rejected.

- As this is the entry point into the ODS process stream, it is also where rejected records, once corrected, will re-enter the ODS processing stream.

▶ **Create and update process:**
- This process commits the create, update, delete, and key change transactions to the ODS after conducting referential integrity checks.
- Any record failing an integrity or data synchronization check will be rejected (these checks ensure that the system of record and the ODS are synchronized).

6.3 Real-time user interface characteristics

In Figure 6-4 on page 184, the reject handling application consists of an online User Interface (UI) along with back-end processing services. Note that these components are shadowed so that they are easier to distinguish from the rest of the ODS architecture. The real-time UI components provide the following functionality (the related architecture components are described in parentheses):

1. Authenticate the end-user (Authentication Services) of the application.

2. Provide the ability to make online record corrections (Presentation Services) through read/write access to reject tables.

3. Enable the end-user to view a list of all rejected records (Presentation Services) in a specific order so that all records belonging to a given client's account is grouped together (for example, business unit identifier, operational system client key, and the change capture timestamp for each transaction record).

4. Permit the end-user to browse the contents of a given rejected record (Presentation Services) and scroll through its associated reject messages. There could be many messages, depending on how many fields failed validation.

5. Provide the end-user the ability to edit a given rejected record (Presentation Services) and fix the problem(s).

6. Allow the end-user the ability to flag the record for reprocessing (Presentation Services) so that it flows through the ODS processing stream once more and successfully enters the ODS database. (Similarly, this includes the ability to set a logical delete flag if the record is not to be reprocessed for entry into the ODS.)

7. Provide an on-line audit of user changes (Presentation Services) that captures, in the audit table, the field that was changed (with before and after values), which user made the change, and when the change was made.

6.4 Back-end processing characteristics

The back-end components, which characterize the reject handling application, consist of the following processes (each item relates to a separate architecture component in Figure 6-4:

1. Records that have been flagged for reprocessing through the UI will be identified, unloaded, sorted, and formatted for reintroduction into the ODS processing stream through the *Reject Unload* process. This process will be scheduled to run every four hours during normal business hours. Records will be sorted in the "natural" change capture timestamp order, where create, update, delete, and key change transactions are sorted in the same order, by day and time, as they occurred in the source.

    Consequently, records that belong together (for example, person record, address record, account record, and so on) for a given client will be processed together. This is especially relevant, since rejected records may take one or more days to be investigated and fixed by the business unit, giving rise to a situation where many days of rejected records could be sent for reprocessing at the same time. Proper transaction sequencing is critical in this situation to ensure that a delete transaction from two days ago does not precede a create transaction for the same client key from three days ago, for instance.

2. So that the records already corrected, flagged, and unloaded for reintroduction no longer appear in the UI, the *Delete* process will logically delete these records in the reject tables. These records should be logically deleted because it may not be possible to recreate them - depending on the business event that occurred to generate them. After some period of time, these records can be safely deleted physically.

3. Once a day, the *Propagate* process copies and incrementally updates all current day reject record data and associated message data from the reporting tables to the reject tables. The reporting tables are used to generate daily reject and warning reports and are subsequently refreshed for the next day's processing.

4. For reject handling, each business unit will receive two *Exception Reporting* reports. These summary reports will assist them in understanding the new rejects from the previous day along with all outstanding rejects:

    a. A summary report, which shows the count of records rejected, by type of reject, for all records rejected during the previous day

    b. A detail report, which shows all rejects still outstanding in the reject tables sorted by the business unit, operational system client key, and change capture timestamp

Finally, the dotted lines represent manual investigation processes that involve:

1. Business unit specific views of the ODS tables that enable a given analyst to check field values of records in the ODS for which an update was rejected.
2. Operational system access to check the current field values of a given rejected record.
3. Manually duplicating corrections, made to the rejected record, on the business unit's operational system. This step is intended to keep the system of record and ODS synchronized. That is, a field in its system of record should have the same value in the ODS.

6.5 Data analysis

The reject handling application must be designed to handle the many reject scenarios possible from the operational systems' data. Some data analysis must be conducted to understand these scenarios. The data gathered through this analysis will form the basis for the reject handling application's functional requirements.

Here are some steps which may be undertaken to identify and document the various reject scenarios:

1. Determine for each field sourced from each operational system the relative risk (Low, Medium, High) of dirty data being introduced through that system's input sources. For example, Figure 6-1 on page 181 shows a number of fields sourced from business unit XYZ and its operational system (in this example the operational system is called ABC). Data enters ABC through three channels: direct data entry into the ABC application; tape transfers from external clients; and, customers entering data through the Internet. The relative risk of dirty data being introduced by each of these channels, for a given field, is shown in the "Risk Level By ABC Source" column.
2. Using test data, identify and group the reject scenarios into similar handling streams (in other words, develop a few high-level reject scenario classifications).
3. So that they will be prepared when the UI becomes available, have each business unit document how they will handle each type of high-level scenario when using the on-line UI. In Figure 6-1 on page 181, the "ABC System Fix" and the "ODS Fix" columns, identify how the rejected record will be corrected through the source applications and the UI respectively. This documentation can also be used later as part of a user guide.

Note: In some cases, you may wish to "tokenize" invalid code values coming from operational systems (this means to set the invalid code to a token such as a '?' in the ODS). This will ensure that an entire change data record does not reject due to some relatively minor coded value (for example, invalid marital status code). However, be aware that there are some risks in doing this:

- The business units are less likely to fix problems in their operational systems, since there is no pressing need to do so, given that no record actually rejected during ODS processing and there is therefore no "outstanding" problem to resolve.
- All consuming applications will have to build their own special "handling" mechanisms for tokenized codes.
- Since the offending erroneous field, that is being tokenized, has had its invalid value replaced by a token value in the ODS, it becomes increasingly difficult for the business unit to conduct a data quality analysis and resolve the operational system data problem. For example, they cannot tell what the invalid code was if they query the ODS, since all invalid codes now have the same value of '?'.

7

Building and managing the ODS population subsystem

The processes needed to capture source data, transform it, and update the ODS, are critical elements in the day-to-day production of updating the ODS. Building and managing these processes can be a daunting task. However, if we view the set of these processes as a whole, we can see some structure, and we can use this structure to develop an architecture for this population subsystem.

In this chapter we discuss why we might need an architecture, explore how the architecture might look and discuss the issues. To illustrate, we use an integrated example based on the two scenarios presented in this book.

7.1 Requirements of a population subsystem

Obviously, the primary purpose of any population subsystem is to extract data from a number of sources, move the data to the destination system, transform the data in various ways, and finally update the target database. This sounds like any number of data conversion projects that have been around for decades. Normally, a data conversion project was a one-time use system. Once the data was converted, we were finished. However, the difference is that for today's data warehouses, we must perform this data conversion over and over. And, in an ODS environment, we must do this data conversion very rapidly.

7.1.1 Data conversion project

Let us take a little look at the characteristics of a typical data conversion project. These projects are created for a variety of reasons, but many are created due to the need to move an application system from one type of storage mechanism to another, for example, from VSAM files to a relational database. The tasks we must accomplish are to extract the data from the old system, change the data to match the new storage structures and to load the data into the new structures. When we develop these functions, we realize that it will only be used once, so we are not overly concerned with structured design, application maintenance issues, performance, and so forth. We will run this conversion and then throw away the code.

7.1.2 Populating a data warehouse

In a general way, the tasks to populate a data warehouse are basically the same as in any data conversion project. We must extract data from some data source, change the data to match the warehouse data structures and then load it into the warehouse. However, the tasks are usually many times more complex:

▶ First, we may have a number of source structures across many systems.

▶ Second, we do many more functions in preparing the data for the warehouse. Not only must we worry about getting the data into a new structure — we must also do much more. We enhance the data by converting codes into something meaningful, calculating new data, adding data from external sources, geo-coding the data, and so forth. We also have to make sure the data is clean and reconciled across sources systems.

▶ Third, we must maintain history. Our conversion project now must be repeatable, as we will be adding data to the warehouse at some periodic interval. On top of all this, we have to maintain this conversion application as new sources are added, as new business rules must be applied, and as new cleansing requirements arise.

7.1.3 Populating an ODS

As in a warehouse, the tasks to populate an ODS are basically the same as in any data conversion project. We must extract data from some data source, change the data to match the warehouse data structures, and then load it into the ODS. Also, many of the same types of tasks are required as in a data warehouse. There may be numerous source structures to be integrated across many systems, as well as many functions needed to prepare the data for loading into the ODS, including data enhancement and possibly some data cleansing.

The ODS population process must also be a repeatable system with the same type of maintenance issues as in the warehouse. However, the ODS population processes are repeated much more frequently that a warehouse. It is not unusual to see data reflected in the ODS within minutes or even seconds after the source system is updated. An ODS must also support a very mixed workload allowing transactions and analyses to read the data in as it is being updated. And, obviously, performance is critical.

A population subsystem for a data warehouse or an ODS can be quite complicated. However, we can apply techniques learned over many decades of developing structured application systems to this daunting task. In particular, we need impose some type of structure to our processes, in other words, we need to develop an architecture for our population subsystem.

7.2 ODS population subsystem architecture

A software architecture represents a framework for the design and construction of some type of run-time system. Overall architectures for ODSs are discussed in Chapter 3, "ODS architectures" on page 33. An architecture describes a system in terms of its components, relationships between those components, patterns that guide their composition, and constraints over those patterns. This consistency allows us to make intelligent decisions regarding the sometimes conflicting requirements of build-time requirements, adaptability, reusability, and testability, as well as the run-time requirements of efficiency, reliability, interoperability, and security.

In this section we take a look at a reference architecture that has been defined for a data warehouse population subsystem and, based on this architecture, we design a population subsystem for an integrated slice of our ODS. Then we consider how to set up an execution schedule to automate our ODS population subsystem processes. Finally, we discuss the role of metadata in an ODS.

7.2.1 Architecture for a population subsystem

In developing any architecture, it is not unusual to start with something that has already been done and customizing it. It is possible to construct a general architecture for a particular type of software system which can then be customized to fit a particular instance. And we happen to have such a reference architecture for a data warehouse population subsystem described in Figure 7-1. If you wish to learn more about architecting a population subsystem, IBM offers a course called *Advanced Data Warehouse Workshop: Extract, Transform, and Load* (course number DW130).

This architecture splits the processing into layers such that each layer performs a specific function which does not overlay into other layers, and the processes in each layer are encapsulated such that what happens in one layer is of no concern to the other layers. This approach allows us to implement a more modular approach, allows the layers to be modified independently, and allows layers to be moved to other platforms with minimal impact to the other layers.

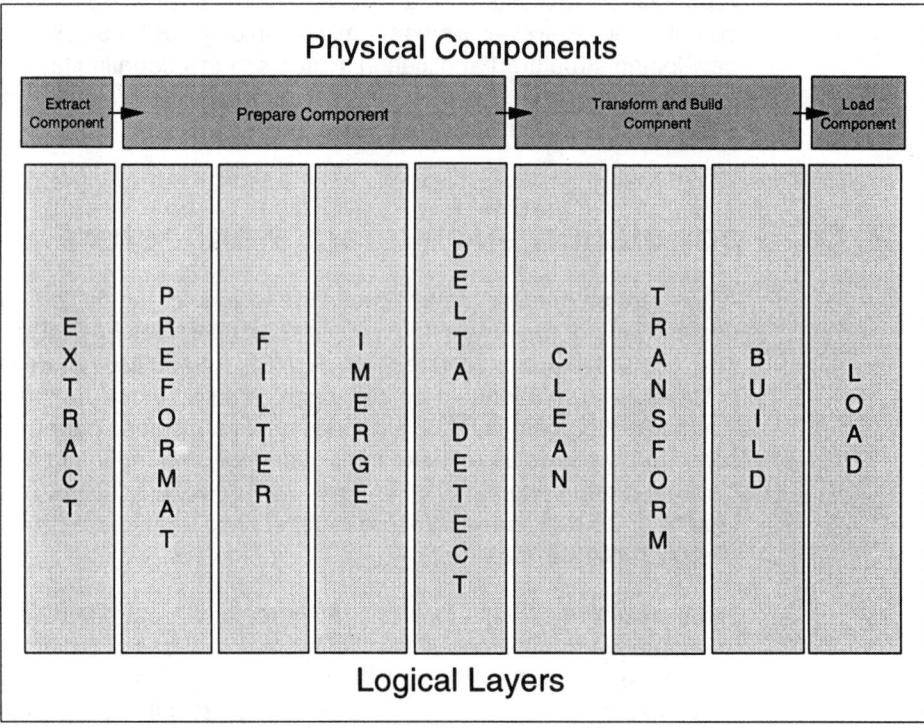

Figure 7-1 The population subsystem reference architecture

As you can see, this architecture has physical components, each of which provides a certain set of services based on its logical layers. Each physical component will likely be one or more technical functions implemented via user programs, database or file utility, services of an ETML tool or, most likely, a combination of all of these.

7.2.2 Designing based on the architecture

We will discuss each component and how it may apply in creating an architecture for our particular ODS. In our previous scenarios, we discuss how to build an ODS using either DB2 Replication or MQ Series queues along with the DB2 Warehouse Center. In this section, we will start with this reference architecture, develop our own architecture to bring all of these capabilities into one integrated scenario and see how we can use it to implement a slice of our ODS. In particular, we will consider how we can implement a population subsystem to capture delta changes about PARTs from three standalone PART systems and consolidate the data into one ODS PART table (see Figure 7-2).

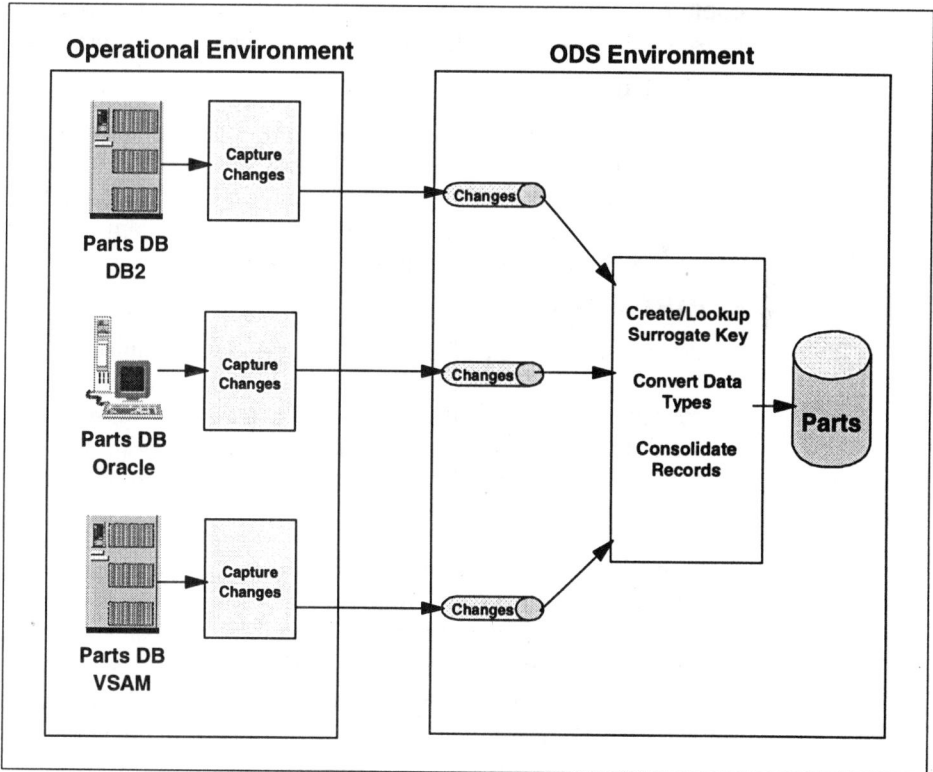

Figure 7-2 High-level view of our PARTs population process

7.2.3 Extract component

The *Extract component* implements the *Extract layer* and provides services that makes the required data available to the population subsystem. These services could be in the form of full/partial snapshots or a set of changes that have occurred in the data source. These services typically would select only the data that is appropriate for the population subsystem, put them is some sort of storage, and transport the data to the ODS system.

In a data warehouse, we find a great amount of snapshot extracts which we usually provide to the population subsystem in large batches. However, in an ODS we want to be able to propagate a change in the operational data very quickly to the ODS. So, to facilitate that, we must be able to somehow capture just those changes and provide those to the ODS population subsystem.

In our example, we have three PARTs systems: one in a DB2 relational database on the mainframe (but it could be any DB2 database); one in an Oracle relational database; and one in a VSAM database on the mainframe. The objective of our *Extract* component (shown in Figure 7-3) would be to provide technology to capture every insert, update, or delete in all three of these systems and make these changes available to our ODS population subsystem:

- **PART table in DB2:**

    We implement the DB2 change capture technology which will monitor the DB2 log for changes to our PART table. When a change is detected, whether an Insert, Update, or Delete, it is captured and inserted into a change table. This table is then made available to our ODS system via a remote DB2 connection back to the operational system.

- **PART table in Oracle:**

    We implement the DataJoiner heterogeneous capture technology which will define triggers on our Oracle PART table which, when fired, will write the appropriate Insert, Update, or Delete to a change table in Oracle. This change table is made available to our ODS system via a remote DB2 connection to our DataJoiner system which provides the gateway function to Oracle.

- **PART file in VSAM:**

    Unfortunately, there is no generic change capture capability for VSAM as there is for relational systems. Typically we would rely on some type of application log or the application itself to provide changes. Also, we would need some type of transport mechanism to make the data available to our ODS system. In our case, as seen previously, we have chosen to implement MQ Series asynchronous messaging along with having the transactional system provide a message that reflects the changes made to the database to the MQ Series queue. MQ Series is the transport mechanism that guarantees delivery of this message to a local queue on our ODS system.

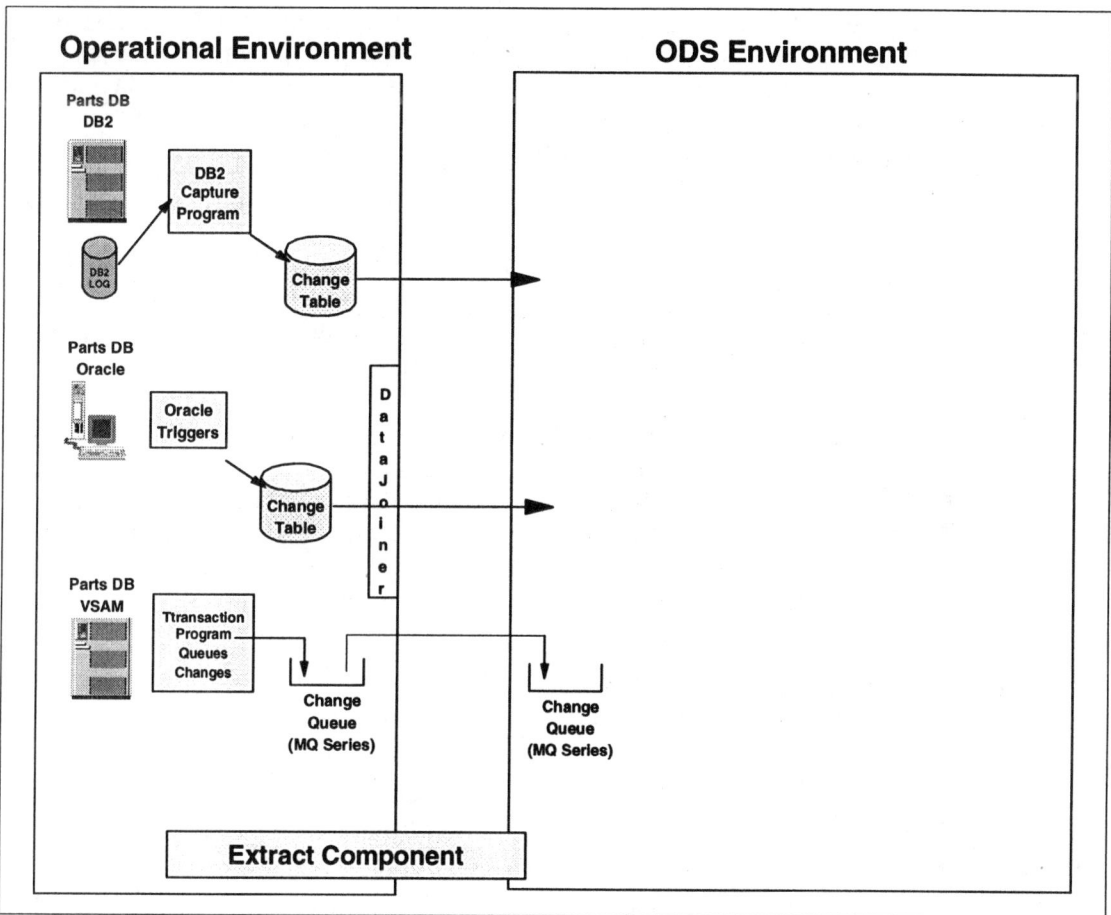

Figure 7-3 The Extract component of our PARTs ODS

Prepare component

The *Prepare component* implements the *Preforrmat, Filter, Intelligent Merge*, and *Delta Detection* logical layers. The objective of this component is to bring the extracted data into a common storage mechanism, filter out records that are not needed, intelligently merge data files together if necessary, and detect changes made since the last extract. The output of this component is a file containing one record for each change from the last extract.

The layers in this component seem to be based on having some type of snapshot extracts from data sources in what would be a typical data warehouse population subsystem. These extracts would have to be manipulated to a point where the individual records can be compared to the appropriate record in the previous extract to detect data changes and to create change records.

In our ODS population subsystem, as most ODS population subsystems, we actually capture changes directly from the source system; therefore we have "automatic" delta detection. So, our ODS *Prepare component* becomes fairly simple (see Figure 7-4). The primary function is to take the source data and pre-format it by putting it in a common storage mechanism, namely DB2 relational tables. In our PART ODS populations subsystem, this is all we must do.

However, other ODS population subsystems may have some amount of filtering or some record merging to do. If we have a relatively long apply interval, we could conceivably have more that one change record for any given key. In this case, we may decide to merge these separate change records into one. Fortunately, DB2 replication technology can do this for us, but we may have to provide this function for other change capture methods.

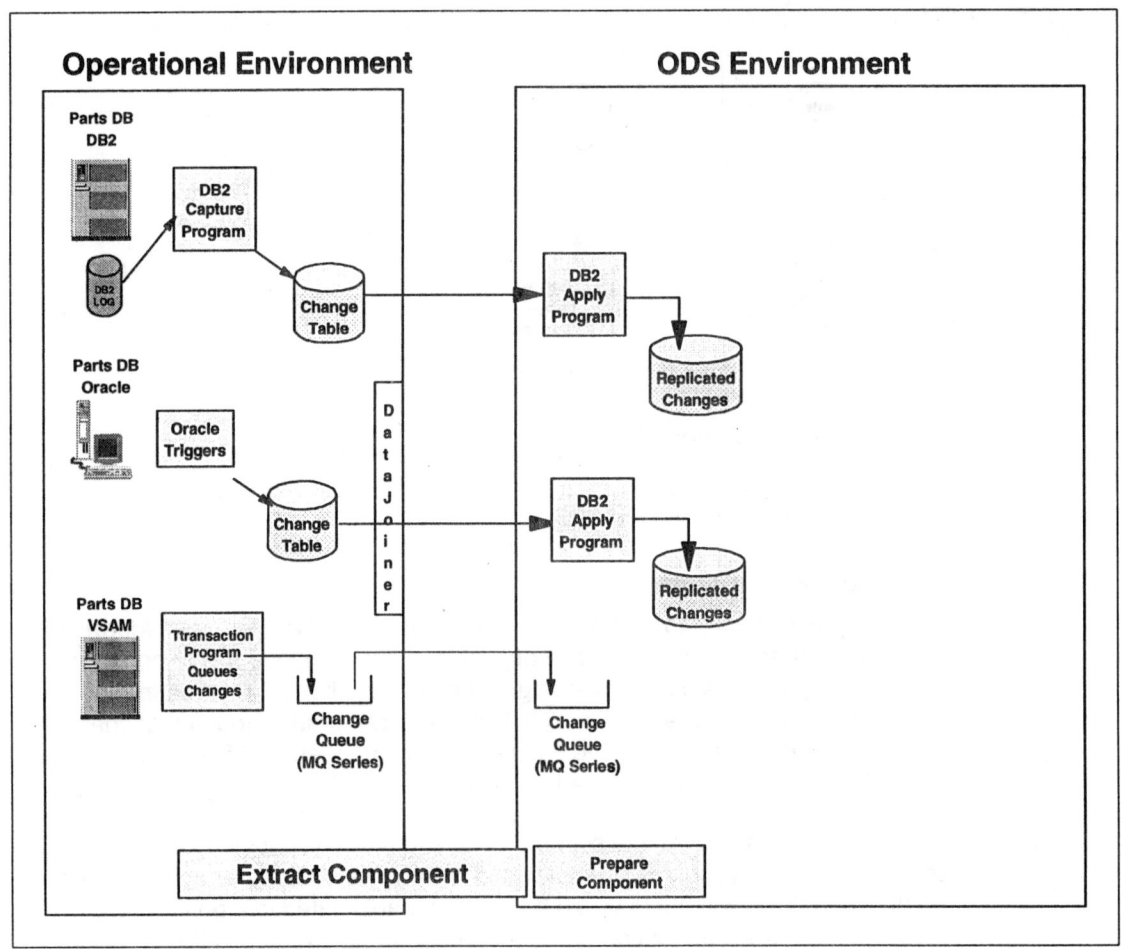

Figure 7-4   Adding the prepare component to our PARTs ODS

Notice that we have added two replication apply programs to our design which will take the change records from the source changed data table and replicate them to a table within our ODS work area which fulfils our preformat function. So why not do that for the change records from the VSAM PARTs database?

Well, we actually have the physical manifestation of the MQ Series queue on our ODS system, and also, we have a DB2 view that makes it look like a DB2 table. In effect, we have virtually accomplished that pre-format step, and we do not actually have to physically store those records in a DB2 table. The benefit of the pre-format step is that we can use common tools across all of the data.

Transform and build component

The *Transform and build component* implements the *Clean*, *Transform* and *Build* layers. This component is the most complex of the components and may involve several steps and, perhaps, very specialized tools. The output of this component would be finalized change records with cleansed, transformed data that will be input to the *Load component*.

In an ODS environment, the amount and complexity of data cleansing and transforming has to be balanced with the need to quickly propagate operational transactions to the ODS. Depending on your business requirements, the data in the ODS should reflect the data in operational systems, so care should be taken that cleansing and transformation activities do not change the intention and meaning of the data.

Typical transformations that usually occur in an ODS might include:

- Assignment or lookup of surrogate keys
- Text case conversions
- US measurements to metric
- Converting cryptic codes into meaningful descriptions
- Separating/concatenating fields
- Normalizing or de normalizing data
- Adding derived data

In our ODS population subsystem, we need to take the change records from each of the staged changed data tables, apply the appropriate transforms and create a standardized change record that feeds to the ODS update process.

Transformations that we need to perform include:

- If a new record, assign a new surrogate key else lookup the surrogate key
- Map the data fields from the input format to the output format
- Do data type conversions where necessary
- Assign the original key to the PART_SOURCE_KEY field
- Populate the PART_SOURCE_SYSTEM with a constant representing the original source system of the data

We, therefore need three transformation functions, one for each data source, that perform the transforms in an appropriate manner for the input source (see Figure 7-5). Each of these three transformation functions may be one executable entity or could be several executable entities with intermediate storage in between. Updated change records are produced and all stored in a common table.

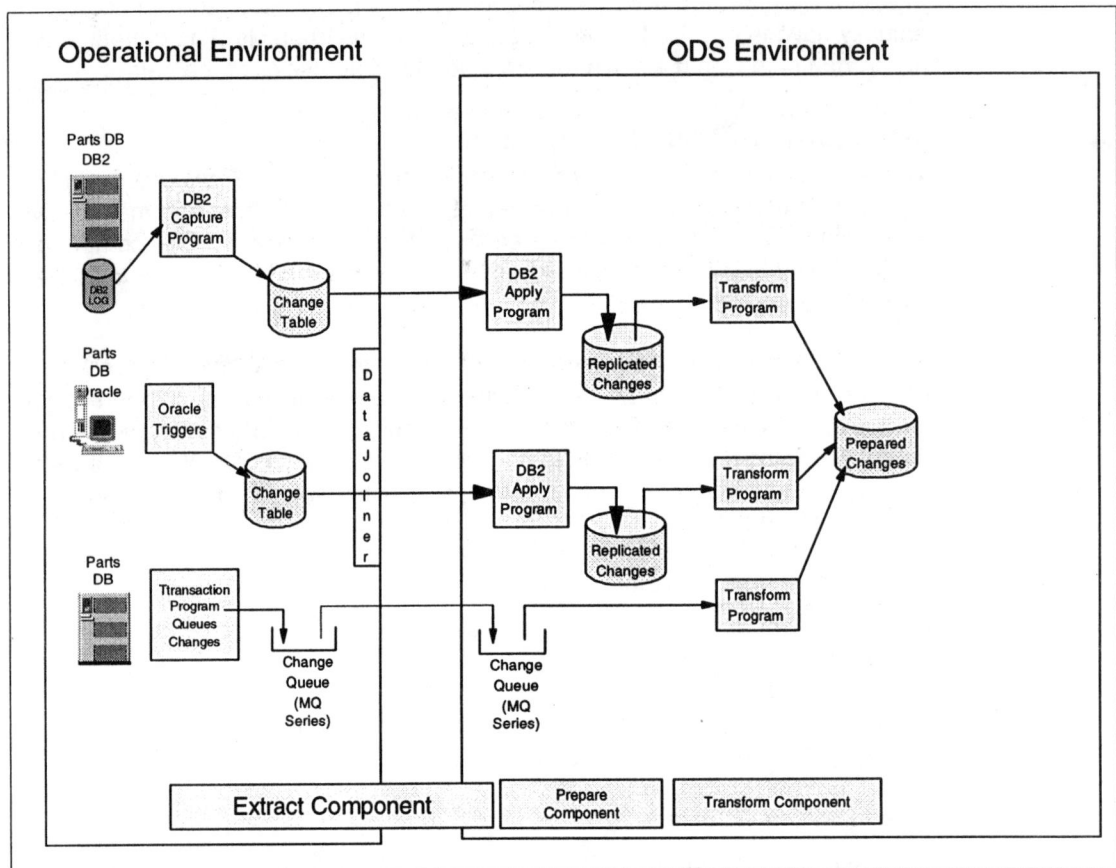

Figure 7-5 Adding the transform component to our PARTs ODS

Load component

The *Load component* implements the *Load layer* and will apply the prepared change records to the ODS as defined by the business requirements. It is no accident that the *Load component*, as well as the *Extract component*, are "thinner" than the other two components, as these two components directly impact live databases.

We want to minimize the time these components impact their respective databases. It is particularly important that the *Load component* does the minimum amount of work to update the ODS tables. That is why we have done all of the preparation of the data ahead of time and stored the prepared changes in one place.

All the *Load component* has to do is to read the changes and apply the appropriate insert/update/delete action to the database with the minimal amount of processing. This component is responsible for committing changes to the database frequently enough not to hold locks to long, but keeping that in balance with the overhead of processing those commits.

In our example ODS population subsystem, we have one function that is responsible for applying all of the prepared change records for PARTs to the ODS database. The reason that we have only program updating all PART changes is so we do not have two programs updating the PARTs table(s) at the same time thus reducing the contention.

However, we would have update programs for other subject areas updating at the same time as they would normally be updating a different set of tables. For example, we may have sales transactions being added to the ODS at the same time that we are applying changes to the PARTs table(s).

In our example, the three transformation functions in the *Transform component* and the *Load Function* are depicted in Figure 7-6.

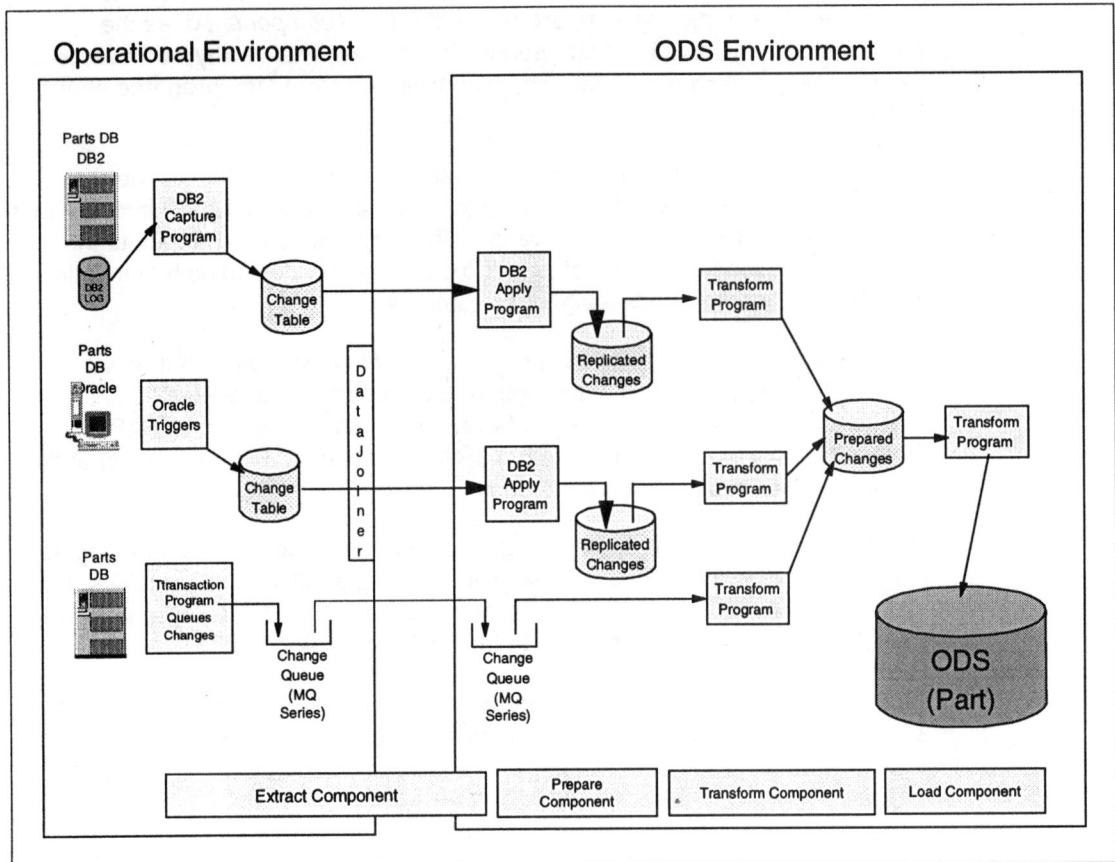

Figure 7-6 Adding the load component to our PARTs ODS

We have a complete picture for our PART slice of our overall ODS. Since we are now ODS population subsystem architects and are into structured design, we will look at our data by subjects and create a similar system for each subject area.

Conclusion

Looking at the final diagram in Figure 7-7, you may think that staging and executing components in this layered approach is just too inefficient. That may be true if you isolate one individual operational update and measure the time it takes to get it from the operational system to the time it is updated in the ODS. But if you consider the system as a whole, you may find that with this approach, we can have almost all of the processes running in parallel. From the final design chart, we should be able to identify operational dependencies between functions and therefore see where there are independently executing units of work.

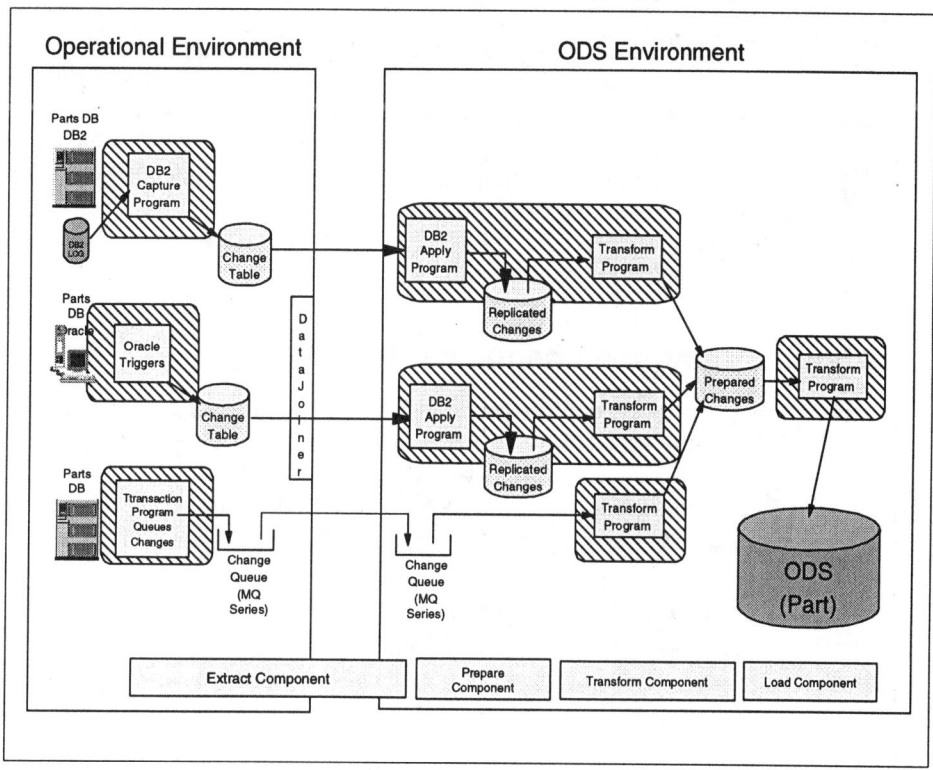

Figure 7-7 Independently executing units of work

Each of these shaded boxes represents a chance to process in parallel. It is obvious that each of the capture processes can execute in parallel, even if they are on the same platform. In our ODS population subsystem, we have four independent processes, one for each of the three Prepare/Transform workflows and one for the *Load component*. For technical and other reasons, the steps in any one of the *Prepare/Transform* workflows should probably be executed serially as a complete unit. It certainly would make recovery easier.

Each of these three workflows can execute in parallel, when adding change records to the same table. Having a short wait on locks at this point does not impact user access. While the *Transform component* adds new change records to the end of the table, the *Load component* reads and deletes change records from the front of the table, making the table act something like a First-In-First-Out (FIFO) queue. An alternative approach would be to use a real MQ Series queue between the *Transform* and *Load components*, taking advantage of the new DB2 MQ Series UDFs.

7.3 Automating the population of the ODS

Once we have designed our population subsystem and implemented the processes, it is necessary to automate those processes so the population subsystem will continue to execute with the minimal amount of human intervention. In this section we show how the DB2 UDB Data Warehouse Center (DWC) can help us automate the execution of the ODS population subsystem processes and monitor the execution. We define a production schedule for our integrated PARTs population subsystem that we designed in 7.2, "ODS population subsystem architecture" on page 191.

7.3.1 Automating the change capture process

The change capture process is actually executed in the operational environment, so from an ODS perspective, we are not concerned with managing that process. However, it is important that we understand to some degree how that operational process works. We now examine each of the three capture functions to see how they work.

PART database in DB2

We have one PART table in a DB2 database, which happens to be on z/OS or OS/390. However, at our level of understanding, the process is the same for any DB2 source.

To capture a change from a DB2 table, that table has to defined as a replication source, which sets up the DB2 environment to start capturing changes to that table. To capture changes, the DB2 *Capture component* monitors the DB2 log to detect any changes that occur for the replication sources, and it inserts those changes into a changed data table for each table. Detecting data changes by monitoring the log has the absolute minimum impact on the operational transaction. This capture program is a continuously running process which will be running anytime the DB2 database is up.

As you can see, this happens with total independence from our ODS population subsystem. When our ODS population subsystem is ready to get those changes, our *Apply* process will access those changed data tables.

PART database in Oracle

We also have a PART table in an Oracle database, which happens to on a Windows NT system, but the process is the same if it is on a UNIX system. While the DWC can access an Oracle database via an ODBC connect, we want to be able to use the DB2 replication technology to capture changes.

With DB2 V7.2, this replication requires the DataJoiner product, which provides a distributed join capability across DB2 and non-DB2 database systems, including heterogeneous replication. We will use this capability to capture changes from our Oracle PART table.

Unfortunately, we cannot capture changes from the Oracle logs as we do in our DB2 capture solution. However, we can create triggers on the Oracle table that will capture changes as they happen to the database during the transaction. But, this does have an impact on Oracle applications, since these triggers must execute during the transaction commit scope. These triggers will insert change records into a changed data table in Oracle, as the *Apply* process can access this Oracle table via the DataJoiner middleware. The DataJoiner Replication Administration (DJRA) tool automates the creation of the triggers and control tables needed to accomplish change capture in Oracle.

Again, this happens independently of the ODS population subsystem and when we are ready to receive the change records our *Apply* process will access the changed data table in Oracle via DataJoiner. Even better, when we set up the *Apply* processes in our ODS population subsystem to access the DB2 and Oracle replication sources, it is done the same way for both.

PART database in VSAM

We also have a PART "database" in VSAM that is simply a keyed VSAM file. Unlike the DB2 or Oracle sources, we have no database log, nor do we have triggers. We must therefore use some other mechanism. Most of these will rely on some type of requirement on the application system to log those changes and then some type of transport system. One excellent solution, the one we have chosen here, is to have the application log the changes to another VSAM file. We then have a CICS transaction that becomes our "*capture*" *component*. This reads the application change log and puts the change record onto an MQ Series queue which has guaranteed asynchronous delivery to a queue in our ODS system.

Our ODS *Apply* process would retrieve these messages from the queue for further processing into the ODS.

7.3.2 Implementing and automating the ODS workflows

As we have seen, the capture PART of our *Extract component* executes in our operational systems independently of our ODS processes. Our concern, then, is to automate the various workflows that occur in our ODS population subsystem.

Referring back to Figure 7-7 on page 201, we see that our ODS population subsystem can be broken down into four independent processes executing in parallel. In this section we discuss each process in more detail and determine how it will be scheduled using DWC.

DB2 PARTs workflow

The purpose of the DB2 replication workflow is to receive the change records from the changed data table in the DB2 source system into the ODS work area, apply transformations to these changed records, and provide them in a common format to the *Load component* by inserting them into a DB2 table.

This workflow consists of two steps which we execute serially:

1. Receiving the change records into the ODS work area. We accomplished this by using the DB2 *Apply* program.
2. Applying the appropriate data transformations and inserting the change record into a common format into a DB2 table. We implemented the transformation logic via a DB2 SQL Stored Procedure.

Once started, we continue to loop through these two processes, as shown in Figure 7-8.

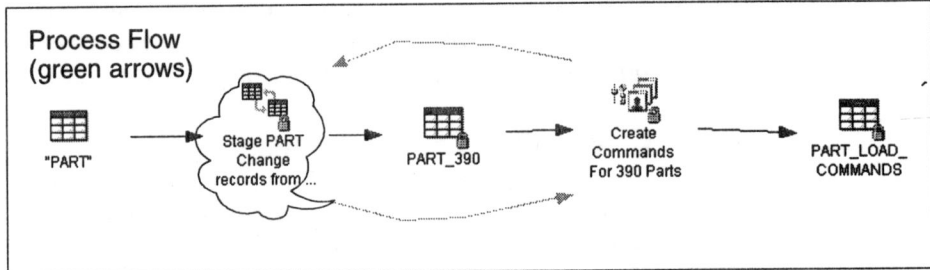

Figure 7-8   The DB2 replication workflow as seen in the DWC

Using the DWC, we use a staging table replication step that will have as input the replication source, which is the PART table in our DB2 database. However, this step does not actually read the PART table, but reads the change records from the changed data table that the capture populates. (Actually, this is more than we really need to know). See 4.1.4, "Populating the ODS using Data Warehouse Center (DWC)" on page 108, for more information about how to set up a replication step.

To the DWC process modeler canvas, we add the icon representing the source table and a Staging Table step icon. We draw a data flow arrow from the source table icon to the step icon. We then open the properties dialog for the replication step and provide the appropriate information, including having the output table automatically generated.

Figure 7-9, Figure 7-10, Figure 7-11, and Figure 7-12 are some screen captures taken from the properties dialog of the replication *Apply* step.

The DWC replication page in the DWC replication step properties is shown in Figure 7-9. Notice that there are two large text fields (Description and Notes) to provide plenty of descriptive metadata.

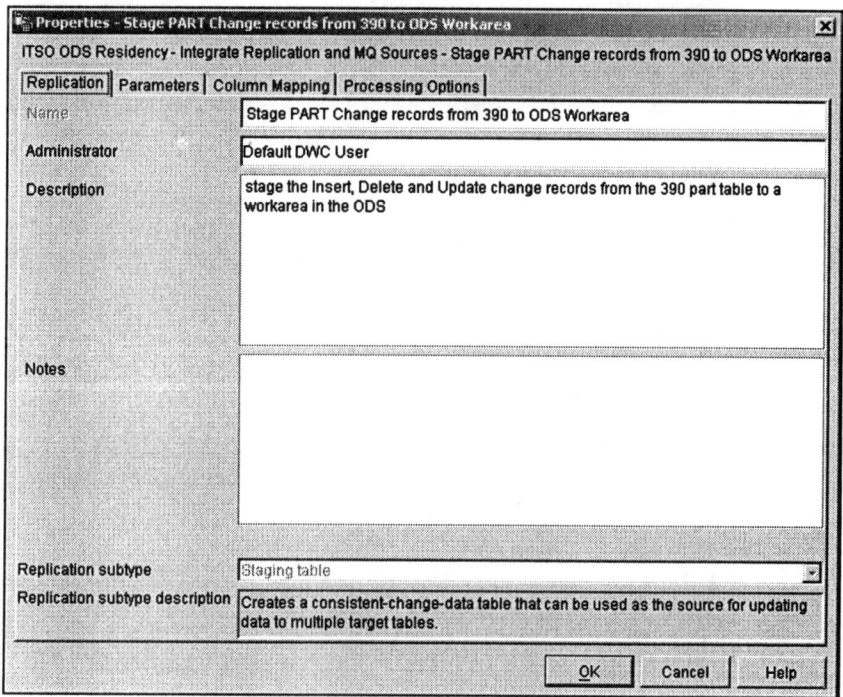

Figure 7-9   DWC replication step properties: replication page

The parameters page in the DWC replication step properties (to select target columns) is shown in Figure 7-10.

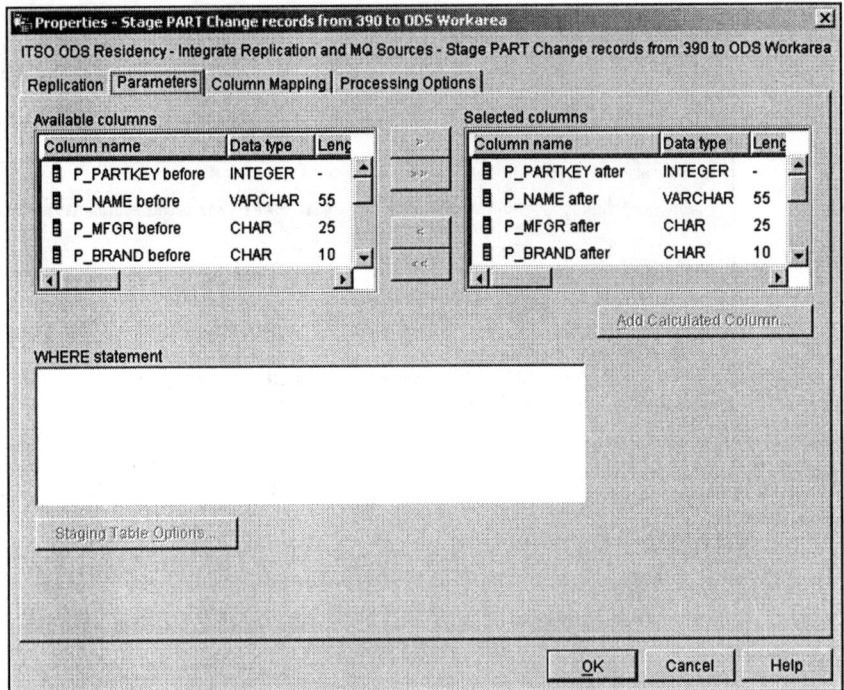

Figure 7-10   DWC replication step properties: parameters page

The mapping page in the DWC replication step properties (to generate the target table) is shown in Figure 7-11.

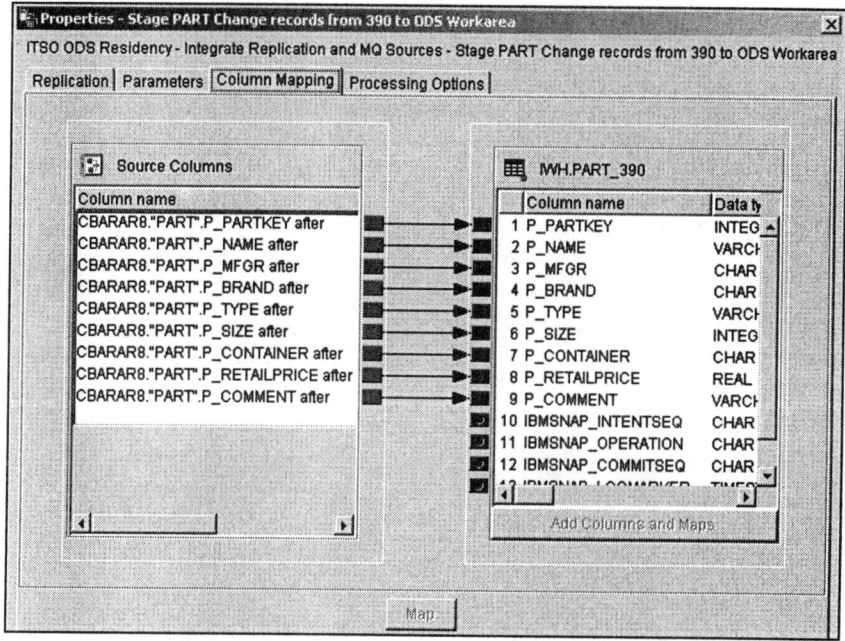

Figure 7-11   DWC replication step properties: column mapping page

The processing options page in the DWC replication step properties is shown in Figure 7-12.

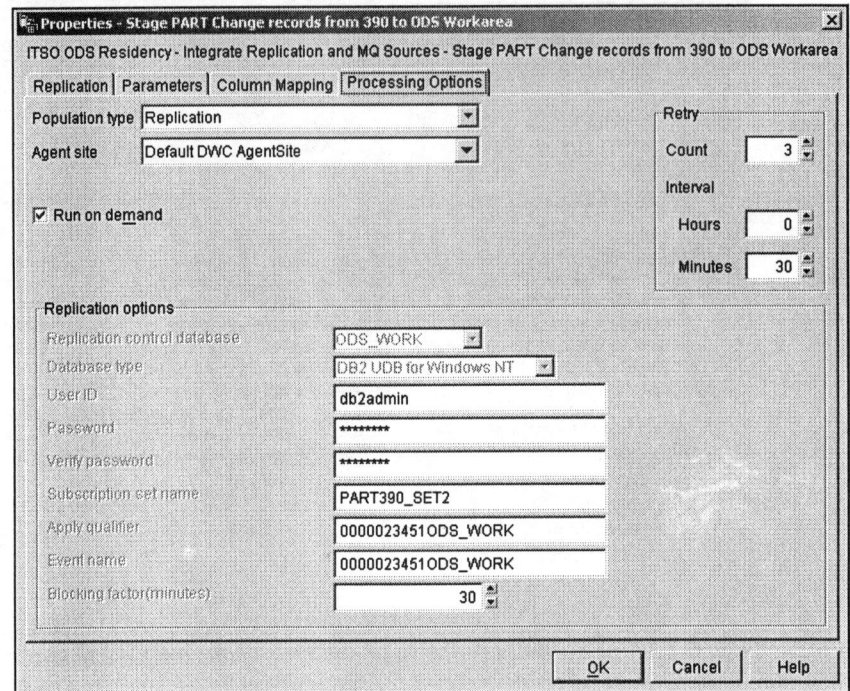

Figure 7-12 DWC replication step properties: processing options page

Due to the type of processing needed for the second step, and the need for the ODS population layer to be thin, we decided to handle all of the transformations in a DB2 SQL Stored Procedure, which is based on the ANSI SQL-PL standard procedure language. See Appendix C, "Population subsystem: tables; SQL stored procedures" on page 293 for the stored procedure listing.

We used the DB2 Stored Procedure Builder shown in Figure 7-13 to define and create the stored procedure — it even has a wizard to provide a skeleton stored procedure.

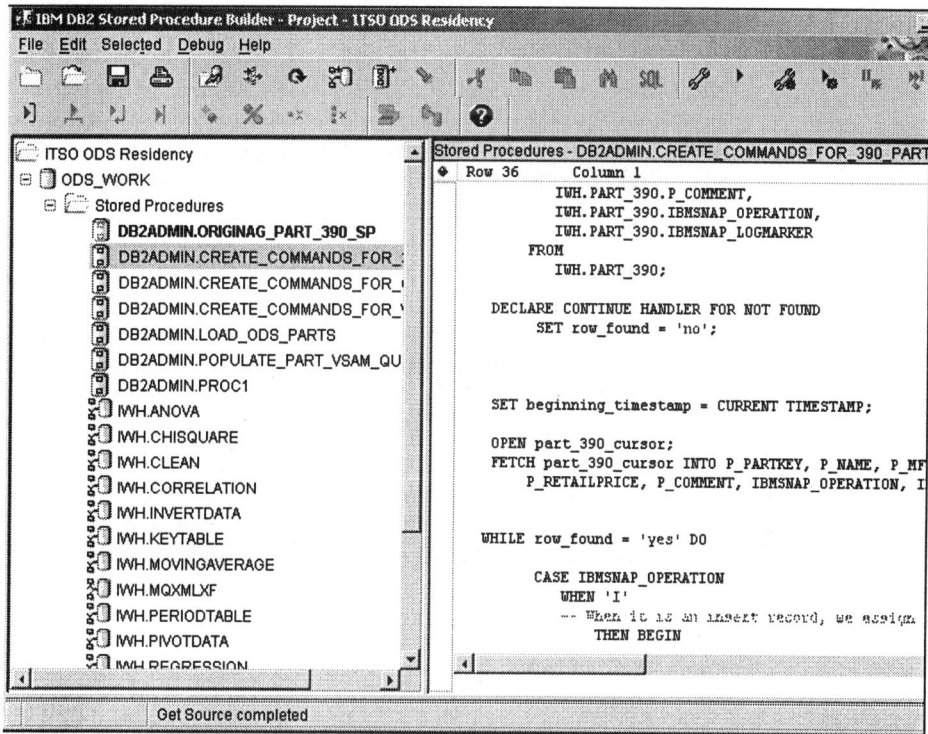

Figure 7-13   IBM DB2 Stored Procedure Builder

Once this stored procedure is created, then we can register it as a User Defined Program to the DWC, and then it becomes available for us to use as an icon in any workflow.

Our next step is to define our execution dependencies between our two steps. When the replication step, named "Stage PART Change records from 390 to ODS work area, completes successfully, we need to execute the stored procedure step, "Create Commands For z/OS and OS/390 PARTs". To do that we use an *On Success Process Flow* arrow to connect the first step to the second. We now have a one-way workflow, but we want to loop back and continuously repeat this to keep those change records flowing into our ODS.

To do this looping, we simply connect the second step back to the first step, using the *On Success Process Flow* arrow. As long as both steps complete successfully, we basically have a never-ending loop. We designed it this way due to the fact that our DB2 operational system has a high transaction rate, and the changed records will be coming into the ODS at a very fast rate also. Therefore, we have decided to have a loop that continuously processes these change records.

The question you are probably asking is, "How do we get that first step to start in order to get the workflow going, and how do we stop it?" There are several ways to start a step that is cannot be started by a dependent flow link from another step. The three most common ways are to start it manually, have it started by an event outside of the Warehouse Manager, or have it started based on some time element. Since this workflow will run continuously once started, we have decided just to have this step started manually using the DWC operations window, the Work In Progress window.

Since we have designed this workflow as a never-ending loop, by definition there is no way to stop it unless one of the steps fails. But there are several ways to address the issue. But we have to consider that, from a logical viewpoint, we should only stop this process after it has finished processing the second step. One way to do this is to demote the first step from what is called the *production mode* to a *test mode* which simply deactivates any automatic scheduling. Therefore, when the second step completes for the last time and tries to use the On Success process flow to start the first step, the first step simply will not start, as it is in *test mode*. The next day, the ODS operator would just simply promote the first step back to *production mode* and manually restart the process.

Oracle PARTs workflow

The purpose of the Oracle replication workflow is to receive the change records from the changed data table in the Oracle source system into the ODS work area, apply transformations to these changed records, and provide them in a common format to the *Load component* by inserting them into a DB2 table.

This workflow (in Figure 7-14) consists of two steps which we execute serially:

1. Receiving the change records into the ODS work area, which is accomplished by using the DB2 *Apply* program.
2. Applying the appropriate data transformations and inserting the change record into a common format into a DB2 table. We implemented the transformation logic via a DB2 SQL Stored Procedure.

This is almost the same as the DB2 workflow.

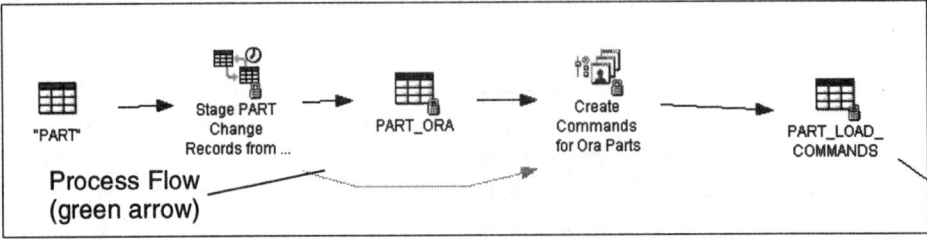

Figure 7-14   The Oracle replication workflow as seen in the DWC

Using the DWC, we use a staging table replication step that will have as input the replication source, which is the PART table in our DB2 database. However, this step does not actually read the PART table, but reads the change records from the changed data table that the capture populates. See 4.1.4, "Populating the ODS using Data Warehouse Center (DWC)" on page 108, for more information about how to set up a replication step.

To the DWC process modeler canvas, we add the icon representing the source table and a Staging Table step icon. We draw a data flow arrow from the source table icon to the step icon. We then open the properties dialog for the replication step and provide the appropriate information, including having the output table automatically generated.

The process is exactly the same as for the DB2 replication step, so we will not repeat the screen shots. See the four screen shots in Figure 7-9 on page 205, Figure 7-10 on page 206, Figure 7-11 on page 207, Figure 7-12 on page 208 for the DB2 replication scenario to see how to define a staging table replication step.

Due to the type of processing needed for the second step and the need of the ODS population layer to be thin, we decided to handle all of the transformations in a DB2 SQL Stored Procedure which is based on the ANSI SQL-PL standard procedure language. We use the DB2 Stored Procedure Builder to define and create the stored procedure. It even has a wizard to provide a skeleton stored procedure.

See Figure 7-13 on page 209 to see how the Stored Procedure Builder looks. Then refer to Appendix C, "Population subsystem: tables; SQL stored procedures" on page 293. If you compare this stored procedure (see "Stored Procedure to process the change records from Oracle" on page 302) with the stored procedure example for the DB2 replication workflow (documented in "Stored Procedure to process the change records from DB2 for z/OS" on page 297), you will see that they are almost the same.

Once this stored procedure is created, we can register it as a User-Defined Program to the DWC. Then it becomes available for us to use as an icon in any workflow.

Our next step is to define our execution dependencies between our two steps. When the replication step (named "Stage PART Change Records from Oracle to ODS Work Area") completes successfully, we need to execute the stored procedure step (Create Commands for Oracle PARTs). To do that, we use an On Success Process Flow arrow to connect the first step to the second.
We now have a one-way workflow. In this workflow, we do have the same kind of transaction throughput requirements as we do for our DB2 replication workflow. Therefore, we do not have to process quite as fast, so we do not need such a tight loop.

We now analyze our expected transaction rates in terms of updates per minute, to understand how many change records we may have to process in any one iteration of the workflow. We also consider how long it would take to process a certain number of updates, and use that information to decide how often to execute this workflow. In our example, we have decided to start the workflow every three minutes (see Figure 7-15). So every three minutes, the Warehouse Server starts the first step in our workflow. After it completes successfully, the second step executes, and then this iteration of the workflow is finished.

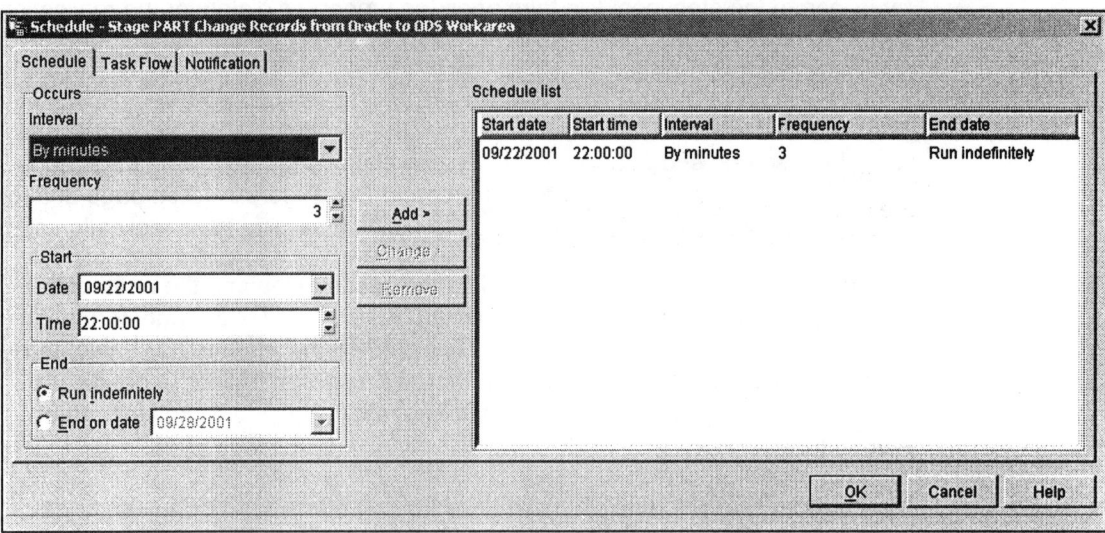

Figure 7-15 Schedule of the first step in the Oracle replication workflow

VSAM PARTs workflow

The purpose of the VSAM PARTs workflow is to receive the change records from a MQ Series queue, which was populated with change records by the operational application system, apply transformations to these changed records, and provide them in a common format to the *Load component* by inserting them into a DB2 table.

This workflow (in Figure 7-16) consists of only one step. Why is there not a staging step? The function of MQ Series asynchronous messaging is to guarantee delivery of messages inserted into one queue on one system to a queue on another system. Therefore, MQ Series delivers those messages to a queue that is local to our ODS system.

Then why do we not have to put those messages from the queue into a common storage mechanism, namely DB2, as defined in the *Pre-Format layer* of our architecture? We have a "virtual" staging table.

As we learned in 5.1.4, "Populating the ODS using the DWC MQ Connector" on page 153, we can use the MQ-Assist Wizard to define a DB2 relational view of the queue, which is materialized by a DB2 table function based on the DB2 MQ User Defined Functions. So, we can use this created view as direct input to our transformation function, which applies the appropriate data transformations and inserts the new change record into a common format into a DB2 table. We have also implemented the transformation logic via a DB2 SQL Stored Procedure.

Again we refer you to Appendix C, "Population subsystem: tables; SQL stored procedures" on page 293. See the section, "Stored Procedure to apply the final change records to the ODS" on page 311. This procedure is very similar to the previous two, with the exception that our capture system does not capture delete records, only insert and update changes.

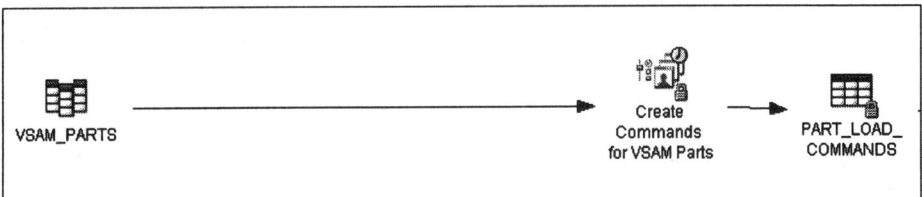

Figure 7-16   The VSAM PARTs via MQ workflow as seen in the DWC

Once this stored procedure is created, then we can register it as a User Defined Program to the DWC and then it becomes available for us to use as an icon in any workflow.

Since we only have one step, we have no execution dependencies. Therefore, we will directly schedule this stored procedure step by some time interval (see Figure 7-17) — specifically, we will schedule it at once a minute until there is an error, or until we demote the step from production to take it out of the production schedule.

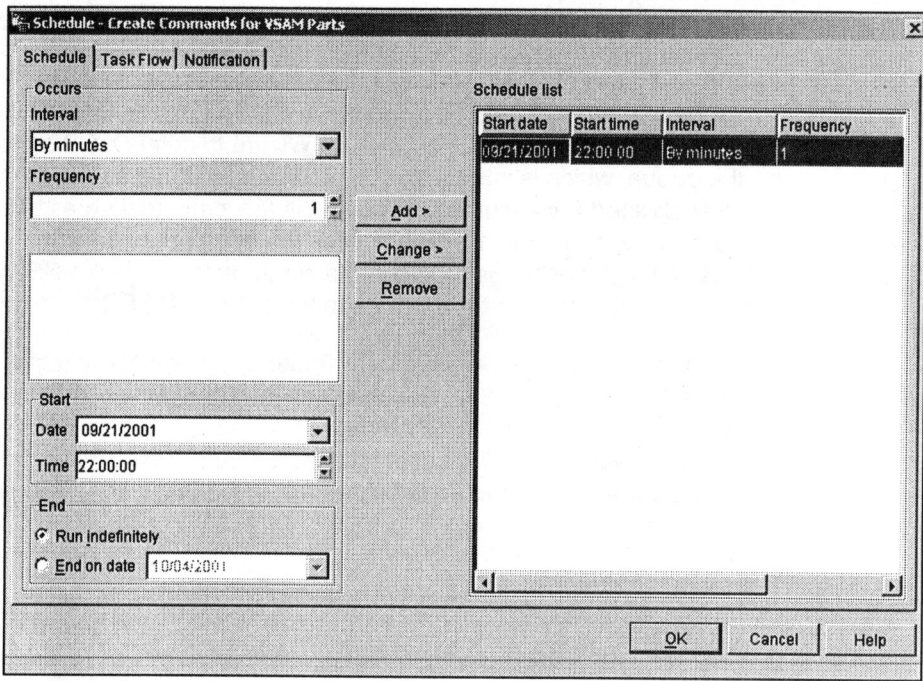

Figure 7-17 Schedule of the VSAM MQ Series workflow

Automating the Load component workflow

Our final workflow to automate (Figure 7-18) is the workflow that takes our transformed change records and applies them to the final ODS table. There will be inserts, updates, and deletes that must be applied appropriately to the ODS. Also, as discussed throughout this book, care must be taken with this step to minimize the impact to other workloads in the ODS. It is desirable to work more frequently with small bundles in order not to hold database locks longer than necessary. We must always balance the number of updates we do between commits against the overhead of commit processing.

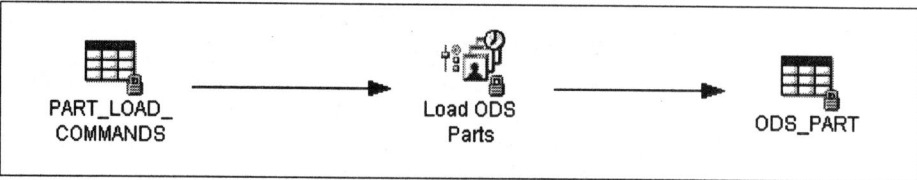

Figure 7-18 The workflow to update the ODS as seen in the DWC

Again, we decided to implement the logic in one step using a stored procedure (see Appendix C, "Population subsystem: tables; SQL stored procedures" on page 293). This stored procedure does not do much more than just check the type of change record and process the appropriate SQL command. There is no actual processing on any of the data, as all of that was done in previous steps. The advantage here is that the heavy duty processing is accomplished against work tables, an approach that does not impact other users' access and allows the final step to do the minimum amount of work to update the live ODS tables.

As in the other steps, we want to schedule this on a time interval basis, and we have chosen to process it every minute, as shown in Figure 7-19.

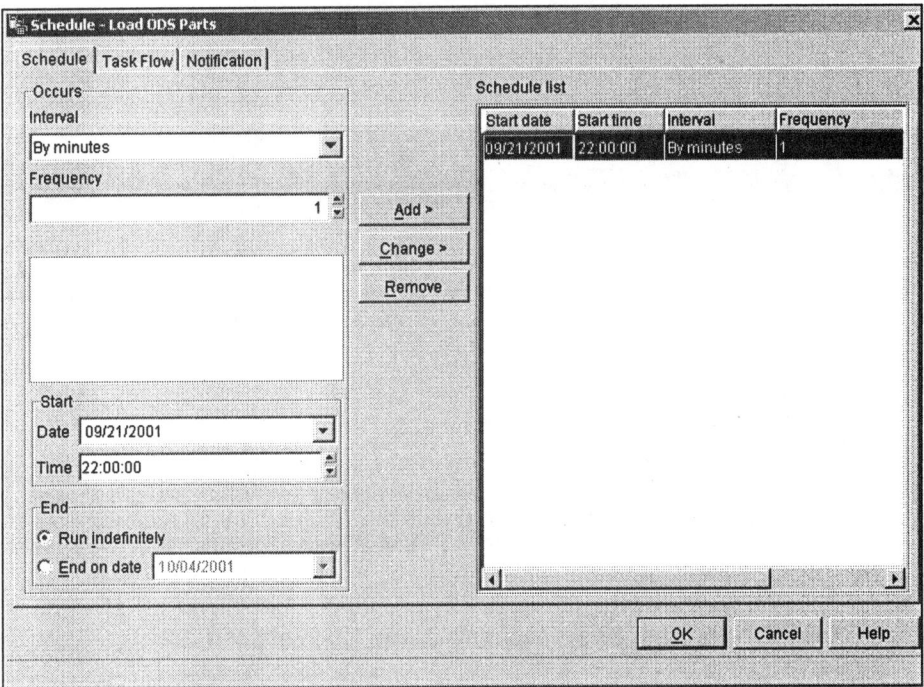

Figure 7-19   Schedule of the load ODS workflow

ODS automation summary

We have discussed each of the population subsystem components individually and have developed and scheduled these process workflows for each. Seven independent concurrent processes now comprise the four components of our ODS population subsystem. In the *Extract component*, we have three processes capturing the change records from the source databases and presenting them to *Prepare component*. Of course, we do not actually see the actual capture process, only the output that represents that capture.

We have three independent process workflows, one for each source database, which implement the *Prepare* and *Transform components*. Finally, we have one process that implements the *Load component*. Each of these processes (see Figure 7-20) executes independently of the others and has its own schedule, passing data to the next component via some type of intermediate storage. In the view of the entire subsystem, it is much easier to see how we have designed our processes to map to the population subsystem reference architecture. But, we have designed it to handle a constant flow of changes from the source systems to the ODS.

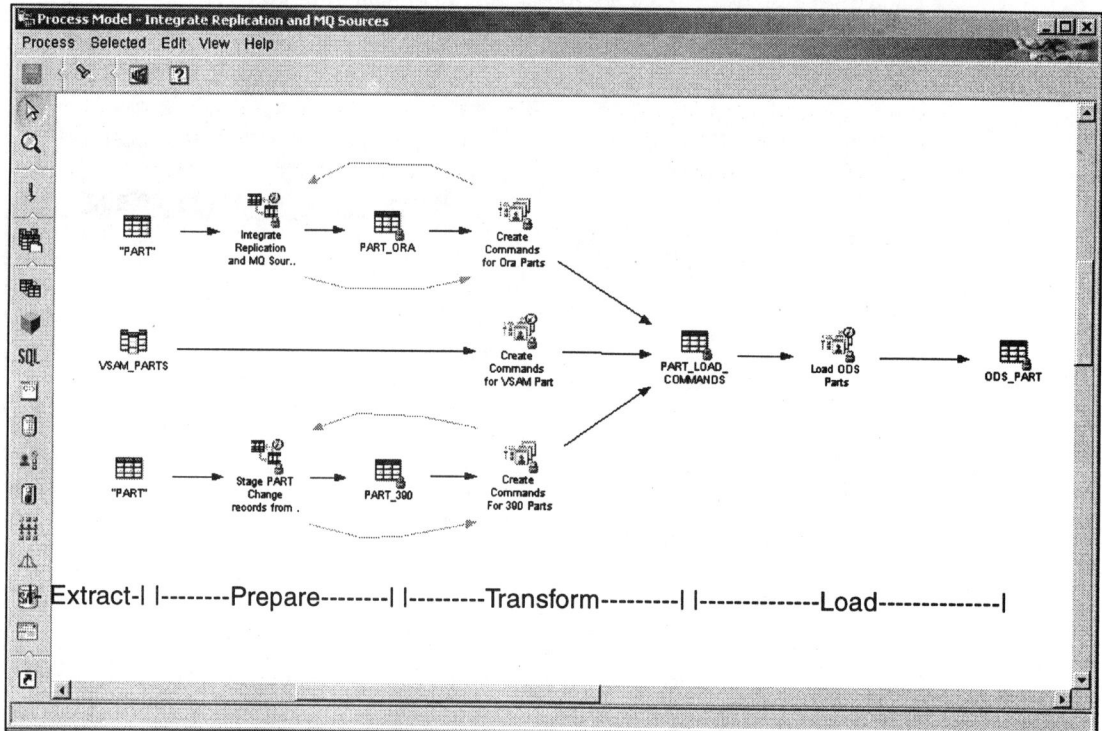

Figure 7-20   The entire ODS population subsystem

Referring back to Figure 7-7 on page 201, you should now be able to map that to our process in the DWC process modeler above. Remember how we scheduled each of the processes, to see how we obtain a high level of parallelism in processing. The *Capture component* processes are continuously populating their changed data tables. The prepare and transform processes take small bundles of these changed records at basically one minute intervals, transforming the change records as necessary and passing them along to the *Load component* via some intermediate storage. And, lastly, the *Load component* reads small bundles at one minute intervals and applies the changes to the ODS.

So, we see that in just a matter of a minute or so, changes in our various PARTs operational systems find their way into a consolidated ODS PARTs table. And we have achieved this with a very maintainable, architected solution.

7.4 ODS metadata

In developing the ODS, we need to obtain information about the data assets that we will use and information about what things we need to do to those data assets. But, we also generate a wealth of information regarding the details of how we accomplish our tasks and the results of those tasks, namely, the ODS tables. All of this information is called *metadata*. When we use the DB2 UDB Data Warehouse Center (DWC) to develop and automate our ODS and its population subsystem, we are really just working with metadata. When end users need metadata about what is in the ODS, then we can selectively publish metadata from the DWC to the Information Catalog Manager (ICM).

In this section, we will explore the kinds of metadata that we see and work with in the ODS as administrators, discuss the various stores of metadata in an ODS, and determine what metadata we need to provide to the ODS end-users.

7.4.1 Usage of metadata in the ODS population subsystem

As developers, administrators, or users of the ODS and its population subsystem, we will be dealing with metadata on a day-to-day basis. But users in each category need different views of the ODS metadata:

- Developers are mostly creators of metadata. They need to obtain metadata about data sources, but working with the DWC GUI, they create metadata that represents the processes to transform the data, the resulting tables, and information about how the processes will behave in a production system.
- Administrators need to know about the production status of processes in the ODS production system in order to monitor the population subsystem.
- End users need to know what data is contained in the ODS, and some need to trace the data lineage back to the source.

Even the warehouse server itself, uses and creates metadata.

- It uses the metadata to determine when it is time to execute a process, as well as to gather information that it needs to execute that process; and it creates metadata on the status of the execution of the process.
- A DB2 WM agent also uses the metadata that is passed to it from the warehouse server to execute the process and passes back metadata regarding the execution status.

In our ODS, there are actually a number of places in which metadata is stored. Of course, the source databases usually have some type of metadata store; most common are the catalogs of relational database systems, which contain metadata about tables and columns. The same is true for our target database systems, which also have catalogs with metadata about its tables and columns.

The primary metadata store in our ODS is the metadata store associated with our warehouse server, known as the Control Database (CDB), as shown in Figure 7-21. The CDB is a special relational database that is used by the warehouse server to store all of the metadata that is needed to develop, administer, and execute the processes needed to take data from data sources and build the ODS tables. We view and manipulate this metadata using the DWC GUI. The CDB is a private metadata store to be used by the warehouse server and is not intended for end users.

For end users, we have a generalized, open metadata store that is known as the Information Catalog. This metadata store is not just for ODS or data warehouse metadata. Metadata for any type of business object can be stored in the Information Catalog.

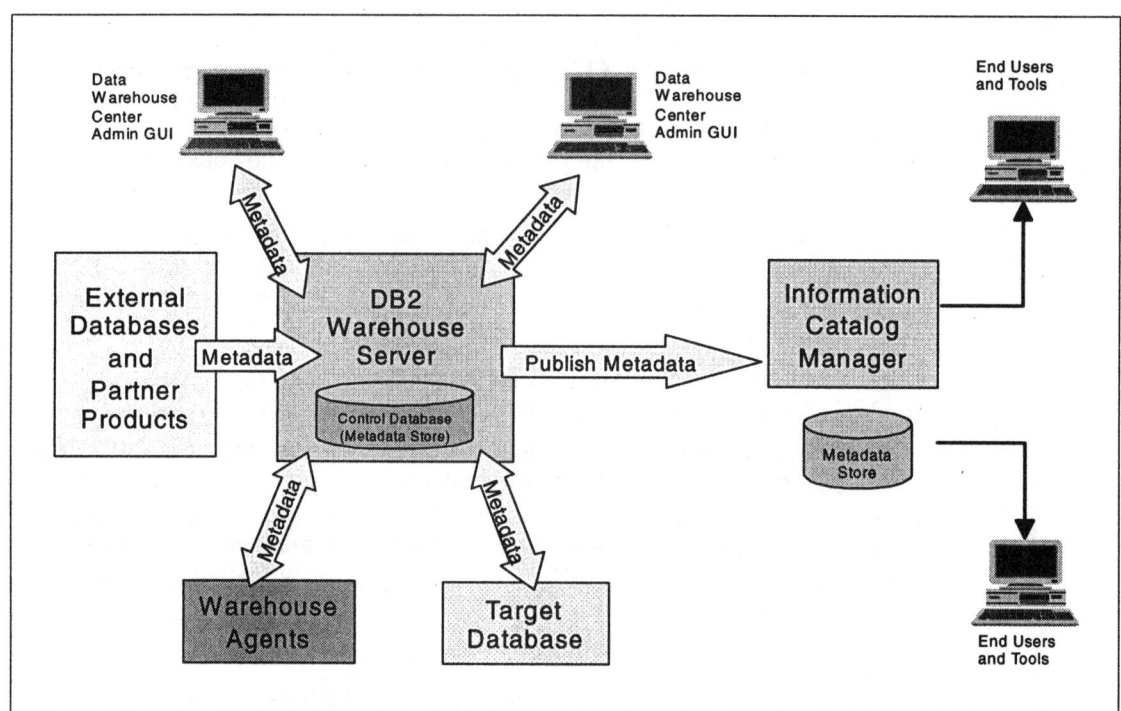

Figure 7-21   Metadata flows using the DWC and the Information Catalog Manager

Metadata needed during development

During the development of our ODS population subsystem, we acquire and generate quantities of metadata. We may not actually be aware that we are working with metadata when using the DWC GUI, in which we deal with icons representing objects, arrows representing data and process flow, and dialogs in which we provide information about those objects. However, all of that information is metadata and is stored in a common metadata store called the Control Database (CDB).

There are many types of metadata with which we work during development:

- **Sources:** One of the first things that we did was to define our source databases and their underlying source tables. We did this using the DWC dialogs for connecting to source databases and importing the definitions for the tables and their columns in which we are interested, resulting in the appropriate source definitions in our CDB.

- **Targets:** We also registered our target database to the DWC and imported the definitions of any existing target tables which populated target metadata in our CDB. We also generated target table definitions as we developed our processes which, again, stored that metadata in the CDB.

- **Processes:** We created a number of steps to represent work activities that need to happen within our ODS population subsystems. As we defined those steps, we connected input and output icons to the step icon, provided information in dialog boxes (for example, creating the SQL statement), and even defined processing dependencies and schedules. Indeed, all of this is metadata that is stored in the CDB.

- **Miscellaneous:** There are also metadata definitions that represent systems where we can actually execute steps, programs that we can execute, and warehouse administrators.

Metadata needed during execution

You have seen much of the DWC GUI which is used to development this metadata. But what you probably do not see is how the warehouse server uses this metadata. When the warehouse server determines that it is time to execute a step, whether via a schedule, manually, or from an external trigger, it reads the CDB to gather all of the metadata needed to execute the step. It needs to know the input tables/files, the output table, the program/stored procedure/SQL statement to execute, on what machine to execute the step, and userid/password information to make all of the log-ins.

After a step executes, the agent passes back to the warehouse server, all the information about the execution of the step, such as whether it was successful or failed, execution time, number of rows, number of bytes, and so forth, depending on the type of step. This is, of course, stored in the CDB and is available for viewing using the DWC GUI component called the Work In Progress window (see Figure 7-22).

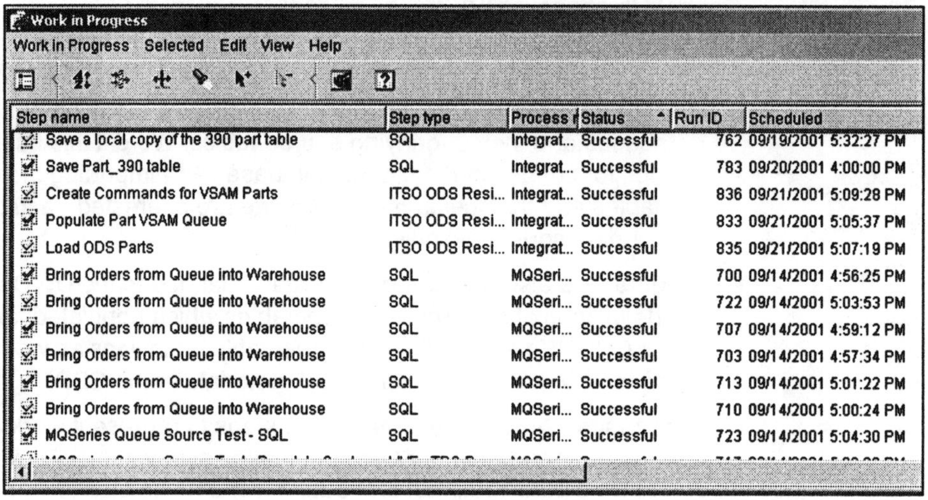
Work in Progress
Work in Progress Selected Edit View Help
Step name Step type Process Status Run ID Scheduled
Save a local copy of the 390 part table SQL Integrat... Successful 762 09/19/2001 5:32:27 PM
Save Part_390 table SQL Integrat... Successful 783 09/20/2001 4:00:00 PM
Create Commands for VSAM Parts ITSO ODS Resi... Integrat... Successful 836 09/21/2001 5:09:28 PM
Populate Part VSAM Queue ITSO ODS Resi... Integrat... Successful 833 09/21/2001 5:05:37 PM
Load ODS Parts ITSO ODS Resi... Integrat... Successful 835 09/21/2001 5:07:19 PM
Bring Orders from Queue into Warehouse SQL MQSeri... Successful 700 09/14/2001 4:56:25 PM
Bring Orders from Queue into Warehouse SQL MQSeri... Successful 722 09/14/2001 5:03:53 PM
Bring Orders from Queue into Warehouse SQL MQSeri... Successful 707 09/14/2001 4:59:12 PM
Bring Orders from Queue into Warehouse SQL MQSeri... Successful 703 09/14/2001 4:57:34 PM
Bring Orders from Queue into Warehouse SQL MQSeri... Successful 713 09/14/2001 5:01:22 PM
Bring Orders from Queue into Warehouse SQL MQSeri... Successful 710 09/14/2001 5:00:24 PM
MQSeries Queue Source Test - SQL SQL MQSeri... Successful 723 09/14/2001 5:04:30 PM

Figure 7-22 Metadata execution using the DWC work-in-progress window

Metadata needed by end users

End users need to understand what data is stored in the ODS. They want to be able to search the metadata using business terms, not by cryptic table or column names. They may also want to understand how some of the data was derived, tracing the data lineage back to the original source and seeing how the data was modified along the way. There is also a need to access metadata about other kinds of objects other than those related to ODS tables. Any kind of object can be created in the Information Catalog and metadata provided for that object (see Figure 7-23).

Figure 7-23   Many objects can be defined in the information catalog

We have some metadata already stored in our CDB, as shown in Figure 7-24.

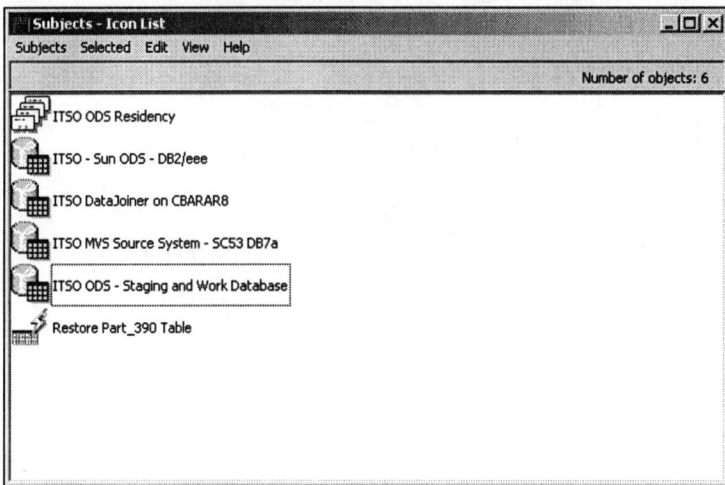

Figure 7-24   Our ODS subjects in the information catalog

Do we want to open up the CDB to users for the querying of metadata? Do we want to be able to define other types of objects in our CDB, even if they are not related to the ODS? *The answer is no!* First of all, the CDB is not a generalized metadata store, but rather a private store that is designed specifically for the day-to-day operation of the warehouse server. Second, we do not want users getting into a critical database that is used to run our ODS production jobs.

What we really want to do is to be able to provide the ODS metadata to some other generalized metadata store that is set up for end users. That is exactly the purpose of the Information Catalog Manager (ICM) product. We use the ICM to administer and query a generalized Information Catalog. The end user can use either the ICM client-server interface or the ICM Web interface to search any or all of the various types of objects in the Information Catalog, including any information we provide about the objects in our ODS. Additionally, some advanced users can use it to trace back a table to its sources (see Figure 7-25).

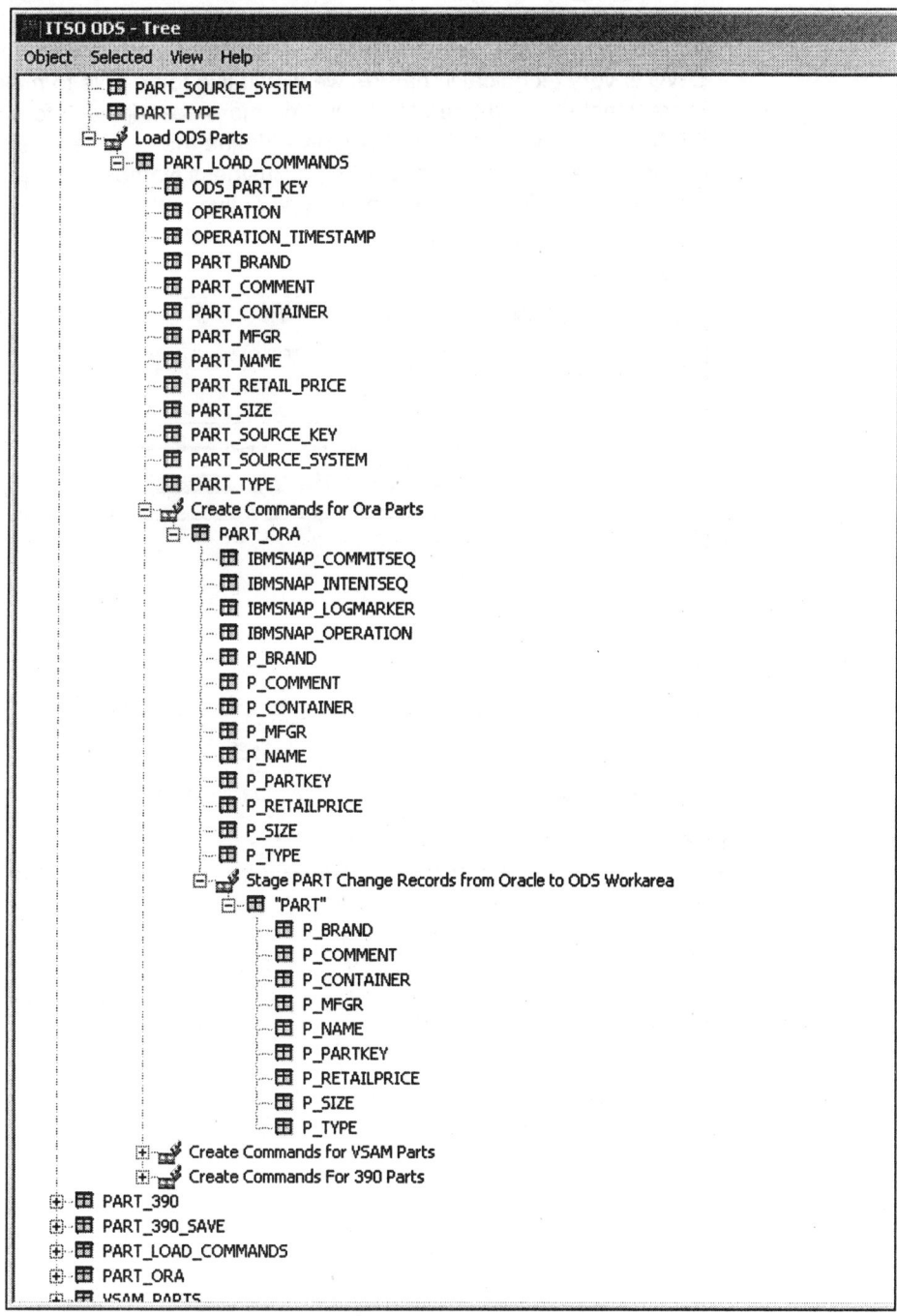

Figure 7-25 Tracing our ODS PART table back to its sources

Publishing ODS metadata to the Information Catalog

We provide ODS metadata to the Information Catalog by using the *Publish* function of the DWC (see Figure 7-26). As the metadata we publish from the DWC is very technical in nature, we would like to be able to make this metadata more usable by end-users, by providing more descriptive information about our ODS objects. We can do that when we define the metadata using the DWC dialogs. There are fields for providing Business Names to objects such as tables and columns. We can also provide descriptive text information and notes on the first page of object dialogs.

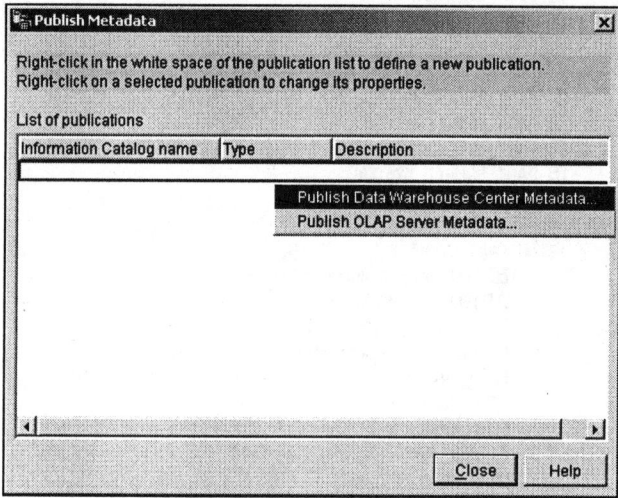

Figure 7-26 Starting the publish DWC metadata dialog

As we work with the publish metadata dialog, we can select the amount and level of metadata to publish (see Figure 7-27).

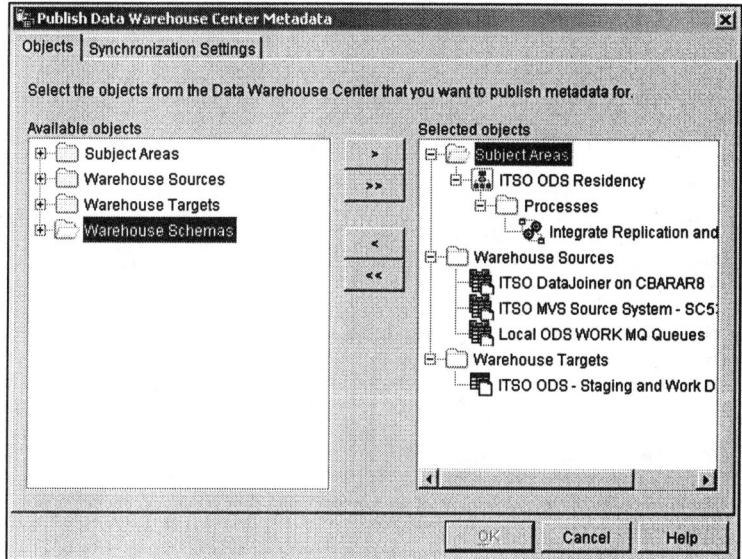

Figure 7-27   Selecting the processes, sources, and targets to publish

We can trace the metadata publishing process using a log as shown in Figure 7-28.

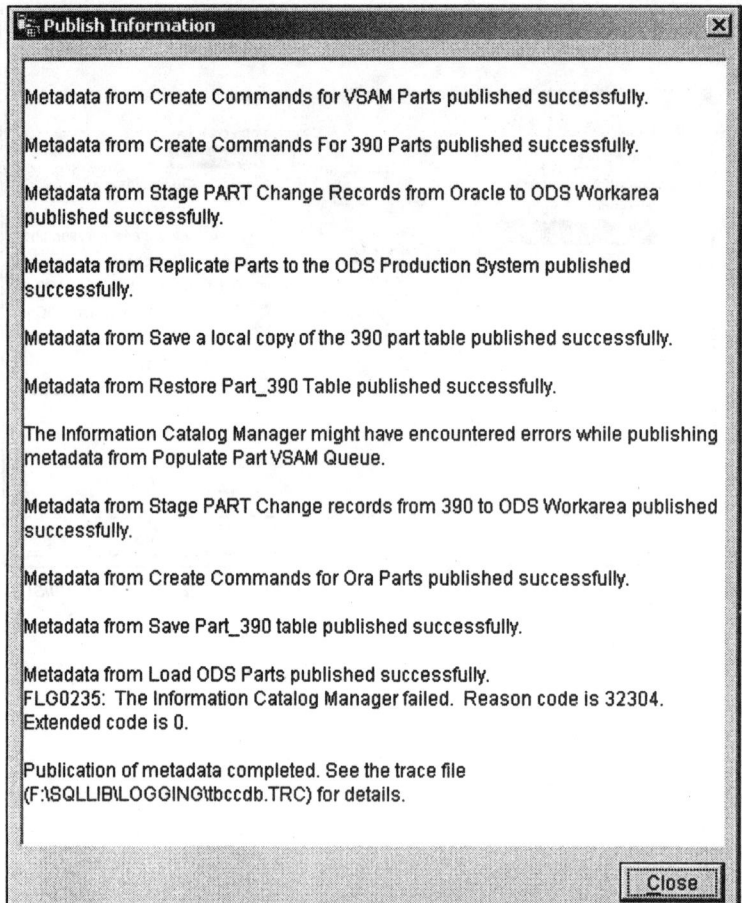

Figure 7-28   Publish metadata processing log

We definitely want to publish metadata about the target tables. But, we may choose not to publish all of the processes and source files. We do not want to overwhelm the end users with too much metadata that does not provide business value to them. We can schedule an automatic process to do it, as shown in Figure 7-29.

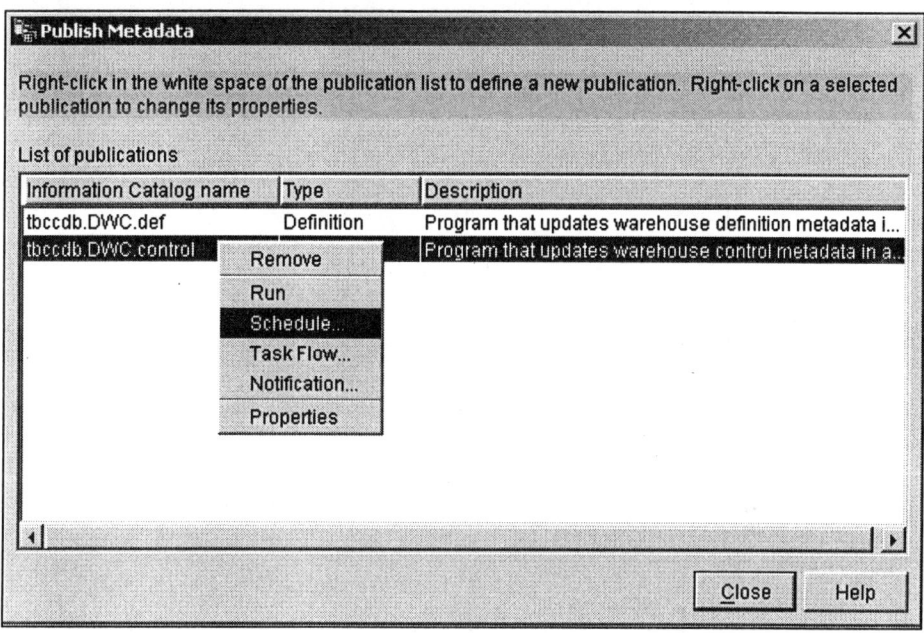

Figure 7-29 Scheduling future metadata updates to be published automatically

Now we have our ODS definitions published to the Information Catalog for end-users. Some of this metadata can change with new definitions and changes to current definitions. In addition, we also have dynamic metadata about the execution of steps that changes constantly in an active population subsystem. We may want to get these definition changes and the dynamic metadata published to the Information Catalog. You can see that we have two separate publishing definitions defined. One is for republishing definition metadata and one is for publishing the dynamic control metadata. These can be scheduled or integrated into a workflow independently.

7.5 Summary

In this chapter we have taken our ODS population subsystem from an idea, designed it using a structured architecture, developed our processes, and grouped them into workflows. We then applied a schedule to the processes and finally we put it all into production. We ended up by letting our users know about what is in our ODS by publishing metadata to a user accessible Information Catalog.

Critical success factors for the target ODS servers

A key component of an ODS solution is a reliable high performance relational database engine. This engine must handle high transaction rates, mixed workloads and large volumes of data. It must be scalable, manageable, and have a very high degree of availability. For additional flexibility, the database should integrate with a wide range of tools in the areas of data acquisition, database maintenance, application development and data access. Industry standards should be followed to leverage current and future skill requirements.

The choice of the target ODS server will also have to take into account many environment factors, including the organization's current skill set, the existing platforms, and the project's budget. The DB2 Universal Database (UDB) family of database engines provide a wide range of functionality and platform support.

In this chapter we discuss ODS issues related to the Relational Database Management System (RDBMS). First we look at the DB2 UDB family in general and how they resolve integrating multiple operational sources, ODS data transformations, and source system synchronization issues. We then discuss how the level of detail, near-current data delivery, mixing updates and queries, flexible growth path, uptime, performance tuning and monitoring, and initial loads are addressed by DB2 UDB Enterprise-Extended Edition (EEE) and DB2 UDB for z/OS.

8.1 DB2 UDB family

Many of the issues related to On-Line Transaction Processing (OLTP) systems have equivalent ODS issues. The DB2 UDB family offers all the advantages of standard relational database management systems. In this section we will relate these ODS issues to the features of an RDBMS by discussing the following points:

- Integrating multiple operational sources
    - Integrating DB2 UDB with data acquisition tools
    - Integrating DB2 UDB with the operational applications
    - Handling concurrency
    - Bundled units of work
- ODS data transformations
- Source synchronization
    - Consistency and integrity points
    - Conceptual units of work
    - Transactional units of work
    - Managing referential integrity
    - Type B ODS synchronization

8.1.1 Integrating multiple operational sources

Data integration is managed by the data acquisition layer of the ODS architecture in conjunction with the database data model. For performance, the process design and choice of tools for this layer must integrate particularly well with the database server. As discussed in 3.4.2, "Data acquisition" on page 61, there exists a plethora of solutions using of many different products. The DB2 UDB family of databases are positioned as middleware servers integrating with a wide range of IBM and third party tools and applications.

The ODS will have varying degrees of integration with the current operational applications depending on the type (A, B or C). For example, in a type C scenario the integration will be very tight since the business requirement requires a single version of the truth. Because of this integration and the operational nature of an ODS it will rapidly become a crucial element of the business process. The DB2 UDB family of industrial strength database products have been used to handle both mission critical OLTP and data warehouse applications.

The database must also integrate the transactions flowing from the data sources with the read and write transactions initiated by the ODS users. DB2 UDB uses RDBMS locking mechanisms to maintain the concurrency of these transactions. Concurrency can be determined by the lock granularity and isolation level. An

ODS will typically use row-level or page level locking versus table level locking (used more in a data warehousing environment). DB2 UDB supports the following isolation levels to give maximum flexibility when deciding the trade-offs between concurrency and integrity:

- Repeatable Read: All rows *referenced* within a unit of work are locked.
- Read Stability: All rows *retrieved* within a unit of work are locked.
- Cursor Stability: This locks the row while the cursor is positioned on that row. Lock is held until the next row is retrieved, or if the row is changed, the lock is held until the change is committed.
- Uncommitted Read: This allows access to uncommitted changes of other transactions.

Your choice of isolation level should be based on the ODS business requirements matched to the concurrency restrictions of each level. Most ODSs will choose cursor stability since it maintains integrity at the transaction level. The uncommitted read is best for decision support queries on read only tables (for example summary tables).

Your locking strategy should be designed in conjunction with the data acquisition process, the physical data model and the ODS data access applications. The design must minimize locking between the transactions coming from the data sources and the updates and queries from the users. Along with the lock granularity and isolation level, DB2 UDB has several configuration parameters like LOCKLIST or LOCKMAX which should also be used as part of the strategy.

Records flowing from the sources will typically be bundled together and applied to the ODS in small bursts. Locks may be held during the entire bundled unit of work or a subset. For example, replication configures the bundle through the subscription set timing and the blocking factor whereas Warehouse Center uses the frequency of the apply schedule.

Each bundle may be applied serially or multiple concurrent bundles may be applied to take advantage of parallel architectures. When designing the bundled records coming from the data sources you must match their size and frequency with the user access requirements. For example, if the user requires a two-second response time, then the size and frequency of the bundles will have to be less than two seconds.

Because an ODS will have records constantly flowing from the data sources it is highly unlikely that you will allow users to lock records for more than a brief period of time. These user transactions should be designed to be very small with minimal locking requirements so as not to affect the data flowing from the data sources.

Of course there will always be exceptions to these rules of thumb. For example, during the nightly operational batch run we may be able to guarantee that no records will flow from the data sources. This would allow us to change the lock granularity to table level and schedule our resource intensive reports.

Deadlocks are handled by an asynchronous process called the deadlock detector. This process monitors transactions waiting on locks and arbitrarily chooses a transaction to release its locks when a deadlock is encountered. Various configuration parameters control lock and deadlock characteristics.

8.1.2 ODS data transformations

Transformation business logic may be built into the database by using triggers, User Defined Functions (UDF), stored procedures and summarization/ aggregation functions (constructs like grouping sets and Automatic Summary Tables (ASTs). Many tools take advantage of these procedural database functions to execute their data transformations. Sections 4.1.2, "ODS data transformations" on page 98 and 5.3.3, "ODS data transformations" on page 172 discuss some of these tools and how their transformations are optimized to take advantage of the database.

> **Note:** Transformations may be performed outside the database, but you may have to write the transform logic or programs yourself. It is very difficult to write such programs which will efficiently make use of the parallel capabilities of large SMP or MPP machines — whereas, this is automatic if the data is first loaded in DB2 UDB EEE, and then transformed. The drawback of this approach is that you need a good SQL programmer to express the transformations in SQL and these are few and far between.

8.1.3 Source synchronization

As Figure 8-1 shows, an ODS contains three synchronization points depending on the type:

1. Data changes in the source systems must be consistently reflected in the ODS (all ODS types)
2. Data changes in the ODS must be consistently reflected back to the source systems (type B)
3. The referential and data integrity of the sources systems must be maintained in the ODS (all ODS types)

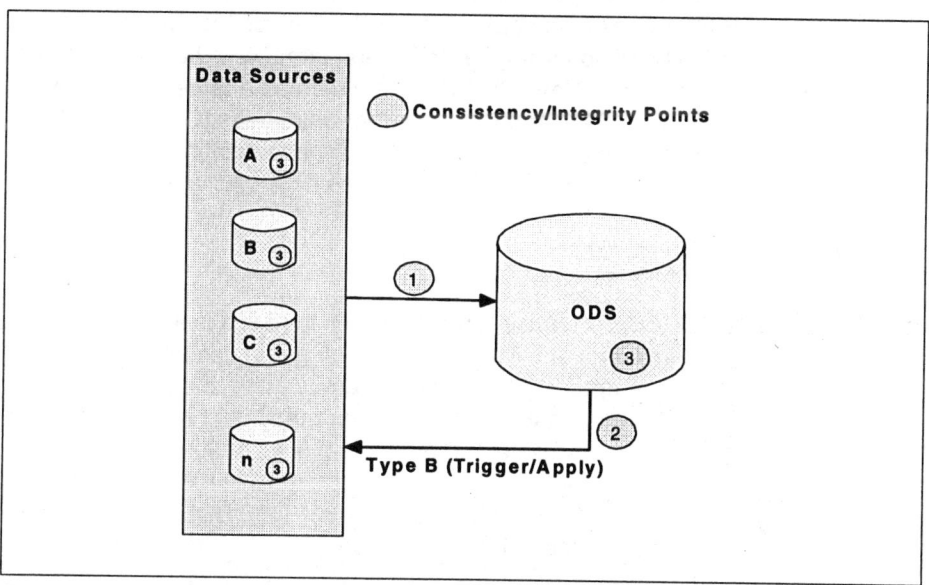

Figure 8-1   ODS synchronization points

The business requirements will guide the ODS rule definitions for the conceptual units of work. The components of a conceptual unit of work will arrive at the ODS at different times because the data is flowing from multiple disparate data sources. The database must be able to handle these missing components (pieces of information) as per the business requirements. Database triggers, UDFs, and exception tables call all be used for this type of processing.

All DB2 UDB databases implement the transactional concept of a unit of work with commit and rollback features. These native functions can be used for regular and distributed units of work by the data acquisition process or the trigger/apply mechanism for coordinated transaction processing. The data acquisition tool must also contain a coordinated commit and rollback function. For example, Replication and Warehouse Manager use the "COMMIT WORK" and "ROLLBACK WORK" RDBMS functions to maintain consistency between multiple sources and targets.

The data integrity within the ODS can be maintained using database referential integrity, column constraints and triggers. However, due to the performance requirements and high transaction volumes, the design of the data acquisition process may be used to guarantee the data integrity. In the same way, to aid the performance of the acquisition process we may partially rely on the integrity of the data sources.

Database triggers can be used to automate the synchronization between a type B ODS back to the data sources. SQL functions, UDFs and/or stored procedures could be used for any reverse transformations, both in the trigger and/or apply mechanisms. See 4.2, "Relational data as a target (ODS type B)" on page 121 and 5.4, "VSAM and IMS as target databases (ODS type B)" on page 174 for other examples of automating the synchronization for a type B ODS.

8.2 DB2 UDB EEE

DB2 UDB Enterprise-Extended Edition (EEE) is an ideal database server for an ODS environment. The shared-nothing architecture of DB2 UDB EEE allows for maximum upgradability over numerous platforms with near linear scalability. It has been the database of choice for many data warehouses and has been successfully implemented on many critical OLTP applications. Many of the ODS issues can be addressed by combining DB2 UDB EEE's OLTP capabilities with its partitioning attributes. We will relate DB2 UDB EEE to an ODS environment by discussing the following issues:

- Level of detail: How to handle detailed data, large volumes of data, and summary data.
- Near-current data delivery and mixing updates and queries: How to maintain high transaction throughputs while meeting data access response times
- Flexible scalability: How to manage incremental data and user growth
- Uptime: How to handle planned and unplanned outages
- Performance tuning and monitoring: How to monitor and maintain database performance

8.2.1 Level of detail

An ODS typically contains very detailed transaction data — thereby indicating the potential for huge volumes of data. At the same time, there may be limited business requirements for point-in-time data consistency (daily balance snapshots), summary information (call center statistics), and aggregate performance tuning (similar types of summary queries). DB2 UDB EEE can manage all these issues by using database partitioning and Automatic Summary Tables (AST).

Figure 8-2 compares DB2 UDB Enterprise Edition (EE), a single partition database, and DB2 UDB EEE, a multi-partition database. DB2 UDB EEE database partitioning refers to the ability to divide the database into separate distinct physical partitions. Database partitioning has the characteristic of storing large amounts of data at a very detailed level while keeping the database manageable. Database utilities also run faster by operating on individual partitions concurrently.

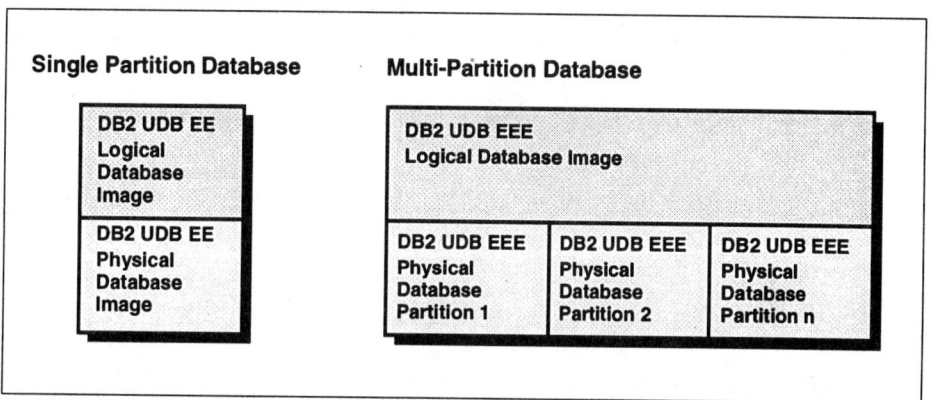

Figure 8-2 Single partition database compared to a multi-partition database

The physical database partitions can then be allocated across an MPP server, a single SMP server, or a cluster of SMP servers. Figure 8-3 shows examples of each of these configurations. The database still appears to the end-user as a single image database, however, the database administrator can take advantage of single image utilities and partitioned utilities where appropriate.

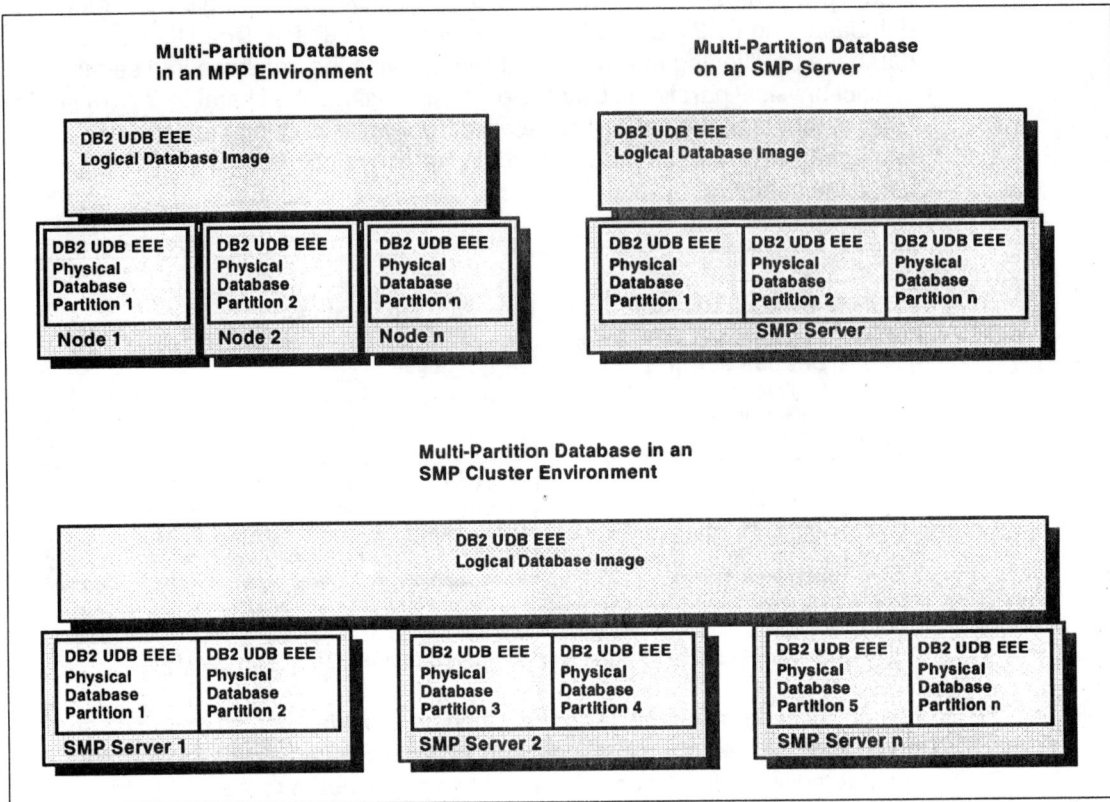

Figure 8-3 Sample MPP and SMP configurations

Typically an ODS will have limited summarization and aggregation requirements. As much as possible, this type of access should use the data warehouse. However, the ODS may be used when near real-time or special operational data is required.

An AST is built using summary criteria on one or more base tables. The summary criteria contains SQL column functions, table joins, predicates and a GROUP BY. After an AST is created, the user has no knowledge of whether their query is using the base tables or the AST. The DB2 optimizer decides whether the AST should be used based on the costing of the various data access paths.

An AST can be updated synchronously or asynchronously by using refresh immediate or refresh deferred. Using the database partitioning capability of DB2 UDB EEE, one or more ASTs can be placed on a separate partition to help manage the workload involved in creating and updating the AST.

These are some examples of using ASTs:

- **Point-in-time consistency**: Managers require a daily snapshot of their product balances for analysis. An AST is built to capture the data grouped by time, department and product. Deferred processing is used with a scheduled daily refresh. The managers then use this table when doing their analysis with the understanding that it does not contain current data.

- **Summary data**: Call center managers would like to analyze their call resolution statistics throughout the day. An AST is built to capture statistics by customer representative and resolution code. Immediate processing is used hence the AST is updated synchronously when the base table changes.

- **Aggregate performance tuning:** The DBA notices that hundreds of queries are run each day asking for the number of customers in a particular department. An AST is built grouping by customer and department. DB2 will now use the AST whenever this type of query is run.

8.2.2 Near-current data delivery and mixing updates and queries

The ODS must handle large transaction throughputs (the number of transactions processed during a specific time period) while maintaining an acceptable response time for the data access applications and user groups. Using DB2 UDB EEE's shared-nothing parallel architecture we can design a physical database environment which will handle both types of ODS access requirements. In this section we expand on the concept of database partitioning. We describe how collocation, replicated tables, local bypass and transaction managers can be used to design a database for maximum transaction throughput while managing a mixed workload. In addition, we discuss the issues surrounding complex transactions and decision support queries.

The majority of transactions coming from the data sources and the data access layers should be designed to be short and simple. The transaction design along with the query requirements must be used to help construct an appropriate database partitioning scheme. The goal is to create a design where the majority of transactions are executed on a single database partition. Your partitioning scheme should avoid the situation where data is shipped from one database partition to another.

Figure 8-4 demonstrates how a table is partitioned across multiple DB2 UDB EEE nodes. First, a nodegroup is created with a specific set of partitions, it does not have to include every partition in the database. One or more tablespaces are then assigned to the nodegroup. Database objects created in this tablespace are then distributed across the partitions included in the nodegroup. When a table is created, one or more columns are assigned as the partitioning key. In our example the "ID" is the partitioning key.

When a nodegroup is created, it is assigned a partitioning map containing 4096 hash buckets (also known as vector positions). This map may be modified by a DBA to take into account intentional or unintentional data skew. A table row's partitioning key value is then hashed to one of the vector positions in the partitioning map. Finally the partition number of the vector is used to place the data on a database partition. Using this scheme, the database engine can manage large amounts of data while maintaining high transaction throughputs.

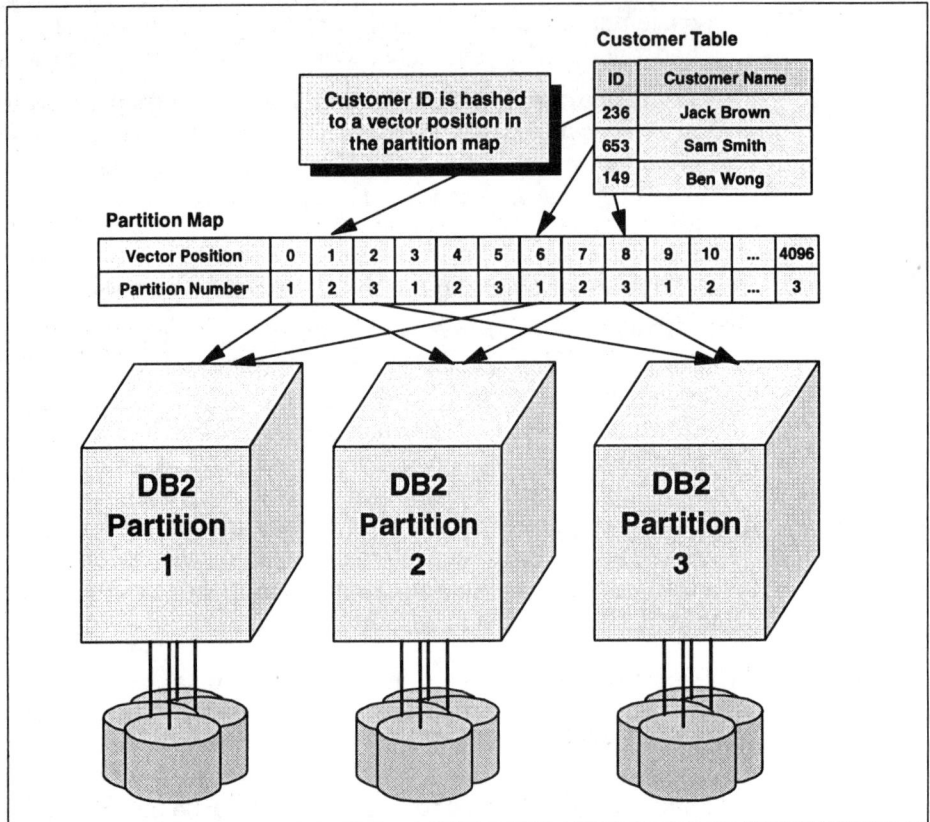

Figure 8-4   DB2 UDB EEE table partitioning

One of the keys to high transaction throughputs is collocation. This technique eliminates the overhead of copying data from one partition to another. Collocation is achieved when a join or subquery contains an equality predicate on the partitioning key columns. The data accessed for each table in the join or subquery is then local to each partition. There are three rules for collocation:

1. Tables must be in the same nodegroup
2. They must have the same number of partition key columns
3. The data types for each pair of columns must be compatible

If these rules are met, then the rows from the different join tables are guaranteed to be placed on the same partition.

> **Note:** Do not confuse replicated tables with replication or data propagation. Replicated tables are database objects implemented through ASTs.

Replicated tables can also be used to help maintain collocation between tables. You should consider replicated tables for situations where a table can not be partitioned on the same columns as the other tables. A replicated table is copied in its entirety to all database partitions in the nodegroup. This implies that they should be of modest size and typically read-only. When a replicated table is updated the data must be copied to all the other partitions in the nodegroup — incurring the associated overhead.

Local bypass extends the characteristics of collocation to OLTP environments by limiting data access to a single partition. In addition to the three collocation rules an equality predicate using the partitioning key must be added to the transaction (for example, WHERE ... AND ID = 51785). The predicate guarantees that the rows required to satisfy the request are on one and only one partition.

To describe more complex collocation scenarios we first define the concept of the coordinator node. The database partition to which the transaction has a physical connection is known as the coordinator node. The coordinator node sends the database request to all required partitions and collects and integrates any results. If required the coordinator will assign subagents to work on the request.

There are three different scenarios for accessing data in a partitioned environment:

- Local bypass
- Non-local
- Non-collocated

Where local bypass has the best performance and non-collocated has the worst performance. Figure 8-5 demonstrates the three scenarios and the overhead involved with each. Local bypass is the best as the coordinator node also contains the data required to fulfill the request. In this scenario, no other database partition is accessed — all access is local. For non-local, the data still resides on a single database partition but its not on the coordinator node. This requires the final result to be shipped to the coordinator node incurring communication overhead. The third type is non-collocated, the data to fulfill the request resides on two or more partitions incurring the communication and integration overhead.

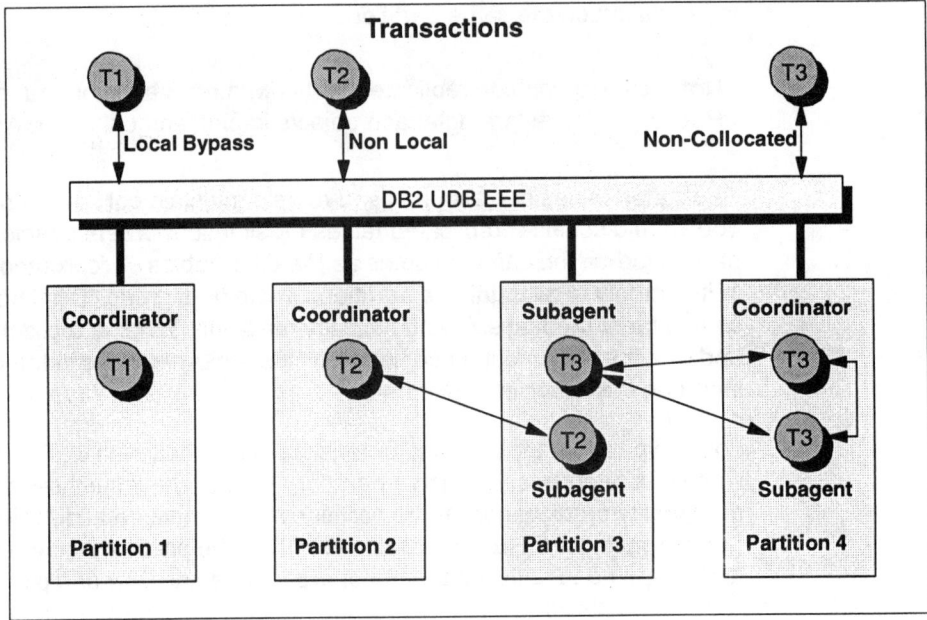

Figure 8-5 Three types of collocation

DB2 UDB EEE contains two APIs which can be used by a transaction manager (or a middle tier application) to implement local bypass at the coordinator level. This is accomplished by obtaining partition map information and routing the application to the partition containing the required rows. The GET_TABLE_PARTITION function obtains the partitioning map by accessing the database, however, it only has to be executed once for each nodegroup. The second function, GET_ROW_PARTITION uses the partition map and a partition key value to obtain the database partition number. This function is called for every transaction and does not require access to the database. Now the application can connect to the database partition containing the data and execute the transaction.

For more complex transactions where collocation and local bypass may not be an option, DB2 UDB EEE takes advantage of other techniques:

▶ Minimizes network traffic through message passing
▶ Function shipping (for example, a query which uses the SUM column function may execute partial sums on each database partition in parallel instead of serially at the coordinator node)

- When data is not located on the required partition, data is shipped to other partitions using one of the following two methods:
  - Directed data access (the coordinator identifies a target partition where only the required data is sent directly)
  - Broadcast data access (data is sent to all partitions dynamically — like replicated tables)

To manage a more complex mixture of long and short transactions, use the DB2 Governor and DB2 Query Patroller. Please refer to "Performance tuning and monitoring" on page 252 for a more detailed discussion of these two tools. The DB2 Governor can be used to monitor resource usage and change application priorities based. DB2 Query Patroller acts as an agent for the end user, prioritizing and scheduling queries in a predictable and more resource efficient manner.

The potential for decision support requirements challenges us to also look at complex long running queries. For these queries we should design the database partitioning structure to maximize query parallelism using the rules defined for collocation. DB2 UDB EEE can manage a mixture of small transactions and massive decision support queries by using local bypass and large scale collocation — the key is to know your query requirements.

8.2.3 Flexible growth path

The ODS must be able to support current workloads while at the same time allow for future data growth and larger user populations. Ideally the ODS should be able to scale without having to migrate to a different platform or architecture. This section describes how DB2 UDB EEE's shared-nothing architecture is especially scalable through the implementation of the following types of parallelism:

- Intra-query parallelism
- I/O parallelism
- Utility parallelism

We then show how these three types of parallelism can be combined with various hardware architectures to produce a highly scalable and flexible database design.

> **Note:** Intra-query parallelism also applies to the updates from the data sources or the data access applications (for example, INSERT, DELETE, and UPDATE).

Intra-query parallelism

DB2 UDB EEE operations scale extremely well when additional database partitions are added because the database engine is designed to take advantage of all dimensions of parallelism. The following section describes how the different forms of parallelism use one or more database partitions. We discuss the various types of query/partition parallelism, and how they take advantage of multiple database partitions.

Intra-query parallelism refers to processing parts of a query at the same time by subdividing a single database operation into multiple tasks and executing them asynchronously and concurrently. Intra-query parallelism uses two types of partition parallelism:

- Intra-partition parallelism
- Inter-partition parallelism

Intra-partition parallelism refers to taking an individual task (for example, (SELECT ... FROM ...) and generate multiple tasks operating on different pieces of the data. These tasks are allocated across multiple CPUs in an SMP server. All types of database operations exploit inter-partition and intra-partition parallelism, for example, SELECT, INSERT, UPDATE, and DELETE. This type of parallelism increases the performance of a task within a single partition.
Figure 8-6 shows a task the is broken down into three sub-tasks, each working on a piece of the overall data required for the task.

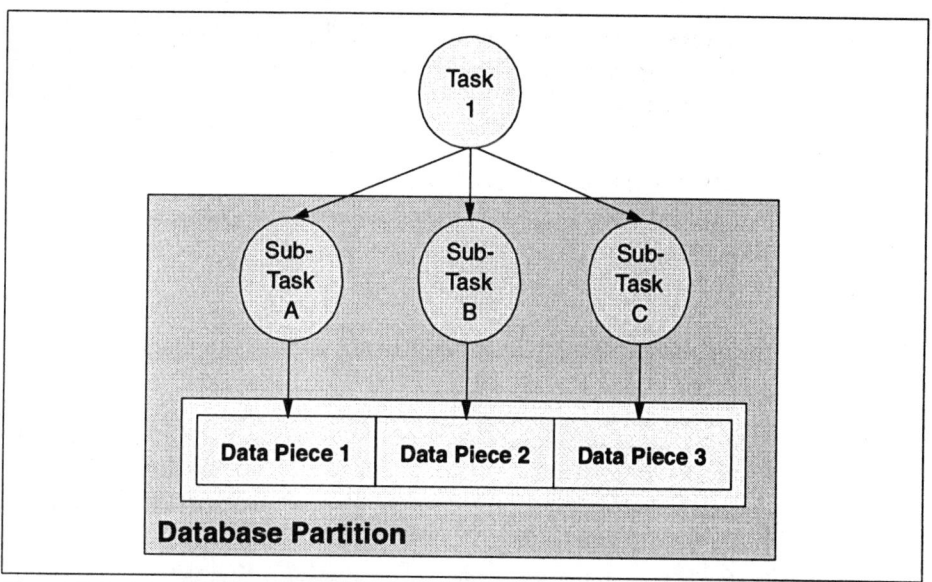

Figure 8-6   Intra-partition parallelism

Inter-partition parallelism refers to the ability to break up a task into multiple parts and allocate the sub-tasks across multiple partitions of a partitioned database. Identical sub-tasks are performed in parallel across all required partitions. Figure 8-7 shows a task that is broken into three sub-tasks, each of which are executing on a different database partition.

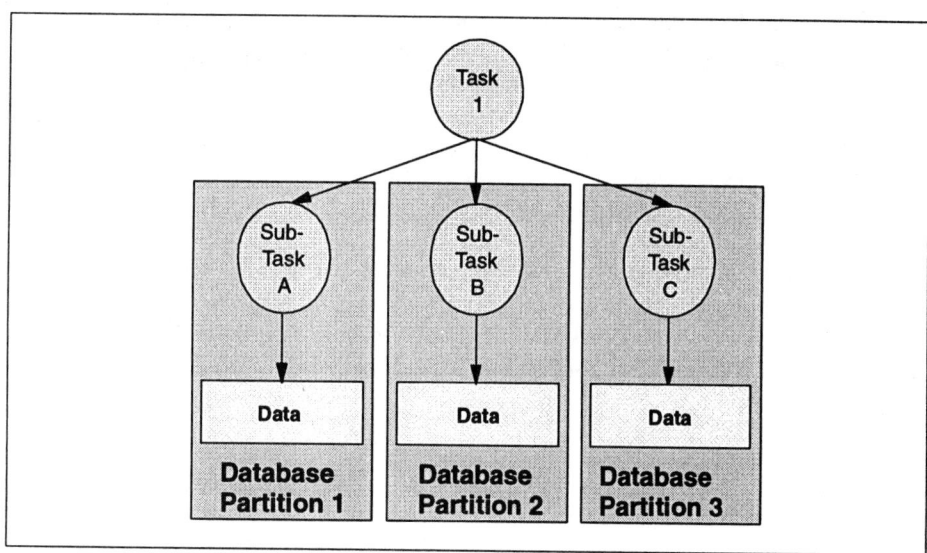

Figure 8-7   Inter-partition parallelism

As shown in Figure 8-8, both types of parallelism can be used in combination to dramatically increasing the speed at which database tasks are processed. This combination of parallelism will take advantage of SMP and MPP hardware architectures simultaneously. The section, "Hardware scalability" on page 245, describes in more detail how DB2 UDB EEE can benefit from these architectures.

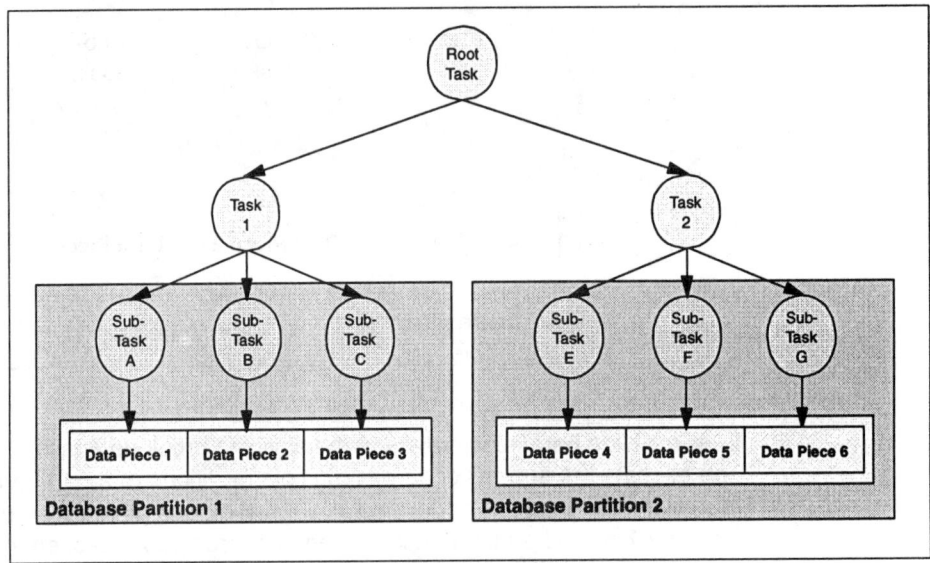

Figure 8-8 Combining inter-partition and intra-partition parallelism

Inter-partition and Intra-partition parallelism will also scale on large SMP boxes by creating multiple logical partitions on the same physical server. Logical database partitions have the identical properties and characteristics of physical database partitions — except two or more logical partitions may be placed on one physical server. By using DB2 UDB EEE's shared-nothing architecture, all the resources of the SMP hardware will have maximum usage while keeping the database granular for manageability.

Coordinating all the tasks and sub-tasks is the job of the coordinator agent running on the coordinator partition. All parallel sub-tasks (or subagents) are run asynchronously, limiting the coordinator agent to the work of initializing subagent tasks and collecting the final results.

I/O parallelism

DB2 UDB uses the concept of a container for the storage of data and indexes in a tablespace. A container is the logical equivalent of a storage device, however, one container may span multiple physical disks and one physical disk may store multiple containers. By assigning multiple containers to a tablespace the database benefits from I/O parallelism by processing several reads and writes from multiple I/O devices simultaneously. This significantly increases the transaction throughput within a database partition. DB2 UDB EEE adds the additional benefit of having multiple transactions use multiple database partitions for I/O parallelism across nodes.

Utility parallelism

Another type of parallelism is utility parallelism. DB2 UDB EEE utilities take advantage of both types of partition parallelism (inter and intra). For example:

- The backup and restore utilities not only backup each data partition in parallel, but also exploit intra-partition parallelism, I/O parallelism and writing to multiple backup media in parallel.
- The data redistribution utility moves data between database partitions when a new partition is added to the database or when the partitioning map changes — for example, the data is not uniform and you want to eliminate any data skew. The redistribution is executed online concurrently with database updates.
- The CREATE INDEX statement scans and sorts the data in parallel across all involved database partitions, exploiting intra-partition and I/O parallelism. DB2 UDB supports unique and non unique indexes.
- The table reorganization utility (REORG) executes in parallel across the all database partitions of the nodegroup for the specified table. REORG also exploits I/O parallelism when the tablespace is spread across multiple containers.

Hardware scalability

DB2 UDB EEE can scale in small increments along all dimensions of a clustered system to service more users and mange increases in data volumes. Some examples:

- Add more CPUs to a current node to service more users
- Add more memory to a current node to reduce I/O
- Add more disks to a current node to reduce I/O
- Add more nodes, which increases CPU, memory and disk

In this section we discuss the concepts of SMP parallelism, simultaneous SMP and MPP parallelism and logical database partitioning on large SMP systems.

Figure 8-9 is an example of SMP parallelism using DB2 UDB Enterprise Edition (EE). By taking advantage of inter-query parallelism, intra-partition parallelism and I/O parallelism, DB2 UDB EE will make maximum usage of the multiple CPUs and physical storage devices.

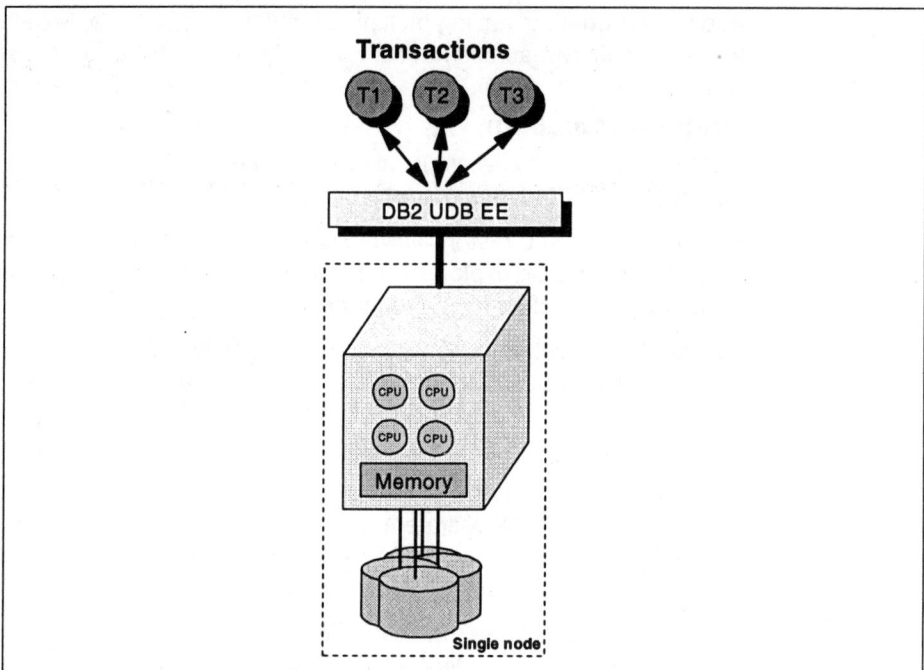

Figure 8-9 SMP scalability with DB2 UDB EE

DB2 UDB EEE extends the functionality of DB2 UDB EE by adding support for multiple database partitions. As shown in Figure 8-10 this added capability allows DB2 UDB EEE to scale across all dimensions, CPU, memory, storage, network and nodes. For example, add storage devices to increase I/O parallelism, add CPUs to increase intra-partition parallelism, add more nodes for inter-partition parallelism.

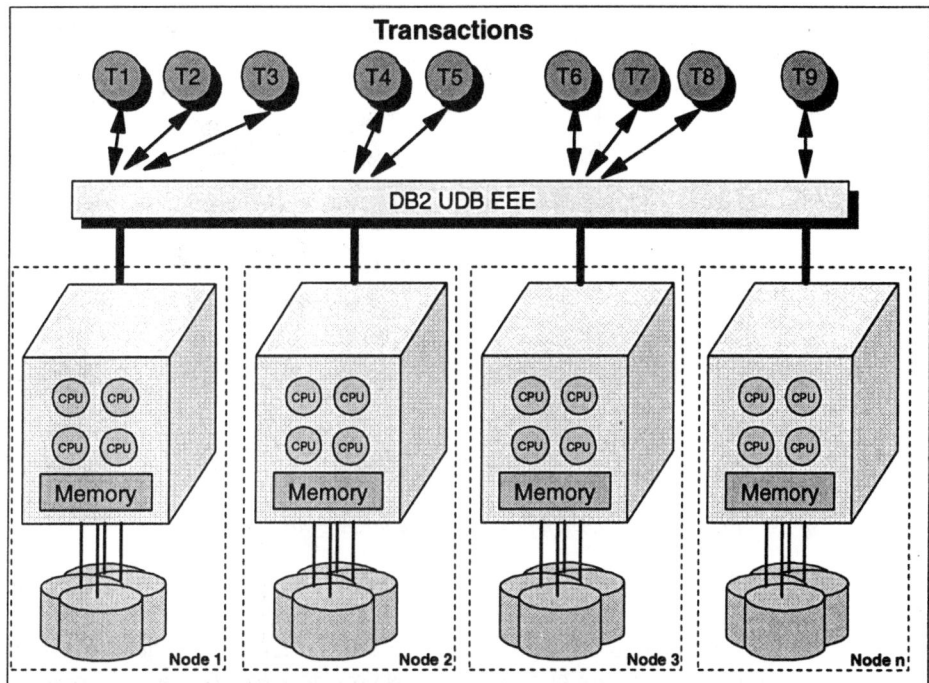

Figure 8-10 SMP and MPP scalability with DB2 UDB EEE

DB2 UDB EEE's shared-nothing architecture is excellent for shared-everything hardware. DB2 UDB EEE may be installed on a large SMP box (as shown in Figure 8-11) or a cluster of large SMP boxes and partitioned into multiple logical database partitions. In the shared-everything environment of an SMP machine, a shared-nothing database implementation is more scalable (as you add more CPUs and disks) than a shared-everything database implementation. Because each database partition is completely independent of the other partitions there is no contention or bottleneck for shared resources such as memory or disk. Another item to note is that when data must be shared across logical partitions DB2 UDB EEE uses shared memory which is very fast.

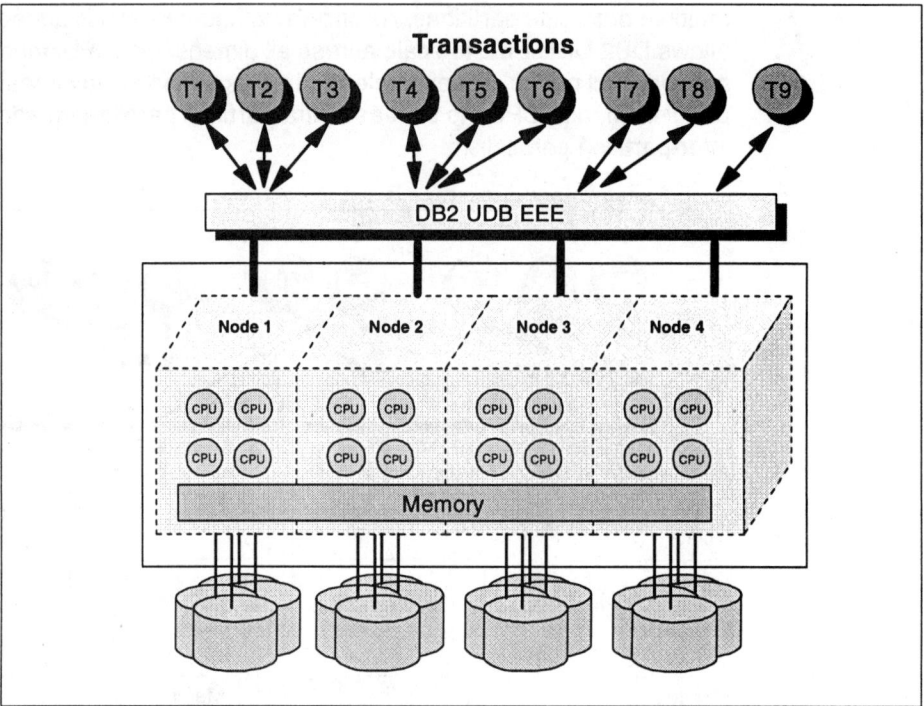

Figure 8-11   DB2 UDB EEE on a large SMP box

By combining the different hardware architectures with DB2 UDB EEE you can design a database which is very scalable, has granular database administration, and will exploit large memory models. Incremental growth can be achieved by adding additional database partitions to the database, changing the partition map to include the new partition and then redistributing the data using standard DB2 UDB EEE utilities. You can start on a single SMP box and migrate to a cluster using standard interconnect protocols such as TCP/IP.

8.2.4 Uptime

Because the ODS will be running the day-to-day operations of the organization, the availability requirements will be very high. The maintenance and batch windows will be extremely small and any unplanned outages will have to be diagnosed and fixed immediately. In this section we discuss the two types of outages, planned and unplanned, and how the features of DB2 UDB EEE can be exploited to keep these outages to a minimum.

Planned outages

For planned outages like batch processing and database maintenance, the goals are to minimize the time of the outage or, if possible, stay online during the process. If the ODS is online during the process, then performance degradation will have to be considered. DB2 UDB EEE uses the following features to address these issues:

- The different types of parallelism
- Granular maintenance utilities
- Parallel backup and restore utilities

By taking advantage of the different types of parallelism (query, I/O, and utility), you can minimize your batch windows. For example, if there is a monthly or daily batch load from the data warehouse to the ODS, you can use autoloader to leverage multiple partitions, CPUs and storage devices. If the data warehouse uses DB2 UDB EEE you have the potential to export and process the data in parallel as well. For the best performance, your batch process must be designed to take advantage of multiple database partitions and scale along with the database.

DB2 UDB utilities, like CREATE INDEX, RUNSTATS and CREATE TABLESPACE all run in parallel at the partition level. If your maintenance window is squeezed, the more partitions you have, the less data per partition, the faster the utilities.

DB2 UDB EEE's backup and restore utilities have the ability to backup and restore multiple database partitions in parallel while at the same time accessing multiple I/O devices in parallel. DB2 UDB EEE also has the facility for delta and cumulative incremental backups. They not only minimize the downtime for a backup but also take advantage of the existing, fully parallel, backup and restore infrastructure. DB2 UDB EEE also has the option for online database or tablespace level backups. Backing up and restoring multiple tablespaces in parallel will exploit the CPU parallelism of SMP boxes.

Unplanned outages

In this section we discuss how to minimize unplanned outages by protecting your data. We describe the different Redundant Array of Inexpensive Disks (RAID) configurations and what the different trade-offs are in the context of an ODS. DB2 UDB EEE contains special parameters which can take advantage of a RAID configuration. We also discuss how DB2 UDB EEE implements a fast roll forward recovery. Finally, we discuss the use of high availability software which can take advantage of the clustering/partitioning aspects of DB2 UDB EEE.

To minimize restores you should protect your data at the source. The three major components of the database are, the database control files, the catalog, the logs, and data (including indexes and other database objects). If your temporary table space is being used regularly, then you may also want to consider protecting it. Make sure none of these components become a single point of failure by following basic data protection rules:

- Keep dual logs
- Put logs and data on separate physical devices
- Perform regular backups — keep logs small
- Balance performance and checkpoint frequency
- Keep backups in a safe place
- Move archived logs to a safe place

To guard against data corruption and to minimize database restores, some form of redundancy should be built into the system. Redundant Array of Inexpensive Disks (RAID) is one of the more popular ways to insure the availability of your data. There are several different ways to configure a RAID system:

- No RAID: Best for performance as DBAs can use DB2 UDB's I/O parallelism capabilities (for example, number of containers, extent size, prefetch size, placement of data) to out perform any of the RAID levels. However, it is not good for availability as there is no redundancy at all.

- RAID level 0: Parallel data striping, controller breaks data into blocks and writes them in parallel. Performs the best from a RAID point of view, but there is again no built in redundancy.

- RAID level 1: Also known as disk mirroring, duplicates a copy of each data block on a separate disk. If a disk fails, then the mirrored disk may continue servicing requests until the failed disk is replaced. Use RAID level 1 (disk mirroring) where performance and high availability is a high priority and cost is a low priority (since twice the disk capacity is required). Reads and writes are almost as good as single non-RAID disk. Because of their importance we recommend the database logs, the catalog, and the database control files use some form of mirroring to handle disk failures.

- RAID level 0+1: Combines the strengths of RAID 0 and RAID 1, it uses I/O parallelism from RAID 0 plus the redundancy of RAID 1. Or put another way, RAID-0+1 mirrors a RAID-0 array. This combination is better than RAID-1 for the important database files in a large OLTP environment like an ODS. With heavy logging requirements and because the logs are striped across several disks, they can be written to faster than single disks — allowing greater transaction throughput.

- RAID level 2, 3 and 4: All use redundancy and striping but are rarely used by databases.

- RAID level 5: Data is striped across all but one disk in the array. A parity is then written to the last disk. With each stripe, the parity disks is rotated using a round-robin scheme. This ensures the data and parity are evenly distributed across all disks. When one disk in the array fails, the information can be re-created using the data and parity information from the remaining disks. For example, in a 4-1 configuration (five disks total) the parity information is spread across all five disks so that if one disk is damaged the data can be re-built from the other 4. Writes are significantly slower due to the computation and writing of the parity data while reads perform relatively good. Space overhead depends on the size of the array. In our example the overhead is 20%, 1 disk divided by 5. Note, the larger the array, the lower the disk overhead, but the higher the write overhead because of the longer parity maintenance.

  The RAID-5 configuration is better for read only databases such as a decision support data warehouse. In an ODS environment which contains numerous writes, you will have to weigh the cost of the disk overhead of RAID-1 or RAID-0+1 with your performance requirements. Your best performance with maximum redundancy is RAID 0 or RAID-0+1, however if cost is a factor, then choosing an optimal RAID-5 array size may be best.

DB2 UDB EEE contains special configuration tuning parameters so that the database engine knows that it is dealing with a RAID device and can act accordingly. First, to improve I/O efficiency, your tablespace extent and prefetch settings should match the RAID stripe size. Then the following two registry variables can be set:

- DB2_PARALLEL_IO: Allows DB2 to issues multiple I/O requests for a single container. Normally a RAID array looks like one container to DB2, this variable allows DB2 to issue an appropriate number of I/O requests using the
- DB2_STRIPED_CONTAINERS: Aligns the tablespace data to the stripe boundary of the RAID array. Without this alignment, DB2 may have to initiate two I/Os to read a page of data.

For a more detailed discussion of these parameters, refer to *IBM DB2 Universal Database Administration Guide: Planning Version 7,* SC09-2946-00.

After an unplanned outage, DB2 UDB EEE will restore each node in parallel (after the catalog node — which should be on a separate database partition). The restore time is then bounded by the recovery time of a single partition which is dependant on the distribution of data. Intra-partition parallelism within a single object is also supported.

After the database is restored, a roll forward recovery is executed. DB2 UDB EEE has implemented a fast parallel roll forward recovery using several techniques. To exploit all CPUs in an SMP environment many recovery processes have been parallelized, for example, parallel prefetching, asynchronous page cleaners and parallel agents. The SOFTMAX database configuration parameter can also be used to increase the number of checkpoints and consequently decrease the amount of time required for recovery. However, you must balance the ODS recovery time requirements with the ODS data delivery requirements since increasing the SOFTMAX also increases the logging overhead. DB2 UDB EEE also triggers additional checkpoints during long transactions.

Clustered nodes can be used to provide automated high availability. Disk devices can be connected to multiple servers, however they are owned by only one server at a time. When it is detected that a server has gone down, the partner server takes over the damaged node and the application is restarted. Clients lose their current connection, but can reestablish a connection after the failover. Note that there will be a degradation in performance after the failover. There are various clustering scenarios such as idle standby, mutual takeover and active standby. High Availability software such as High-Availability Cluster Multi-Processing (HACMP), Microsoft Cluster Services, MC/Service Guard or Sun Enterprise Cluster High Availability software can all be used to automate the failover. Refer to redbook *Managing VLDB Using DB2 UDB EEE, SG24-5105-00* for a discussion on using high availability software with DB2 UDB EEE.

8.2.5 Performance tuning and monitoring

DB2 UDB EEE's parallel technology is a key factor for implementing a high performance ODS. However, there are many other aspects of DB2 UDB which can be used to monitor and maintain the performance of an ODS. This section highlights some of the add-on tools and built in performance features. For a more in depth look at tuning and managing DB2 UDB EEE, refer to the redbooks, *DB2 UDB V7.1 Performance Tuning Guide,* SG24-6012-00 in conjunction with *Managing VLDB Using DB2 UDB EEE,* SG24-5105-00.

Much of the performance tuning for an ODS will take place during the design and initial development phases of the project. The most important consideration for DB2 UDB EEE is the design of the partitioning scheme. The goal is to maximize collocation and local bypass. The majority of transactions applied against the ODS should be designed to be short and simple in the context of the partitioning scheme and database design. More complex transactions will require more advanced techniques such denormalization and replicated tables.

As with the data warehouse but to a lesser extent, the ODS will contain some access which will require an ongoing monitoring and maintenance strategy. The usage of the ODS may change over time. This requires a proactive strategy to understand how the data is being accessed and to change the database structures, if required, to meet these new requirements. The rest of this chapter describes the various DB2 UDB tools and features which can be used as part of your overall performance tuning strategy:

- The database system monitor
- DB2 Governor
- DB2 Query Patroller
- AIX 5L Workload Manager
- Various built-in performance features

The DB2 system monitor gathers data about the operation and performance of the database and the transactions using it. This data contains valuable information which can be used for activity monitoring, troubleshooting, and performance tuning. There is some overhead when tracking this data, however, monitor switches are available to control the categories of information collected. The information gathered by the system monitor is accessed using either snapshots (information for a specific point in time) or event monitors (automatically logs monitor data when specific events occur). A snapshot takes a picture of the current state of the database manager for a specific object, group of objects, or transactions. Event monitors allow you to track transient events that are difficult to monitor using snapshots, such as deadlocks and transaction completion.

The DB2 Governor (available with DB2 UDB EEE) can be used to monitor and change the behavior of transactions running against the database. A governor daemon can be started on all partitions or specific partitions (for example, a coordinator node) of a partitioned database. The governor daemon collects statistics about the transactions and applications running against the database and checks them against rules specified in a governor configuration file. The governor can track resource usage such as, CPU, number of locks held, number of rows returned, time per unit of work (UOW), and idle time. The governor then acts based on these rules. For example, based on resource usage, the governor could lower an applications priority, change its schedule, or force it off the database to make sure transactions from the data sources are applied on time. A log is used to keep track of all changes made by the governor.

DB2 Query Patroller (available in the DB2 Warehouse Manager as a separate product) improves the performance of the ODS by managing both queries and hardware resources. The ODS application queries and the tactical decision support queries fall into this category. DB2 Query Patroller controls and monitors query execution while exploiting the capabilities of various hardware architectures like SMP and MPP.

Queries are trapped, their costs are assessed and then their execution is prioritized. Priorities can be set for individual users and users classes as well as setting query limits. DB2 Query Patroller provides load leveling across MPP systems by tracking node usage and routing queries to idle nodes, effectively spreading the query load across the system.

The AIX 5L Workload Manager controls the resource consumption when there is contention from competing concurrent processes. It allows the system administrator to place priorities and limits on CPU, memory, and I/O bandwidth. For example, when the ODS is on an SMP box shared by other applications or databases, Workload Manager can be used to make sure the ODS has the top priority. This allows the ODS to have all the resources it needs to maintain the required level of performance. For a more in depth look at the workload balancing possibilities and configurations, see *AIX 5L Workload Manager (WLM)*, SG24-5977-01.

DB2 UDB also has the following built-in performance features which can be used as part of your ODS performance maintenance strategy:

- DB2 UDB provides a variety of indexing technologies for use in performance tuning. For example, clustered indexes, index-only access, index includes, dynamic bitmap indexing (which is handled automatically by the optimizer), on-line index reorgs, and bi-directional indexes.

- DB2 UDB's cost based optimizer chooses the most efficient access path. The advanced algorithms take into account all aspects of the environment, for example, the number and speed of the CPUs, the I/O bandwidth, the distribution of the data values, triggers which will be fired, and all the available types of parallelism. The optimizer also uses the information from distributed environments when assessing a distributed query.

- The DB2 UDB EEE SQL compiler includes a query rewrite phase which transforms the query into a less costly logical equivalent. This can be extremely useful for complex queries such as those generated from ODS query tools. Rewriting the query allows DB2 UDB EEE to maximize performance regardless of the query's structure. The query rewrite phase uses techniques like, operation merging, operation movement, and predicate translation. For more information on the query rewrite phase and the SQL compiler refer to the *DB2 UDB Administration Guide: Performance*, SC09-2945.

- The visual explain facility provides a graphical display of the access path chosen by the optimizer. The graphical display contains a very detailed, tree structure which breaks down the access path into all of its many sub-components. Each node of the tree has a drill down capability to display more and more detailed information.

- The index wizard can be used to suggest indexes. When given a query or a set of queries, the wizard uses the optimizer to calculate an optimum configuration of one or more indexes to maximize the performance.
- Asynchronous page cleaners enable DB2 UDB to write modified data in memory back to disk asynchronously and in parallel with other database operations.
- Sequential prefetch and index prefetch allows the DB2 UDB optimizer to choose, where appropriate, to retrieve more data than is required. The decision is based on the probability that the data will be required in the near future. This results in the retrieval of large block I/O while other data is already being processed.
- Star-join techniques for decision support queries. DB2 will recognize a star schema and execute an appropriate join strategy using a combination of hash joins and dynamic bitmap indexes.

8.2.6 Initial load

DB2 UDB EEE includes an utility called DB2 autoloader for fast parallel data loading. The high performance DB2 autoloader bypasses the SQL engine and formats and loads data pages directly to disk. Autoloader can load data from files, pipes or devices (such as tape). Using pipes or devices avoids having to stage any data before it is loaded, for example, loading directly from the z/OS operational system. Autoloader can operate in two load modes, load insert, which appends data to the end of a table, and load replace, which truncates the table before it is loaded. There are also two different indexing modes, rebuild, which rebuilds all indexes from scratch and incremental, which extends the current indexes with the new data.

8.3 DB2 UDB for z/OS

DB2 UDB for z/OS (DB2) runs as a subsystem in several different address spaces along with CICS, IMS, or TSO address spaces. DB2 works with other z/OS subsystems in the enterprise server with new technologies, such as, the parallel sysplex cluster that provides the availability 24 hours a day, 7 days a week which is mandatory to a production ODS environment. ODS applications in z/OS can share DB2 resources with other subsystems or batch environments, or remote databases on other operating systems through DB2's Distributed Data Facility (DDF).

There are many factors that the ODS implementation can be benefited to utilize DB2 as the target ODS platform with the fact that many companies maintain a huge and constantly growing operational databases and data warehouses in z/OS platform that can be shared locally among other subsystems. We will relate DB2 UDB for z/OS to an ODS environment by discussing the following issues:

- Level of detail: How to handle detailed data, large volumes of data, and summary data.
- Near-current data delivery and mixing updates and queries: How to maintain high transaction throughputs while meeting data access response times.
- Flexible scalability: How to manage incremental data and user growth
- Uptime: How to handle planned and unplanned outages
- Performance tuning and monitoring: How to monitor and maintain database performance

8.3.1 Level of detail

A typical ODS may contain very detail data from the operational transactions, therefore the volumes of ODS tables could be huge. We need to be able to manage huge tables in small pieces to support ODS applications without affecting the entire table while some required operations are in progress, such as, maintenance, recovery, or batch loading.

By utilizing the table partitions, you can efficiently support a very large ODS table with a fine grain. For example, you do not have to reorganize the whole partitioned table if only one or few partitions need to be reorganized. It may take 5 hours to reorganize the entire table if it is not partitioned, but it may take only one hour to reorganize one partition that is disorganized, thereby ODS users can have the table back 4 hours earlier from the REORG utility.

Partitioned table lets a utility job work on a partition of the table, while allowing ODS applications to concurrently access data on other partitions. Because you can work on part of your data instead of the entire table, your operation on the table will require less time.

DB2 V7 made improvements to manage partitioned tables increasing efficiency of the granularity and parallelism. Combined with the improvements of independency of partitions and Parallel Sysplex cluster technology ("Parallel Sysplex" is introduced more detail in the 8.3.3, "Flexible growth path" on page 265), a very large ODS data can be managed in partitions, with the following advantages:

- Enable DB2 utility parallelism to reduce the elapsed time than running the same utility against the entire table.
- You can break mass update, delete, or insert operations into separate jobs, each of which works on a different partitions. Breaking the job into several smaller jobs that run concurrently can reduce the elapsed time for ODS population task.
- You can plan for growth. You can define more partitions than you need now and use only partitions you need. Over time, the distribution of the data might become uneven, as inserts and deletes occur in ODS. Then you can rebalance partitions using the same number of partitions or use more partitions that you defined in advance but left empty if some partitions grew too big.
- Enable query parallelism for faster response time.
- Enable spreading I/Os across DASD volumes.
- Enable large table support (up to 64 Gigabytes in each of 254 partitions ==> 16 Terabytes).

Important: The volumes of ODS tables differ considerably. Some tables can be large enough to take several hours to load, which might be unacceptable to an ODS operation. Those tables may utilize the parallel load of a partitioned table, and the elapsed time of the LOAD utility of a partitioned ODS table is reduced, as you can see in Figure 8-12.

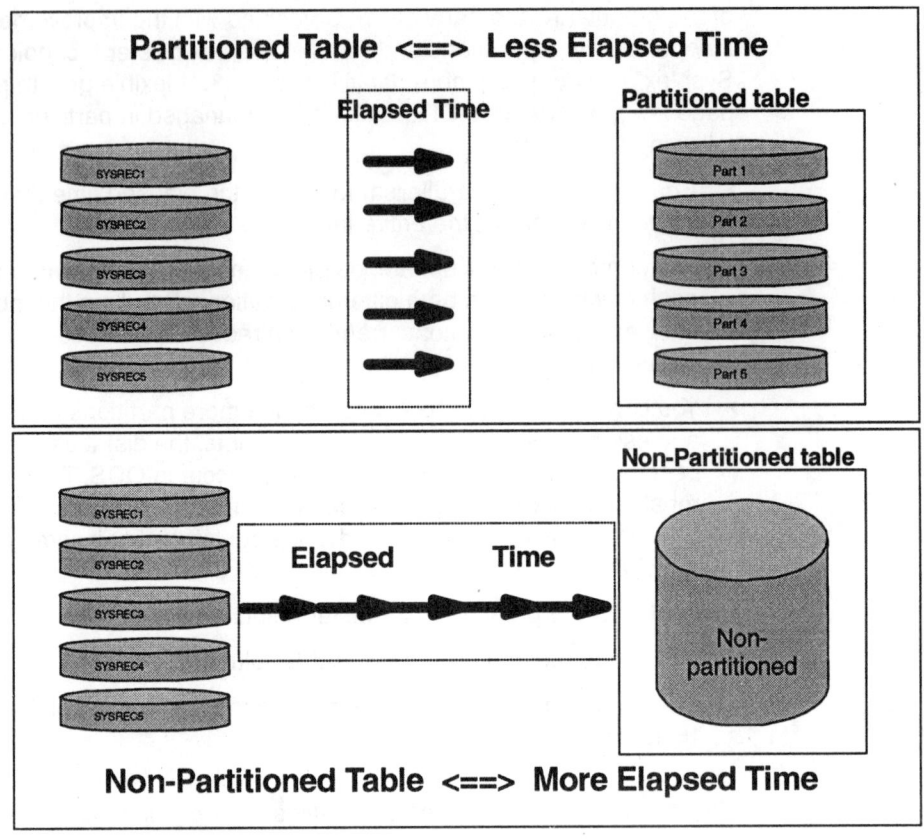

Figure 8-12   Partitioned table granularity

8.3.2 Near-current data delivery and mixing updates and queries

The ODS must handle a very mixed workloads: bursts of insert/update/delete to replicate from the operational sources, updates coming from the high transaction processing (high-volume and real-time performance), limited in an ODS environment but few resource consuming DSS/EIS processing, end user queries, and small batch loads while providing adequate response time to ODS online users and ODS applications.

As we have discussed in Chapter 3, "ODS architectures" on page 33, the ODS architecture is very important step to structure an ODS logical/physical designs to address the mixed workload and volatility by disparate processing in an ODS environment. All of the disparate processing that goes into the daily workload mix should be considered before building an ODS.

However, there are tools to help running ODS applications in the best possible performance objective that can be easily understood in the business-oriented term. We discuss how DB2 would support an ODS with mixed workloads and support disparate processing concurrently for a volatile ODS environment.

DB2 and workload manager

The workload management basically is act of trade-offs to handle ODS workloads. With the tight integration of DB2 and Work Load Manager (WLM) for z/OS, the ODS can perform better to process the diversified workloads including the works from the stored procedure address spaces (which will be used by Warehouse Manager to integrate and populate ODS data) based on the priorities that you set.

DWC will manage most of the ODS population, but WLM controls the execution of DB2 work at the system level below the ODS population, and WLM ensures that incoming mixed workload to ODS is optimally balanced to perform as planned across the systems.

WLM enables the ODS administrator to manage easily resources according to the performance objectives of the workloads and you can balance the *system resources* based on the performance requirements in a service policy that expressed in terms commonly used in Service Level Agreements (SLA) from the ODS user community. (Now, it is easy to tell WLM what your objective is in a business-like terms, although it is still not a drag-and-drop interface. Before the introduction of WLM, MVS required you to translate your data processing goals from high-level objectives into the extremely technical terms that the system can understand.)

WLM provides a way to define z/OS or OS/390 externals and tune z/OS or OS/390 without having to specify low-level parameters. The focus is on setting performance goals for work, and letting the workload manager handle processing to meet the goals. The PARMLIB members in the Installation Performance Specification and Installation Control Specification need *no longer* to be used to specify resource management goal.

With the goal-oriented systems management, WLM manages workloads that share system resources and have different priorities and resource usage characteristics which is a typical ODS workloads. Example: Assume that a limited but a query with a low priority in ODS is running on the same system as online update transactions with a higher priority. WLM can ensure that a long query (perhaps with no index) doesn't monopolize resources and does not prevent the online ODS transactions from achieving acceptable response times.

WLM adapts as needed to manage the trade-offs between meeting your service goals for work and making efficient use of system resources. It also provides feedback to support performance reporting and analysis which describes performance achievements in the same terms as those used to express goals for work.

For details of the WLM support, please refer to *DB2 UDB for OS/390 and z/OS V7 Administration Guide,* SC26-9931 and *OS/390 MVS Planning: Workload Management,* GC28-1761.

ODS scheduling while building an ODS

The objective of the scheduling is to control the processes and optimize resource utilization. We discuss the scheduling and controlling outside of the Data Warehouse Center (DWC) in this section to avoid overlaps in the book. Using DWC and OS/390 agent, the batch job scheduling can work together with DWC.

Z/OS tools for the Operation Automation, such as OPC/ESA, can assist ODS administrator to utilize the resources to the maximum by helping to setup regular schedules for ODS production jobs. It can help ODS administrator to plan and automatically schedule the production workload, such as regular refresh jobs, it drives and controls the mixed workload processing at both local and remote sites to manage your production workload across the system if you have a distributed ODS in a different node.

Any ODS jobs can be scheduled to run during the day, night shift or weekend to mix workloads at the right time. For example, you can set to run regular production jobs, such as massive update jobs, after most users leave the office at 9:00PM.

ODS jobs can be scheduled to run automatically at a certain time or after a certain event. (For example, a successful execution of a predecessor job or a group of jobs.) One special query could be set to the scheduler during the day to run once automatically at midnight as an on-demand job, and the user can check the result in the next morning.

If there is an exceptional massive update job, it may be scheduled to run on Saturday while weekend CPU utilization is low. It could be set to run regularly during every second and third saturday in a month to avoid a busy month-end period.

If there is a certain group of jobs to run serially, such as loading an ODS subject data from different sources, all those jobs can be set to run as a single group with predecessors and successors defined and can be monitored. If there is any problem in the job flow, it goes into an error queue prompting to notify the responsible staffs for their attention and resolution of problems.

In summary, any ODS job that are not controlled by DWC can be scheduled to run at a point-in-time, either triggered by event(s), time and calendar day or combinations of time and event(s), and run it automatically without manual intervention once it is setup in the scheduling system. The entire ODS production can be scheduled to run orderly to meet the business requirement and to mix the workloads to maximize the resource utilization.

For details of OPC/ESA, please refer to *OPC/ESA General Information,* GH19-6715.

DB2 for z/OS data sharing: flexible workload balancing and growth

Another feature, DB2 data sharing provides flexibility for workload balancing as data in a DB2 data sharing environment does not need to be redistributed when you add a new subsystem or when the workload becomes unbalanced.

The new DB2 member has the same direct access to the data as all other existing members of the data sharing group. You do not have to migrate or port to a different platform or architecture because your data grew considerably. We introduce more of the data sharing in 8.3.3, "Flexible growth path" on page 265.

ODS near currency and concurrency

We discuss the near currency and concurrency in regard to the performance to respond to the ODS volatility with lock management and parallelism. The ODS needs to handle the volatility to be able to access current or near-current data with frequent updates to an ODS unlike data warehouses environment. In a typical ODS environment, legacy transactions will flow into an ODS with burst of data updates from the integration and transformation layer, and most of them should be populated within a short response time depending on the business requirement. In the mean time, update transactions may be running along with a special analytical processing that may sweep ODS at the same time.

Again, an ODS needs to be built right first to give an optimal response time to support the ODS volatility. No one can expect to win a race with a poorly designed car by compensating its faulty engine with a higher octane gas. It is imperative to have everything looked during the ODS development before building an ODS, such as frequent commits preventing a total refresh with massive inserts/updates/deletes without intermediate commits, physical database design including partitioning and denormalization for the performance reasons, using the right isolation level (such as Uncommitted Read where possible) and locking strategy, and index designs, and so on.

In addition, all ODS transactions need to be analyzed for their access patterns, frequency, and program efficiency. The ODS administrator should assign a proper priority to the online transactions and balance scheduling to avoid a performance bottleneck. Otherwise, there is a good possibility that ODS users may suffer a long response time when updates and other simultaneous accesses are pouring into an ODS, and unfortunately, even dead-locks. Even with a well planned schedule and priorities of ODS workloads, there is no escape from the peaks and valleys and we need to respond to the volatility by utilizing DB2 functions wisely. Let us look at the locking management and parallelism to provide a good performance and concurrency ensuring the ODS data integrity.

DB2 UDB for z/OS lock management and concurrency

There are various features that DB2 can help the ODS volatility by providing mechanisms to allow frequent updates made to ODS while other processing require to update/read the ODS at the same time.

DB2 uses a lock management on user data to ensure the integrity of the data. Two or more independent application processes must be prevented from simultaneously accessing and updating specific rows in DB2. The state of a lock tells what access to the locked object is permitted to the lock owner and to any concurrent processes.

Depending on the lock state, the data can be read or updated by the lock owner, or can be denied to access to protect the data integrity. You may compare this lock to your certified check in the bank. Once you have your certified check drawn, you cannot use the amount from your account balance because the bank put a lock on it until you clear the certified check. Your bank does not put a lock on your account because you are merely checking your balance.

However, despite the importance of data integrity, locking can be too restrictive in a volatile ODS environment with lots of update. If an application process locks too much, other ODS users, utilities, and application processes must wait for the locked data. This may result in poor concurrency. Then, how do we start to place a locking strategy?

Initial lock management strategy for ODS

Concurrency is the ability to allow ODS users to access the same data at essentially the same time while the data integrity is ensured. To have a proper balance, you need to choose a right locking strategy. Generally, use LOCKSIZE ANY which is the default for CREATE TABLESPACE until you have reason not to use the default value.

The best of locking strategy depends on the ODS application and other transactions hitting the same data at the same time, therefore there is no simple or good way to describe a general rule of thumb. For example, the control tables (ASN.IBMSNAP_*) of the replication could be used in a very different pattern than the usual ODS data for end users. Because there are two asynchronous processes, apply and capture, which use the control tables by different tasks.

Those control tables with a small data, but referenced very frequently with occasional updates by different transactions are a good candidates for the LOCKSIZE ROW. Some of the replication control tables belong to the same category. Consequently, you will likely to have a different LOCKSIZE on different control tables for the replication. Again, it is important to understand the data characteristics, and when and how the tables are being accessed before you decide the LOCKSIZE. For the replication control tables, please refer to the referenced redbooks or manuals in the "Related publications" on page 323.

However we try to understand the ODS data to find an initial locking strategy to start. Since most of ODS updates will come as a burst in a small group of update/insert/delete from a same source through the replication processes (Apply Subscriptions) or through some processes of Warehouse Manager, such as stored procedures with a regular COMMIT in the logic by subject area data, there is a good chance not to hit many rows in a same page by different apply processes. And ODS data is usually detail and tend to be large. Initially, there are not many update OLTP transactions within ODS. Then starting with LOCKSIZE ANY might be a good initial strategy instead of ROW level locking. If queries are running against ODS, a good portions of ODS query might use 'UR' and some will use 'CS' as the isolation level, which should result a reasonably good performance with LOCKSIZE ANY.

A careful consideration of the trade-off has to be given when you decide to use the ROW level locking as the locks cost the overhead of crossing the region to Internal Resource Lock Manager (IRLM), which raises the CPU consumption, and ROW level results more number of locks to maintain.

It is important to maintain as small number of locks to support the ODS volatility and concurrency, but we cannot hurt the ODS data integrity on the other hand. A careful consideration for the locking and isolation level must be given by the ODS designer during the ODS development. The frequency of capture/apply processes depends on the requirements of the ODS users who can decide the tolerance of the lagging between the operational source and ODS data.

Accordingly the frequency of replication or population into the ODS and the frequency of the COMMIT within the burst of inserts/updates/deletes from the apply processes by WHM will also impact the number of locks held at a given point and duration of the locks held. You should stop anything that holds too many locks or change it to do COMMIT frequently. Do not refresh tables with massive inserts/updates/deletes, rather refresh it using the LOAD utility if possible. Consider using the ASNLOAD user exit to use the LOAD utility during for the initial full refresh. As a next step, a question will arise as to how many locks we can afford.

Number of locks held and lock escalation

The number of locks held may be limited by the LOCKMAX which specifies the maximum number of page or row locks that a single application process can hold on the table space before those locks are escalated. Lock escalation is the act of releasing a large number of page or row locks, held by an application process on a single table or table space, to acquire a single table or table space lock to prevent maintaining too many locks.

The data-blocking value in the subscription will affect the LOCKMAX in an ODS operation. The bigger the value, the more locks you hold, but you do not go through the frequent COMMIT overhead. It is a balance between one trip with ten in your hand or ten trips with one in your hand. If a human being with two hands delivers to the target, it may be best to make five trips with two for each trip. You need to monitor the system and related threads during the design validation or stress test.

Monitor to learn the right lock management for your ODS

To use the right values for LOCKSIZE and LOCKMAX if you do not use the default, you should base your choice upon the results of monitoring ODS applications that use the table space. The default value of LOCKMAX for LOCKSIZE ANY is SYSTEM which is set by the system programmer during the installation of the subsystem. The value need to be adjusted based on your ODS activity and should be monitored to find the right value. We hope you find a reasonable value during the stress test before the production deployment.

For a certain ODS online transactions that tend to hit different rows in a same page at the same time may need to use ROW level lock and higher number of LOCKMAX explicitly specified, although the ROW level usage might be a rare case except the type C ODS where the production OLTP transactions hit the ODS in a real-time access with a high volume.

Since the initial deployment of the ODS is likely to roll out the type A, ODS designers would learn from the type A ODS implementation and gradually progress to more of the type B and the final integration to the type C ODS. To become a true type C ODS, all updates in ODS should be made synchronously within the same UOW at the same time with the legacy operational data updates, or the legacy applications should update the type C ODS database only. Essentially, it would mean that most of legacy applications will be ceased or migrated to use the ODS database as the operational production database. By then, the locking strategy will be based on the continuous monitoring, that will allow ODS designers to adjust the locking parameters to perform optimally.

Need to process more work in less time

Partitioning is another way to increase concurrency for ODS users by shortening the response time, thereby increasing the chance of other ODS processes to access ODS data concurrently. You can break mass update, delete, or insert operations into separate jobs, each of which works on a different partitions to reduce the elapsed time. The partitioning has been discussed in detail in 8.3.1, "Level of detail" on page 256.

Although a typical ODS includes a large number of updates and relatively less queries than the data warehouse, nonetheless, fast query response always help other ODS transactions in the concurrency perspective. When DB2 plans to access data from a table or index in a partitioned table space, it can initiate multiple parallel operations. The response time for data or processor-intensive queries can be significantly reduced which should help to support the ODS volatility. Sysplex query parallelism can expand even farther the processing capacity available for processor-intensive queries. DB2 can split a large query across different DB2 members in a data sharing group. For an application process that is using Sysplex query parallelism, the lock count is maintained on a data sharing member basis, not globally across the group for the process. Thus, escalation on a table space or table by one member does not cause escalation on other members. Parallel Sysplex and data sharing will be discussed below.

8.3.3 Flexible growth path

As the operational data grows, the ODS will grow along with the user populations. The ODS architecture must be able to support the current workload as well as the future data volume and increased data access. DB2 data sharing in the Parallel Sysplex cluster can be a key technology to support the ODS architecture for the scalability to grow ODS without migrating to a different platform or architecture.

The Parallel Sysplex cluster can grow incrementally. You can add a new DB2 subsystem onto another central processor complex and access the same data through the new DB2 subsystem. You no longer need to manage copies or distribute data to a system in a next room. This combination will let ODS respond to the future growth with no effort to migrate ODS to a different architecture.

A data sharing group is a collection of one or more DB2 subsystems that access shared DB2 data, which runs on a z/OS Parallel Sysplex cluster. A Parallel Sysplex is a cluster of z/OS systems that communicate and cooperate with each other which consists of two key pieces of technology as described below. Basically, it is a group of S/390s that communicate and synchronize very well, can share all workloads dynamically, and can expand smoothly. The concept of the Parallel Sysplex and DB2 subsystem with the data sharing to support ODS is shown with two key technologies in Figure 8-13.

1. **Coupling facility:** Provides specialized hardware, specialized high-speed links and a shared storage for fast inter-system data sharing protocols.
2. **Sysplex timer:** Provides a common time source across all of the systems in the cluster, which offers an efficient way to provide log-record sequencing and event ordering across the different systems.

With this technology, you can configure your server in many different ways in any combination of CPU and memory and dynamically add more power to match to the workload growth incrementally. With DB2 data sharing members, you can easily add or rebalance the ODS workloads with a great scalability. The flexibility of the configuration allows to respond to an unplanned outage too. If an entire Central Processor Complex (CPC) fails, your ODS work can be routed to another CPC which might squeeze out test jobs to take the routed workloads.

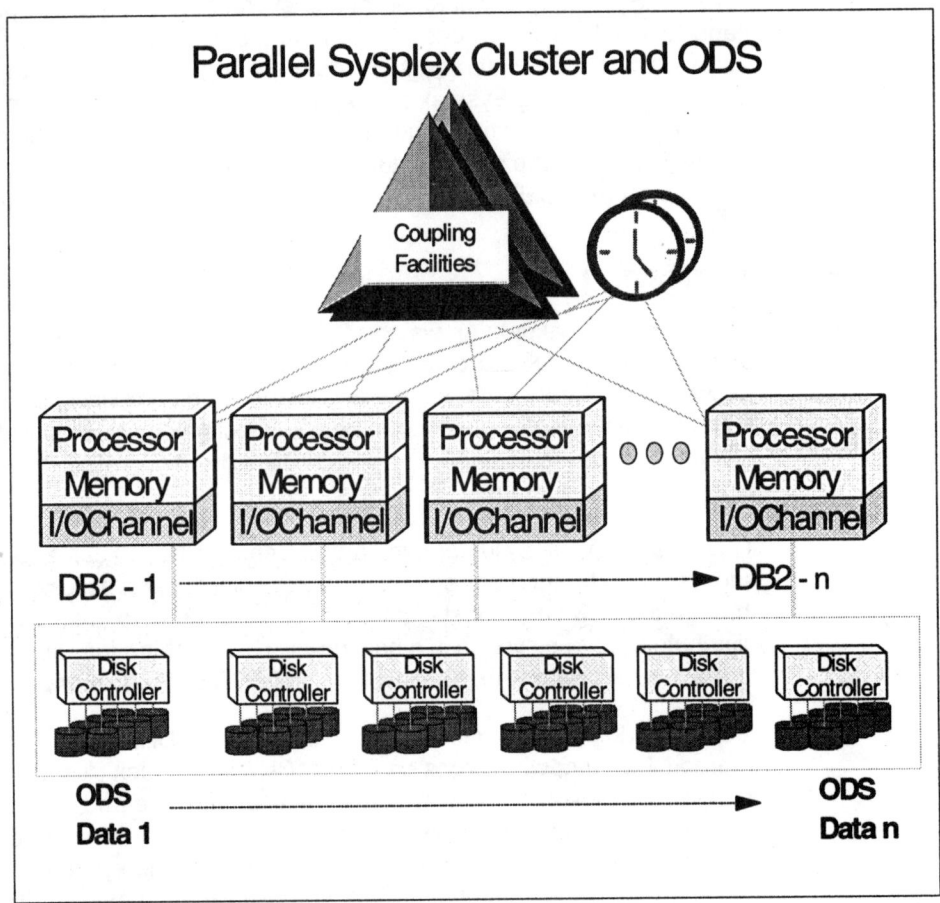

Figure 8-13 Parallel Sysplex cluster architecture and ODS

Each DB2 subsystem that belongs to a particular data sharing group is a member of that group. All members of a data sharing group use the same shared DB2 catalog. The ODS data in a DB2 data sharing environment does not need to be redistributed when you add a new subsystem or when the workload becomes unbalanced.

The new DB2 member has the same direct access to the ODS data as all other existing members of the data sharing group and the parallel sysplex can grow incrementally. This gives an easier scalability to ODS. For more detailed information, please refer to *DB2 UDB for OS/390 and Z/OS V7 Data Sharing: Planning and Administration,* SC26-9935 and *DB2 UDB for OS/390 and z/OS V7 Administration Guide,* SC26-9931.

The scalability is there not only to help the future growth of ODS, but also to ease to handle peak loads, such as end-of-quarter processing, by starting data sharing members to handle peak loads, and then stop them when the peak passes. You can take advantage of all of these benefits, whether your workloads are for OnLine Transaction Processing (OLTP), or a mixture of OLTP, batch, and queries which are all part of an ODS.

In summary, DB2 provides a good scalability to ODS. ODS can run and grow without having to migrate or port to a different architecture. Data sharing gives ODS opportunities to put more work through the system. you can run the same ODS application on more than one DB2 subsystem to achieve transaction rates that are higher than is possible on a single subsystem. Sysplex query parallelism enables DB2 to use all the processing power of the data sharing group to process a single query. For ODS users who do complex data analysis or decision support though not frequent like the data warehouse, Sysplex query parallelism is a scalable solution.

8.3.4 Uptime

Since the ODS may be supporting the daily operation of the entire enterprise, the ODS requires the availability 24 hours a day, 7 days a week with minimal planned outages. There are two kinds of the uptime (continuous availability) as far as ODS users concerned.

- ODS system-wide availability
  - Daily operation
  - Batch window for backup and recovery, reorganization
- ODS table availability
  - Locks and concurrency
  - Utilities

ODS system-wide availability

If a DB2 subsystem is down which holds all ODS data in a non-data sharing environment, then it is a system-wide problem that affects all ODS users. If a table or few are not available due to the locks held, it may affect some group of ODS users. Let us take a look at both aspects of the availability issue.

The Parallel Sysplex provides cluster technology that achieves 24 hours a day, 7 days a week, so that ODS can be accessed without a possible outage. With two coupling facilities and group buffer pools duplexed, a significant operating system availability can be achieved. If we combine the parallel sysplex with DB2 data sharing, a significant ODS availability benefit can be achieved.

During a planned or unplanned outage of a DB2 group member, ODS data remains available through other DB2 group members. Some common situations when you might plan for an outage include applying software maintenance, or migrating to a new release. For example, during software maintenance, you can apply the maintenance to one member at a time, which always leaves DB2 members available to run works as shown in Figure 8-14. If a DB2 subsystem or the entire Central Processor Complex (CPC) fails, work can be routed to another system.

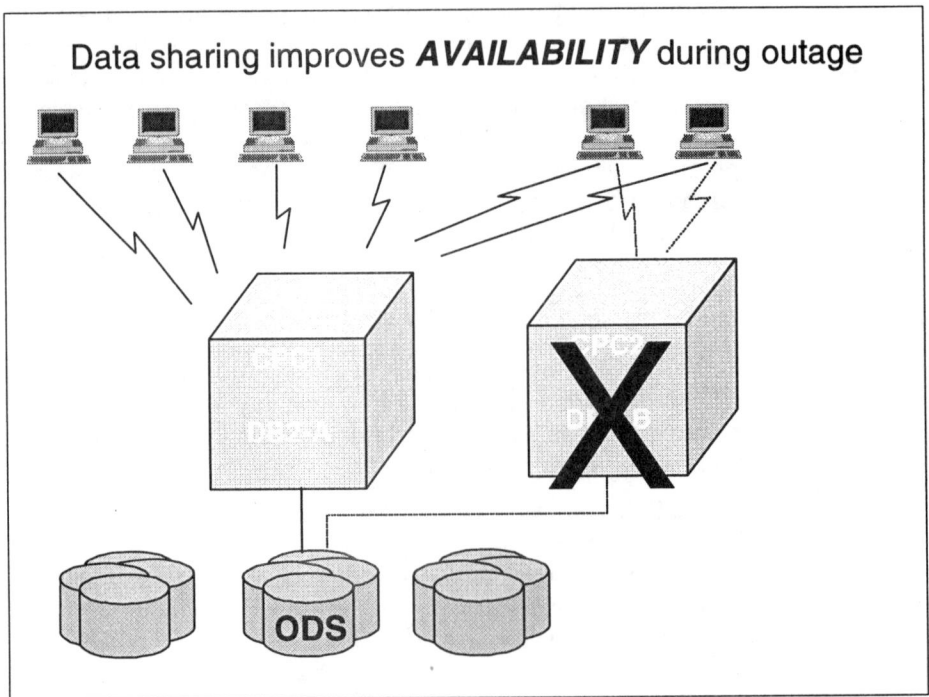

Figure 8-14 Parallel Sysplex with data sharing improves availability

The ODS can be served better with this technology to improve system availability and concurrency. And you can configure your system environment more flexibly and grow your system incrementally.

ODS table availability and concurrency

Let us look at the availability of ODS data from the concurrency perspective.

Concurrency is the ability to allow ODS users to access the same data at essentially the same time while other users or even utilities are running against same tables. As discussed in the ODS volatility issue, some of the availability is enhanced by CPU and I/O parallelism by allowing more users to access ODS concurrently. Another consideration of the availability is the enhancement of DB2 utilities and other function to continue to make ODS data available.

- **Parallelism**

    You can break mass update, delete, or insert operations into separate jobs, each of which works on a different partitions to reduce the elapsed time.

    The volumes of ODS data differ considerably, and some tables may need to utilize the parallel load with multiple inputs in a single step. The elapsed time of the LOAD utility is reduced when parallel loading and parallel index build of multiple indexes are used, which thereby increases the availability.

- **Online REORG enhancement**

    To improve the access response time, DB2 tables need to be reorganized after inserts/delete operations. It is more critical in ODS considering the massive inserts/delete operation. The Online REORG improves the availability of ODS data while running the REORG utility for a maintenance by allowing access to ODS.

- **Online LOAD RESUME**

    Online LOAD RESUME might be used in the ODS building to add data from non-relational sources daily or even hourly. For example, you may need to load some interface data on a flat file to a certain ODS table regularly. DB2 allows you to choose to read and write access to the table during the LOAD utility is running. This allows ODS data available to ODS users or transactions to continue the access, thus increasing the availability of the ODS data, while the data is being loaded at the same time.

- **Online subsystem parameters**

    The DB2 sub-system may have to be taken down to alter one or more of the subsystem parameters known as ZPARMs. DB2 V7 enables you to change many ZPARMs without stopping DB2, thus enhancing the ODS availability.

8.3.5 Performance tuning and monitoring

To support the mixed workloads of ODS and variety of ODS users with a satisfactory response time, the performance of ODS needs to be maintained in a best possible condition based on the continual performance monitoring.

A typical ODS may contain fast transaction processing, burst of inserts/update/delete from continuous ODS population, incremental batch loadings (LOAD RESUME), a refresh load of a large data (LOAD REPLACE), I/O or CPU intensive queries, apply/capture running frequently, special ODS administration transactions with updates, and few DSS/EIS transactions running in a given day competing system resources.

Obviously, there is a complexity in ODS operation, but there should be an order in the complexity. To have a proper performance in the complex ODS operation, a well-planned order must control the complexity. If the complexity seeps into the order in place, it could be the beginning of the disorderly processing of an ODS that will result a poor performance.

Planning for performance

Managing the ODS performance should involve the following steps:

- Understand the ODS workloads including all replications and ODS population.
- Analyze the characteristics and resource usage patterns of the ODS workloads.
- Classify profiles of the ODS workloads.
- Schedule the ODS workgroups for the optimal system usage.
- Run the proper maintenance processes including replication control tables.
- Establish performance criteria and objectives.
- Plan how to monitor performance.
- Carry out the performance monitoring plan.
- Analyze the monitoring report.
- Adjust the monitoring activities depending on the performance results as monitoring itself uses resources.
- Continue monitoring to generate a history of performance to compare with future results. Use historical statistics provided by V7. (You can predict the future space requirements for the table and index spaces more accurately and run utilities to improve performance. DB2 Visual Explain utilizes statistics history for comparison with new variations that you enter to improve your access paths and aid the future design for the iterative ODS development.)

- Post performance reports to the ODS community and provides the performance feedback to ODS designers or programmers.

Having listed all the necessary steps to maintain a good performance environment for ODS, this is a good place to remind that a careful ODS development with the performance in mind and workload management must precede the performance monitoring. The ODS development should include the performance review phase and the performance validation phase.

Of course, the performance analysis should provide feedbacks to improve the ODS design once the monitoring and performance corrections begin. However, remember that correcting problems after a production implementation costs considerably more than fixing problems during the ODS design phase.

There are many functions and enhanced features from DB2 to help ODS designers or programmers to meet the ODS performance objective. One of the example for ODS is the star join that was discussed in 3.3, "Data modeling" on page 52: a new way of processing multiple-table joins was added as an option to DB2, known as the star join performance enhancement because it is oriented to improve star join performance. The improvement also applies to joins of tables using the snowflake schema design which involves one or more extra levels of dimension tables around the first level of dimension tables. In DB2 V7, the parameter that enables or disables this feature is changed from a hidden to an externalized keyword.

We discuss some of the performance considerations for the ODS and steps to correct performance problems if performance is not satisfactory in this section. For detailed performance information, please refer to these IBM Redbooks:

- *DB2 UDB Server for OS/390 and z/OS Version 7 Presentation Guide*, SG24-6121
- *DB2 UDB for OS/390 and z/OS V7 Administration Guide*, SC26-9931
- *DB2 UDB for OS/390 and Z/OS V7 Data Sharing: Planning and Administration*, SC26-9935
- *DB2 UDB for OS/390 Version 6 Management Tools Package*, SG24-5759
- *DB2 for z/OS and OS/390 Version 7 Performance Topics*, SG24-6129.

Performance considerations

During the ODS design phase, ODS designers must deal with the compromise and trade-off to accommodate the disparate processing of an ODS. The same will apply to the performance improvements. The trade-off is a way of improving performance of one process which may affect other processing, as all ODS threads compete for the system resource and ODS data.

The performance touches every technical subject and we have already introduced Parallel Sysplex, DB2 Data Sharing, WLM, and Parallelism in previous sections that touched some performance implications. Essentially, it all comes down to the ODS architecture and how to balance system resources, mainly, CPU, I/O, and memory.

We introduce several subjects that need to be considered during the ODS development and performance corrections after an implementation. This section is not exhaustive and does not include all descriptions and measurements related to the performance. We will not cover all performance techniques as the detail information can be found in other publications including those referenced above. We will not discuss any network performance in this book either.

We will only look at subjects that will clearly affect ODS performance and we may repeat few subjects from the previous sections for the completeness.

- Understand the implication of the high volume of inserts in ODS. It directly relates to the number of I/O:
    - If your application needs a clustering sequence on the table where high volume inserts occur, you should create only one clustering type 2 index on the table where high volume inserts occur.
    - Consider maximizing the insert frequency by partitioning the table according to the key distribution of insert transactions. Multiple transactions can concurrently insert rows of different key ranges to different partitions.
    - If your application needs other indexes to retrieve data for a tactical query/DSS/EIS at night that might need to access ODS, then you should consider creating them when there is SQL activity and create index when you need them using CREATE INDEX DEFER YES and REBUILD INDEX.
    - Use the PREFORMAT as described in 8.3.6, "Initial load" on page 275.
    - Use LOAD utility during the full refresh for a large table or during nightly batch load, which is more efficient that massive inserts.
- Reserve free space in table spaces and indexes as ODS population uses INSERT frequently.
- Avoid hot spots. They are portions of a table that are continuously and repeatedly updated by the applications, for example, a total column in ODS. A contention is likely to occur when accessing that data, and updates must serialize. To avoid host spots, you have to spread updates across the table, by reducing the total scope. For example, if you have a corporate-wide sales total in your ODS table, every sale transaction will update this total, which becomes a hot spot. Spread updates by using geographic total, division total, regional total, and so on.

- Use asynchronous INSERT preformatting that will asynchronously preformat the next range of new pages during INSERT processing. This may speed up ODS populations that use bursts of inserts.
- Ensure sufficient primary allocation for table spaces and do not let any reorganization job reduce the primary allocation automatically to fit the size at a point.
- Speed up preformatting by allocating in cylinders rather than blocks or tracks.
- Make buffer pools large enough for the workload. This is a trade-off between I/O and memory. With high volume inserts in ODS, you can minimize the impact of asynchronous insert I/O's by defining a sufficient buffer pool.
- Use partitioning for optimal parallel processing.

    This is a key technology that ODS designer may utilize in building physical ODS tables. Please refer to 8.3.1, "Level of detail" on page 256 and 8.3.2, "Near-current data delivery and mixing updates and queries" on page 258.

- Use Utility parallelism.

    The volumes of ODS data differs considerably, and some tables may need to utilize the parallel load with multiple inputs in a single step. You may choose to use the LOAD utility instead of massive inserts in ODS population for a full refresh or nightly loading. The elapsed time of the LOAD utility is reduced when parallel loading and parallel index build of multiple indexes are used. DB2 utilities support the partition-independency and inline functions to reduce the elapsed time. Please refer to 8.3.4, "Uptime" on page 267, and the IBM Redbooks, *DB2 for z/OS and OS/390 Version 7 Using the Utilities Suite,* SG24-6289, and *DB2 UDB for OS/390 and z/OS V7 Utility Guide and Reference,* SC26-9945. Here is an example of the utility functions that utilize the parallel/inline technology.

    – Loading partitions of a partitioned table space in parallel
    – Unloading partitions of a partitioned table space in parallel
    – Inline COPY with LOAD REPLACE and REORG TABLESPACE
    – Inline RUNSTATS with LOAD,REORG TABLESPACE,REORG INDEX and REBUILD INDEX
    – Building the indexes of a table space in parallel during LOAD or REORG TABLESPACE
    – Rebuilding a partitioned index in parallel during REBUILD INDEX
    – Rebuilding multiple indexes in parallel with REBUILD INDEX

- Use Workload Manager to set performance objectives.

- Reduce I/Os. Generally speaking, most performance problems begin with excessive I/Os. Thus, reducing the number of I/O operations is one way to improve response time of ODS transactions.
    - Use NO Logging when possible to reduce DB2 logging activities, such as initial loading using LOAD utility.
    - Reorganize tables on time.
    - Use RUNSTATS to keep access path statistics current.
    - Avoid running wild queries, which generate excessive I/O operations:
        - Do not let queries run in the production ODS unless it is tuned. Use tools such as DB2 SQL Performance Analyzer, Resource Limit Facility (Governor), DB2 Query Monitor, or DB2 Bind Manager. Refer to *DB2 UDB for OS/390 and z/OS V7 Administration Guide,* SC26-9931, and *New Tools for DB2 for OS/390 and z/OS Presentation Guide,* SG24-6139.
        - Build indexes when you need to avoid the overhead while you are populating using inserts, and use them during the query. Use Visual Explain to display and analyze information on access paths chosen by DB2. An index can improve the access path in several ways. For example, it can reduce the number of pages and rows scanned (by changing a table space scan into a matching index scan).

Performance corrections

If the ODS performance is not satisfactory, take the following steps:

- Trace the slow performing processes and ask the following questions:
    - Have we analyzed the characteristics and resource usage patterns using EXPLAIN and other monitoring tools?
    - Is an index being used?
    - Should we reclassify its profile?
    - Should we reschedule it for the optimal system usage?
    - Have we run the proper maintenance?
- Determine the major constraints in the system.
- Decide where you can afford to make trade-offs and which resources can bear an additional load. Nearly all tuning involves trade-offs among system resources. Change or adjust the slow performance.
- Tune your system where necessary by adjusting its characteristics to improve performance.
- Continue to monitor the system.

There are abundant books and classes available for learning the details of performance monitoring and tuning, so we do not discuss every performance monitoring and tuning technique here.

8.3.6 Initial load

Some of the ODS tables will be populated by loading data from a sequential file acquired from the ODS ETML layer rather than by replication or inserts due to a performance reason or the input source has to be converted before being loaded to ODS. If it is a huge and hopefully partitioned table, then a batch load can be the best performing method. We discuss the batch initial loading here, however we will not discuss any transformation in this section.

The primary method for the initial loading to ODS is the LOAD utility. You can load data to populate ODS tables in two ways:

- From a sequential data set. This is an efficient tool to populate an ODS from legacy flat files.
- From a result set of an SQL query launched against tables. This is a new function called Cross Loader. This new DB2 Utility statement allows the input of the LOAD utility to be on a local or remote DRDA compliant databases. For the Cross Loader, please refer to the Appendix D, "DB2 UDB for z/OS Cross Loader" on page 317.

When you use the LOAD utility for the initial loading to ODS, you can:

- Load rows into an empty table (LOAD REPLACE) which will be used mostly for the initial loading, or add new rows to a table that is not empty (LOAD RESUME)
- Filter the input data using criteria supplied by the user
- Check the input data on unique, referential, and other constraint violations
- Place failing records to a sequential data set so that you can review errors

We discuss few performance tips and other options when you use the LOAD utility for the initial loading to ODS.

Performance tip to use LOAD Utility for ODS initial loading

There are few tips to consider before you use the LOAD Utility for ODS initial loading. Basically, it is an effort to keep ODS available as much as possible by performing the necessary tasks in a short elapsed time. We will discuss the parallelism and inline functions.

Use partition parallelism

This is the best way to load a huge, but partitioned table. With DB2 UDB for z/OS V7, partitions can be loaded in parallel in the same job even with Non-Partitioned Index (NPI). This single job will now read one input data set per partition and launch multiple subtasks, optimally one for each partition.

In order to allow each partition to be loaded from a separate data set, with discards (optionally) written to discard data sets for that partition, the LOAD syntax allows the specification of the INDDN and DISCARDDN keywords as part of the INTO TABLE PART specification.

DB2 determines the degree of parallelism, that is, the number of load subtasks, based on the system resources available, such as the followings:

- Number of CPUs
- Available virtual storage in the batch region
- Available number of DB2 threads

If ODS operation can afford only small window for the batch load, then you should consider to make large tables as partitioned to take advantage of the parallelism.

Use Inline COPY and Inline RUNSTATS

Use the inline functions whenever possible to reduce the total elapsed time and unavailability of your table spaces during LOAD. To avoid having the copy pending after the LOAD utility, either you run the ImageCopy or force the copy pending off without an ImageCopy if you are not concerned the recovery of the table using the ImageCopy. If it is your choice to run the ImageCopy, then you run the LOAD utility with Inline Copy as it is more efficient and reduce the elapsed time than you run the LOAD and ImageCopy serially in a separate job.

You also need to run the Runstats after the loading anyway, and the same reason applies to use inline Runstats rather than two separate jobs serially.

Use LOG NO, COPYDDN

If you run the LOAD REPLACE, then consider to run with LOG NO, COPYDDN, and REUSE. This is the most *effective* way to LOAD your table space and the table will be fully available to all applications and fully recoverable after the LOAD is done. Of course, you can use Inline Runstats with your Load Replace if you want to keep the catalog current.

Load Resume allows to access table while being loaded

Although you will use mostly LOAD REPLACE for the initial ODS loading, but you may need to load incrementally to reflect the current updates after an initial loading. LOAD RESUME is to allow add data to an existing table.

The Online LOAD RESUME allows you to access the ODS table while it is being loaded. The Online LOAD RESUME works internally like a mass INSERT and allows other SQL calls to access the table. This is a good technique to increase the ODS availability and this is a new feature added in V7. However, because the Online LOAD Resume internally works like a SQL INSERT, it is slower than the classic LOAD. This is a trade off between the performance and availability.

May use Preformat option

Since ODS tends to have more inserts than read, you may consider to use the PREFORMAT to improve the insert SQL later against the table you are loading.

The PREFORMAT option will preformat a table space and its associated index spaces during LOAD time and prepare it for INSERT processing. It reduces execution time delays due to formatting and eliminates the need to preformat new pages in a table space during INSERT processing, but add extra processing time to reformat during the load.

Preformatting is only recommended for table spaces and index spaces that has a very high INSERT applications where normal INSERT formatting can cause considerable delays or inconsistent elapsed times. It is not recommended for tables that are mainly used for query processing. The additional preformatted pages can cause table space scans to read additional empty pages, extending the elapsed time for these queries. Also it does not make sense to use Preformat for the tables that are only populated by the LOAD REPLACE without using INSERTS as it can cause an additional elapsed time of the LOAD processing.

Use the PREFORMAT with care and only when you are sure that there is an obvious benefit. Preformatting can only be used with LOAD SHRLEVEL NONE.

Note: There is a way to reduce the insert preformatting which may be beneficial to the ODS inserts. DB2 V7 introduced asynchronous INSERT preformatting and this new function will asynchronously preformat the next range of new pages during INSERT processing if the current page is within a predefined range from the end of the formatted pages. This could cut down the response time for the burst of inserts during the ODS population.

UNLOAD Utility

To prepare the input data for the initial ODS loading, there might be many ways to acquire ODS data from operational sources. The UNLOAD utility could be one way to collect data to prepare an initial loading.

The new UNLOAD utility works faster than DSNTIAUL program which has been widely used. It now allows to unload data from an image copy, so you can expand your ODS data source to ImageCopies. This function may be used in pair with LOAD utility for the initial ODS data loading.

DB2 Unload can do the following:

- Rapidly unload tablespaces.
- Simultaneously execute several unloads accessing the same tablespace.
- Do unload against an image copy to eliminate interference with DB2 production databases. The image copy can be:
    - Any full image copy
    - An incremental image copy
- Unload selected rows and columns.
- Unload every n rows and maximum rows.
- Generate load control statements for subsequent reload.
- Using the DB2 Unload user exit, inspect, modify, or discard DB2 rows.

It provides an extremely fast way to sequentially read and share a DB2 tablespace among multiple unloads. DB2 Unload scans a tablespace and creates the number of output files you specify, in the format you specify. The output format can be:

- DSNTIAUL compatible
- VARIABLE, which lets you create variable-length records
- DELIMITED, which lets you create a delimited file that can be exported to another platform
- USER, which lets you specify virtually any type of conversion so that your output appears as you want it

Implementing message flows with MQSI

This appendix describes the steps to follow to design and deploy a message flow in the broker domain where the ODS resides.

MQSeries Integrator (MQSI) provides a great deal of flexibility and functionality with respect to message handling. In 5.1.3, "Populating the ODS using MQSI" on page 134, we described and demystified how an MQSI message flow is used to accept a message from a queue, parse it, do some data transformation on it, provide some error handling capabilities, and finally, output the record to the ODS. In the following sections, we describe how that message flow was created and deployed.

Assumptions

We assume that the MQSI code is already installed on the NT platform where the MQSI Control Center resides. It is the MQSI Control Center GUI that is used to connect together the message flow design. We also need DB2 and MQSeries to be installed on that machine. On the target machine you also need to have installed the MQSI product and databases as described in the Installation Guide for that particular platform where the ODS resides.

Using the MQSI Control Center

From the desktop. select:

Start -> Programs -> IBM MQSeries Integrator 2.0 -> Control Center

You should get the MQSI Control Center panel shown in Figure A-1.

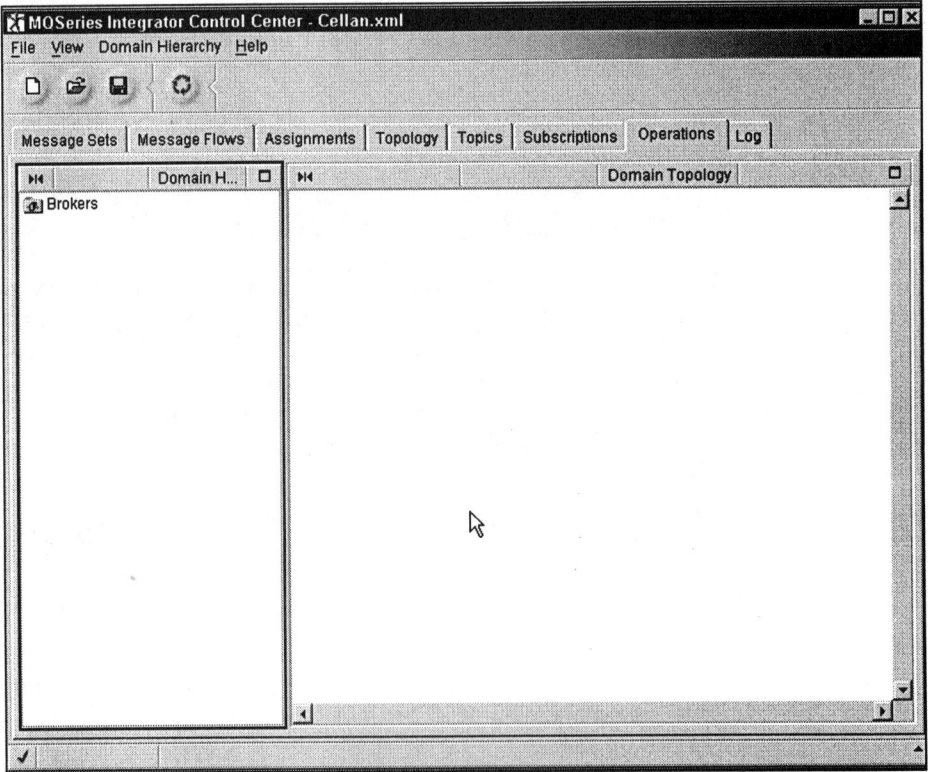

Figure A-1   Control center panel

Note the tabs near the top of the screen. These allow you to navigate easily around the Control Center.

Steps required to implement an MQSI flow

In order to implement a MQSI flow, the following steps need to be executed:

- Configure the broker domain and topology
- Define message sets
- Define message flows
- Assign message sets and flows to the broker
- Deploy the broker domain

Configuring the broker domain and topology

The broker may be on the local (NT) queue manager or a remote one. Assuming it is remote, as it would be for our ODS, then you need to define a pair of send and receive channels between the local queue manager (using MQSeries Explorer) and the remote queue manager (using RUNMQSC and DEF CHANNEL command on that system).

Now select the **Topology** tab in the Control Center. Right-click on the **Topology** folder and check out, then right-click again to create broker as shown in Figure A-2. There is always one broker per queue manager.

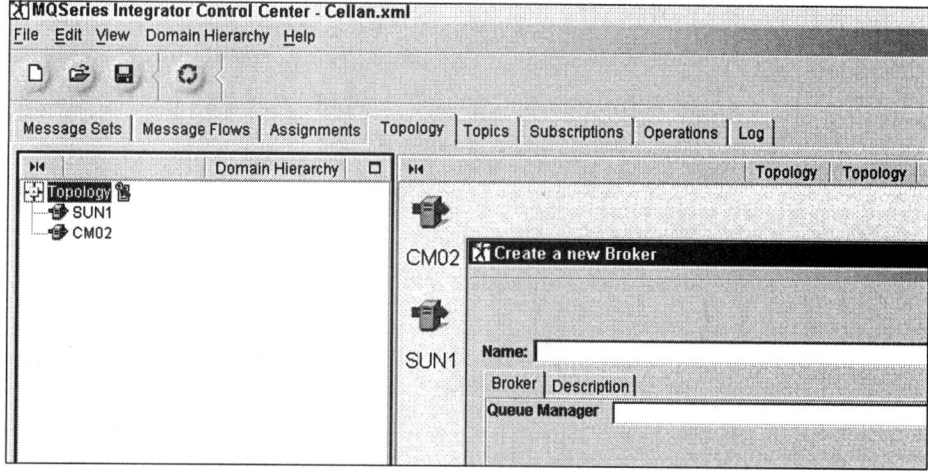

Figure A-2 Creating a broker

Creating a message set

First of all, create your message (in this example, the input message) in a text file like our example PART in Figure A-3.

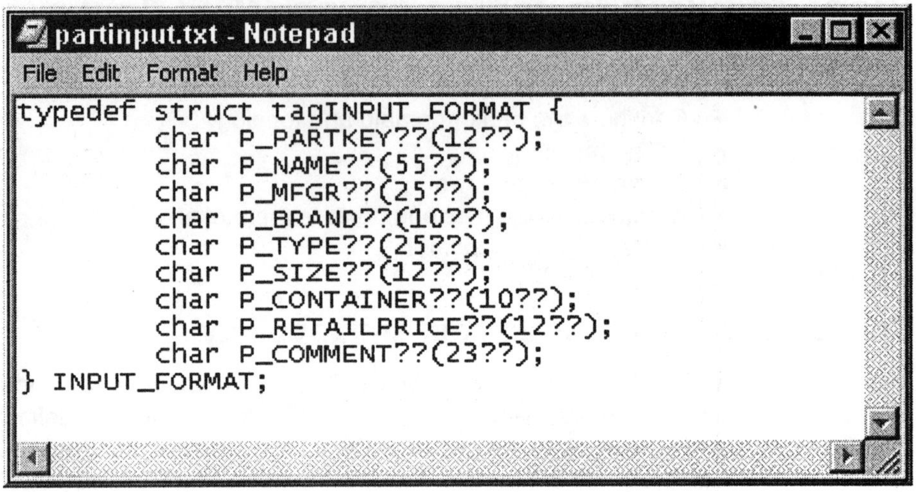

```
typedef struct tagINPUT_FORMAT {
        char P_PARTKEY??(12??);
        char P_NAME??(55??);
        char P_MFGR??(25??);
        char P_BRAND??(10??);
        char P_TYPE??(25??);
        char P_SIZE??(12??);
        char P_CONTAINER??(10??);
        char P_RETAILPRICE??(12??);
        char P_COMMENT??(23??);
} INPUT_FORMAT;
```

Figure A-3 PART input file

To define a message set, as shown in Figure A-4, follow these steps:

- Click on **Message Sets** tab.
- Right-click **Message Sets** folder and select **Create Message Set**.
- Provide a name (PART_SET).
- Right-click the new message set and select **Import to Message Set**.
- Click **Browse** and enter the file name of your text file (.txt) and select **Finish**.
- Expand the message set.
- Right-click on the **Types** folder and select **Add to Workspace**.
- Select PART_SET.
- Right-click **Messages** folder and select **Create-->Message** to create a message format.
- Provide a name (PART_INPUT_FORMAT_MSG) and an identifier (PART_INPUT_FORMAT_MSG).
- From the Type drop-down box, select the created type (INPUT_FORMAT_TYPE).
- Select **Finish**.

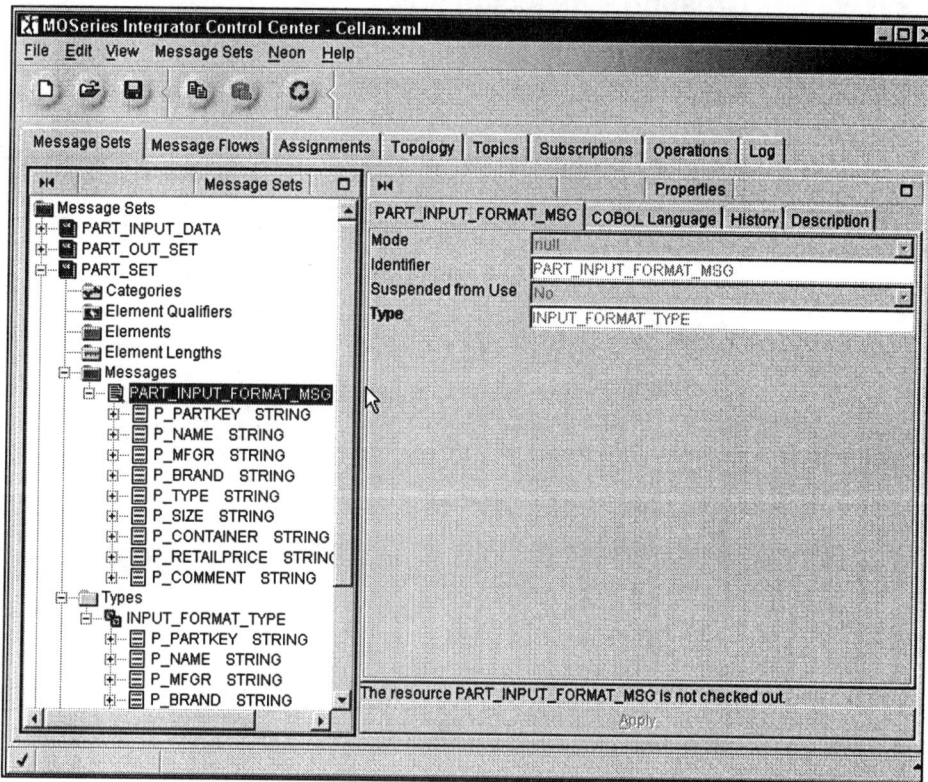

Figure A-4 Defining a message set

Creating a message flow

To create a message flow:

- Click on the **Message Flow** tab as shown in Figure A-5.

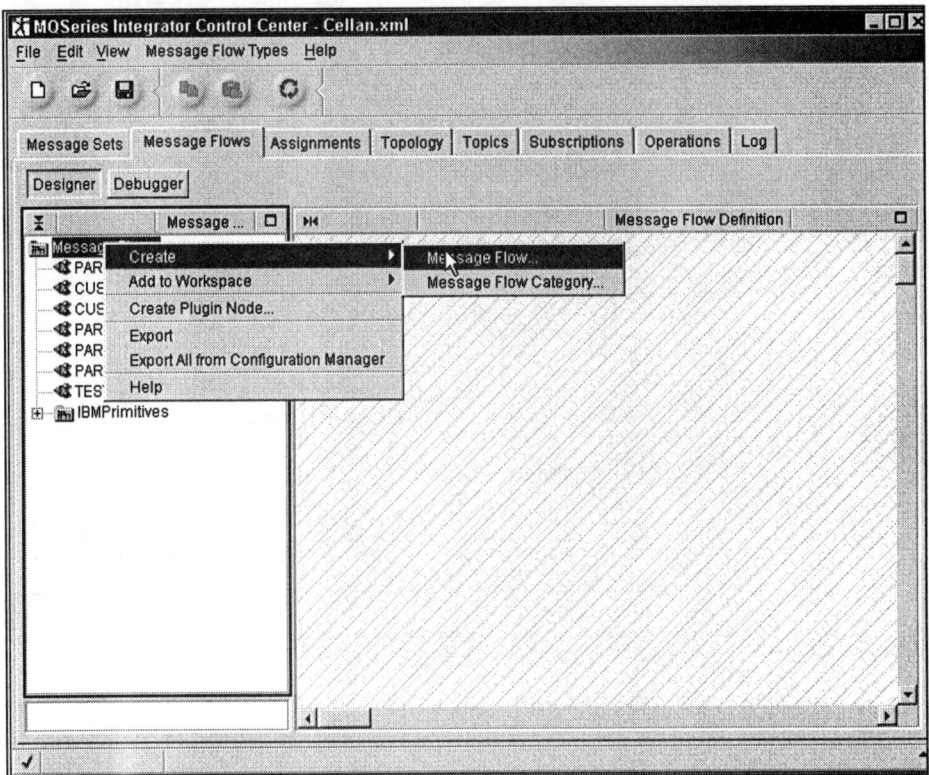

Figure A-5   Defining a message flow

- Provide a name (PART1)
- Expand the **IBM Primitives** folder and drag elements from it to the workspace in the right hand screen. For our ODS example, we created the screen in Figure A-6.

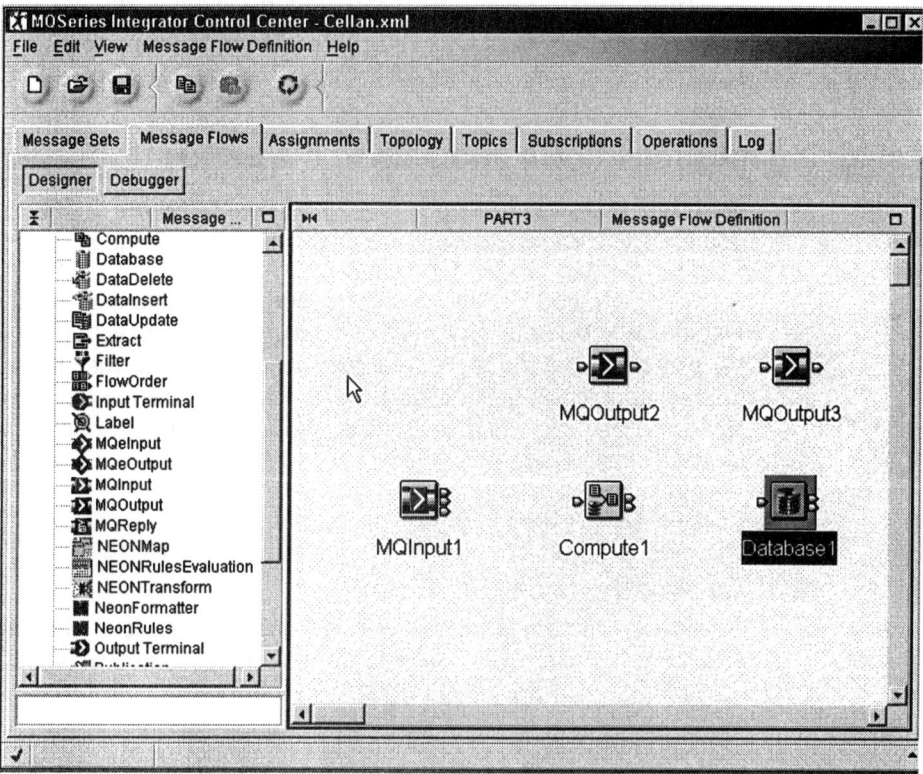

Figure A-6   Designing the message flow

- Right-click on each node to rename them to something meaningful, then right-click on each again to connect them up together.
- Again right-click on each and select *properties*. With the MQInput nodes select the **Basic** tab and provide a queue name. This queue must exist in MQseries. On the MQOutput nodes the queue can exist on a remote queue manager, that is on the same machine or a different one.

The Database node and Compute nodes are more complex and are explained in detail in MQSI manuals such as *Using the Control Center*, SC34-5602.

This message flow is saved by doing:

File -> Check In -> All in Workspace

> **Note:** Whenever you wish to update a resource, you must check it out by right-clicking on it. This locks the resource so that no-one else can update it. To save, you must check it back in.

Assigning message flows and sets to the broker

To assign message flows and sets to the broker, on the MQSI Control Center, you have to click on the **Assignments** tab and to define an execution group.

An execution group is the *container* process into which all message flows are instantiated. A default execution group will be created with your new broker. You have to check out the broker and execution group you wish to update and also the message flows and message sets which you wish to include in that broker. Now drag the flow and message sets from the center panel into the default execution group and save everything by checking them back in again

(File---> Check In ---> All in Workspace).

Deploy the broker domain

Now deploy the broker domain by right-clicking the broker and clicking **Deploy** and then 'Complete Assignments Configuration' as shown in Figure A-7.

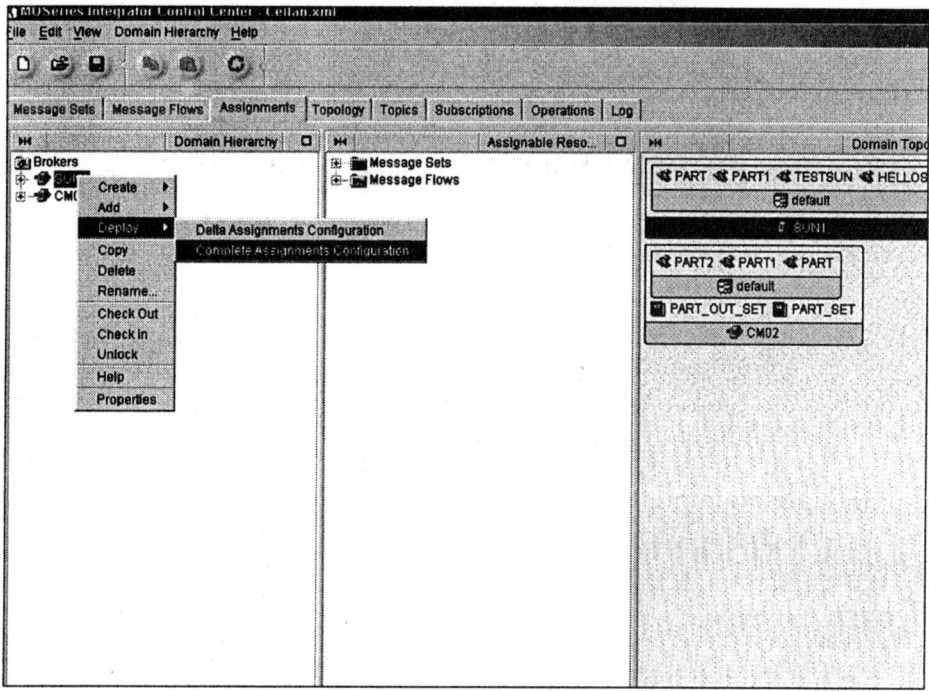

Figure A-7   Deploying the message flow

The message flow is now operational in the target broker domain.

Example CICS program

This appendix contains the listing of the program PARTQ1. This is also known as the PART transaction in CICS, which was used to read data from the VSAM delta file and to write it to a queue called PARTQ1 on the local z/OS machine.

Example: B-1 PARTQ1 CICS program

```
PARTQ1: PROC (PARAM) OPTIONS(MAIN);
 DCL   PARAM CHAR(100) VARYING;

  DCL SYSPRINT   FILE STREAM OUTPUT PRINT;

 /**********************************************************************/
 /*       Copy file of MQ definitions                                  */
 /**********************************************************************/
 %include syslib(cmqp) ;
 %include syslib(cmqepp) ;


 /*******************************************************/
 /* WORKING STORAGE DECLARATIONS                        */
 /*******************************************************/
   DCL MQMNAME                CHAR(48) INIT('MQ7A');
   DCL QUEUE_NAME             CHAR(6) INIT('PARTQ1');
   DCL COMPCODE               BINARY FIXED (31);
   DCL REASON                 BINARY FIXED (31);
   DCL HCONN                  BINARY FIXED (31);
   DCL HOBJ                   BINARY FIXED (31);
```

```
   DCL OPTIONS              BINARY FIXED (31);
   DCL BUFFLEN              BINARY FIXED (31);
   DCL BUFFER               CHAR(190);
   DCL PARTQ1               CHAR(45);
   DCL QMGR                 CHAR(4);
 /***********************************************************/
 /* LOCAL COPY OF OBJECT DESCRIPTOR                         */
 /***********************************************************/

 DCL 1 LMQOD   LIKE MQOD;

 /***********************************************************/
 /* OPEN YOUR QUEUE                                         */
 /***********************************************************/


 /***************************************************************/
 /* SET UP OBJECT DESCRIPTOR FOR OPEN OF REPLY QUEUE            */
 /***************************************************************/


 LMQOD.OBJECTTYPE = MQOT_Q;
 LMQOD.OBJECTNAME = QUEUE_NAME;
 OPTIONS = MQOO_OUTPUT;

 CALL MQOPEN (HCONN,
              LMQOD,
              OPTIONS,
              HOBJ,
              COMPCODE,
              REASON);

 /***********************************************************/
 /* CREATE YOUR MESSAGE                                     */
 /***********************************************************/

   DCL KEY CHAR(8) INIT('        ');
 /***************************************************************/
 /* LOCAL COPY OF MESSAGE DESCRIPTOR                            */
 /* AND PUT MESSAGE OPTIONS                                     */
 /***************************************************************/

   DCL 1 LMQMD   LIKE MQMD;
   DCL 1 LMQPMO LIKE MQPMO;
 /***************************************************************/
 /* SET UP MESSAGE DESCRIPTOR                                   */
 /***************************************************************/
 LMQMD.MSGTYPE = MQMT_DATAGRAM;
 LMQMD.PRIORITY = 1;
 LMQMD.PERSISTENCE = MQPER_PERSISTENT;
```

```
       LMQMD.REPLYTOQ = PARTQ1;
       LMQMD.REPLYTOQMGR = QMGR;
       LMQMD.MSGID = MQMI_NONE;
       LMQMD.CORRELID = MQCI_NONE;
       LMQMD.FORMAT = MQFMT_STRING;

       /***********************************************************/
       /* SET UP PUT MESSAGE OPTIONS                              */
       /***********************************************************/
         LMQPMO.OPTIONS = MQPMO_NO_SYNCPOINT;

       /***********************************************************/
       /* SET UP LENGTH OF MESSAGE BUFFER AND THE MESSAGE         */
       /***********************************************************/

       BUFFLEN = LENGTH(BUFFER);
       BUFFER = PL1_TEST_MESSAGE;

       /***********************************************************/
       /*                                                         */
       /* HCONN WAS SET BY PREVIOUS MQCONN REQUEST.               */
       /* HOBJ WAS SET BY PREVIOUS MQOPEN REQUEST.                */
       /*                                                         */
       /***********************************************************/
       EXEC CICS STARTBR FILE('PARTFIL3') RIDFLD(KEY);
       I = 0;
       EXEC CICS HANDLE CONDITION ENDFILE(ENDBR);
       DO WHILE (I < 1000);
       EXEC CICS READNEXT FILE('PARTFIL3') RIDFLD(KEY) INTO(BUFFER);
       CALL MQPUT (HCONN,
                   HOBJ,
                   LMQMD,
                   LMQPMO,
                   BUFFLEN,
                   BUFFER,
                   COMPCODE,
                   REASON);
         LMQMD.MSGID = MQMI_NONE;
         LMQMD.CORRELID = MQCI_NONE;
       /***********************************************************/
       /* TEST THE COMPLETION CODE OF THE PUT CALL.               */
       /* IF THE CALL HAS FAILED ISSUE AN ERROR MESSAGE           */
       /* SHOWING THE COMPLETION CODE AND THE REASON CODE.        */
       /***********************************************************/
       I = I + 1;
       END; /* END DO WHILE */
       ENDBR:
       EXEC CICS ENDBR FILE('PARTFIL3');
       EXEC CICS START TRANSACTION('PART') INTERVAL(000030);
```

```
END PARTQ1;
```

Population subsystem: tables; SQL stored procedures

This appendix contains the listing of the SQL Stored Procedures developed for use in the integrated example which was presented in Chapter 7, "Building and managing the ODS population subsystem" on page 189, as well as definitions of the tables.

Example tables

This section describes the definitions of the PART tables used in DB2 for z/OS and Oracle as the definition of the PART file used in VSAM.

Part source table in DB2 for z/OS

The definition of the PART table in DB2 for z/OS is shown in Figure C-1.

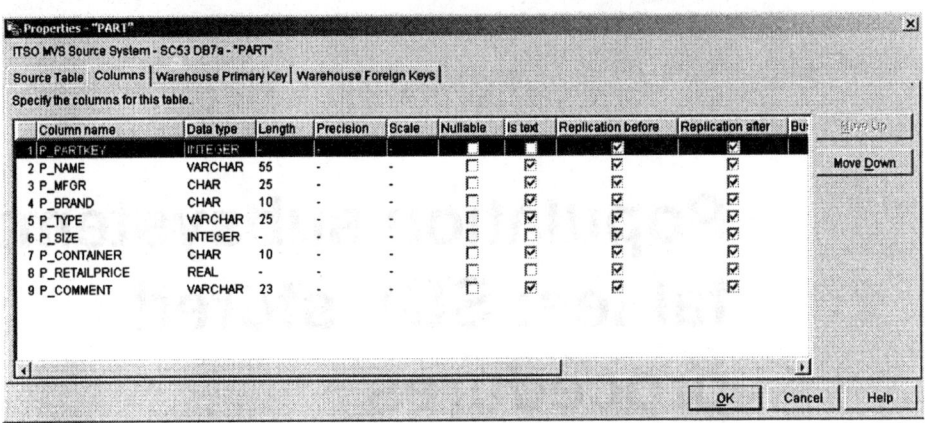

Figure C-1   Table definition for the PART table in the DB2 for z/OS database

PART source table in Oracle

The definition of the PART table in ORACLE is shown in Figure C-2.

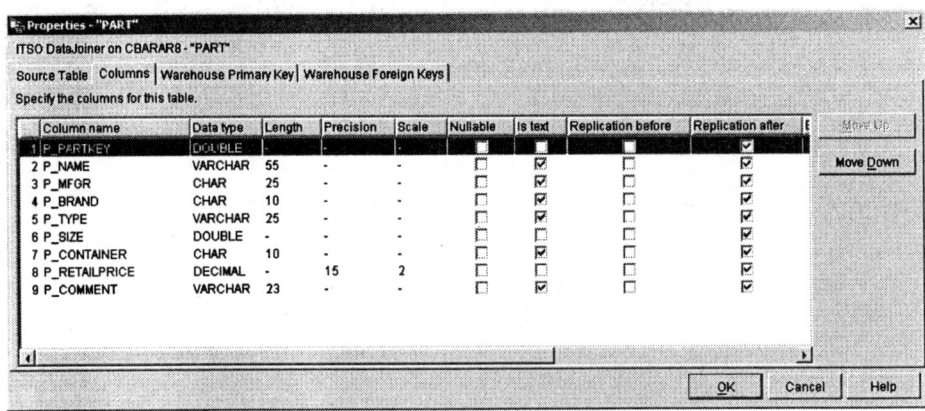

Figure C-2   Table definition for the PART table in the Oracle database

PART source in VSAM file

The definition of the PART file in VSAM is shown in Figure C-3.

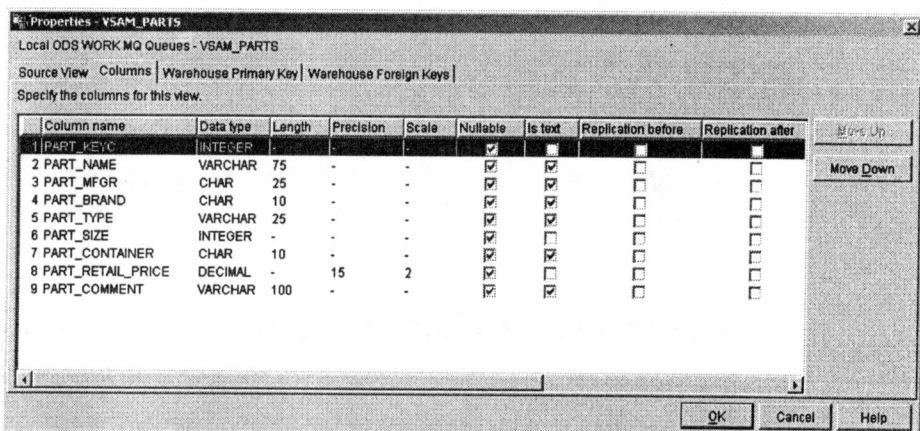

Figure C-3 Relational view of the MQ queue representing the VSAM PART file

DB2 for z/OS PART staging table

The definition of the staging area in DB2 used for the DB2 for z/OS table is shown in Figure C-4.

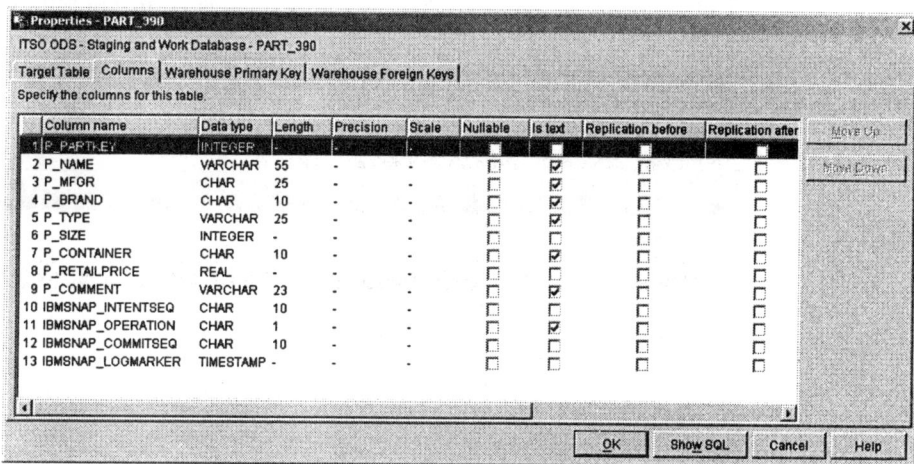

Figure C-4 Table used for staging change records from the DB2 PART table

Oracle PART staging table

The definition of the staging area in DB2 used for the ORACLE table is shown in Figure C-5

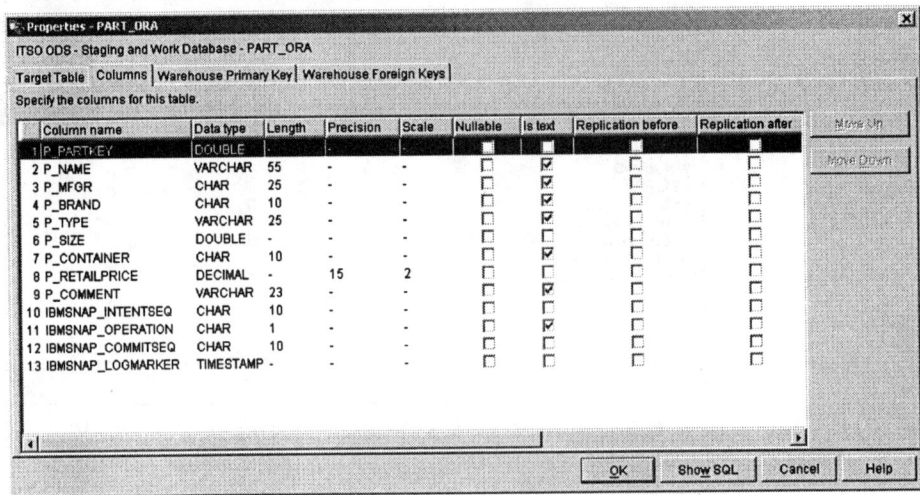

Figure C-5 Table used for staging change records from the Oracle PART table

Common changed data table

The definition of common changed data table is shown in Figure C-6

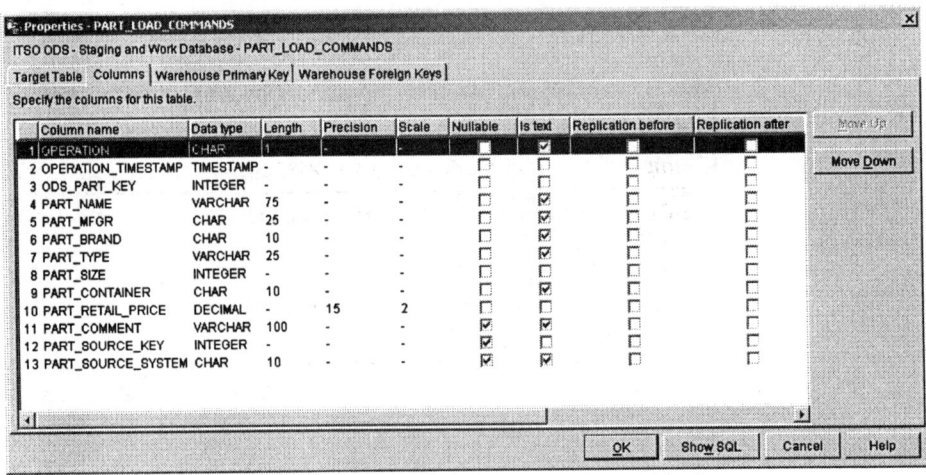

Figure C-6 Table used to store the common change records

ODS PART table

The definition of the final consolidated table in the ODS is shown in Figure C-7

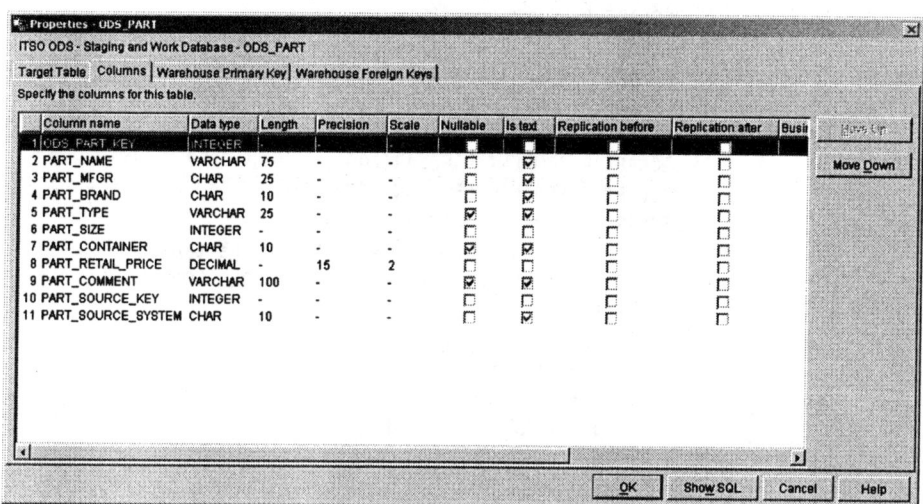

Figure C-7   The final consolidated PART table in the ODS

Stored Procedures

This section provides the stored procedures listings.

Stored Procedure to process the change records from DB2 for z/OS

The Stored Procedure in Example C-1 process the change records from DB2 for z/OS.

Example: C-1   Stored procedure for DWC Step: "Create Commands for 390 PART"

```
CREATE PROCEDURE DB2ADMIN.Create_Commands_For_390_Parts ( )
    RESULT SETS 1
    LANGUAGE SQL
------------------------------------------------------------------
-- SQL Stored Procedure
------------------------------------------------------------------
P1: BEGIN

    DECLARE insert_count, delete_count, update_count, error_count, total_count,
surrogate_key, uncommitted_records INTEGER DEFAULT 0;
    DECLARE beginning_timestamp TIMESTAMP;
    DECLARE commit_count INTEGER DEFAULT 100;
```

```
        DECLARE row_found CHAR(3) DEFAULT 'yes';
        DECLARE P_PARTKEY INTEGER;
        DECLARE P_NAME VARCHAR(75);
        DECLARE P_MFGR CHAR(25);
        DECLARE P_BRAND CHAR(10);
        DECLARE P_TYPE CHAR(25);
        DECLARE P_SIZE INTEGER;
        DECLARE P_CONTAINER CHAR(10);
        DECLARE P_RETAILPRICE DECIMAL (15,2);
        DECLARE P_COMMENT VARCHAR(100);
        DECLARE IBMSNAP_OPERATION CHAR(1);
        DECLARE IBMSNAP_LOGMARKER TIMESTAMP;
-- Loop thru all rows in the PART_390 change table
        DECLARE part_390_cursor CURSOR WITH HOLD FOR
            SELECT
                IWH.PART_390.P_PARTKEY,
                IWH.PART_390.P_NAME,
                IWH.PART_390.P_MFGR,
                IWH.PART_390.P_BRAND,
                IWH.PART_390.P_TYPE,
                IWH.PART_390.P_SIZE,
                IWH.PART_390.P_CONTAINER,
                IWH.PART_390.P_RETAILPRICE,
                IWH.PART_390.P_COMMENT,
                IWH.PART_390.IBMSNAP_OPERATION,
                IWH.PART_390.IBMSNAP_LOGMARKER
            FROM
                IWH.PART_390;

        DECLARE CONTINUE HANDLER FOR NOT FOUND
            SET row_found = 'no';

        SET beginning_timestamp = CURRENT TIMESTAMP;

        OPEN part_390_cursor;
        FETCH part_390_cursor INTO P_PARTKEY, P_NAME, P_MFGR, P_BRAND, P_TYPE,
P_SIZE, P_CONTAINER,
            P_RETAILPRICE, P_COMMENT, IBMSNAP_OPERATION, IBMSNAP_LOGMARKER;

        WHILE row_found = 'yes' DO

            CASE IBMSNAP_OPERATION
                WHEN 'I'
                    -- When it is an insert record, we assign a new key using the
ods_part_seq sequence
                    THEN BEGIN
                        INSERT INTO IWH.PART_LOAD_COMMANDS
                            (
                                OPERATION,
```

```sql
                        OPERATION_TIMESTAMP,
                        ODS_PART_KEY,
                        PART_NAME,
                        PART_MFGR,
                        PART_BRAND,
                        PART_TYPE,
                        PART_SIZE,
                        PART_CONTAINER,
                        PART_RETAIL_PRICE,
                        PART_COMMENT,
                        PART_SOURCE_KEY,
                        PART_SOURCE_SYSTEM
                    )
                VALUES
                    (
                        IBMSNAP_OPERATION,
                        IBMSNAP_LOGMARKER,     -- we do not have an update
timestamp as part of the data, so we use the replication-provided timestamp
                        NEXTVAL FOR ODS_PART_SEQ,
                        P_NAME,
                        P_MFGR,
                        P_BRAND,
                        P_TYPE,
                        P_SIZE,
                        P_CONTAINER,
                        P_RETAILPRICE,
                        P_COMMENT,
                        P_PARTKEY,
                        'DB7A'


                    ) ;
                SET insert_count = insert_count + 1;
                END;
            WHEN 'U'
            -- When it is an update record, we need to lookup the surrogate key
                THEN BEGIN

                    SET surrogate_key = (SELECT ODS_PART_KEY
                                    FROM IWH.ODS_PART
                                    WHERE PART_SOURCE_KEY = P_PARTKEY AND
PART_SOURCE_SYSTEM = 'DB7A');
                    INSERT INTO IWH.PART_LOAD_COMMANDS
                        (
                            OPERATION,
                            OPERATION_TIMESTAMP,
                            ODS_PART_KEY,
                            PART_NAME,
                            PART_MFGR,
```

```
                            PART_BRAND,
                            PART_TYPE,
                            PART_SIZE,
                            PART_CONTAINER,
                            PART_RETAIL_PRICE,
                            PART_COMMENT,
                            PART_SOURCE_KEY,
                            PART_SOURCE_SYSTEM
                          )
                        VALUES
                          (
                            IBMSNAP_OPERATION,
                            IBMSNAP_LOGMARKER,    -- we do not have an update
timestamp as part of the data, so we use the replication-provided timestamp
                            surrogate_key,
                            P_NAME,
                            P_MFGR,
                            P_BRAND,
                            P_TYPE,
                            P_SIZE,
                            P_CONTAINER,
                            P_RETAILPRICE,
                            P_COMMENT,
                            P_PARTKEY,
                            'DB7A'



                          );
                    SET update_count = update_count + 1;
                  END;
               WHEN 'D'
                    -- When it is a delete record, we need to lookup the surrogate
key
                  THEN BEGIN
                    SET surrogate_key = (SELECT ODS_PART_KEY FROM IWH.ODS_PART
WHERE PART_SOURCE_KEY = P_PARTKEY AND PART_SOURCE_SYSTEM = 'DB7A');
                       insert into db2admin.my_messages values (current timestamp,
'surrogate key: [' concat char(surrogate_key) concat ']');
                       insert into db2admin.my_messages values (current timestamp,
'operation: [' concat ibmsnap_operation concat ']');
                       INSERT INTO IWH.PART_LOAD_COMMANDS
                         (
                            OPERATION,
                            OPERATION_TIMESTAMP,
                            ODS_PART_KEY,
                            PART_NAME,
                            PART_MFGR,
                            PART_BRAND,
                            PART_TYPE,
```

```
                        PART_SIZE,
                        PART_CONTAINER,
                        PART_RETAIL_PRICE,
                        PART_COMMENT,
                        PART_SOURCE_KEY,
                        PART_SOURCE_SYSTEM
                    )
                VALUES
                    (
                        IBMSNAP_OPERATION,
                        IBMSNAP_LOGMARKER,     -- we do not have an update
timestamp as part of the data, so we use the replication-provided timestamp
                        surrogate_key,
                        P_NAME,
                        P_MFGR,
                        P_BRAND,
                        P_TYPE,
                        P_SIZE,
                        P_CONTAINER,
                        P_RETAILPRICE,
                        P_COMMENT,
                        P_PARTKEY,
                        'DB7A'


                    ) ;
                SET delete_count = delete_count + 1;
                END;
            ELSE SET error_count = error_count + 1;  -- we would also put the
bad record in a reject table
        END CASE;
        DELETE FROM IWH.PART_390 WHERE CURRENT OF PART_390_CURSOR;

            SET uncommitted_records = uncommitted_records + 1;
        IF uncommitted_records > commit_count
            THEN
                commit;
                SET uncommitted_records = 0;
            end if;
    FETCH part_390_cursor INTO P_PARTKEY, P_NAME, P_MFGR, P_BRAND, P_TYPE,
P_SIZE, P_CONTAINER,
            P_RETAILPRICE, P_COMMENT, IBMSNAP_OPERATION, IBMSNAP_LOGMARKER;


    END WHILE;
-- create log entry

    INSERT INTO IWH.ODS_PART_LOG
        (
```

```
                STEP,
                TIMESTAMP,
                BEGIN_TIMESTAMP,
                END_TIMESTAMP,
                NUMBER_INSERTS,
                NUMBER_DELETES,
                NUMBER_UPDATES,
                NUMBER_ERRORS
            )
        VALUES
            (
                'Commands for 390 Parts',
                CURRENT TIMESTAMP,
                beginning_timestamp,
                CURRENT TIMESTAMP,
                insert_count,
                delete_count,
                update_count,
                error_count
            );

        COMMIT;

    END P1
```

Stored Procedure to process the change records from Oracle

The Stored Procedure in Example C-2 process the change records from Oracle.

Example: C-2   Stored procedure for DWC Step: "Create Commands for Ora PARTS"

```
CREATE PROCEDURE DB2ADMIN.Create_Commands_For_Ora_Parts ( )
    RESULT SETS 1
    LANGUAGE SQL
------------------------------------------------------------------------
-- SQL Stored Procedure
------------------------------------------------------------------------
P1: BEGIN

    DECLARE insert_count, delete_count, update_count, error_count, total_count,
surrogate_key, uncommitted_records INTEGER DEFAULT 0;
    DECLARE beginning_timestamp TIMESTAMP;
    DECLARE commit_count INTEGER DEFAULT 100;
    DECLARE row_found CHAR(3) DEFAULT 'yes';
    DECLARE P_PARTKEY INTEGER;
    DECLARE P_NAME VARCHAR(75);
    DECLARE P_MFGR CHAR(25);
    DECLARE P_BRAND CHAR(10);
    DECLARE P_TYPE CHAR(25);
```

```sql
        DECLARE P_SIZE INTEGER;
        DECLARE P_CONTAINER CHAR(10);
        DECLARE P_RETAILPRICE DECIMAL (15,2);
        DECLARE P_COMMENT VARCHAR(100);
        DECLARE IBMSNAP_OPERATION CHAR(1);
        DECLARE IBMSNAP_LOGMARKER TIMESTAMP;
-- Loop thru all rows in the PART_ORA change table
        DECLARE PART_ORA_CURSOR CURSOR WITH HOLD FOR
            SELECT
                IWH.PART_ORA.P_PARTKEY,
                IWH.PART_ORA.P_NAME,
                IWH.PART_ORA.P_MFGR,
                IWH.PART_ORA.P_BRAND,
                IWH.PART_ORA.P_TYPE,
                IWH.PART_ORA.P_SIZE,
                IWH.PART_ORA.P_CONTAINER,
                IWH.PART_ORA.P_RETAILPRICE,
                IWH.PART_ORA.P_COMMENT,
                IWH.PART_ORA.IBMSNAP_OPERATION,
                IWH.PART_ORA.IBMSNAP_LOGMARKER
            FROM
                IWH.PART_ORA;

        DECLARE CONTINUE HANDLER FOR NOT FOUND
            SET row_found = 'no';

        SET beginning_timestamp = CURRENT TIMESTAMP;

        OPEN PART_ORA_CURSOR;
        FETCH PART_ORA_CURSOR INTO P_PARTKEY, P_NAME, P_MFGR, P_BRAND, P_TYPE, P_SIZE, P_CONTAINER,
            P_RETAILPRICE, P_COMMENT, IBMSNAP_OPERATION, IBMSNAP_LOGMARKER;


        WHILE row_found = 'yes' DO

            CASE IBMSNAP_OPERATION
                WHEN 'I'
                -- When it is an insert record, we assign a new key using the ods_part_seq sequence
                THEN BEGIN
                    INSERT INTO IWH.PART_LOAD_COMMANDS
                        (
                            OPERATION,
                            OPERATION_TIMESTAMP,
                            ODS_PART_KEY,
                            PART_NAME,
                            PART_MFGR,
                            PART_BRAND,
```

```sql
                              PART_TYPE,
                              PART_SIZE,
                              PART_CONTAINER,
                              PART_RETAIL_PRICE,
                              PART_COMMENT,
                              PART_SOURCE_KEY,
                              PART_SOURCE_SYSTEM
                              )
                      VALUES
                          (
                              IBMSNAP_OPERATION,
                              IBMSNAP_LOGMARKER,    -- we do not have an update
timestamp as part of the data, so we use the replication-provided timestamp
                              NEXTVAL FOR ODS_PART_SEQ,
                              P_NAME,
                              P_MFGR,
                              P_BRAND,
                              P_TYPE,
                              P_SIZE,
                              P_CONTAINER,
                              P_RETAILPRICE,
                              P_COMMENT,
                              P_PARTKEY,
                              'ORA'


                          ) ;
                 SET insert_count = insert_count + 1;
                 END;
               WHEN 'U'
               -- When it is an update record, we need to lookup the surrogate key
                      THEN BEGIN

                      SET surrogate_key = (SELECT ODS_PART_KEY
                                           FROM IWH.ODS_PART
                                           WHERE PART_SOURCE_KEY = P_PARTKEY AND
PART_SOURCE_SYSTEM = 'ORA');
                      INSERT INTO IWH.PART_LOAD_COMMANDS
                          (
                              OPERATION,
                              OPERATION_TIMESTAMP,
                              ODS_PART_KEY,
                              PART_NAME,
                              PART_MFGR,
                              PART_BRAND,
                              PART_TYPE,
                              PART_SIZE,
                              PART_CONTAINER,
                              PART_RETAIL_PRICE,
```

```
                          PART_COMMENT,
                          PART_SOURCE_KEY,
                          PART_SOURCE_SYSTEM
                     )
                 VALUES
                     (
                          IBMSNAP_OPERATION,
                          IBMSNAP_LOGMARKER,    -- we do not have an update
timestamp as part of the data, so we use the replication-provided timestamp
                          surrogate_key,
                          P_NAME,
                          P_MFGR,
                          P_BRAND,
                          P_TYPE,
                          P_SIZE,
                          P_CONTAINER,
                          P_RETAILPRICE,
                          P_COMMENT,
                          P_PARTKEY,
                          'ORA'


                     ) ;
               SET update_count = update_count + 1;
               END;
            WHEN 'D'
               -- When it is a delete record, we need to lookup the surrogate key
               THEN BEGIN
                  SET surrogate_key = (SELECT ODS_PART_KEY FROM IWH.ODS_PART
WHERE PART_SOURCE_KEY = P_PARTKEY AND PART_SOURCE_SYSTEM = 'ORA');
                  insert into db2admin.my_messages values (current timestamp,
'surrogate key: [' concat char(surrogate_key) concat ']');
                  insert into db2admin.my_messages values (current timestamp,
'operation: [' concat ibmsnap_operation concat ']');
                  INSERT INTO IWH.PART_LOAD_COMMANDS
                     (
                          OPERATION,
                          OPERATION_TIMESTAMP,
                          ODS_PART_KEY,
                          PART_NAME,
                          PART_MFGR,
                          PART_BRAND,
                          PART_TYPE,
                          PART_SIZE,
                          PART_CONTAINER,
                          PART_RETAIL_PRICE,
                          PART_COMMENT,
                          PART_SOURCE_KEY,
```

```
                        PART_SOURCE_SYSTEM
                    )
                VALUES
                    (
                        IBMSNAP_OPERATION,
                        IBMSNAP_LOGMARKER,     -- we do not have an update
timestamp as part of the data, so we use the replication-provided timestamp
                        surrogate_key,
                        P_NAME,
                        P_MFGR,
                        P_BRAND,
                        P_TYPE,
                        P_SIZE,
                        P_CONTAINER,
                        P_RETAILPRICE,
                        P_COMMENT,
                        P_PARTKEY,
                        'ORA'


                    ) ;
                SET delete_count = delete_count + 1;
                END;
            ELSE SET error_count = error_count + 1;   -- we would also put the
bad record in a reject table
        END CASE;
        DELETE FROM IWH.PART_ORA WHERE CURRENT OF PART_ORA_CURSOR;

            SET uncommitted_records = uncommitted_records + 1;
        IF uncommitted_records > commit_count
            THEN
                commit;
                SET uncommitted_records = 0;
            end if;
    FETCH PART_ORA_CURSOR INTO P_PARTKEY, P_NAME, P_MFGR, P_BRAND, P_TYPE,
P_SIZE, P_CONTAINER,
            P_RETAILPRICE, P_COMMENT, IBMSNAP_OPERATION, IBMSNAP_LOGMARKER;


    END WHILE;

    -- create log entry

    INSERT INTO IWH.ODS_PART_LOG
        (
            STEP,
            TIMESTAMP,
            BEGIN_TIMESTAMP,
            END_TIMESTAMP,
```

```
                NUMBER_INSERTS,
                NUMBER_DELETES,
                NUMBER_UPDATES,
                NUMBER_ERRORS
            )
        VALUES
            (
                'Commands for Ora Parts',
                CURRENT TIMESTAMP,
                beginning_timestamp,
                CURRENT TIMESTAMP,
                insert_count,
                delete_count,
                update_count,
                error_count
            );

        COMMIT;


END P1
```

Stored Procedure to process the change records from VSAM

The Stored Procedure in Example C-3 processes the change records from VSAM.

Example: C-3 Stored procedure for DWC Step: "Create Commands for VSAM Parts"

```
CREATE PROCEDURE DB2ADMIN.Create_Commands_For_VSAM_Parts ( )
    RESULT SETS 1
    LANGUAGE SQL
------------------------------------------------------------------------
-- SQL Stored Procedure
------------------------------------------------------------------------
P1: BEGIN

    DECLARE insert_count, delete_count, update_count, error_count, total_count,
 surrogate_key, uncommitted_records INTEGER DEFAULT 0;
    DECLARE beginning_timestamp TIMESTAMP;
    DECLARE row_found CHAR(3) DEFAULT 'yes';
    DECLARE commit_count INTEGER DEFAULT 100;
    DECLARE INPARTKEY INTEGER;
    DECLARE INPARTNAME VARCHAR(75);
    DECLARE INPARTMFGR CHAR(25);
    DECLARE INPARTBRAND CHAR(10);
    DECLARE INPARTTYPE CHAR(25);
```

```
            DECLARE INPARTSIZE INTEGER;
            DECLARE INPARTCONTAINER CHAR(10);
            DECLARE INPARTRETAILPRICE DECIMAL (15,2);
            DECLARE INPARTCOMMENT VARCHAR(100);
            declare drow_count integer default 0;    --debug

              DECLARE C1 CURSOR WITH HOLD FOR
                 SELECT
                    PART_KEYC,
                    PART_NAME,
                    PART_MFGR,
                    PART_BRAND,
                    PART_TYPE,
                    PART_SIZE,
                    PART_CONTAINER,
                    PART_RETAIL_PRICE,
                    PART_COMMENT
                 FROM
                    DB2ADMIN.VSAM_PARTS;

            DECLARE CONTINUE HANDLER FOR NOT FOUND
            begin -- debug
              insert into db2admin.my_messages values (current timestamp,'handler for not
found');   -- debug
                 SET row_found = 'no';
            end; -- debug



            SET beginning_timestamp = CURRENT TIMESTAMP;
              insert into db2admin.my_messages values (current timestamp,'start SP');   --
debug

            OPEN C1;
                 FETCH C1 INTO INPARTKEY, INPARTNAME, INPARTMFGR, INPARTBRAND,
INPARTTYPE, INPARTSIZE, INPARTCONTAINER, INPARTRETAILPRICE,INPARTCOMMENT;

              -- Loop thru all rows in the VSAM_PARTS change table
            WHILE row_found = 'yes' DO
                   Insert into db2admin.my_messages values (current
timestamp,char(inpartkey) concat ' -- inpartkey');    -- debug

                    SET surrogate_key = (SELECT ODS_PART_KEY
                             FROM IWH.ODS_PART
                            WHERE PART_SOURCE_KEY = INPARTKEY AND PART_SOURCE_SYSTEM =
'VSAM');

                      CASE
                         WHEN surrogate_key is null
```

```
                    -- Then it is an insert record, we assign a new key using the
ods_part_seq sequence
                THEN BEGIN
                    insert into db2admin.my_messages values (current
timestamp,'row not found leg of case');  -- debug
                    INSERT INTO IWH.PART_LOAD_COMMANDS
                        (
                        OPERATION,
                        OPERATION_TIMESTAMP,
                        ODS_PART_KEY,
                        PART_NAME,
                        PART_MFGR,
                        PART_BRAND,
                        PART_TYPE,
                        PART_SIZE,
                        PART_CONTAINER,
                        PART_RETAIL_PRICE,
                        PART_COMMENT,
                        PART_SOURCE_KEY,
                        PART_SOURCE_SYSTEM
                        )
                    VALUES
                        (
                        'I',
                        CURRENT TIMESTAMP,       -- we do not have Atimestamp
as part of the data, so we use the current time
                        NEXTVAL FOR ODS_PART_SEQ,
                        INPARTNAME,
                        INPARTMFGR,
                        INPARTBRAND,
                        INPARTTYPE,
                        INPARTSIZE,
                        INPARTCONTAINER,
                        INPARTRETAILPRICE,
                        INPARTCOMMENT,
                        INPARTKEY,
                        'VSAM'


                        ) ;
                    SET insert_count = insert_count + 1;
                    END;

                ELSE BEGIN
                    insert into db2admin.my_messages values (current
timestamp,'record found - surrogate_key = ' concat char(surrogate_key));  --
debug
                    -- Then it is an update record, we need to use the surrogate key
                    INSERT INTO IWH.PART_LOAD_COMMANDS
```

```
                        (
                            OPERATION,
                            OPERATION_TIMESTAMP,
                            ODS_PART_KEY,
                            PART_NAME,
                            PART_MFGR,
                            PART_BRAND,
                            PART_TYPE,
                            PART_SIZE,
                            PART_CONTAINER,
                            PART_RETAIL_PRICE,
                            PART_COMMENT,
                            PART_SOURCE_KEY,
                            PART_SOURCE_SYSTEM
                        )
                    VALUES
                        (
                            'U',
                            CURRENT TIMESTAMP,      -- we do not have Atimestamp
as part of the data, so we use the current time
                            surrogate_key,
                            INPARTNAME,
                            INPARTMFGR,
                            INPARTBRAND,
                            INPARTTYPE,
                            INPARTSIZE,
                            INPARTCONTAINER,
                            INPARTRETAILPRICE,
                            INPARTCOMMENT,
                            INPARTKEY,
                            'VSAM'


                        ) ;
                    SET update_count = update_count + 1;
                    END;

        END CASE;
        -- this is where we would normally delete the just-processed row, but
the input is actually a desctructive read from a MQ Queue

            SET uncommitted_records = uncommitted_records + 1;
        IF uncommitted_records > commit_count
            THEN
                commit;
                SET uncommitted_records = 0;
        end if;
```

```
        FETCH C1 INTO INPARTKEY, INPARTNAME, INPARTMFGR, INPARTBRAND,
INPARTTYPE, INPARTSIZE, INPARTCONTAINER, INPARTRETAILPRICE,INPARTCOMMENT;

    END WHILE;
-- create log entry
INSERT INTO IWH.ODS_PART_LOG
        (
            STEP,
            TIMESTAMP,
            BEGIN_TIMESTAMP,
            END_TIMESTAMP,
            NUMBER_INSERTS,
            NUMBER_DELETES,
            NUMBER_UPDATES,
            NUMBER_ERRORS
        )
    VALUES
        (
            'Commands for VSAM Parts',
            CURRENT TIMESTAMP,
            beginning_timestamp,
            CURRENT TIMESTAMP,
            insert_count,
            delete_count,
            update_count,
            error_count
        );
COMMIT;
END P1
```

Stored Procedure to apply the final change records to the ODS

The Stored Procedure in Example C-4 applies the final change records to the ODS.

Example: C-4 Stored procedure for DWC Step: "Load ODS Parts"

```
CREATE PROCEDURE DB2ADMIN.LOAD_ODS_PARTS ( )
    LANGUAGE SQL
------------------------------------------------------------------------
-- SQL Stored Procedure
------------------------------------------------------------------------
P1: BEGIN
    -- Declare variable

    DECLARE insert_count, delete_count, update_count, error_count, total_count,
uncommitted_records INTEGER DEFAULT 0;
```

```
    DECLARE commit_count INTEGER DEFAULT 100;
    DECLARE beginning_timestamp TIMESTAMP;
    DECLARE IN_OPERATION CHAR(1);
    DECLARE IN_OPERATION_TIMESTAMP TIMESTAMP;
    DECLARE IN_ODS_PART_KEY INTEGER;
    DECLARE IN_PART_NAME VARCHAR(75);
    DECLARE IN_PART_MFGR CHAR(25);
    DECLARE IN_PART_BRAND CHAR(10);
    DECLARE IN_PART_TYPE CHAR(25);
    DECLARE IN_PART_SIZE INTEGER;
    DECLARE IN_PART_CONTAINER CHAR(10);
    DECLARE IN_PART_RETAIL_PRICE DECIMAL (15,2);
    DECLARE IN_PART_COMMENT VARCHAR(100);
    DECLARE IN_PART_SOURCE_KEY INTEGER;
    DECLARE IN_PART_SOURCE_SYSTEM CHAR(10);
DECLARE row_found CHAR(3) DEFAULT 'yes';

-- Declare cursor

DECLARE part_cmd_cursor CURSOR WITH HOLD FOR
    SELECT
        IWH.PART_LOAD_COMMANDS.OPERATION,
        IWH.PART_LOAD_COMMANDS.OPERATION_TIMESTAMP,
        IWH.PART_LOAD_COMMANDS.ODS_PART_KEY,
        IWH.PART_LOAD_COMMANDS.PART_NAME,
        IWH.PART_LOAD_COMMANDS.PART_MFGR,
        IWH.PART_LOAD_COMMANDS.PART_BRAND,
        IWH.PART_LOAD_COMMANDS.PART_TYPE,
        IWH.PART_LOAD_COMMANDS.PART_SIZE,
        IWH.PART_LOAD_COMMANDS.PART_CONTAINER,
        IWH.PART_LOAD_COMMANDS.PART_RETAIL_PRICE,
        IWH.PART_LOAD_COMMANDS.PART_COMMENT,
        IWH.PART_LOAD_COMMANDS.PART_SOURCE_KEY,
        IWH.PART_LOAD_COMMANDS.PART_SOURCE_SYSTEM
    FROM
        IWH.PART_LOAD_COMMANDS;


    DECLARE CONTINUE HANDLER FOR NOT FOUND
    begin
        insert into db2admin.my_messages values (current timestamp,'entering not found handler');  -- debug
        SET row_found = 'no';
    end;
    insert into db2admin.my_messages values (current timestamp,'start load ods sp');  -- debug


    SET beginning_timestamp = CURRENT TIMESTAMP;
```

```
    OPEN part_cmd_cursor;
        FETCH part_cmd_cursor INTO IN_OPERATION, IN_OPERATION_TIMESTAMP,
IN_ODS_PART_KEY,
            IN_PART_NAME, IN_PART_MFGR, IN_PART_BRAND, IN_PART_TYPE,
IN_PART_SIZE,
            IN_PART_CONTAINER, IN_PART_RETAIL_PRICE,IN_PART_COMMENT,
IN_PART_SOURCE_KEY, IN_PART_SOURCE_SYSTEM;


    -- Loop thru all rows in the VSAM_PARTS change table
    WHILE row_found = 'yes' DO
       insert into db2admin.my_messages values (current timestamp,'entering
while loop');  -- debug
           CASE IN_OPERATION
              WHEN 'I'
                 THEN BEGIN
                   insert into db2admin.my_messages values (current
timestamp,'entering I leg');  -- debug
                     INSERT INTO IWH.ODS_PART
                         (
                             ODS_PART_KEY,
                             PART_NAME,
                             PART_MFGR,
                             PART_BRAND,
                             PART_TYPE,
                             PART_SIZE,
                             PART_CONTAINER,
                             PART_RETAIL_PRICE,
                             PART_COMMENT,
                             PART_SOURCE_KEY,
                             PART_SOURCE_SYSTEM
                         )
                     VALUES
                         (
                             IN_ODS_PART_KEY,
                             IN_PART_NAME,
                             IN_PART_MFGR,
                             IN_PART_BRAND,
                             IN_PART_TYPE,
                             IN_PART_SIZE,
                             IN_PART_CONTAINER,
                             IN_PART_RETAIL_PRICE,
                             IN_PART_COMMENT,
                             IN_PART_SOURCE_KEY,
                             IN_PART_SOURCE_SYSTEM
                         ) ;
                   SET insert_count = insert_count + 1;
                   END;
```

```
            WHEN 'U'
                THEN BEGIN
                    insert into db2admin.my_messages values (current
timestamp,'entering U leg');   -- debug

                    UPDATE IWH.ODS_PART
                    SET PART_NAME = IN_PART_NAME,
                        PART_MFGR = IN_PART_MFGR,
                        PART_BRAND = IN_PART_BRAND,
                        PART_TYPE = IN_PART_TYPE,
                        PART_SIZE = IN_PART_SIZE,
                        PART_CONTAINER = IN_PART_CONTAINER,
                        PART_RETAIL_PRICE = IN_PART_RETAIL_PRICE,
                        PART_COMMENT = IN_PART_COMMENT
                    WHERE ODS_PART_KEY = IN_ODS_PART_KEY;
                    SET update_count = update_count + 1;
                END;
            WHEN 'D'
                THEN BEGIN
                    insert into db2admin.my_messages values (current
timestamp,'entering D leg');   -- debug

                        DELETE FROM IWH.ODS_PART
                        WHERE ODS_PART_KEY = IN_ODS_PART_KEY;
                        SET delete_count = delete_count + 1;
                    END;
            ELSE SET error_count = error_count + 1;
        END CASE;

        DELETE FROM IWH.PART_LOAD_COMMANDS WHERE CURRENT OF part_cmd_cursor;

        SET uncommitted_records = uncommitted_records + 1;
        IF uncommitted_records > commit_count
            THEN
                commit;
                SET uncommitted_records = 0;
            end if;

        FETCH part_cmd_cursor INTO IN_OPERATION, IN_OPERATION_TIMESTAMP,
IN_ODS_PART_KEY,
                IN_PART_NAME, IN_PART_MFGR, IN_PART_BRAND, IN_PART_TYPE,
IN_PART_SIZE,
                IN_PART_CONTAINER, IN_PART_RETAIL_PRICE,IN_PART_COMMENT,
IN_PART_SOURCE_KEY, IN_PART_SOURCE_SYSTEM;


        END WHILE;
```

```
        -- create log entry


        INSERT INTO IWH.ODS_PART_LOG
            (
                STEP,
                TIMESTAMP,
                BEGIN_TIMESTAMP,
                END_TIMESTAMP,
                NUMBER_INSERTS,
                NUMBER_DELETES,
                NUMBER_UPDATES,
                NUMBER_ERRORS
            )
        VALUES
            (
                'Process Part Commands',
                CURRENT TIMESTAMP,
                beginning_timestamp,
                CURRENT TIMESTAMP,
                insert_count,
                delete_count,
                update_count,
                error_count
            );

        COMMIT;

END P1
```

DB2 UDB for z/OS Cross Loader

The new utility named Cross Loader, from DB2 UDB for z/OS V7 after GA, with PTF UQ55541 for APAR PQ45268 and PTF UQ55542 for APAR PQ46759, can be used to load DB2 for z/OS tables from DB2 UDB tables on distributed platforms as NT and UNIX or another DV2 for z/OS system. The Cross Loader is a new function that has been added to the DB2 UDB Load utility. It combines the efficiency of the IBM LOAD utility with the robustness of DRDA and the flexible SQL. It is an extension to the IBM LOAD utility that now enables the output of any SQL SELECT statement to be directly loaded into a table on DB2 UDB for z/OS V7.

Since the SQL SELECT statement can access any DRDA server, the data source may be any member of DB2 UDB family, DataJoiner, or any vendor products that has implemented DRDA server capabilities. That makes a good additional technique that can be used in the ODS architecture to load small volumes of data from DB2 distributed platforms or another DB2 for z/OS in a DB2 for z/OS database seen as an ODS data source or the staging area before the ODS itself in the ODS architecture.

Using the Cross Loader is much simpler than unloading the data, transferring the unloaded file to the target site, and then running the LOAD utility.

Refer to Figure D-1 for a diagram of the Cross Loader.

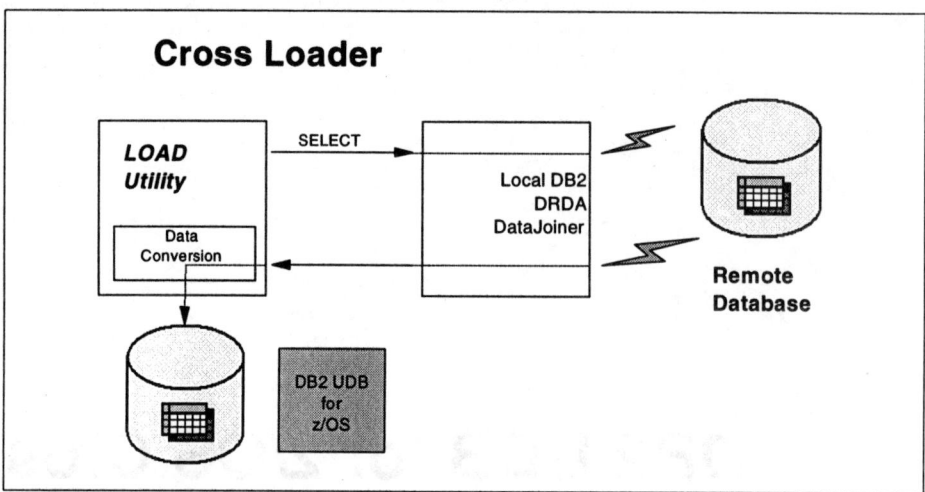

Figure D-1   Cross Loader

Example D-1 shows the exact syntax of the LOAD utility statement, which was tested in our ODS test environment. The resident table in DB7B in z/OS was loaded into a table in a DB2 subsystem in another z/OS.

Example: D-1   Syntax of the LOAD utility statement

```
EXEC SQL
DECLARE C1 CURSOR FOR
SELECT * FROM DB7B.S950.RESIDENT
ENDEXEC
LOAD DATA INCURSOR(C1) REPLACE LOG NO NOCOPYPEND
INTO TABLE CBARAR8.RESIDENT STATISTICS
```

Please notice that there is a three-part name for the source table with the location name.

When loading data from a remote location, you must first bind a package for the execution of the utility on the remote system, as in:

```
BIND PACKAGE (location_name.DSNUTILS) COPY(DSNUTILS.DSNUGSQL) - ACTION(REPLACE)
OPTIONS(COMPOSITE)
```

Table D-1 shows batch statistics after loading the same 80,000 rows using either the local LOAD (reading the same data from a table and loading to another table with the same columns within the same DB2 subsystem) or Cross Loader.

Table D-1   Cross-Loader statistics

Cross/Local	EXCP	CPU	CLOCK
Cross Load	620	0.17	2.3
Local Load	60772	0.03	0.5

The testing environment

This appendix describes the hardware, software, and entities used to test many of the ODS data acquisition scenarios discussed in this book. The following ODS data source platforms were utilized:

- DB2 UDB for OS/390 and z/OS
- VSAM on OS/390 and z/OS
- Oracle on AIX
- DB2 UDB EE on AIX

The integration and transformation software included:

- DB2 DPROP included with DB2 UDB EEE
- DB2 DataPropagator for OS/390 and z/OS
- WebSphere MQSeries and MQSeries Integrator
- DB2 Warehouse Manager
- DataJoiner, to replicate from Oracle to DB2

For the population management and control we used:

- DB2 Warehouse Manager

The following ODS target platforms were dealt with:

- DB2 UDB V7.1 for OS/390 and z/OS
- DB2 UDB EEE V7.2 on SunOS

Figure 8-15 describes the technical architecture of the testing environment.

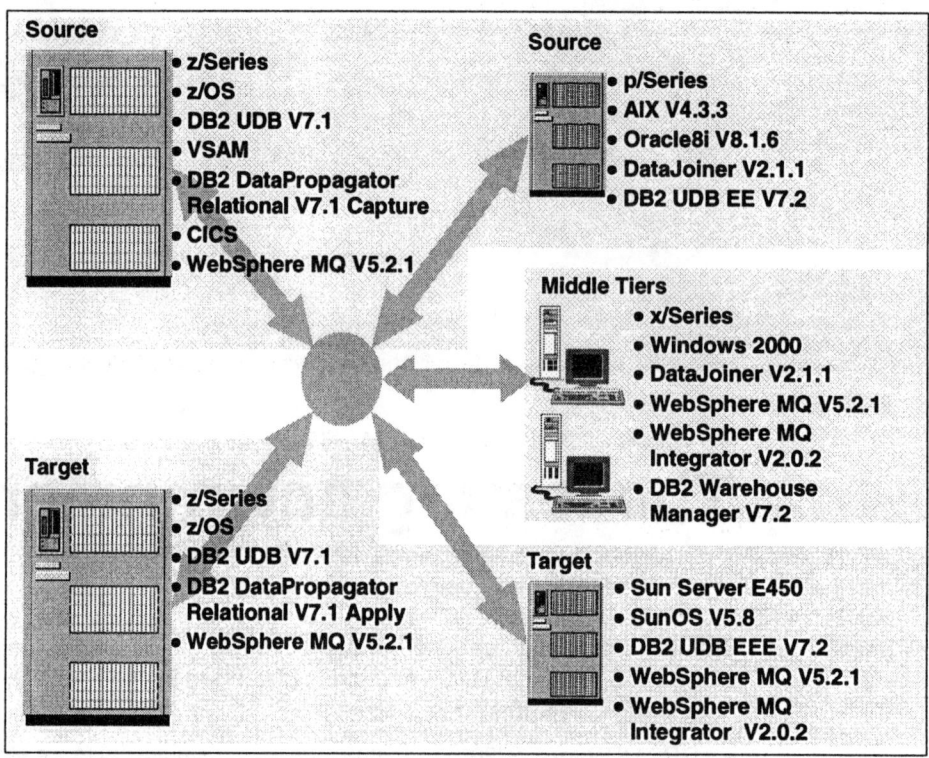

Figure 8-15   Testing environment

We used the Order Maintenance ODS (from the Parts-r-Us business scenario in 3.1.2, "Consolidated customer and order information" on page 35 to describe many of the different data acquisition solutions. Figure 8-16 shows the entities and their relationships that were used to test ODS types A and B.

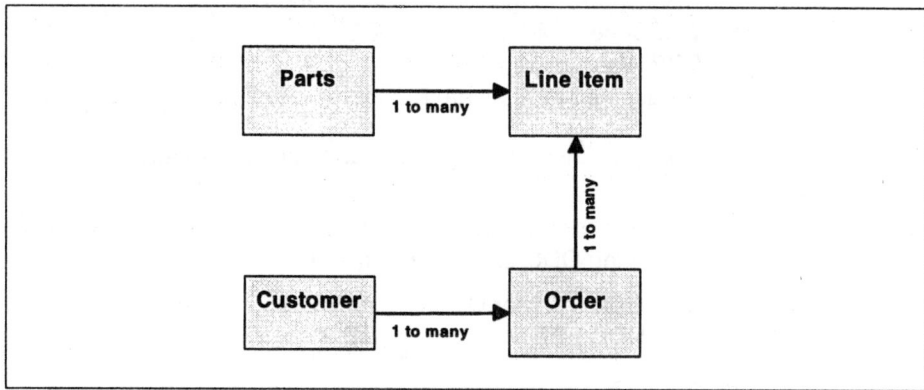

Figure 8-16   Parts-r-Us entity-relationship diagram

Related publications

The publications listed in this section are considered particularly suitable for a more detailed discussion of the topics covered in this redbook.

IBM Redbooks

For information on ordering these publications, see "How to get IBM Redbooks" on page 326.

- *My Mother Thinks I'm a DBA!*, SG24-5463
- *Business Integration Solutions with MQSeries Integrator*, SG24-6154
- *DB2 UDB V7.1 Performance Tuning Guide*, SG24-6012-00
- *Managing VLDB Using DB2 UDB EEE*, SG24-5105-00
- *DB2 UDB Server for OS/390 and z/OS Version 7*, SG24-6121
- *Business Intelligence Architecture on S/390*, SG24-5641
- *New Tools for DB2 for OS/390 and z/OS Presentation Guide*, SG24-6139
- *DB2 UDB for OS/390 and Continuous Availability*, SG24-5486
- *DB2 Universal Database in Application Development Environments*, SG24-6009
- *Database Performance on AIX in DB2 UDB and Oracle Environments*, SG24-5511
- *DB2 UDB for OS/390 Version 6 Management Tools Package*, SG24-5759
- *DB2 for z/OS and OS/390 Version 7 Performance Topics*, SG24-6129
- *DB2 UDB for OS/390 Version 6 Performance Topics*, SG24-5351
- *Migrating to DB2 UDB Version 7.1 in a Visual Warehouse Environment*, SG24-6107
- *DB2 for OS/390 and Data Compression*, SG24-5261
- *DB2 for OS/390 Application Design Guidelines for High Performance*, SG24-2233
- *Locking in DB2 for MVS/ESA Environment*, SG24-4725
- *S/390 WLM Implementation and Exploitation*, SG24-5326

Other resources

These external publications are relevant as further information sources:

- *Building the Operational Data Store, second edition.* W.H.Inmon. John Wiley & Sons, 1999. ISBN: O-471-32888-X
- *Data Warehouse: From Architecture to Implementation.* Barry Devlin. Addison-Wesley, November 1998. ISBN: O-201-96425-2

These IBM publications are also relevant:

- *DPROPR Planning and Design Guide,* SG24-4771
- *DB2 UDB Replication Guide and Reference,* SC26-9920
- *The DB2 Replication Certification Guide,* SC09-2802
- *DB2 Universal Database Version 6.1 Certification Guide,* SC09-2915
- *Getting Started with Data Warehouse and Business Intelligence,* SG24-5415
- *Migrating to the IBM Replication Solution,* SG24-6140
- *IBM ESS and IBM DB2 UDB Working Together,* SG24-6262
- *WOW! DRDA Supports TCP/IP: DB2 Server for OS/390 and DB2 Universal Database,* SG24-2212
- *DB2 UDB Administration Guide: Planning,* SC09-2946
- *DB2 UDB Administration Guide: Performance,* SC09-2945
- *DB2 UDB Administration Guide: Implementation,* SC09-2944
- *DB2 UDB System Monitor Guide and Reference,* SC09-2956
- *AIX 5L Workload Manager (WLM),* SG24-5977-01
- *DB2 UDB Data Warehouse Center Administration Guide,* SC26-9993
- *DB2 UDB Data Warehouse Center Application Integration Guide,* SC26-9994
- *DB2 Warehouse Manager Managing ETI Extract Conversion Programs with DB2 Warehouse Manager,* SC27-1268
- *An introduction to MQSeries,* GC33-0805
- *MQSeries Application Programming Guide,* SC33-0807
- *MQSeries Application Programming Reference,* SC33-1673
- *MQSeries System Administration,* SC33-1873
- *MQSeries for OS/390 System Administration Guide,* SC34-5652
- *MQSeries for Window NT and Window 2000 V5R2 Quick Beginnings,* GC34-5389
- *MQSeries Integrator Using the Control Center,* SC34-5602

- *MQSeries Integrator ESQL Reference*, SC34-5293
- *MQSeries Integrator Sun Solaris Installation Guide*, GC34-5842
- *MQSeries Integrator Window NT Installation Guide*, GC34-5600
- *DB2 UDB for OS/390 and z/OS V7 Administration Guide*, SC26-9931
- *DB2 UDB for OS/390 and z/OS V7 Application Programming and SQL Guide*, SC26-9933
- *DB2 UDB for OS/390 and Z/OS V7 Data Sharing: Planning and Administration*, SC26-9935
- *DB2 UDB for OS/390 and z/OS V7 Utility Guide and Reference*, SC26-9945
- *DB2 UDB for OS/390 V7 An Introduction to DB2 for OS/390*, SC26-9937
- *DB2 UDB for OS/390 and z/OS V7 ODBC Guide and Reference*, SC26-9941
- *DB2 UDB for OS/390 and z/OS V7 Reference for Remote DRDA Requesters and Servers*, SC26-9942
- *DB2 UDB for OS/390 and z/OS V7 Release Planning Guide*, SC26-9943
- *OS/390 MVS Planning: Workload Management*, GC28-1761
- *QMF High Performance Option User's Guide for OS/390*, SC27-0724
- *DB2 High Performance Unload*, SC27-0965
- *DPROPNR V2R2 Administrators Guide*, SH19-5036
- *IMS DAta Propagator for z/OS: Administrator's Guide for MQSeries Asynchronous Propagation*, SC27-1217

Referenced Web sites

These Web sites are also relevant as further information sources:

- IBM Software Homepage

  http://www.software.ibm.com/

- IBM Database Management Homepage

  http://www.software.ibm.com/data/

- IBM DProp Homepage

  http://www.software.ibm.com/data/dprop/

- IBM DataJoiner Homepage

  http://www.software.ibm.com/data/datajoiner/

- IBM Data Management Performance

  http://www.software.ibm.com/data/db2/performance

- IBM DataPropagator Relational Performance

  http://www.software.ibm.com/data/db2/performance/dprperf.htm

- IBM Enterprise Storage Server

  http://www.ibm.com/storage/hardsoft/diskdrls/technology.htm

- IBM DB2 and IMS

  http://www.software.ibm.com/data/db2imstools

- IBM MQSeries

  http://www-4.ibm.com/software/ts/mqseries/platforms

- IBM WLM/SRM

  http://www.ibm.com/s390/wlm

- IBM MQSeries SupportPac

  http://www-4.ibm.com/software/ts/mqseries/txppacs/txpm1.html

- Bill Inmon's Web site

  http://www.billinmon.com/library

How to get IBM Redbooks

Search for additional Redbooks or Redpieces, view, download, or order hardcopy from the Redbooks Web site:

ibm.com/redbooks

Also download additional materials (code samples or diskette/CD-ROM images) from this Redbooks site.

Redpieces are Redbooks in progress; not all Redbooks become Redpieces and sometimes just a few chapters will be published this way. The intent is to get the information out much quicker than the formal publishing process allows.

IBM Redbooks collections

Redbooks are also available on CD-ROMs. Click the CD-ROMs button on the Redbooks Web site for information about all the CD-ROMs offered, as well as updates and formats.

Index

A

acquisition
    from non-relational data sources 87, 89
    from relational data sources 85, 91
ADABAS 82
adding
    new sources 25
    new targets 25
aggregation 27, 92, 232, 236
AIX 59, 150
AIX 5L Workload Manager 253
analysis 2, 27, 56
ANSI SQL-PL 208, 211
Apply 47, 74, 84, 86–87, 93–94, 96, 101–102, 108–109
    DB2 for z/OS 94
    event-triggered 104
    multiple 104
    pull mode 102
    qualifier 104
    scheduled 104
ASCII 141
AST 232, 234, 236
audit 47, 61
autoloader 249, 255
Automatic Summary Tables 232
automation 215
availability 7, 21, 27–28, 164, 229, 252, 267
    24x7 7, 19

B

BAAN 61
backup 66, 68, 249–250
banking/finance
    business questions 18
batch 44, 66, 249
    window 28, 61, 248
block fetch 102
business
    challenges 1
    priorities 17
    process 23
    questions 17
    requirements 23, 29, 33, 46, 48
    scenarios 34
        banking 45
        retail 35, 48
        telecommunications 37, 50
    users 45–46, 70, 72
Business Intelligence 1

C

call center 34, 72, 237
campaign management 72
Capture 74, 84, 86–87, 93, 95–96, 101–102, 104, 108–109
CCD tables 106, 110
    pruning 108
CD tables 74, 93
CDB 218–219
changes
    back to the operational sources 24, 46, 86, 122, 174
    capture process 202
    capturing 26, 47, 61–62
    log 62
CICS 87, 128, 130, 165, 176, 203
clustered 245
code page 144
columns 224
commit 214, 233, 261
concurrency 230, 262
condensed copy 110
consistency 61, 230
consolidated view 18
conversions 25
cost 7
CRM 18
customer
    product portfolio 34
    service 23
Customer Relationship Manager 18
customers
    calling card fraud 37
    increased customer service 34
    track their orders 35

D

daily 237
data
    access 27, 56, 70
    aggregation 60
    archiving 26
    characteristics 19, 26
    consolidation 23
    conversions 60, 190
    currency 27
    current 2, 19–20, 26
    delivery timing 25, 111
    dirty 29, 179
    elements 24
    filter 24
    formats 25
    frequency 25
    integration 2, 23, 27, 61
    integrity 23, 26, 47, 68, 173, 230, 233
    invalid 180
    level of detail 2, 20, 26–27
    model 30, 33, 52, 63, 66, 230
        dimensions 52, 54–55
        enterprise 23
        entities 53
        facts 54–55
        measures 54
        relationships 53
        star 55
    moving 26
        from the data sources to the ODS 22
    near real-time 39
    near-current 2, 20, 26, 145, 261
    non-relational 23
    operational 17, 58
    overlapping 23
    ownership 29
    purging 26
    quality 19, 29, 47
    read-only copies 24
    real-time 39
    reformatting 60
    requirements 24
    sampling 60
    source types 20
    steward 29
    structures 25, 30
    subject area 2, 20
    transferring 19, 22
    transformations 20, 22, 24, 139, 230, 232
        aggregating 62
        cleansing 25, 62
        consolidating 62
        conversions 25
        converting physical structures 25
        decoding 25
        denormalizing 62
        encoding 25
        formatting 25, 62
        reconciling 62
        summarization 25
    types 25
    velocity 25
    volatile 2
Data Difference Utility 75, 87
data flow
    between operational system and ODS 40
data sources 22, 40, 60, 109, 218
    DB2 92, 95
    deltas 62
    external 22, 44, 73
    heterogeneous 48
    homogeneous 50
    internal 42, 44
    many different platforms 25
    multiple 230
    non-DB2 92, 95–96
    non-relational 84
    operational 22
    relational 84, 111
    Web 61, 111
data warehouse 2, 7, 17, 23, 25–26, 28, 42, 45, 51, 190, 230, 236
    updates 24
Data Warehouse Center 60, 92, 108, 202
database
    design 30
    hot-swap 28
DataJoiner 60, 74, 84, 86, 91–92, 96, 100, 108, 194, 203
    database 95
DataJoiner Administration Tool 92
datamart 2, 26, 51
DataRefresher 75, 87
DataStage 82
DB2
    Control Center 108
DB2 DataPropagator 60, 74, 84, 91–92, 99–100

DB2 for z/OS
    data sharing   261
DB2 Governor   253
DB2 MQ Series UDF   201
DB2 MQ User Defined Functions   213
DB2 Stored Procedure Builder   208, 211
DB2 UDB   194
DB2 UDB EE   235
DB2 UDB EEE   84–86, 89, 95, 132, 171, 234–235
    configuration tuning parameters   251
    logical partitions   247
    nodegroup   237
    nodes   247
    redistributing data   248
DB2 UDB family   59, 230
DB2 UDB for z/OS   84–85, 87, 89, 95, 130, 169, 255
    coupling facility   266
    level of detail   256
    Parallel Sysplex   265
    parallelism   269
    partitioning   256, 276
    workload manager   259
DB2 Warehouse Manager   60–61, 80
DB2 WM   84, 91–92
    agents   164, 217
DDF   255
DDU   75, 87
deadlock   232
delta file   176
direct access
    from front-end applications   40
DJRA   92, 96, 203
DL/I   59, 75
DSS   70
DWC   108, 155, 202, 259
    MQ Connector   153
    process modeler   160, 211, 216
    workflow   120, 162

E
EBCDIC   141
end-users   70, 73, 185, 217
Entity Relationship Model   52
environments
    heterogeneous   23, 25, 60, 82
ERM   52–53
ESQL   140, 142
ETI

EXTRACT   80, 82
ETML   25, 73, 82, 275
Evoke   82
exception handling   47
Extended SQL   140
Extract Transform Move Load   25

F
failure   68
fault tolerance   7
flat files   23, 111, 127, 165
    z/OS and OS/390   128
flow control   29–30

G
granularity   26–27
growth path   21, 164, 267
    flexible   27–28, 241

H
HACMP   28, 252
hardware   69
High Availability Cluster Multi-Processing   28
high updates
    volumes   18, 104
history   26, 67, 110
    accounting period   26

I
I/O   30, 64
IBM Data Replication   73, 91
IBM partner products   81
IBM products   73, 81
ICM   217
    web interface   222
Image Copy   68
IMS   23, 59, 75, 87, 89, 111, 127, 166
IMS DataPropagator   60, 75, 87, 89, 166
    log asynchronous   168
    near real-time asynchronous   169
    Relational Update Program   170
    synchronous   167
inconsistencies   46
index   102, 254
information
    consolidation   18
information catalog   29, 42, 64

Information Catalog Manager   217
Informix   59, 74, 97
infrastructure   30
initial loads   29, 31, 60, 62, 229, 275
insurance
   business questions   18
Internet   72
intranet   72
inventory
   co-manage   18
i-series   59
isolation level   261

J
JD Edwards   61

L
LAN   72
latency   174
layer
   administration   22
   data access   43, 70
   data acquisition   22, 42, 61, 172, 179, 230
      build   61
      capture   61
      extract   61
      transformation   61
      trigger updates   61
   data enhancement   41
   data sources   22, 42
   datamart   41–42
   enterprise data   22, 42
   external   42
   extract   47, 194, 215
   load   47, 198, 216
   maintenance   22
   preformat, filter, merge and delta detection   195
   prepare   215
   transform   216
   transformation   24
   transport   79
legacy   24–26
   applications   19, 23, 27, 169
   systems   18, 20, 26, 47, 73, 180
      integration   35
level of detail   229, 234
Linux   59
load
   massive load   60
Local Area Network   72
locks   27, 214, 232, 262, 264
log   74, 85, 95, 168, 203, 226, 250

M
maintenance   66, 248–249
mapping   173
Massively Parallel Processing   28
message   137, 139
   flow   135, 138, 153
   models   154
   XML   142
Message Queue Interface   76
messages
   persistence   145
messaging system   49
metadata   30, 64, 84, 109, 112, 217
   build-time   64
   control   64
   Control Database   218
   dynamic   227
   processes   219
   publishing   224
   scheduling   226
   sources   219
   targets   219
   usage   64
Microsoft Cluster Services   252
Microsoft SQL Server   59, 74
mirroring   28
mixed workload   27
mixing
   updates and queries   27
MPP   28, 235, 244
MQ Message Descriptor   141
MQ trigger   163
MQ-Assist Wizard   154, 162, 213
MQ-ASYNC   166, 170
MQCONN   77
MQGET   77, 139
MQMD   141
MQOPEN   77, 130
MQPUT   77, 131
MQSeries   91, 132, 134
   queue   75–77, 86–87, 169
      queue-local   131
      queue-remote   123, 131, 175

queue manager   77–79, 122, 146, 175
queues
    queue-local   139
    source to an ODS   161
MQSeries Integrator   76
MQSI   76, 78, 86, 89, 122, 127, 132, 134
    brokers   79, 138, 146
    control center   79, 135, 137, 142
    data transformations   139
    message repository manager   79
    message set   135, 142
        input   144
    multi-broker domain   138
    nodes   139
    parser   144
multiple operational sources
    integrating   20
multiple platforms   47

N
near current data   20, 229
near real-time   25, 44, 62, 236
    asynchronous   166
nicknames   95–96
nodes   135, 139
    compute   135, 140
    database   135, 142
    filter   144
    MQInput   135, 139
    MQOutput   135, 140
non-pruning mode   101
NOPRUNE   101
numbers of users   28

O
ODBC   72, 142, 146, 202
ODS   2, 7
    administration   21, 28–29
    architectures   22, 33, 73, 84
    deploying   153
    environment   27
    growth   21, 27
    inconsistency   24
    incremental changes   26
    initial load   21
    issues   17, 91
    layers   22, 33, 57
    maintenance   19, 28, 68

manage user updates   20
multiple   23
population   22, 26, 62, 66, 108, 127, 134, 161, 191
population control   21
population subsystem   190, 203, 219
    architecture   191
real-time   2
refreshment   26
single version of the truth   20, 23–24, 50
synchronization   20
system of record   23–24, 47
timing delivery   26
transactions   27
type A   39, 43, 73, 84, 87, 91
type B   39, 43, 46, 48, 61, 73, 84–85, 91, 121, 153, 177, 230
type C   39, 43, 49, 73
types   33, 38, 73, 230
    selecting   51
validating   66, 70
workflows
    automating   203
    implementing   203
workload   63, 72
off-peak periods   44, 63
OLAP   70
OLTP   17, 230, 234
On-Line Transactional Processing   17
OPC/ESA   260
operational applications
    heterogeneous   18
operational sources   41
    integrating   22–23
operations
    day-to-day   28
optimizer   254
Oracle   59, 61, 74, 97, 119, 194, 202
OS/400   59
outages
    planned   248, 268
    unplanned   248, 268

P
parallel   104, 146–147, 164, 174, 203, 237, 249, 252
parallelism   249, 261
    I/O   245

inter-partition 242
intra-partition 242
intra-query 242
query 242
utility 245
partitioning 234–235, 237
PeopleSoft 61
performance 24, 26, 60, 63, 66, 68, 72, 94, 100, 102, 104, 125, 144, 153, 174, 177, 229–230, 237, 252, 259, 270–271
    bottleneck 63
    tuning and monitoring 21, 29–30, 69, 270
PL/I 131
planning 24
population subsystem 191
    automating 202
priorities 102
production 120, 189, 213
products
    cross-product selling 34
pruning 66–67, 105
pruning mode 101

Q
QSAM 165
queries 2, 27, 63, 229
query 70
    response time 18
quiesce 68

R
RAID 28, 249
read and write 43, 45–46
real-time 19, 26, 44, 51, 62
recovery 68
    replication 68
Redbooks Web site 326
    Contact us xx
redundancy 56
referential integrity 233
refreshes
    full 68
reject handling application 187
rejected records 29, 179
relational data sources
    non-DB2 74, 84
reorganization 66, 68
replication 50, 92

Base Aggregate 110
CD table 96, 101, 105
Change Aggregate 110
Change Data table 68, 74, 95
Committed Change Data table 106
control server 94, 105
control tables 66
DB2 UDB EEE 85
execution 121
from VSAM to DB2 UDB EEE 88
heterogeneous 2
homogeneous 2
Point-In-Time copy 110
sources 109–111
spill file 94, 105
staging tables 74, 110
subscription 93, 105
subscription sets 93, 104, 106
Unit Of Work table 68, 93
UOW table 102
User Copy 110
requirements 7
response time 7, 64
restore 249
retail
    business questions 18
rollback 233
runstats 68

S
SAP 61
scalability 28, 146, 164, 234, 245, 267
scheduling 61, 63, 66, 84, 101, 109, 161, 260
service level 7
service level agreement 28
Service Level Agreements 2
serviceability 7
shared-everything hardware 247
shared-nothing architecture 234, 237
Siebel 61
SLA 2, 28
SMP 28, 235, 244, 246–247
snapshots 44–45, 194, 237
Solaris 148
source
    synchronization 20
SQL statements 154
staging table 171, 173, 204, 211, 213

standards 30
stored procedures 122, 164, 208, 232, 234
subject area 23
summarization 27, 232, 236
summary tables 67
Sun Enterprise Cluster High Availability 252
suppliers 18
surrogate keys 197
Sybase 59, 97
Symmetric MultiProcessing 28
synchronization 24, 26, 45, 48, 50, 62, 125, 173, 229–230, 232, 234
system management 66
systems
    consolidation 18

T

table function 213
tables 224
TCP/IP 72
telecommunications
    business questions 19
Teradata 59
throughput 7, 69, 147, 153, 237, 245
transaction 60, 64, 66, 128
    processing 30
    rate 165, 229
transactional updates 27
transformations 61, 99, 111, 119–120
    requirements 62
    tools 25
triggers 47–48, 96, 101, 121, 131, 203, 232–234
    asynchronous trigger 40, 46

U

UDF 154, 232, 234
units of work 230
UNIX 59
UOW 170, 174, 177
update anywhere 50
updates 27, 39, 64, 121, 229
    asynchronous 130, 132
    back to a data source 46, 48
    batch 43–44
    batch/store and forward 43
    capturing 128
    cyclical data update 47
    daily 129

    frequency 63
    from the ODS 48
    independent 122, 175
    massive 101, 104
    near real-time 101–102, 129, 153, 183
    partitioning 164
    real-time 40, 43
    scheduling 28
    segmenting 164
    small rates 177
    store and forward 43
    synchronous 130
    timing of operational system updates 40
    user 23–24, 45
uptime 21, 27–28, 164
User Defined Functions 154
User Defined Program 163, 209, 213

V

Vality
    Integrity 80, 82
view 160
    consistent 18
    up-to-date 18
visual explain 254
VM 59
volatile 25
volatility 261
volumes 27–28, 60, 153, 174, 234, 269
    high update 25
VSAM 23, 59, 82, 87, 89, 111, 127, 175, 194, 203
    delta file 129

W

WAN 72
weblogs 2
WebSphere MQ 60
WebSphere MQ family 76
WebSphere MQ Integrator 60, 127
Wide Area Network 72
Windows NT/2000/XP 59
WLM 259
Work Load Manager 259
workflow 120, 201
    automating 214
    DB2 204
    Oracle 210
    VSAM 212

workload 8, 73
    balancing 261
    growth 261
    mixed 27, 164, 229, 259, 270

Z
z/OS 59
zero latency 2
Zero Latency Enterprise
    service offering 2
ZLE 2